Performing the Temple of Liberty

EARLY AMERICA: HISTORY, CONTEXT, CULTURE
Joyce E. Chaplin and Philip D. Morgan, Series Editors

Performing the Temple of Liberty

of Liberty

Slavery, Theater, and Popular Culture
in London and Philadelphia, 1760–1850

JENNA M. GIBBS

JOHNS HOPKINS UNIVERSITY PRESS   BALTIMORE

© 2014 Johns Hopkins University Press
All rights reserved. Published 2014
Printed in the United States of America on acid-free paper

2 4 6 8 9 7 5 3 1

Johns Hopkins University Press
2715 North Charles Street
Baltimore, Maryland 21218-4363
www.press.jhu.edu

Library of Congress Cataloging-in-Publication Data

Gibbs, Jenna M., 1961–
Performing the temple of liberty : slavery, theater, and popular culture in
London and Philadelphia, 1760–1850 / Jenna M. Gibbs.
pages cm. — (Early America: history, context, culture)
Includes bibliographical references and index.
ISBN 978-1-4214-1338-9 (hardcover : alk. paper) — ISBN 978-1-4214-
1339-6 (electronic) — ISBN 1-4214-1338-8 (hardcover : alk. paper) — ISBN
1-4214-1339-6 (electronic) 1. Theater—England—London—History—
18th century. 2. Theater—England—London—History—19th century. 3. Theater—Pennsylvania—Philadelphia—History—18th
century. 4. Theater—Pennsylvania—Philadelphia—History—19th century. 5. Slave trade in the theater. 6. Race in the theater. 7. London
(England)—Social life and customs. 8. Philadelphia (Pa.)—Social life and
customs. I. Title.
PN2596.L6G46 2014
792.09421'09033—dc23   2013033294

A catalog record for this book is available from the British Library.

*Special discounts are available for bulk purchases of this book. For more information,
please contact Special Sales at 410-516-6936 or specialsales@press.jhu.edu.*

Johns Hopkins University Press uses environmentally friendly book materials,
including recycled text paper that is composed of at least 30 percent
post-consumer waste, whenever possible.

For my father and mother, Jim and Dorothy,
and for Peter, my true love

CONTENTS

Every first-time author owes a primary debt to her teachers, and my debt is unusually deep. When, in 1996, I decided to leave behind a career in the theater to go back to school and acquire a bachelor's degree, I had the good fortune to take my first undergraduate history classes at Moorpark College, California, with Ranford Hopkins, professor of American and African American history. Ranford is the reason I became a historian. He ignited my passion for history and also insisted that I "belonged" in a graduate program, which, at the time, was news to me. I still aspire to teach as inspirationally as he does, and I remain deeply indebted to him for pushing me to major in history and, later, to pursue a Ph.D. Shortly after transferring to the University of California, Los Angeles, to complete my bachelor's in history I began studying with Lynn Hunt and Margaret C. Jacob. I am grateful to Lynn Hunt for first suggesting that I combine my background in theater with my curiosity about antislavery politics. As a result, I wrote a senior honors thesis on the role of the London theaters in mobilizing antislavery sentiment in parliamentary debates of the 1780s. This thesis was the genesis of my dissertation topic and, eventually, of this book. Lynn Hunt, Margaret Jacob, and Felicity Nussbaum co-supervised the thesis and taught me how to do research. As well as being excellent mentors, they also endorsed my application to the Ph.D. program at UCLA, for which I remain very grateful.

I have had encouragement at every stage of this project, beginning with writing my dissertation. I thank Margaret Jacob, my dissertation advisor, for her insightful historical imagination and stalwart support, both then and since. I also greatly appreciate her immediate enthusiasm for my eleventh-hour proposal to take the project "transatlantic"—a leap of faith on her part, as I trained to be an early modern Europeanist. I also had a fabulous committee. Gary B. Nash made my transatlantic conversion possible as no one else could. He introduced me to American historiography, shared with me his knowledge of the Philadelphia archives, and was and still is an unstintingly generous mentor. Felicity Nussbaum's knowledge of eighteenth- and nineteenth-century theater and blackface performance, so liberally shared, was invaluable, as was her pragmatic "how to" advice on fellowship applications. Erika Rappaport guided me in nineteenth-century British cultural history and offered me particularly astute advice about how to turn the dissertation into a book. David W. Sabean generously opened up his home for weekly dissertation reading groups, accompanying his insightful critiques with good wine, food, and conviviality. Fellow members of the reading group also offered constructive criticism and camaraderie: Teresa Barnett, Sung Choi, Sean Guillory, Kelly Maynard, Ben Marshke, Kris Pangburn, Ritika Prasad Dan Ryan, Tami Safarti, Daniella Saxton, Simon Teuscher, and Claudia Verhoeven. Too many UCLA scholars to list lent me their time and advice despite not being my formal mentors, but I particularly want to thank Anne Mellor for being a keen supporter ever since I was an undergraduate in her memorable class on British Romantic literature and for her unflagging interest in my project and progress.

I have enjoyed both financial and intellectual support when researching and writing this study. Several short-term fellowships got me off to a great start: a Kanner Fellowship at the William Andrews Clark Memorial Library, UCLA; a Sylvia Thayer Fellowship at the Young Research Library, UCLA; and a Mayers Fellowship at the Huntington Library in San Marino, California. At the Huntington I had the benefit of good intellectual company, especially in Fiona Ritchie and Laura Stephens, and the support of Robert Ritchie, who was then the director. An Albert Greenfield Dissertation Fellowship funded my Philadelphia research at the Library Company of Philadelphia and the Historical Society of Pennsylvania. Philip Lapsansky, who was then curator of the Afro-Americana collection at the Library Company but who has since retired, was generous in pointing me, time and again, to invaluable sources. Connie King, who was then reader services librarian, was also extremely helpful. Director John Van Horne made a point of interacting with each fellow individually and was always warm and accessible. I was also a research associate at the McNeal Center for Early American Studies, where Dan Richter, in his capacity as director, made me very welcome. Michael Zuckerman's salons also made my Philadelphia sojourn stimulating. I conducted my London research in the British Library, the Friends Library, the Hoxton Public Library, and in what was then the Covent Garden Theatre Library, and the staff in all these establishments helped me greatly. A year-long Ahmanson-Getty Postdoctoral Fellowship at the William Andrews Clark Memorial Library and UCLA's Center for Seventeenth- and Eighteenth-Century Studies in 2009–2010 facilitated early revisions of the manuscript. Susanne Tatian, Scott Jacobs, and head librarian Bruce Whiteman made the Clark Library a productive and pleasant place to work. Thanks also to Michael Meranze and Saree Makdisi, who organized the program of which I was a part, and my fellow postdocs, Sarah Crabtree, Anthony Galuzzo, and Aris Sarafinianos, who were especially congenial intellectually and socially. The Wissenschaftskolleg zu Berlin was a wonderfully supportive environment in which to do the final revisions and copy edits of the manuscript in 2013.

I appreciate having had the opportunity to give papers on aspects of this project at various conferences, workshops, and events where audiences and commentators offered thought-provoking comments and asked challenging questions: the Clark Library "British Atlantic in an Age of Revolution and Reaction" conferences, organized by Michael Meranze and Saree Makdisi; the Consortium on the Revolutionary Era; the American Society for Eighteenth-Century Studies; the British Society for Eighteenth-Century Studies; the International Society for Eighteenth-Century Studies; the Atlantic Emancipations conference, co-sponsored by the Library Company of Philadelphia, McNeil Center for Early American Studies, and the Rochester Institute of Technology; the American Historical Association; the Society for Caribbean Studies; the Amerika Institute at Ludwig-Maxmillian University; the Bay Area Early American Seminar; "The Eighteenth-Century Cosmopolis," a conference organized by Kathleen Wilson at the State University of New York at Stony Brook Humanities Institute; the University of Miami's Atlantic Studies Seminar; and Göttingen University Department of History, at a seminar organized by Isabel Richter.

Friends and colleagues have read and commented on this project at different stages of its development. My friends and fellow graduate students at UCLA, Arthur Rolston and John Dixon, both Americanists, were tremendous sources of brainstorming and patient advice when I was first navigating my late-adopted American field. Kathleen Wilson challenged me at an early point to break down the bifurcation between street and theater performances. Christopher Looby gave me excellent advice on nineteenth-century American literature and invaluable research leads. Rose Beiler, Marie-Jeanne Rossignol, and Jessica Lepler, during the time we were all fellows at the Library Company, spurred me on my way with engaging exchanges about early American history. Dee Andrews has been a staunch supporter, as have Christopher Brown, Aaron Fogleman, and Rich Newman. I cherish Sarah Crabtree's friendship and she read my entire dissertation with a critical eye and super suggestions for revisions. John Davies kindly shared his research on Gabriel's rebellion, and I also value Marc Lerner's friendship and our constant exchange of ideas about Atlantic theater. I have also enjoyed invigorating conversations about Atlantic theater with Peter Reed, Fiona Ritchie, and Miles Grier, among others. Martha Schulman read and helped edit successive drafts and her skills contributed enormously to the lucidity of my prose and thought. Gary B. Nash continues to be a tireless champion who has read several drafts of the manuscript and offered erudite and probing feedback.

I am privileged to be part of a vibrant group of Atlanticists and Americanists in Miami. My department at Florida International University has a Ph.D. program in Atlantic history that is a stimulus for both research and teaching, and I have excellent colleagues. I particularly want to thank Ken Lipartito for supporting my research both as a friend and as department chair, and Kirsten Wood, April Merleaux, and my emeritus colleague, Howard Rock, for their friendship and for reading and commenting on my work. Howard read the entire manuscript and helped me refine my arguments in crucial ways. I have also received encouragement and good cheer from colleagues at the University of Miami, especially from Ashli White and Tim Watson, who run an Atlantic Studies group. Richard Godbeer has been extraordinarily generous and given me excellent advice at every step. His friendship is a priceless gift, and I hope he knows how much I treasure it.

As I draw this project to a close, it is a great pleasure to thank Robert J. Brugger at Johns Hopkins University Press for his immediate and sustained enthusiasm for my project, his patience and confidence in me as I worked through various drafts, and his good sense about how to tackle the revisions. Joyce Chaplin and Philip Morgan are ideal series editors; both have been encouraging from the start and quick to communicate smart suggestions. Melissa Solarz has been extremely efficient and easy to work with on the preparation and submission of the images and manuscript. A special thank you to Glenn Perkins, whose judicious and thorough copy editing clarified and enlivened my prose and saved me from embarrassing citation errors. The marketing folks—Brian Gilbert and Vanessa Kotz among them—have been helpful and communicative throughout. From beginning to end, Johns Hopkins University Press has been a wonderful home for an author producing her first book.

I thank my family for their unerring faith in me during my twelve-year "back to school" odyssey and as I went through the challenges of being a junior professor these past four years. Throughout, my brothers and sisters-in-law Steve Gibbs, Veronique Gailly, Tom Gibbs, and Veronique Timmermans, and, above all, my parents, James and Dorothy Gibbs, have cheered me on and nourished me with their love. Kenneth and Ellen Hart, my aunt and uncle, and my lovely cousins Daniel and Justin Hart (a fellow historian) have also supported me. Dominique Reill is a cherished family member and loyal friend; her intellectual passion has stimulated my own, and she has often buoyed my spirits with her abundant optimism, energy, and love. I have saved my most important thanks until last: my husband, partner, and soulmate, Peter Reill. His intellectual companionship, his readings of my work at critical junctures, his abiding love, and his amazing culinary talents have seen me through many ups and downs. He has endured the writing of this book with more patience, humor, and precious love than I have any right to expect.

Political and Cultural Exchange in the British Atlantic

Come with me and stroll along the Thames River to the Haymarket Theatre Royal on August 4, 1787. Shackled African slaves are being marched to Greenwich, where a ship will transport them to the Americas. The streets teem with pedestrians, peddlers, and pickpockets; bawdy drunks spill out of taverns; rakes and painted women pack brothels; playwrights and wits mingle at coffee houses. Cobbled streets lead to St. Paul's Church with its Tuscan-style portico and Italianate square, the south side of which houses a bustling open-air fruit and vegetable market. Demobilized and desperately impoverished veterans of the war against the former American colonies—many of them African American ex-slaves who fought on Britain's side for the promise of freedom—beg. Theatergoers stroll along Strand Street, a major thoroughfare, before turning off for the Haymarket to see the debut of George Colman Jr.'s *Inkle and Yarico*. The play tells the story of British merchant, Inkle, who is shipwrecked off the coast of Barbados and saved by Yarico, a noble African maiden; she becomes his mistress, but he heartlessly sells her into plantation slavery. A street minstrel belts out the show's ballads to the multiracial, cross-class, male and female ticketholders milling outside under the theater's neoclassical colonnades. Playgoers buy song sheets from the orange girl, who also hawks illustrated broadsheets to advertise the play to the illiterate. Peddlers sell cartoons featuring images of popular theatrical characters used to satirize topical political issues.

Inside, the pianoforte is barely audible above the rowdy audience of over two thousand. Oil-lamps cast flickering light on the cavernous stage, and middling sorts and high-end women of ill repute are seated in the main gallery above the lower-priced orchestra pit. Three tiers of gilded boxes flank the right and left of the hall, allowing the upper sorts, nobility, and even royalty to overlook the stage. Alas, King George III and Queen Consort Charlotte are not in attendance on August 4. In any event, the plebeian "gods" in the upper balconies rule the theater. Their raucous boos, hisses, taunts, and cheers determine the success or failure of any performance. As the play starts, the gods, boxes, galleries, and pits guffaw at the blackface Wowski—with her childlike, lisping "black" pidgin English—and her romance with Trudge, Inkle's cockney manservant. The gods' boos and heckles indict the cruelly mercenary Inkle when he sells Yarico. Sympathetic sighs greet her ballad, a pathetic plea for Inkle's continued love:

> For him by day with care conceal'd
> To bring him food I climb the mountain
> And when the night no form reveal'd
> Jocund we fought the bubbling fountain
> Then wou'd joy my bosom fill.
> Ah! Think of this and love me still.

After the governor of Barbados, Sir Christopher Curry, saves Yarico from slavery and shames Inkle into marrying her, the curtain falls, to wild applause.

In the crowded, smoke-filled Bedford Coffee House, literati and artisans enjoy their post-show punch and buzz with gossip of sexual scandals, the stock market, politics, and the crowd-pleasing *Inkle and Yarico*. Here, patrons can read newspapers reporting that antislavery philanthropists have raised money to rescue black ex-soldier slaves from penury by sending them to West Africa where they will found a colony. Patrons hotly debate these loyalists' presence on the streets of London and the rights and wrongs of African slavery. William Wilberforce, a Tory member of Parliament who helped found the new London Society for the Abolition of the Slave Trade, has just proposed that Parliament ban the trade. Excited chatter turns to Colman's musical opera. Some claim it will stir support for the slave-trade ban—even though Wilberforce, in keeping with the precepts of the Church of England's evangelical Clapham sect to which he belongs, finds the theater immoral.[1] A theater aficionado has a hot-off-the-press edition of *Inkle and Yarico* and reads from its preface, written by famous playwright Elizabeth Inchbald: "This is a drama which might remove from Mr. Wilberforce his aversion to theatrical exhibitions, and convince him that the teaching of moral duty . . . is most effectually inculcated [in] the resorts of the gay, the idle, and the dissipated."[2] Discussion returns to the play's antislavery message, heightened by Colman's decision to change Yarico's original Native American identity to African, at Inchbald's behest.[3] Patrons read theatrical reviews like those in *Lloyd's Evening Post*, which declares, "Cold must that heart be which does not warmly interest itself in such a Yarico," and the *Daily Register*, which lauds the musical's "many noble and liberal sentiments" and their "striking effect on the audience, who received them with the most hearty approbation."[4]

In eighteenth-century London, *Inkle and Yarico*'s antislavery sentiment reached the illiterate and literate alike through performances to boisterous audiences and through offstage reverberations in broadside images, newspapers, and coffee shop repartee. Colman's musical opera opened at the Haymarket Theatre in 1787 at a pivotal moment of antislavery momentum. Contemporaries enthused that the play, performed 164 times between 1787 and 1800, drummed up support for slave-trade abolition.[5] Playwright Inchbald, an antislavery advocate, claimed *Inkle and Yarico* was "the bright forerunner of the alleviations to the hardships of slavery."[6] Actress Frances Maria Kelly took on the part of Yarico explicitly out of sympathy for the "ill used African" and took pains to "carefully put on a Brown-Sherry complexion" so as to be "excessively African."[7] Bards used Yarico's story as the basis of antislavery poems.[8]

Yet while London reporters boasted of *Inkle and Yarico*'s "noble and liberal sentiments" and their "striking effect" on the audience, when the play migrated across the Atlantic to Philadelphia, thespians diluted the piece's antislavery message through textual, costume, and set alterations. They likely did so to avoid inflaming offstage tensions over slavery. In 1790, *Inkle and Yarico* debuted in the Southwark Theatre in Philadelphia, then the seat of national government and a seaport of roughly thirty thousand people. At that time, the city boasted a thriving shipping trade, daily newspapers, numerous printers, two circuses, houses of musical entertainment, a public library, two theaters, and scores of inns and taverns. The play was performed in the early 1790s amid heightened racial anxieties as refugees from the Saint Dominguan slave rebellion flooded the city. In 1792 alone, six hundred Saint Dominguan émigrés—roughly 450 whites and 150 African slaves—sought refuge in Philadelphia.[9] Their presence in Philadelphia unsettled race relations in the city and evoked the specter of slave revolt in the South, especially as the white émigrés told horrifying tales of how "the innocent as well as guilty [were] butchered . . . [and] as far as the eye could reach, everywhere presented to us ruins still smoking, and houses and plantations at that moment in flames."[10] At the same time, Philadelphians were as enthused about the French Revolution, which stirred up newly partisan politics, as they were appalled at the slave rebellion on Saint Domingue. Democratic-Republican plebeians in the cheaper galleries and pit clamored for the orchestra to play French revolutionary songs.[11] Since the New Theatre had been established in 1792, under the patronage of a newly formed Dramatic Association composed of wealthy Federalist sponsors, theater managers had incentives to tamp down the politics of slavery, and partisan politics more generally, onstage.[12] Stage manager Charles Durang summed up the managerial intention: "Political questions, where two large parties are neatly balanced, should be warily touched on the stage."[13]

While evidence about the play's reception is fragmentary—in contrast to London, theatrical reviews were uncommon in Philadelphia of the 1790s—the edition of the play published in the city and playbills offer clues about how its antislavery potential was diminished. From its 1790 debut onward, the Southwark Theatre advertised its production as *A School for Avarice, Adapted from George Colman's Comic Opera,* a title more relevant to Inkle's greed than to the problem of slavery.[14] The rudiments of Colman's storyline remained intact, but Philadelphia thespians added dialogue that laid the blame for the slave trade at the feet of the British. For example, when the Barbados governor, Sir Christopher Curry, chastises Inkle for his intent to sell Yarico, he declares, "An Englishman. More shame for you . . . Men who so fully feel the blessings of liberty, are double cruel in depriving the helpless of their freedom."[15] Unlike the African Yarico of the Haymarket, the Southwark's wore a feathered headdress evoking a Native American.[16] The sentimental effect of the climactic scene of Inkle's marriage to Yarico was superseded by the spectacle of "a military scene in the denouement of the play, far surpassing any thing of the kind that [had previously] appeared on this stage."[17]

When it opened its version of Colman's play in 1792, Philadelphia's Lailson's Circus also emphasized fantastic extravaganza over antislavery fable, boasting that its production was "a Grand Historic and Military Pantomime—Ornamented with military Evolutions and Fights."[18] Nor was the Southwark alone in defining Yarico as Native American.[19] The Lailson Circus version was titled *The American Heroine,* and its playbill described Yarico as an "Indian savage maiden."[20] The New Theatre's 1793 production was similarly billed as *The Indian Heroine.* As Durang admitted, "This very excellent piece . . . by George Colman . . . was very much altered for [Philadelphia] representation."[21] Plays like *Inkle and Yarico* crossed the ocean back and forth during this period. So, too, did people: thespians, abolitionists, artists, and poets. But evidence shows that the ways theatrical narratives—and attendant ballads, poems, broadsheets and cartoons—intersected with political discourse about slavery differed dramatically on the two sides of the Atlantic.

The contrasting performances of *Inkle and Yarico* in 1787 London and 1790s Philadelphia invite several questions that this book seeks to answer: How did discourses of slavery and race develop differently in disparate geopolitical sites and constituencies, and what insight into this problem can we gain by using transatlantic theater and popular culture as our lens? How and why did many Britons' and Americans' attitudes toward slavery evolve from widespread complacency to bloody contestation of the institution in the late eighteenth to mid-nineteenth centuries? Did the theater between the 1770s and 1850s play a role in transmuting individual antislavery sentiment into mobilized political constituencies? This startling sea change in Great Britain, the United States, France, Ireland, and elsewhere in the Atlantic world has still not been satisfactorily explained by industrialization, shifts in moral economy about free labor, enlightenment sensibilities, religious revivalism, or the impact of the eighteenth-century revolutions. Close examination of theater and popular culture shows that they had a critical part to play in the development of transatlantic antislavery feelings.

This book examines the performance of slavery, race, and rights in theatrical and popular culture in relation to the political enactment of slave-trade abolition and emancipation in order to understand the transatlantic development of realities and discourses of race and slavery; the relationship between abolitionism and blackface performance; and the role of theater and popular culture in shaping and popularizing debates about slavery. The narrative spans the eighteenth-century revolutions through to the transatlantic antislavery efforts of the 1850s, offering a comparative, transatlantic analysis of how thespians, poets, cartoonists, and abolitionists in the two of the most populous and cosmopolitan British Atlantic cities, London and Philadelphia, depicted free and enslaved blacks in the process of weighing in on the contested issues of slavery, rights, and polity.

I examine predominantly white cultural productions of human difference, slavery, and antislavery in print, visuals, and performance, albeit contextualized in relation to the lived realities of people of African descent in London, Philadelphia, and the British Caribbean. Debates about slavery evolved quite distinctively in each city's social, political, and cultural contexts, but transatlantic exchange had its own dramatic impact, as theatrical producers and performers in London and Philadelphia created a constellation of images, tropes, and perspectives on issues of slavery and race that Britons and Americans shared. Philadelphians and Londoners contributed to the creation of a lexicon of recognizable meanings and symbols that co-mingled Enlightenment notions of natural rights and antislavery, neoclassical motifs (such as the Roman-derived Temple of Liberty as a metaphor for polity), and blackface burlesque.

The contrasting signification of theatrical antislavery sentiment in London and Philadelphia, voiced by white actors in blackface and brownface, also raises questions of the relationship between the transatlantic slavery discourse, racial burlesque, and the development of racist explanations of human difference. During the eighteenth century, on both sides of the Atlantic, human difference was commonly explained by environment and culture. A widely read discussion was that of the Comte de Buffon, whose *Histoire naturelle* (1799) claimed that people who lived in extreme hot or cold climates—be they Africans or Scandinavians—were less advanced than peoples in more moderate climates.[22] During the period slave-trade abolition was effected and emancipation began, racial categories rigidified into biologically based explanations that fixed people of different skin complexions and physiognomic features in a hierarchical order related to geography.[23] Long before *Uncle Tom's Cabin*, not only proslavery but also antislavery discourse used racial burlesque.[24] This study demonstrates that eighteenth-century transatlantic blackface performances first set this interplay in motion and were instrumental in animating incipient notions of racialized human difference.

The eighteenth-century productions of *Inkle and Yarico* in London and Philadelphia underscore the need for sustained analysis of this latter proposition. In London, the *Morning Chronicle* enthused about the "pathetic" but "tawny" and "delicate" Yarico. Wowski, her lisping maidservant, was instead "dingy" black, "thick-lipped, and flat-nosed" and incurred derogatory jibes about her perceived idiocy.[25] While her description seems prophetic of nineteenth-century biologically defined categories of human difference, on the eighteenth-century London stage ethnic identities were still flexible and depended partly on the socioeconomic status of the characters. Noble or heroic African characters like Yarico (along with Shakespeare's Othello and Juba in Addison's *Cato*) were often distinguished from menial characters like Wowski by their lighter, "tawny," complexions. By contrast, in Philadelphia, red, black, and white were already on their way to being distinct "racial" categories. American actress Olive Logan reminisced about how eighteenth-century actors donned "black gloves" and "arms of black silk" and "covered the face and neck with a thin coat of pomatum . . . then burned a cork to powder for the sables of Wowski."[26] Even heroic "Moors" like Othello were clearly demarcated from characters like the "Indian maiden" Yarico. Thus, by 1800 a reviewer criticized popular actor Mr. Farewell's Othello as unacceptably pale: "He was rather a Red-man than a Moor; and this inconsistency was the less pardonable, on account of the references so frequently made to the black complexion of Othello."[27] Plays like *Inkle and Yarico* demonstrate that theater and popular culture played a critical role in how ideas about human variety and race developed differently in Great Britain and the United States.

Yesterday's television, theater was consanguineous with politics and print culture, making it an especially potent barometer of and participant in the period's battles over polity, slavery, and rights. From the eighteenth century onward, politics infused the choice of theatrical subject matter. But theater did not simply reflect political events and debates; rather, it played an active role in steering them and shaping how they were understood. Its impact extended far beyond the physical environs of the theater and its catholic audiences, as theatrical idioms, images, and characters were ubiquitous in political and popular culture. Even Edmund Burke and Thomas Paine used theatrical analogies in their famous volleys over competing visions of polity. Burke castigated the French Revolutionaries for acting "like the comedians of a fair before a riotous audience . . . a mixed mob of ferocious men and of women lost to shame . . . As they have inverted order in all things, the gallery is in place of the house."[28] Paine countered by calling for a democratic "open theater of the world" where rational political performers on an egalitarian stage would replace the "cant and sophistry" of royalty who performed their rule "behind a curtain."[29] Both skilled rhetoricians, Paine and Burke well understood the theater's pervasive reach. Ballads sung on street corners, cartoons of blackface theatrical characters, broadsides intended to be read aloud, poetry and art using theatrical tropes, street parade floats featuring theatrical set-pieces, and polemical pamphlets—these were the theatrically infused media prevalent in a public sphere that, in its inclusion of all walks of life, all ethnicities, and both genders, was far more expansive than the oft-cited male, bourgeois, print-oriented civic culture.[30]

But the path from theatrical images, stories, metaphors, and tropes infusing these varied media to political and philosophical discourse was not a one-way street. There was a fluid circulation between theater and philosophical works, missionaries' and explorers' reports, abolitionist activities, blackface minstrel shows, street parades, fine art, political cartoons, scientific treatises, hymns, patriotic anthems, and political tracts. One example of this permeability between document and performance is the way the theater transmuted philosophical tracts, political discourses of rights, and scientific theories of race into popular form for the literate and illiterate alike, which helps explain how ideas of about race, rights, and slavery gained currency outside educated literati and scientific circles. Theater and popular culture powerfully animated these discourses as race relations in both cities evolved under pressure from demographic and economic factors. Crucially, theatrical performances were woven into the larger cultural fabric of politics, visual, print, and street performances, and the exchanges between these media helped create a transatlantic lexicon of slavery and antislavery.

This study concentrates on the two most important cities in the eighteenth-

and nineteenth-century British Atlantic—London and Philadelphia—and the exchange between them. This approach has both strengths and shortcomings. The plays, cartoons, ballads, broadsides, and political tracts all traveled far and wide to multiple cities and countries. For example, the New Theatre ensemble, composed predominantly of British-imported actors, traversed an annual off-season circuit that included Baltimore, Boston, and Alexandria, and plays and players from the company also migrated to New York. Meanwhile, the plays and performers of the three London theaters royally patented to perform narrative dramas (Drury Lane, Covent Garden, and the Haymarket) spent their off-seasons touring Dublin, Bristol, Liverpool, Bath, Calcutta, Senegal, and other parts of the British empire. The limitation of the approach taken in this book is thus obvious: one cannot extrapolate directly or neatly from the exchange between London and Philadelphia to full-blooded conceptualizations of the early American republic, eighteenth- and nineteenth-century Britain, or "the" British Atlantic world more generally. Plays, cartoons, poetry, and abolitionist pamphlets were published in multiple cities and countries and their creators traveled far and wide within the Atlantic and Pacific worlds and beyond.

Yet the exchanges between the two cities nonetheless offer a window into the British Atlantic cultural production of race and slavery. London and Philadelphia were the two largest cities in the eighteenth- and early nineteenth-century British Atlantic world.[31] As such, the theatrical and political exchange between them was vital to the development of both antislavery and popular culture in Great Britain and North America from the 1760s to the 1850s. The world's first antislavery organizations were birthed in Philadelphia in 1775 and in London in 1787. Moreover, both cities had sizeable black populations by the late eighteenth century —roughly 10,000 in London and over 6,400 in Philadelphia—the noticeable presence of whom amplified the politics of "race," slavery, and abolition.[32] And because of Pennsylvania's Gradual Emancipation Act of 1780, the city had a free black population of over twelve thousand by 1820.[33] London abolitionists, after successfully agitating for slave-trade abolition in 1807, pushed through the 1833 Emancipation Bill, which set in motion freedom for slaves in the British West Indies. London was host to seething parliamentary debates on slavery and abolition, while Philadelphia, although it relinquished its role as constitutional seat of the United States to Washington, DC, in 1801, was still a hotbed of abolitionism and political exchange. And, crucially, these two port cities sustained flourishing theater and print culture and enjoyed a constant circulation of culture, goods, and travelers. This fruitful interchange was essential to the creation of a con-stellation of shared British-American images, tropes and perspectives on race, slavery, and citizenship—highly recognizable on both sides of the ocean—that thespians, poets, cartoonists, and politicians articulated and popularized through plays, poems, polemical tracts, visuals, and theatrical performances.

The abundant political-cultural exchange between London and Philadelphia is, however, only one reason for taking this two-city approach: another motivation was to ground the ideas and cultural forms in local social and material realities in juxtaposition to their transatlantic reach. The interplay between transatlantic exchange and the contingent local adaptations—such as the disparate iterations of *Inkle and Yarico* in the two cities—was what produced a British-American popular culture. The political and cultural exchanges between the two cities shed light on the emergence of a British-American popular culture precisely because it was born of the tensions between the regional factors *peculiar* to each locale and the transatlantic themes of debate *common* to the two cities between the 1760s and 1850s. Through the exchange of transatlantic theater and related media, cultural interlocutors in London and Philadelphia contributed to the invention of a peculiar-yet-common lexicon of neoclassical motifs, blackface burlesque, Enlightenment notions of natural rights, and antislavery. Abolitionists, thespians, poets, artists, cartoonists, and pamphleteers used these tropes, images, and discourses (equally recognizable in eighteenth- and nineteenth-century Great Britain and the United States) to further contrasting, and often competing, political ends.

Well into the nineteenth century, the interchange between the two metropoles was still framed by cultural competition over definitions of liberty and polity that had their inception in the American Revolution. In this competition, the interconnected theater, print, and visual cultural exchange between London and Philadelphia (a microcosm of that between Great Britain and the United States more generally) was a key site of contest. Onstage and off, John Bull faced off against Jonathan, a comic character British performers created to mock Americans' supposed vulgarity and lack of culture. The two became stock characters in a British-American lexicon of race and slavery forged in the fires of the utopian discourse of the eighteenth-century revolutions in France, Haiti, and especially America. The American Revolution powerfully reshaped debates about slavery, polity, and cultural identity on both sides of the Atlantic. Britons agonized over the loss of the American colonies and embraced abolitionism as a way to regain the moral high ground as a liberal empire.[34] In the context of postwar anxieties about becoming American, Americans both perpetuated and altered British culture, as evidenced in Philadelphians' alterations to *Inkle and Yarico*.[35] Decades after American independence, America's "great experiment" in democracy, as the British Fanny Trollope described it in 1832, was the lasting benchmark for popular reformulations of both British and American notions of slavery, liberty, and polity.[36]

This volume pivots around axes of transatlantic disputation over slavery and polity between the 1760s and 1850s. Part I spans the 1760s to the aftermath of the War of 1812, with three interrelated chapters that examine the contestation over polity and slavery that originated in the American Revolution and culminated in slave-trade abolition in 1807–1808 and the imperial civilizing missions in Africa in the 1810s and 1820s. In this period, London and Philadelphian thespians, artists, abolitionists, and poets fashioned anthropomorphic representations of competing political ideologies in the figures of Columbia and Britannia bestowing freedom to supplicant blackface slaves. These motifs helped shape peculiarly British and American constructs of citizenship/subjecthood and became recognizable Atlantic tropes and characters wielded in disputes over slavery between London and Philadelphian playwrights, abolitionists, poets, painters, and cartoonists.

Part II explores British travel to America and curiosity about the democratic experiment across the ocean in the 1820s and 1830s and their connection to the transatlantic development of new genres of racial burlesque in variety shows and cartoons. Two interrelated chapters explore the growth of urban picaresque in prose, cartoons, stage plays, broadsides, and the relationship of early blackface minstrel performances in variety shows to racist cartoons. These chapters situate the development of blackface minstrelsy in a larger cultural context that includes neoclassical drama, abolitionist rhetoric, and politically diverse transatlantic performance spaces and audiences. In these disparate ludic spaces, blackface minstrel performances offered a variety of sales pitches about slavery and race to a range of audiences, just as their earlier cartooning and variety show cousins had. Thespians, comedians, and artists used this new genre to react to slave emancipation in the British West Indies and to black freedom in Philadelphia in the 1830s.

Part III investigates how burlesque and utopian discourses of slavery and race emerged in response to renewed revolution and revolt in the 1830s and 1840s: the second French Revolution of 1830; Nat Turner's revolt and a massive slave revolt on British Jamaica in 1831; and the Chartist movement in England and labor unrest in Philadelphia as the revolutions of 1848 swept through Europe. Radical-leaning playwrights, abolitionists, lecturers, and novelists resuscitated American, French, and Haitian revolutionary rhetoric to promote a racially inclusive brotherhood of industrial "wage slaves" and chattel slaves, yet on stage and in print, this utopian vision was performed in blackface burlesque that embod-

ied hardened racial categories. This section demonstrates that utopian radicalism and racial burlesque, often studied separately, were interwoven, imbricated
threads of the larger fabric of Atlantic political and racial ideology and discourse.
I conclude by discussing iterations of Uncle Tom and the revolutionary legacy
of antislavery and rights as British abolitionists joined forces with the Union
against the antebellum South and demonstrate how the revolutionary-era lexicon
of images and tropes enduringly shaped cultural understandings of race and
slavery.

It took recurrent slave revolts throughout the Americas, decades of abolitionist campaigning, and a bloody civil war to dismantle slavery and the slave trade in
the Anglo-American world. But before this happened, a British-American popular culture that synthesized antislavery, democratic precepts, and racial burlesque
produced transatlantic performances of slavery, liberty, and polity in theater, images, and song—always with transatlantic competition over their meanings. The
fusion of radical and reformist thought with "scientific" constructs of race would
have lasting implications for modern thought and culture. Indeed, only in 2005
would the Covent Garden Royal Opera House, where many eighteenth-century
dramatizations of slavery first debuted, finally abandon the practice of blackface
performance as an "out of date and insensitive artistic tradition" after public
furor erupted over the casting of a white mezzo-soprano as a black woman.[37] Still
shaped by its eighteenth- and nineteenth-century legacies, popular performative
culture today remains a powerful conduit for reshaping the common assump-
tions and implicit rules of a society.

PART ONE

SLAVE-TRADE ABOLITION
Pageantry, Parody, and the Goddess of Liberty
(1790s–1820s)

Transatlantic abolitionist, revolutionary, and pamphleteer Thomas Paine envisaged the origins of republican liberty in a poem first published in the *Pennsylvania Magazine* in June 1775 under the pseudonym "Atlanticus." The "Goddess of Liberty," he enthused, had descended from the heavens in her "chariot of light" and transplanted the "fair budding branch" from the "gardens above" to the "peaceable shores" of America. Once the liberty tree was planted, the "fame of its fruit" drew a fraternity of brothers "unmindful of names of distinctions . . . from the east to the west" to found a democratic, egalitarian republic, for their "Temple was Liberty." Set to the popular tune of "The Gods of the Greeks," Paine's widely reprinted canto used neoclassical imagery to define and promote an American republic founded on the self-evident truths of natural and equal rights to life, liberty and the pursuit of happiness, and to advocate the enactment of those rights throughout the Atlantic world. Paine's lyrics captured not only his utopian vision of the American Revolution but also the democratic precepts that precipitated the first movements to abolish slavery and the slave trade in the Atlantic world, established in Philadelphia in 1775 and in London in 1787. These early antislavery efforts led to the gradual abolition of slavery in Pennsylvania and other northern states in the late eighteenth century and to the abolition of the slave trade by Great Britain in 1807 and the United States in 1808.

Paine's Atlanticus moniker was entirely fitting, because both British and American poets, artists, and playwrights used the shared metaphor of the goddess in her Temple of Liberty to contest the meaning of liberty and slavery during and after the American, French, and Haitian revolutions. On both sides of the Atlantic, slavery was critical to the formation of modern civic identities. Nowhere was this more evident than in revolutionary-era Philadelphia and London, hotbeds of antislavery zeal. In reaction to the slave-trade bans, playwrights, poets, artists, architects, and antislavery advocates in both cities utilized Britannia and Columbia in their Temples of Liberty to reconfigure British and American mythologies of liberty, citizenship, and subjecthood. The theaters of London and Philadelphia staged Britannia and Columbia in their Temples of Liberty in allegorical dances, pantomimes, and "transparencies" (backlit, painted set pieces) just as the British and American bans on the slave trade went into effect. Yet the theaters of London and Philadelphia performed their goddesses in Temples of Liberty that excluded blacks from civic rights and benefits. Indeed, not only in theater but also in architecture, art, and poetry, Britannia boasted her national liberty while promoting an imperial ethno-cultural superiority that legitimated continuing colonial slavery. Columbia, meanwhile, had been celebrated by revolutionary-era painters, poets, and abolitionists for her republican values of liberty and equality, with antislavery signification. But when thespians staged the goddess in her temple on the Philadelphia stage in 1808, they fêted her as a symbol of political independence but *not* of personal abolitionist liberty, a performance that reinforced whiteness and masculinity as the defining qualifications of American citizenship.

The popular language and symbols Londoners and Philadelphians used to articulate these contrasting civic constructs and slavery's place within the polity were not just neoclassical representations of modern civic constructs. Poets, playwrights, and abolitionists also deployed blackface burlesque to negotiate the racialist anxieties about slavery, liberty, and rights unleashed by the American Revolution and the subsequent French and Haitian Revolutions and capped off by renewed hostilities between Great Britain and the United States in the War of 1812. During these revolutionary years, British artists, thespians, poets, and abolitionists used the blackface supplicant slave for mutating and overlapping meanings: as a proto-minstrel blackface clown, as a symbol of xenophobic fears about racial miscegenation (especially after the influx of former American slaves into Great Britain), and as an abolitionist spokesman reconfiguring Britannia's liberty as antislavery to rebut American accusations of British tyranny. In the early years of the American republic there was a brief utopian moment that seemed to promise the extension of republican "life, liberty, and the pursuit of happiness" to Africans, but by the early nineteenth century, Americans, using British blackface stage characters, created a newly virulent form of racial derogation through blackface cartoons and broadsides that was symptomatic of rescinding the radical revolutionary hope of liberty and rights for African Americans.

After slave-trade abolition, Philadelphians and Londoners followed these national trends when they brought mythologies of British and American liberty into contrapuntal dialogue with fantasies of Christianizing and "civilizing" the "dark continent" of Africa. The works of nineteenth-century artists, poets, and thespians sympathetic to slave-trade abolition helped focus the hope of saving the African from the ravages of war, paganism, and the interior African slave trade. For Londoners, this vision of redemptive liberty for Africa was intricately bound up in the celebration of slave-trade abolition and the way it served to reconcile Britannia's liberal nation with its slaveholding empire. In Philadelphia, by contrast, evangelical missions inspired by the Second Great Awakening were intertwined with efforts to "repatriate" free blacks to Africa, efforts undergirded both by racist impulses to expurgate African Americans from Columbia's Temple and by the desire to spread democracy and Christianity to Africa. The Goddess of Liberty and the blackface supplicant slave were key motifs in a shared Atlantic lexicon employed by Britons and Americans in both pageantry celebrating slave-trade abolition and the spread of liberty to Africa and in parody that figuratively denied Africans either British subjecthood or American citizenship.

As Britons and Americans physically battled in the American revolutionary years, they also engaged in creative and discursive combat over the meanings of slavery, liberty, and tyranny. The spectacular events and rhetorical contests of the French and Haitian revolutionary years not only amplified tensions over slavery and polity but also brought Great Britain and the United States back to war in 1812. Yet during this era of British-American acrimony and war—bookended by the American colonial protests of the 1760s and the aftermath of the War of 1812—transatlantic exchanges produced images and discourse of slavery, race, and polity in poems, cartoons, plays, and pamphlets common to and recognizable on both sides of the ocean. British and American artists, playwrights, poems, missionaries, travelers, and abolitionists produced, albeit with dueling significations, a common lexicon of images, ideas, and printed matter: the blackface slave as a symbol of slavery, the neoclassical Goddess in her Temple as a metaphor for polity, and an imperial, civilizing mandate toward Africa.

CHAPTER ONE

Celebrating Columbia,
Mother of the White Republic

On December 26, 1807, just as Congress passed legislation to ban the foreign slave trade, Philadelphia's New Theatre on Chestnut Street performed *The Spirit of Independence*, which featured "a grand emblematical transparency of the GENIUS OF AMERICA" and a "characteristical dance" set in the "TEMPLE OF LIBERTY, according to the playbill."[1] During and immediately following the American Revolution, Philadelphia artists, balladeers, thespians, and participants in festive civic parades created performances of Columbia, the "Genius of America," as an anthropomorphic symbol of the aspiring nation and a guardian of the natural right to political and personal liberty. Stirred by the revolution's democratic precepts, Philadelphians began depicting Columbia bequeathing personal liberty to supplicant slaves from her throne in the temple, seen as a metaphor for the body politic. The thespians at the New Theatre, however, stripped Columbia of her emancipatory powers in *The Spirit of Independence*. Their Genius of America dispensed no liberty: representations of supplicant slaves were nowhere to be seen. This enactment of Columbia glorified national unity but evaded the strife-ridden question of slavery by removing the slaves from the Temple of Liberty. Columbia's guarantee of political liberty was divorced from her previously inclusive mandate of personal liberty for all.

The theater's depiction of Columbia was both a gauge and propellant of the nation's political pulse; the removal of slaves from the temple mimicked post-abolition shifts in the larger body politic, including a lull in antislavery activities and newly violent attempts to restrict the political participation of free blacks. This backlash was sparked by slave-trade abolition, which had been passed just as a visible growth of the free black communities in the northern cities was drawing negative attention, and amid whites' fears that the spirit of rebellion would spread from Saint Domingue to free blacks and slaves in the United States. In this context, some white Philadelphians perceived slave-trade abolition as raising the threatening possibility of eventual emancipation and, therefore, of large numbers of free blacks flooding into the city and demanding their civic rights in the body politic.

Columbia's post-abolition Temple of Liberty—performed in theater, print, fine art, polemical pamphlets, comical broadsides, and street parades—promoted a vision of citizenship as a white and male prerogative. By excluding slaves from the temple, the New Theatre thespians expunged the slaves' claim to the "inalienable right" to liberty, as well as to civic participation in the republic they had helped found. Moreover, although at the birth of the nation cultural producers had often depicted Columbia as Native American, by the time of slave-trade abolition, they were consistently fashioning her as a Greco-Roman Goddess. This whitened Columbia better represented new ideas about white women's special role as republican mothers and also symbolized white Americans' claim to the Indian maiden's ancestral lands. The newly whitened Columbia appeared not only in *The Spirit of Independence* but also in related artwork, parades, and prose. But when artists, thespians, abolitionists, and others sought to create an emergent American idiom that celebrated the revolutionary heritage and republican nation, they reached to their British heritage to do so; the Greco-Roman goddess was closely related to Britannia, whose use as an anthropomorphic symbol of liberty originated in the Glorious Revolution, a political legacy shared by Britons and Americans alike.[2]

Side by side with the whitening of Columbia and the figurative removal of the slaves from her temple, white Philadelphians unleashed a newly virulent form of racial burlesque that disparaged free Northern blacks' civic participation in the polity and their celebration of slave-trade abolition. This racial burlesque, too, borrowed from British cultural traditions, as it featured blackface theatrical characters from British stage plays to satirize American blacks. When blacks paraded in celebration of the abolition legislation, white Northerners lampooned them in broadsides depicting malapropism-prone blackface characters celebrating the abolition bill with civic activities modeled on supposedly Native American rituals. Whites' mockery of black civic participation simultaneously derided both Native and African Americans and combined with the erasure of blacks in performances of Columbia to promote constructions of citizenship defined by whiteness, masculinity, and newly rigidified edifices of racial codification.

Natural Rights, Antislavery, and Revolutionary Columbia

Modern Columbia began emerging as a potent symbol of the colonists' right to political liberty during the imperial crisis that precipitated the American Revolution. Starting from the Stamp Tax protests of 1765, revolutionary era artists began creating a peculiarly American Goddess of Liberty. They depicted the would-be nation in a variety of shifting iconographic faces—plumed Greek goddess and

Indian princess—before her ultimate metamorphosis into a Greco-Roman deity derived from the Roman figure of Libertas.[3] This evolution was not linear, and the disparate personifications of the nation overlapped in the revolutionary and immediate postrevolutionary years, but all Columbia's visages symbolized political freedom from British imperial "tyranny" grounded in precepts of natural rights.

To achieve this meaning of Columbia, American revolutionary patriots—a name they adopted in opposition to those who wanted to remain loyal to Great Britain—depicted her alternately as an Indian maiden and a European neoclassical deity, but they invested both these visages with claims to political liberty. The Native American Columbia's "natural" indigenous identity was intended to symbolize the New World's "natural rights" to liberty and its spurning of the political hierarchies of the Old World. Appropriating Indian identity—whether to represent America or to masquerade as Mohawks at the Boston Tea Party— allowed the patriots to protest against the British from a uniquely American position.[4] This meaning of political liberty was also paramount in the early depictions of Columbia as a European American wielding a pole topped with the liberty cap. Her first visual appearance as a neoclassical deity, Libertas, was on a coin commemorating American victories at Saratoga and Yorktown in 1776, commissioned by Benjamin Franklin and minted in 1782 to celebrate American political independence.[5] Art, poetry, and songs, such as Francis Hopkinson's "oratorical entertainment," *America Independent; or, The Temple of Minerva* (1781), also sang the praises of the goddess and her temple as a motif for enlightened, republican polity and political liberty.[6] Patriots used Columbia as Indian maiden, Minerva, or Libertas interchangeably as proxies for political liberty.

But revolutionary patriots also used Columbia (in her various guises) as a potent symbol of personal liberty, a dual meaning Thomas Paine had made clear in his Goddess of Liberty ballad, in which he advocated an egalitarian polity with liberty and rights for all, "unmindful of names and distinctions." And Paine's was not a lone voice. His fellow patriot-turned-playwright John Leacock also linked the goddess with natural rights for all humankind in "The Goddess of Liberty," the poetic preface to his pro-revolutionary *The Fall of British Tyranny; or, American Liberty Triumphant* (1776). *The Fall of British Tyranny* was a complex five-act drama that began with the British parliamentary debates about the American colonies in the 1750s and 1760s and culminated with the first patriot military campaign at Lexington. Leacock, a member of the Philadelphian patriot group, the Sons of Saint Tammany (an offshoot of the Sons of Liberty), was also part of the pro-patriot reading circle of Benjamin Rush, Francis Hopkinson, Leacock's brothers-in-law David Hall and James Reade, and his cousin-in-law Benjamin

Franklin, almost all of whom were opposed to slavery.[7] Franklin's opposition was equivocal: he was a slave owner in 1776 but eventually became president of the Pennsylvania Abolition Society.[8] Although Leacock utilized slave labor in his gold and silversmith business until at least 1767, property records reveal that by the time he wrote "The Goddess of Liberty" and his play in 1776, the upwardly mobile Leacock had become a vintner who no longer owned slaves, although whether that was a matter of conscience or pragmatism is unclear.[9] What is clear in his play, however, is that he was disturbed by slavery.

At first glance, the poem and play could be construed as unabashed pro-patriot propaganda, but Leacock's poetical exaltation of the goddess was more compli-cated, as the play it introduced pointed a satirical barb at the Whig-patriot ideals of liberty and complaints of political "enslavement" by juxtaposing them to the reality of chattel slavery.[10] *The Fall of British Tyranny* included one of the earliest known theatrical depictions of American slavery: a striking dramatization of Lord Dunmore's proclamation of 1775 offering freedom to slaves who fought for the British. In Leacock's version, "Lord Kidnapper" enlists rebel slaves and tells their leader, Cudjo, in language echoing the patriots' complaints, "they have no right to make you slaves." Leacock then conflates the cause of rebel slaves with that of the rebel colonists when Lord Kidnapper boasts to the Chaplain that arming the fugi-tive slaves pits "the servant against his master—rebel against rebel." The Chap-lain's rejoinder, "a house divided thus against itself cannot stand," voices not only the patriots' worst fears about the ramifications of Dunmore's proclamation but also the threat chattel slavery posed to the nascent nation. The scriptural refer-ence to "a house divided" was a recurrent refrain in Philadelphian antislavery circles. Abolitionist John Parish, for example, in his 1806 *Remarks on the Slavery of Black People*, warned, "A house divided against itself cannot stand; neither can a government or constitution."[11] Thus, when Leacock's prefatory encomium to the Goddess of Liberty exhorted American colonists to "wish, talk, write, fight, and die—for Liberty," it also introduced a problem: to whom, exactly, did that liberty extend?

That question vexed Thomas Paine, Benjamin Rush, and other Philadelphia patriots and was at the heart of their antislavery agitation. Even before Jefferson enshrined the "inalienable right to life, liberty, and the pursuit of happiness" in the Declaration of Independence in 1776, these patriots had loudly protested slavery as antithetical to the natural right to liberty. On these grounds, Benjamin Rush excoriated the hypocrisy of rebel patriots and vehemently argued against the belief in innate racial difference in *An Address to the Inhabitants of the British Settlements in America on Slavekeeping*, published in Philadelphia in 1773. Rush condemned slavery as a "national crime" and challenged his fellow "Advocates for American Liberty [to] rouse up and espouse the cause of Humanity and Liberty."[12] Paine passionately echoed Rush's sentiments in his antislavery tract, *African Slavery in America*, published in the widely read *Pennsylvania Journal and Weekly Advertiser* in March 1775. In it, he denounced slavery as a horrible contradiction to the natural right to liberty, asking, "With what consistency or decency [can American slaveholders] complain so loudly of attempts to enslave them, while they hold so many hundred thousand in slavery? We have enslaved multitudes and shed much innocent blood in doing it, and now are threatened with the same."[13]

Philadelphian antislavery revolutionaries soon turned their fervent words into actions. In 1775, ten white "Advocates of American liberty" met in the Rising Sun Tavern and founded the first ever antislavery organization, the Society for the Relief of Free Negroes Unlawfully Held in Bondage, to advocate American liberty for African slaves.[14] The high-water mark of antislavery clamor came in 1780 when the Pennsylvania General Assembly, with Paine as clerk, passed a Gradual Abolition bill. The bill's preamble made clear that the legislators' impetus was their heightened awareness of slavery's incompatibility with revolutionary principles of liberty, which they felt keenly, having been "enslaved" themselves under the British occupation of Philadelphia, ended only four months earlier:

> When we contemplate our abhorrence of that condition, to which the arms and tyranny of Great Britain were exerted to reduce us . . . we conceive that it is our duty, and we rejoice that it is in our power, to extend a portion of that freedom to others, which hath been extended to us; and a release from that state of thralldom, to which we ourselves were tyrannically doomed, and from which we have now every prospect of being delivered.[15]

Despite this stirring foreword, the bill freed no slaves: indeed, it stipulated that all children of slave mothers serve their mother's master until age twenty-eight, and it kept all children born before the bill was passed enslaved. The 1780 law nonetheless marked a sea change of public opinion about slavery; it also meant that by the early nineteenth century Philadelphia had a sizeable free black population. All the other Northern states passed similar gradualist abolition bills, and even in the Southern states republican ideals inspired a higher rate of individual manumissions. Amid the tumult of revolution, many Americans had come to idealize a "Temple of Liberty" in which slavery was an aberration, an ugly blemish on the very liberty the temple enshrined. And, although the fledgling abolition society accomplished little in the turmoil of revolution, it was formally incorporated as the Pennsylvania Abolition Society (PAS) in 1788 and began launching legal challenges to slavery. Paine, Rush, Franklin, and other revolutionary patriots—like Thomas Mifflin and Samuel Mifflin, Leacock's and Rush's co-conspirators in the Sons of Saint Tammany—all became members of the PAS.[16]

Party Politics, Columbia's Liberty, and the Federalist Constitution

The heated debates in 1787 and 1788 over the proposed new constitution took place against this backdrop of antislavery fervor. Pro-constitution advocates prominently featured the Temple of Liberty in propaganda intended to promote the writing of a new constitution that would empower stronger centralized government as an antidote to the dire economic distress and widespread social unrest of the postwar years while also vouchsafing personal liberty. The drafters of the Articles of Confederation of 1776 had intended to protect the sovereignty of the states by preventing the federal government from imposing taxation, raising a national army, or exercising fiscal control over interstate and foreign commerce. But staggering inflation, stagnant trade, massive war debts, and demobilization of the Continental troops—many of whom had not been paid—all contributed to a wrenching economic crisis that the government, drowning in debt and not empowered to tax or regulate trade, was ill-equipped to tackle. Horrified by the specter of class-based civil strife, the self-proclaimed Federalists advocated limiting the franchise to ensure that an aristocratic elite would rule the country and writing a constitution that empowered this elite-led government to take charge of fiscal and foreign affairs. Anti-Federalists, suspicious of political elites, upheld the primacy allotted to the states in the Articles of Confederation and opposed the idea of a new constitution. The Federalists won out, and in 1788 Congress drafted a constitution for a bicameral Congress; separate legislative, executive, and judicial branches of government; and congressional power to control fiscal and foreign affairs by imposing national taxes and conducting international trade. The influential Federalist Papers, authored by James Madison, Alexander Hamilton, and John Jay, helped convince a majority that a stronger federal government would foster stability, and in so doing would, as the preamble of the constitution they authored put it, "secure the blessings of liberty to ourselves and our posterity."[17]

Federalists used images, songs, and poems featuring Columbia and the Temple of Liberty to publicize this vision of a strong central government as the guarantor of personal liberty. For instance, in the widely read and reprinted poem *The New Roof: A Song for Federal Mechanics* (1788), Francis Hopkinson likened the need for a new constitution to the need for a new roof. Once the new roof was raised, Hopkinson enthused, "The sons of Columbia shall view with delight / Its pillars and arches, and towering height . . . The world shall admire Columbia's fair seat." The recurring chorus forcefully claimed that the Temple's "new roof" would secure and protect personal liberty: "For our roof we will raise, and our song still shall be / A government firm, and our citizens free."[18] Advocates of the new constitution also conveyed these ideas through visual depictions of the Temple of Liberty, with one neoclassical pillar representing each state of the federation, and columns added as each state ratified the constitution. Many of these images were accompanied by popular ballads. Accompanying the image depicting North Carolina's ratification, for example, were these lyrics from "The Federal Edifice": "Eleven columns strike our wondrous eyes / Soon o'er the whole, shall swell the beauteous DOME / COLUMBIA's boast—and FREEDOM's hallow'd home." Image and lyric sought to persuade both literate reader and illiterate viewer that each state pillar should not only support but also be subordinate to the central dome of government and, in so doing, provide the political and economic structures necessary for Columbia's dome, or temple, to safeguard personal liberty.

Even though Hopkinson was fiercely opposed to slavery, neither he nor other antislavery Federalists made explicit the relevance of Columbia's personal liberty for African slaves in their visual and aural pro-ratification iterations of Columbia and her temple. Perhaps this is unsurprising, given that their task was to persuade recalcitrant Southern slaveholding citizens, among whom anti-Federalism was dominant, to ratify the constitution.[19] Sectional and political affiliations were not absolute when it came to slavery, but the majority of those who supported limiting the trade were Northern and Federalist. This trend held true in Philadelphia, where many PAS members were affiliated with the Federalists, along with the few blacks enfranchised to vote.[20] As James Madison observed in his notes from the convention, "the division of interests did not lie between the large and small States. IT LAY BETWEEN THE NORTHERN AND SOUTHERN."[21] When drafted, the constitution contained controversial compromises: the slave trade would continue for a minimum of twenty years; for the purposes of taxation and representation, three-fifths of slaves would be counted; and it would be a crime to aid an escaped slave. Philadelphian antislavery delegates like Benjamin Rush and Tench Coxe (both members of the PAS), as well as James Wilson, chafed at these compromises but viewed them as necessary concessions to the South and touted the possibility of ending the slave trade twenty years hence as a step toward gradual abolition.[22]

Prominent critics of slavery even led the public civic celebrations of the constitution's ratification in Philadelphia, including Hopkinson and Charles Willson Peale, one of the best-known artists of the revolutionary era. After the required nine states had ratified the Constitution and when it became clear that enough states would approve it in time for Independence Day, 1788, Hopkinson convened a committee that included Peale, which planned and designed a magnificent ratification parade.[23] Although Peale was not formally associated with the Federalists, he already had celebrated the new constitution in a transparency—a large, backlit painting—titled *Horrors of Anarchy and Confusion and Blessings of Order* (1788), no doubt a reference to Shays's Rebellion and widespread postwar unrest, and had designed floats for ratification parades in Baltimore and Annapolis.[24] Peale had grave misgivings about slavery. He freed one of his slaves in 1787 and had appealed to the Acting Committee to Prevent the Distress of Negroes (an arm of the PAS) for help in emancipating another.[25] He decried the moral effects of slavery on slave owners, whom he claimed grew "dissipated" through being "accustomed to tyrannize and domineer over . . . these unhappy wretches," and advocated instead relations "where mankind are . . . on greater equality."[26]

Despite their antislavery sympathies, Hopkinson and Peale did not *explicitly* bring Columbia's personal and political liberty to bear on questions of slavery, liberty, and citizenship in the celebratory parades, yet they did so *implicitly*. On July 4, 1788, seventeen thousand people, ranging from the city's elites to carpenters, shoemakers, and shipbuilders, participated in the Grand Federal Procession. The festive parade prominently featured several floats designed by Peale, including the Federal Ship, which took the form of a ship symbolizing the new government; a nine-foot-square transparency Peale had designed for parades in Annapolis and Baltimore featuring the "genius of America"; and the float that Hopkinson, in his account of the parade, dubbed the "Grand Federal Edifice," featuring Columbia in her Temple of Liberty, which was the centerpiece of the Philadelphia parade.[27] As Peale noted in his diary, he called this float "the Temple of Immograntz [*sic*]," a title that suggests he intended to stress Columbia's inclusive liberty. Peale's Temple of Immigrants was constructed of thirteen Corinthian columns to represent the thirteen states, with ten delegates seated below the figure of Columbia, who was positioned on top of a dome as "A goddess of Plenty bearing her cornucopia and other emblems of her character."[28] The cornucopia derived from Greek mythology but had come to symbolize to Americans the botanical abundance of the New World, their horn of plenty. Augmenting "immigrant" Americans' symbolic claim to the New World was an adjacent float on which rode "Peter Baynton, esquire, as a citizen, and colonel Isaac Melchor as an Indian chief [who were] smoking the calumnet of peace together."[29] Although black Philadelphians did not march with the Temple of Immigrants float, pulled by six white horses on a three-mile march through the city, they engaged in a civic performance of citizenship as spectators to the parade.[30]

For all Philadelphians' self-conscious use of American and Enlightenment symbols in the Federalist parade, they also drew on British festive traditions, such as Lord Mayor's Day parades and craft processions, and a class-based hierarchy to celebrate the new republic's supposed constitutional equality.[31] As well as patriotic floats like Peale's Temple of Immigrants, the procession included troops of light dragoons, corps of infantry, a herald and trumpeter proclaiming a new era, and a band of music performing a march composed by Alexander Reinagle, the New Theatre's co-manager. But perhaps most striking were the craftsmen participants.[32] House-carpenters, architects, saw-makers, weavers, calico printers, boatbuilders, ropemakers, cordwainers, cabinetmakers, gold- and silversmiths, tanners, and stocking manufacturers were among the forty-four crafts represented. Each craft marched alongside horse-drawn floats carrying insignia and symbols of their trades; on some floats artisans actually performed their crafts in a fusion of manufacturing, theater, and nation-building. Led by the master craftsmen, the journeymen and apprentices marched several steps behind, in a show of deference.[33] Toward the end of the parade came lawyers, headed by the attorney general and followed by law students; the college of physicians, headed by the president and followed by the students; students of the university led by the vice-provost; and all the city's schools, headed by the principals.[34] The organizers fixed the order of the march by lot.[35] While this democratic gesture departed from the British tradition, the procession nonetheless separated Philadelphians by occupation and demarcated rank within each craft or profession. The parade thus retained an ordered hierarchy reminiscent of British society while celebrating American republican principles, and it built on British traditions while also departing from them with peculiarly American symbols like the thirteen columns, the cornucopia, and the Indian chief.

The oratory and music that ended this pageant, however, stressed the new nation's inclusive liberty and citizenship. At parade's end, Senator James Wilson stood atop Peale's float and, in a speech filled with allusions to Roman classical republicanism, evoked "a warm and uniform attachment to liberty." Wilson enunciated all-encompassing ideals of meritocratic equality: "Let no one . . . harbour, for a moment, the mean idea, that he is and can be of no value to his country . . . every one can at many times, perform, to the state, useful services; and he, who steadily pursues the road of patriotism, has the most inviting prospect of being able . . . to perform eminent ones."[36] Capping off the festivities were toasts to "the whole family of mankind" and the singing of Hopkinson's ode, written for the occasion. Participants, reading from the thousands of copies organizers distributed, sang, "Columbia's standard on her roof display; / And let the people's motto ever be, / 'United thus, and thus united, free.' "[37] Such processional performances of Columbia and her temple, with their symbolism and rhetoric of inclusive citizenship and liberty, were a regular part of Independence Day celebrations, which included blacks until 1805.[38]

The following year, pro-ratification ballads written for the parade were performed in the theater as renewed partisan conflict blazed over Pennsylvania's new constitution and the advent of the French Revolution. Pennsylvania legislators were embroiled in dismantling the egalitarian constitution drafted by the Pennsylvania Assembly and replacing it with a more conservative one. Meanwhile, widespread celebration of the fall of the Paris Bastille soon took on partisan dimensions when anti-Federalists donned the French revolutionary tricolor cockade, renamed themselves the Democratic Republicans to suggest their greater allegiance to *liberté, egalité,* and *fraternité,* and feted the revolution in street parades and festivals.[39] Democratic-Republican plebeians seated in the New Theatre's cheaper pit and gallery showed their solidarity with French republicanism by demanding that the orchestra play French revolutionary songs.[40] Federalist supporters, for their part, were alarmed by the dangerous possibility that these same plebeians would renew their demands to "level" rank and distinction. As the Federalist-leaning *Pennsylvania Gazette* noted with trepidation, "Among the many changes in public opinion . . . that of the people of France and America, on the subject of personal rank and distinction, is not the least striking . . . the most enthusiastic Leveller that ever existed could never have hoped for a change such as has been the effect of the recent convulsion."[41] Seeking to dampen political controversy and foster patriotic unity, Reinagle, a staunch Federalist and co-manager, with Thomas Wignall, of the New Theatre on Chestnut Street, instructed the theater orchestra to play the *Federal March*—which Reinagle had written in 1788 to support ratification—and other patriotic songs.

> Behold Columbia's empire rise,
> On Freedom's solid base to stand
> Supported by propitious skies,
> And seal'd by her deliverer's hand.[42]

With his invocation of "Freedom's solid base," Reinagle offered Columbia as a symbol of both liberty and security. Francis Hopkinson's *New Roof* and Reinagle's *Federal March*, first performed by the marching band in the 1788 Federalist Parade before its revival in the New Theatre, symbolized Philadelphian Federalists' contradictory impulses. They supported the elite political hierarchy embedded in the new state constitution despite its conflict with more inclusive notions of Columbia's liberty like those performed in Peale's Temple of Immigrants. The two ballads were also indicative of the fluid exchange between street and stage, print and theater, and rhetoric and civic ritual—a fluidity that would help turn Columbia in her temple into a recognizable antislavery motif.

Republican Motherhood and Abolitionist Columbia in the Early American Republic

While antislavery advocates Paine, Peale, and Hopkinson had touted Columbia's inclusive temple and patronage of personal liberty without naming African slavery, in the early to mid-1790s antislavery proponents made Columbia's emancipatory qualities *explicit* using the whitened figure of Columbia, the idealized republican mother of the nation. The Indian princess and plumed Greek goddess fell into disuse and a whitened, neoclassical deity emerged to represent the new nation, with both gendered and ethnic implications. There were several reasons for a whitened Columbia. First, once the republic had been established, there was no longer the same need to insist on an American uniqueness predicated on borrowing an indigenous identity to oppose neoclassical Britannia's hierarchies and customs. Additionally, the Indian maiden was an increasingly troubling symbol for a nation engaged in the large-scale displacement of Native Americans that began after the war when white settlers—both the "loyalists" who had fought with the British and the "patriots" who allied with the Americans in the revolutionary war—flooded into the Ohio River valley, the Northwestern territories, and the former lands of Iroquois nations.[43] The founding elite generation faced the task of creating and wielding unifying symbols of republican citizenship predicated, both symbolically and practically, on whiteness and traditional social strata, while also conveying the unique republican nature of the new nation. Artists, poets, orators, and architects began experimenting with the creation of an independent political culture. The challenge for politicians and cultural producers was to create a language that was uniquely republican yet also preserved as a sturdy edifice the young nation's foundational legal, political, and cultural heritage. One solution was to employ and popularize neoclassical motifs, including iconographic representations of national identity.[44] Thus, when construction began in 1791 on the Washington, DC, Capitol building, popularly referred to as the Temple of Liberty, the architectural plan proudly featured a sculpture of a neoclassical Columbia on a pedestal in the foreground.[45]

But perhaps the most significant reason for whitening Columbia was that this enabled artists and thespians to use the figure as a strong visual symbol of the emergent ideal of republican motherhood and the mother's special role in train-ing her sons for civic participation, even while she herself lacked political rights. The American Revolution had unleashed the notion of women's rights, and women like Abigail Adams, Judith Sargent Murray, playwright Mercy Otis War-ren, and novelist Hannah Webster Foster challenged the notion of political rights as exclusively masculine.[46] Yet, despite Abigail Adams's famous plea in 1776 to "remember the Ladies" and the active role the Daughters of Liberty had played in boycotts of British goods and as suppliers of provisions to revolutionary sol-ders, the American Revolution did little, other than instituting small changes in divorce and inheritance laws, to change women's legal or political status. New Jersey provided a temporary exception when its constitution allowed women who met the property requirements to vote, a right rescinded in 1807.[47] The common consensus was that women's rights were distinct and separate from those of men: men's were political and legal, based on a Lockean conception of rights that emphasized equality and individual liberty, while women's were nonpolitical benefits conferred by God and expressed in the performance of their duties to society as wives and mothers.[48]

With the establishment of the republic and the need to train Americans to be republican citizens, however, the role of mothers as educators of their sons came to the fore. Women needed to be educated so they could be good republican mothers. Newly founded female academies reflected this new ethos, epitomized by Noah Webster's opinion that "the education of females, like that of males, should be adapted to the principles of the government, and correspond with the stage of society [in which they live.]."[49] Benjamin Rush, Webster, and others argued that teaching females the aristocratic skills of French, music, drawing, and dancing was inadequate; their education should prepare them for republi-can motherhood. John Poor founded an academy for girls in Philadelphia in the mid-1780s on this premise. Rush, meanwhile, in *Thoughts upon Female Education* (1787), prescribed a female education of English, geography, history, science, and bookkeeping so that wives could manage their husbands' property and educate their children in civic polity. A whitened, maternal Columbia thus embodied the new ideal of the republican mother as purveyor of civic virtue and morality.

Samuel Jennings was one of the antislavery sympathizers who used this pre-scriptive role of the whitened, maternal Columbia in her temple to call for liberty to be defined not only as political freedom but also as freedom from enslave-ment. A Philadelphian and transatlantic traveler, Jennings painted his abolition-

Figure 1. Samuel Jennings, *Liberty Displaying the Arts and Sciences* (1790–92). Jennings created this overtly abolitionist painting while in London, just as the first British parliamentary debates were under way and the fledgling London Society for Effecting the Abolition of the Slave Trade was founded. He also created a second painting that was all but identical, save that a shield bearing the Union Jack was prominently displayed at the goddess's feet. For Jennings, Columbia and Britannia were interchangeable icons of abolitionist liberty in the early 1790s, demonstrating the continuing cultural affinity between Great Britain and United States despite the war. Courtesy of The Library Company of Philadelphia

ist *Liberty Displaying the Arts and Sciences; or, The Genius of America Encouraging the Emancipation of the Blacks* (1790–92) (fig. 1) in England in 1789 as the English Parliament was seething with its first debates about abolition. He first conceived of the painting after learning that the Library Company of Philadelphia (founded by Benjamin Franklin in 1731) was to be moved to a new purpose-designed building in 1789.[50] Jennings proposed to the Library Company directors that he present them a painting appropriate to "so noble and useful an Institution." As possible subjects to hang in their new, "Elegant Building," he suggested Clio, the muse of history; Calliope, the muse of harmony; and Minerva, the goddess of wisdom.[51] The Library Company promptly accepted Jennings's offer, but took "the liberty of suggesting an Idea of Substituting the figure of Liberty (with her Cap and proper insignia) . . . [with] a Broken Chain under her feet, and in the distant back Ground a Groupe of Negroes sitting on the Earth, or in some attitude expressive of Ease and Joy." They also requested the painting include "striking Symbols of Painting, Architecture, Mechanics, [and] Astronomy," and tht Liberty "place on the top of a Pedestal, a pile of Books, lettered with Agriculture, Commerce, Philosophy and Catalogue of Philadelphia Library."[52] Jennings complied and depicted the young nation through Enlightenment symbols of art, science, and abolitionist liberty. He portrayed the book-holding Columbia as an educated republican mother of the nation, receiving appeals from Africans for their freedom and citizenship, full civic rights which she herself was denied.

Jennings also added his own Atlantic antislavery touches. He alluded to British antislavery by placing a bronze bust of British abolitionist Henry Thornton in the foreground of the painting.[53] Thornton was the chairman of the Sierra Leone Company, which had founded the Sierra Leone Colony as a refuge for impoverished free London blacks in 1791, just as Jennings was painting. Thus, Jennings's encomium to Columbia also conveyed the transatlantic nature of the antislavery movement. He went on to produce a smaller replica of the painting that differed from the original only in that Liberty became Britannia, identified by the addition of her usual shield bearing the Union Jack.[54] His depiction—as late as 1792—of the Goddess of Liberty as interchangeably Columbia and Britannia is striking, given that the revolution had prompted British and American artists to create competing anthropomorphic civic identities. But it makes sense, given Jennings's transatlantic training. At the time of Jennings's London sojourn, George Richardson's stock images of liberty in his Iconologia (1779) were still the templates for the codification of Libertas as a female holding a pole topped by the Phrygian cap of liberty for artists on both sides of the ocean.[55] Even though British and American poets, thespians, and artists exploited the plastic Goddess of Liberty to represent competing civic ideologies and geopolitical spaces, in the years between 1789 and 1792 they still drew on a common lexicon in their depictions of Columbia, the republican mother, and Britannia, icon for a monarchical empire, as symbols of emancipationist liberty. The Library Company thus hung an allegory of republican national identity and American Enlightened antislavery that was painted using British-originated symbols to American ends.

Practical Slavery, Professional Liberty, and Columbia's Black Threat

Jennings had employed the Atlantic trope of the Goddess of Liberty to praise America's republican principles, but in the build-up to the United States' ban on the slave trade, antislavery activists instead began to use Columbia in her temple to critique the shortcomings of America's republican practices. Among them was Philadelphian Thomas Branagan, a former slave-trader and Antigua planter who came to believe, as he said in the preface to his poem *The Penitential Tyrant; or, Slave Trader Reformed* (1807), that "slavery and tyranny" were "completely inseparable" and as such antithetical to both American liberty and his Methodist faith. As "there cannot be a slave without a tyrant," Branagan proclaimed, he himself was a "penitential tyrant" determined to expiate his guilty past by working against slavery in the present.[56] He made particular note of the fact that slavery, rather than being expunged as a result of revolutionary-era antislavery, had instead vastly expanded after the invention of Eli Whitney's cotton gin in 1793, which had made the cultivation of cotton by slave labor unprecedentedly profitable. Branagan's poem highlighted the discrepancy between America's boast of political liberty and its denial of personal liberty to African slaves through a satirical depiction of Columbia in her temple. At the same time, however, he used the portrayal to argue that the temple of American liberty could only be maintained by making America a *white* republic. *The Penitential Tyrant* was one of several pamphlets and poems in which Branagan invoked Columbia in her Temple of Liberty to agitate against slavery while simultaneously advocating for the removal of free blacks from the republic.[57]

Both the frontispiece of *The Penitential Tyrant* (fig. 2) and Branagan's accompanying description boldly attacked the discrepancy between Columbia's political and personal liberty, articulated as the contrast between the practice of African slavery and the profession of republican liberty. The engraving by David Edwin was titled *Practical Slavery and Professional Liberty* and depicted a slave trader and newly imported slaves coming ashore to greet Columbia, the Goddess of Liberty. Columbia is seated in her temple in front of a column inscribed "Liberty, Virtue, and Independence," which, as Branagan explained, was the motto of the Commonwealth of Pennsylvania. In case the illustration was not clear enough, Branagan went to some lengths to explain it:

> It is intended as a contrast between Practical Slavery and Professional Liberty, and suggests to the citizens of the American States the following important distich: "Sons of Columbia, hear this truth in time, He who allows oppression shares the crime." The temple of Liberty, with the motto of the Commonwealth of Pennsylvania, which would as well become her sister states, is displayed; the Goddess, in a melancholy attitude, is seated under the Pillar of our Independence, bearing in her hand the Sword of Justice surmounted by the Cap of Liberty, while one foot rests

on the Cornucopiae, and the Ensigns of America appear at her side. She is looking majestically sad on the African Slaves, landed on the shores of America, who are brought into view, in order to demonstrate the hypocrisy and villainy of professing to be votaries of liberty, while, at the same time, we encourage, or countenance, the most ignoble slavery.

By calling on the "Sons of Columbia," Branagan harked back to the revolutionary Sons of Liberty and the republic's foundational principle of an inalienable right to liberty. By directing his readers' attention to Pennsylvania's motto, "Liberty, Virtue, and Independence," he juxtaposed the gradual emancipation laws of the state, an example of "professional liberty," with the economic reality of "practical slavery" in the nation at large. Branagan's arresting use of Pennsylvania's motto suggests that he wished to convey that liberty—including for slaves—was integral to republican virtue and independence, and to offer his adopted state and its gradual emancipation laws as the standard for the nation. Columbia in her temple let Branagan mount a two-pronged attack. First, he indicted the nation's "hypocrisy and villainy" by pitting Americans' claims of being "votaries of liberty" against their practice of "ignoble slavery." Second, he contrasted this hypocrisy with the abolitionist example set by Pennsylvania and other Northern states that, by passing abolitionist laws, were practicing "professional liberty" and republican virtue.

But Edwin's image and Branagan's poem also transmitted the idea of a national Temple of Liberty in which black Americans had no voice or place. In contrast to Jennings's portrayal of African slaves appealing to Columbia in her temple, Edwin depicted a white abolitionist appealing to Columbia on behalf of arriving slaves who are positioned outside the temple. Branagan made clear that this placement was no accident, emphasizing white agency and black exclusion in the body of the poem. In *The Penitential Tyrant*, he pleaded with the "Sons of Columbia [to] forsake your lust / Oh! That my late example might impart / This noble valour to each tyrant's heart."[58] The fight to end slavery was thus a matter for the white Sons of Columbia. Moreover, while Branagan positioned himself in his "Preliminary Remarks" as a defender of the "lives and liberties of his fellow men," the men he worried about were his fellow white men, in need of protection from the slaves who posed a threat to the American republic. Branagan's vehement opposition to the slaves' determination of their own "lives and liberties" was induced in part by Saint Domingue, the former French colony where what began in 1793 as a slave revolt had birthed the independent black republic of Haiti in 1804. He feared the "anarchy and intestine commotions" of another

Figure 2. David Edwin, *Practical Slavery and Professional Liberty*, frontispiece for Thomas Branagan's *The Penitential Tyrant; or Slave-trader Reformed* (1807). Edwin's image and Branagan's text lambast American slavery and its contradiction to republican principles by invoking Columbia, the Goddess of Liberty, as a symbol of the ideal, "liberty for all." Courtesy of The Library Company of Philadelphia

"St. Domingo." It was on these grounds that he insisted, "The slave trade in the American republic . . . is to the body politic what the yellow fever is to an individual. Every slave ship that arrives at Charleston is to our nation what the Grecians' wooden horse was to Troy. The fate of St. Domingue will abundantly demonstrate this hypothesis."[59] For Branagan, both slaves and free blacks were a threat to racial harmony, a potential contaminant in the white body politic.

Branagan was reacting not only to the slave trade but also to the white refugees from Saint Domingue who swarmed into Philadelphia, telling tales of bloodshed and massacre. The refugees brought their slaves with them in the mistaken belief they could evade Pennsylvania's emancipation law, which stipulated that slaves brought into the state would become free after six months' residence. These new arrivals swelled Philadelphia's black population—and conspicuously so, for they were light-complexioned French-speaking Creoles and dark-complexioned Yoruba and Ibo born in Africa. They also appeared frequently in the vagrancy docket on charges of conspiring against or disobeying their masters.[60] These highly noticeable, rebellious immigrant slaves stimulated whites' fears that they would instigate Philadelphia-born free blacks to violence.[61]

Branagan and other white Philadelphians' fearful reactions to the Saint Domingue refugees were also framed by the larger drama of the French Revolution. After 1793, when the full horrors of the Jacobins' Reign of Terror became clear and war between revolutionary France and Great Britain erupted, enthusiasm for the revolution had waned, even among noisy plebeian theatergoers.[62] As William McKoy observed,

> The afterward excesses of the Revolutionists in France—Marat, Danton, Robespierre, and the rest . . . operated at last with a cooling effect upon . . . the public rejoicing as expressed in the theater. From the loud and deafening calls from all parts of the house, for Ci Ira Carmagnole and the Marseilles Hymn, they dwindled away to some half dozen voices. Finally, one night . . . the spontaneous, simultaneous, overwhelming hiss of a whole audience consigned them theatrically to total oblivion.[63]

According to McKoy, the Terror revealed a more savage France than even the plebeian audience in the pits or gallery could stomach. Thereafter, he observed, "public opinion having thus released itself suddenly from a passion for French Revolutionary music and song [the vacuum] was immediately supplied by the new national song of Hail Columbia, Happy Land," written in 1798 by Philadelphian Joseph Hopkinson and set to the music of "President's March."[64] Philip Phile wrote the "President's March" for George Washington's inauguration in 1789, which thereafter was regularly played by marching bands on ceremonial occasions, such as Fourth of July events. Joseph Hopkinson (Francis Hopkinson's son) set his 1798 lyrics to its popular melody and intended his ballad to keep Americans unified at a time when Great Britain and France were at war.

For in contradiction to McKoy's assertion that the entire theater spurned French revolutionary songs, American sympathies were divided even after sensational news of the Terror reached Philadelphia. Democratic Republicans continued to be more sympathetic to France, while Federalists were more likely to support Great Britain. In *Hail Columbia*, Hopkinson harked back to the revolutionary experience as a unifying memory, and called on "heroes . . . who fought and bled in freedom's cause" to be "ever grateful" for independence. The rousing chorus featured a blatant plea for political unity: "Firm, united let us be / Rallying round our liberty / As a band of brothers joined / Peace and safety we shall find." Despite Hopkinson's plea and the Anglo-Federalist theater managers' instructions to the orchestra to play "Hail Columbia," Reinagle's "Federalist March," and other patriotic songs, the partisan divisions over the French Revolution persisted from the late 1790s through the early 1800s.

These divisions, in which Saint Domingue served as a litmus test, were visible at the national abolition convention held in Philadelphia in 1797, an annual meeting of all the state-level societies begun in 1794 to call attention to "the principles of the American Revolution and the incongruity of slavery in a land which based her own liberty on the rights of man."[65] Playwright William Dunlap, a delegate who favored gradual abolition, vehemently disagreed with Benjamin Rush, Robert Paterson, and others who called for immediate abolition. Paterson praised the French National Convention's 1794 abolition of slavery in her colonies and advocated a similar "sudden and total abolition of slavery as it respects the Southern states." Rush agreed and went further. According to Dunlap, Rush repeated "with enthusiastic admiration a sentiment attributed to [French abolitionist] Condorcet, 'Perish the colonies rather than we should depart from principle.'" Dunlap and other gradualists were horrified. They interpreted Rush's invocation of Condorcet's "principle" of republican rights as legitimating the disunion of the North and South in order to end slavery.[66] But for gradualists, the even deeper fear was that sudden emancipation would unleash blacks' violent retribution on whites. As Dunlap explained to a British antislavery advocate, immediate emancipation would "perish the unity" of the United States and "inflict misery and death upon thousands," as it had in Saint Domingue.[67]

Even in 1807, as Branagan was writing *The Penitential Tyrant*, these alarmist fears persisted, although by then the national political scene had shifted. The Federalists were out of power: Thomas Jefferson and his Democratic Republicans had won the presidential election of 1800. The change in presidential politics did not, however, alter many Americans' fears that reverberations from the French and Saint Domingue revolutions would incite sectional strife and spread a contagion, as Branagan called it, of slave uprisings to the Southern states. In the North, this fear was compounded by the enormous growth in the free black population. In 1800, Philadelphia's black population had been 6,436, fifty-five of whom were still enslaved. By 1810, the free black population of the city had swelled to

9,656, of whom only three were slaves. The city's sizeable free black population was in part an outcome of Pennsylvania's gradual emancipation legislation. But the striking increase in the free black population was also because the city had become a magnet for black migrants drawn by its thriving dock economy and reputation for abolitionism and philanthropy. Fugitive slaves from the South, emancipated slaves from rural Pennsylvania and the Northern states, and freed slaves from the upper South, where masters in Delaware, Virginia, and Maryland had eased restrictions on manumission, all flocked to Philadelphia.[68]

Free blacks had a very visible presence in the city and had founded a plethora of churches and other institutions. In the 1790s, Absalom Jones and Richard Allen had founded the African Episcopal and African Methodist churches respectively, partially in response to the segregation of the white-led St. George's Methodist Church, but also because of an intensifying desire for churches of their own making. Free black Philadelphians also formed philanthropic and educational societies like the Society of Free People of Color for Promoting the Instruction and School Education of Children of African Descent, charitable societies to aid the poor, and—because blacks were denied membership in white lodges—established black freemason lodges.[69] These institutions caught the attention of residents and travelers alike. Pavel Petrovich Svinin, the Philadelphia-based secretary to the Russian Consul General in the United States, was intrigued by free black life in Philadelphia, recording it in his paintings and travelogues.[70] Based in Philadelphia from 1811 to 1813, Svinin painted a series of watercolors that documented quotidian life in the city, both black and white. He even made note of the new black institutions in paintings such as his *Black Methodists Holding a Prayer Meeting* (1811–13), in which he captured a scene of ecstatic religious enthusiasm while simultaneously providing an indelible record of the formation of black churches in nineteenth-century Philadelphia.

For Branagan, this pronounced free black presence was a threat to the republic. In his view, it was not just the specter of slave revolt that posed a threat to the republic but the mere presence of people of African descent. In his 1804 antislavery pamphlet *A Preliminary Essay on the Exiled Sons of Africa*, he had argued that the "oppressed Africans" were not inherently "inferior kind of men" but were "degraded" because they had been enslaved.[71] His pamphlet was even sponsored by Richard Allen, pastor of the African Methodist Church.[72] But Branagan's view of American blacks was fully exposed in his subsequent *Serious Remonstrances Addressed to the Citizens of the Northern States* (1805), in which he proposed that free blacks be resettled outside of the republic. In prurient language, Branagan dwelt on the horrors of miscegenation that were bound to arise if free black men, whom he characterized as hypersexed, remained in the city to "prey" on white women and produce "mongrels and mulattoes." He also argued that blacks were a burden to the city of Philadelphia, as many were in "penury and want," and that the presence of "the revengeful negro in the city" constituted a threat.[73] Therefore, Branagan argued, it would be ideal "to send the blacks to some distant island, out of our territories altogether." Conceding that it would be "unjust and cruel" to expel them from the Americas, he proposed resettling free blacks to "the most distant part of Louisiana" because it was "upwards of two thousand miles from our population . . . farther from us than some parts of Europe." Branagan demanded that the "free country where our motto is virtue, liberty [and] independence" end its "contradiction in republican ideals," but *not* by extending the temple's shelter to black Americans. "The glorious palladium of our liberty . . . is not only endangered but undermined," he concluded, and the *only* way to reconcile the "contradiction in republican ideals" is for the Temple to purge itself of "the contamination . . . to sacred liberty."[74]

Columbia's Slave-Trade Abolition and Freedom Day

Civil rituals and theater performed some of the same ideas Branagan had articulated in print. For Branagan was not alone in his desire to exclude blacks from the white body politic, and one way this manifested itself was that white Philadelphians began prohibiting black Philadelphians from participating in civic performances in which they had previously been involved. From the Grand Federal Procession of 1788 onward, blacks had participated in annual Independence Day celebrations featuring processional performances of the Temple of Liberty. But on July 4, 1805, on the eve of slave-trade abolition, white mobs forced black would-be participants out of the parade. This violent ousting of blacks from the festive public sphere was in part retaliation for an episode that had taken place the previous year. On July 4, 1804, several hundred black youths formed military-style groups and marched through the streets beating up whites. When they reassembled the following day, they harassed a group of whites and threatened to "shew them San Domingo."[75] These events (and probably also Gabriel's attempted revolt in Virginia in 1800) played on and increased the anxieties of white Philadelphians, who, as Branagan had put it, feared "the revengeful negro in the city."

The forcible exclusion of black Philadelphians from Independence Day celebrations was one reason why African American pastor Absalom Jones called for "Freedom Day" celebrations to commemorate the abolition of the slave trade. In 1787, amid furious debate about the place of slavery in the new republic, Congress had compromised by agreeing to end the foreign trade in slaves within twenty years. The ban went into effect January 1, 1808. Preaching from his pulpit at St. Thomas's African Episcopal Church that day, Jones's *Thanksgiving Sermon* drew on the book of Exodus to compare American slavery with the Israelites' delivery from Egypt. He hailed the abolition legislation as a step toward African American deliverance and salvation for Africa. He called upon his congregation to "unite, with our thanksgiving prayer to Almighty God, for the completion of his begun goodness to our brethren in Africa," and asked them to "be grateful to our benefactors," both "abolition societies and individuals." Then, in an allusion to the recent British abolition bill, he implored his parishioners to "beseech God to extend to all nations in Europe, the same humane and just spirit towards them, which he has imparted to the British and American nations." He concluded by announcing that from then on, "the first of January, the day of the abolition of the slave trade in our country, be set apart in every year, as a day of publick thanksgiving for that mercy."[76] The following January 1, the anniversary of both the day the prohibition took effect and the 1804 proclamation of Haitian independence, would mark the start of blacks' celebration of abolition. New Year's Day freedom celebrations created a collective counter to the white Independence Day public rituals from which blacks had been ejected.[77]

Despite their ejection from civic celebrations of the Temple of Liberty, Philadelphian blacks still hoped for a future in which their liberty and citizenship would be vouchsafed in Columbia's constitution. Michael Fortune made this clear. Fortune, evidently an African American parishioner at St. Thomas's, wrote a *New Year's Anthem* celebrating the United States' prohibition of the African slave trade that was published with Absalom Jones's "thanksgiving" sermon. The hymn's title was annotated by the statement, "Sung in St. Thomas's, or the African Episcopal Church in Philadelphia, January 1, 1808."[78] In it, Fortune echoed Jones's conviction that abolition would rescue Africa and lauded "God on high . . . who, with a tender father's eye / Look'd down on Afric's helpless race." Fortune thanked the "nations that to us restore / The rights which God bestow'd on all." Like Jones, Fortune praised the British abolition bill as well as the American. To do so, he summoned the Atlantic Goddesses of Liberty: "The nations heard His stern commands / Britannia kindly sets us free; / Columbia tears the galling bands / And gives the Sweets of Liberty."

Fortune's verse reveals that black Philadelphians' abolitionist prose, music, and performances employed some of the same tropes and images as those of whites. Yet Fortune used the Goddess of Liberty for a more radical message of freedom. By imagining Columbia as tearing "the galling bands" and giving the

"Sweets of Liberty," Fortune invoked her as an emancipationist icon. But his Columbia, *tearing* the galling bands, was far more active than most white abolitionists' renderings, which usually depicted Columbia *encouraging* emancipation, in keeping with the idealized white republican mother's encouragement of civic virtues in her sons. Surely this must have been a conscious choice to emphasize the nation's capacity to effect emancipation—an expression of optimism about the young nation's potential to keep its promises of liberty and rights for all, despite expanding chattel slavery, growing animosity toward black Philadelphians, and increasingly violent repression of free black men and women. In reality, Columbia's "Sweets of Liberty" had barely been given at all. But Fortune's invocation of her illustrated his belief that the principle of liberty on which her temple had been founded would ultimately be extended to black Americans. It was in this spirit, presumably, that the congregation performed Fortune's hymn and marched in Freedom Day parades.

Theatric Celebration and Columbia's Political Liberty

In contrast to the black community's jubilant celebration of abolition and Fortune's praise of emancipationist Columbia and Britannia, when white Philadelphians performed Columbia in her temple they made no mention of abolition. In *The Spirit of Independence*, which debuted at the New Theatre on Chestnut Street on December 26, 1807, on the eve of slave-trade abolition, the goddess and her temple were performed to lionize the liberty of independence, not manumission from slavery. The piece brought Columbia out of print and into embodied form on the theatrical stage. The performance featured songs, dances, and an enormous backlit transparency that, according to the playbill, contained "180 square feet of canvas—in the centre of the picture is the GENIUS OF LIBERTY, environed by a portico of her Temple, holding the arms of the union with ancient and modern trophies of war. On the right side is supported by the Goddess of Wisdom, bearing the spear and shield, on the left by Justice, with her balance."[79]

Of course, Philadelphian audience members, both black and white, familiar as they were with Columbia as an emancipationist icon, may have read abolitionist resonance into the performance as an unstated subtext precisely because of the glaring absence of slave characters on stage. Perhaps this would have been especially true for the black audience members, who comprised a segregated minority of the New Theatre's predominantly white audiences. In the 1780s and 1790s, black attendees had been interspersed in the same seating areas with whites, and included both free men—like sailmaker James Forten—and slaves.[80] Even two of George Washington's slaves enjoyed the theater when he and Martha stayed home.[81] By the early nineteenth century, however, blacks were generally restricted to the gallery.[82] Just as white thespians removed the slaves from Columbia's temple in *The Spirit of Independence*, theater managers had removed blacks from the "white" seating areas in another rejection of blacks' full participation in the public sphere, indicating that the managers intended their productions to cater to the tastes and concerns of white Philadelphians.

Not only the transparency but also the songs and dances used in *The Spirit of Independence* enunciated this intention. The musical numbers had originally been created for William Dunlap's *The Glory of Columbia; Her Yeomanry* (1807), a piece that glorified the white founding fathers and their utopian discourse of liberty without ever mentioning slavery. The play was performed in honor of the late George Washington and Independence Day, and the playbill for the July 5, 1807, debut of *The Glory of Columbia* describes the transparency that later appeared in Philadelphia in *The Spirit of Independence*:

> The anniversary of the independence of the United States: the theater in Chestnut Street will, in honor of the day, by, be ornamented with an emblematical transparent painting, representing LIBERTY, COLUMBIA AND JUSTICE, when will be presented, an historical play, founded on an interesting act, during the period of the American revolution, called THE GLORY OF COLUMBIA; HER YEOMANRY.[83]

Neither the playbills for *The Glory of Columbia* nor those for *The Spirit of Independence* list the painter, but Thomas Sully is a likely candidate, as he was the in-house painter for Dunlap's New Street Theatre when *The Glory of Columbia* debuted there in 1806 before migrating to Philadelphia in 1807.[84] While the transparency is no longer extant, Henry Dean's untitled contemporaneous painting bears a striking similarity to the detailed descriptions of it in the playbills (fig. 3).

The five-act historical drama featuring General Washington, Major André, and the turncoat Benedict Arnold used the revolutionary language of political slavery, liberty, and tyranny to glorify George Washington and American independence. The play ended with the American victory at Yorktown, with Washington giving the final speech. The general's final words were to his "brave countrymen," calling on them to ensure that "the spirit which has animated the sons of Columbia" would "remain pure and unimpaired." As Washington spoke, the transparency of the "GENIUS OF LIBERTY" descended.[85] The public would have readily recognized the association between the temple's symbology and the heroic valorizing of the country's founder. Indeed, portraits of Washington commonly featured classical emblems such as the eagle, the laurel wreath, and the liberty cap balanced on the point of a sword.[86] Performances of *The Glory of Columbia* and *The Spirit of Inde-*

Figure 3. Henry Dean, untitled (1807). Dean's etching bears a striking resemblance to the description of the backlit "transparency" used in the staging of the *Spirit of Independence* in Philadelphia in 1808. The similarity suggests that the Goddess of Liberty, Greco-Roman figures, and past presidents were common symbols of the young nation. Given that earlier depictions (see figs. 1 and 2) prominently featured African slaves appealing to the goddess for their freedom, the absence of slaves in Dean's painting and the similar theatrical transparency for *Spirit of Independence* are arresting erasures. Courtesy Yale University Art Gallery, Mabel Brady Garvan Collection

pendence ended with "a characteristic dance in the TEMPLE OF LIBERTY," as well as "The Standard of Freedom," recited or sung "in the character of the Genius of Liberty."[87]

Along with strong connections with the public civic celebrations of Independence Day, the performance of Columbia in her Temple of Liberty at the New Theatre may have evoked the symbols of Freemasonry. The transparency almost certainly did not employ any official Masonic emblems, as the brotherhood expressly prohibited unauthorized use of Masonic regalia in performance or exhibit.[88] In a general sense, however, the structure of the temple, with its portico and pillars, resembled Masonic architectural symbolism. Of course, this could also be said of numerous other depictions and performances of the Temple of Liberty, including abolitionist iterations. Samuel Jennings's *Liberty Displaying the Arts and Sciences*, for example, was replete with columns, architectural instruments, and globes, all known Masonic symbols.[89] Similarly, Masonic meaning resonated in the inclusive Temple of Liberty designed by Peale, a freemason, for the 1788 Federalist parade, as well as in his 1788 sculpture of Columbia, *Genius of America*, which employed—like Jennings's painting—Masonic allusions, showing Columbia pointing to Agriculture, Commerce, Arts, and Science.[90]

But the possible Masonic implications of *The Spirit of Independence* and its magnificent backlit transparency had as much to do with its historical commemorative function and authorial origins as with its visual symbolism, per se. Playwright William Dunlap was well known as a Masonic "brother," one of numerous visual and performing artists drawn to Freemasonry's cosmopolitan membership and celebration of the arts.[91] These interlinked associations had a tacit subtext of black exclusion from the polity. There were, of course, black Masonic lodges in Philadelphia, but when Absalom Jones, Richard Allen, and James Forten, among others, founded the black lodges, they did so in defiance of the white lodge's rejection of their membership and refusal to grant them a license to organize.[92] Freemasonry in Philadelphia obviously had exclusionary connotations. Meanwhile, the construction of the U.S. Capitol, another Temple of Liberty in Washington, DC, was under way, and it had strong associations with George Washington, Freemasonry, and racial exclusion. Freemason George Washington laid the cornerstone of the Capitol in a ceremony of Masonic rites, but it was slaves who constructed it brick by brick.[93] Indeed, James Madison's secretary complained of the "revolting sight" of "gangs of Negroes" working to build a capitol for a nation founded on liberty and democracy.[94] Philadelphian Jesse Torrey, too, abhorred the use of slave labor to build the Capitol, decrying "the contradiction of erecting and idolizing this splendid . . . temple of freedom and at the same time oppressing with the yoke of captivity . . . our African *brethren*."[95] *The Spirit of Independence* and its "emblematical" Temple of Liberty were closely associated with Dunlap, with the construction of the Capitol, and with the veneration of Washington, who figured in *The Spirit of Independence* as "the bust of the president of the United States." And Washington, Dunlap, and the Temple of Liberty all had ties to Freemasonry, with its practice of racial exclusion. And just as slaves were building the real-life Temple of Liberty, free blacks were being expelled from the body politic—a bitter irony embedded in the figurative removal of the slaves from the theatrical stage.

Abolition and the question of slavery fared no better on the national political stage in the next few years. The slave-trading ban proved a hollow victory, as it did little to impede the continued illegal trade in slaves and burgeoning internal slave trade to the plantation economy.[96] And in the years following its passage, there was a lull in public interest in antislavery because the act served, as W. E. B. Du Bois wryly noted, "to quiet the public conscience" by fostering the myth that "slavery would gradually disappear in the wake of the slave-trade."[97] In Philadelphia, abolitionists found both public opinion and the courts to be less sympathetic to their cause than previously. Meanwhile, an unintended consequence of abolitionists' earlier legislative successes was the influx of penurious blacks into the city.[98] The presence of these poor immigrants from other states and unease stirred by the 1790s surge of Saint Dominguans of color fostered the racial anxieties expressed so vituperatively by Branagan but shared by other white Philadelphians.[99]

Columbia, Mother of the White Republic

Columbia's whitening and the excision of her emancipatory appeal came at the same time as the development of a new and potent form of racial mockery that borrowed from British blackface theatrical characters to articulate the exclusion of blacks from the American civic polity. The ebb in antislavery fervor was accompanied by a surge in racialist resistance to the idea of eventual black freedom, the possibility of which, however illusory, abolition had posed. One measure of this hardening was whites' continued virulent opposition to and mockery of blacks' attempts at civic participation. Such opposition was both literal and figurative. In a literal sense, blacks continued to be forcibly excluded from Independence Day celebrations, prompting one black citizen to snort sarcastically, "Is it not wonderful that the day set apart for the festival of liberty, should be abused by the advocates of freedom, in endeavoring to sully what they profess to adore?"[100] And figuratively, white Northerners developed a genre of performative racial ridicule that derided blacks' attempts to belong to the civic polity by mocking the civic rituals—commemorative hymns, Freedom Day parades, public toasts—with which blacks commemorated the slave-trade abolition. This derision came in the form of broadsides consisting of dialogues between two "black" characters celebrating "Bobalition." This malapropism was typical of the broadsides' use of "black" dialect comprised of grossly mispronounced and misused language. In Philadelphia, this new genre of parody was first published in a series in the *Tickler* on July 19, 1809. The genre has been dubbed "literary blackface," but it can also be considered "oral blackface" because the malapropisms would have been particularly humorous (to white audiences) when read aloud.[101] The comic dialogues were written in the form of a theatrical script, suggesting they were intended to be spoken aloud.[102] The genre took aim at black civic organizations and festivities, ridiculed black attempts to participate in the civic life of Philadelphia, and rejected black claims to citizenship in the American republic.

Such malapropism-ridden "black" speech was not new, but its antecedent theatrical usage was by slave characters in British-penned plays critiquing black slavery rather than mocking black freedom. Perhaps the most famous progenitor of antislavery appeal in blackface and "black" dialect was the character Mungo in Isaac Bickerstaffe's *The Padlock*, which debuted at Philadelphia's Southwark Theatre in 1769. An importation from London, where it had opened to great acclaim the year before, the play became a perennial favorite on the stages of the early republic.[103] Philadelphia theater manager Charles Durang confirmed that it "was performed several times almost every season from its debut to 1800."[104] The music from *The Padlock* also sold well, and the songs were published in anthologies, newspapers, and magazines.[105] Adapted from Miguel de Cervantes's *El celoso extremeño*, this musical comedy, a short afterpiece usually performed following a full-length drama, was set in Salamanca, Spain, and featured an abusive relationship between Don Diego and his African slave, Mungo.[106] The aging Don Diego, secretly plotting to marry his young ward, Leonora, keeps her under lock and key to ensure her chastity. When he leaves to ask Leonora's parents for permission to marry her, he padlocks her and Mungo in the house. Mungo assists Leander, Leonora's would-be suitor, in climbing over the wall to woo Leonora. A recent escapee from Algerian pirates, where his master was a "cruel and malicious Turk," Leander empathizes with Mungo over his enslaved state. Leander's reference to the systematic enslavement by Barbary pirates of white sailors off the coast of North Africa invoked a familiar antislavery trope in which Algerian captivity was likened to chattel slavery.[107] Although Mungo fantasizes about revolt, he is there waiting on Don Diego's return. The Don, although forced to acknowledge that his padlocked jail has failed to subjugate either his fiancée or his slave, releases only Leonora. Ultimately, *The Padlock* staged resistance to the harsh conditions of slavery rather than emancipation from its state.

The play nonetheless introduced the question of slavery and the first theatrical blackface slave to the early American stage. Lewis Hallam's portrayal of a clown-like Mungo was replete with "black" dialect, and reviews and contemporaries' anecdotes are filled with favorable comparisons of Hallam's supposedly authentic impersonation of a slave to that of Charles Dibdin, who essayed the role in London. Durang declared that "Hallam's Mungo was the originator of the negro character on the stage, and having an opportunity of studying the African race in this country, was a better representative of the character than the English Mungo, who had probably never seen a negro."[108] Playwright William Dunlap agreed, claiming that Hallam gave "Mungo a truth derived from study of the negro slave, which Dibdin . . . could not have conceived."[109] Although a comic character, Mungo bemoaned his enslavement, overwork, and harsh treatment throughout the play, sentiments made popular through the chorus of one of the character's bestselling songs: "Mungo here, Mungo dere, Mungo everywhere . . . me wish to de Lord me was dead."

Philadelphian playwrights like John Leacock and John Murdock probably modeled the speech of their blackface slave characters on Mungo. Leacock's depiction of fugitive slaves fleeing their masters to fight for the British in exchange for their freedom in his *The Fall of British Tyranny* featured a rebellious slave leader, Cudjo, whose malapropism-filled dialogue closely resembled Mungo's. Like Mungo, Cudjo had minstrel-like dimensions as a result of Leacock's clumsy imitation of "black" dialect. Later playwrights followed suit, with the blackface characters in John Murdock's abolitionist dramas fitting the mold and limitations of Leacock's Cudjo and Bickerstaffe's Mungo with their mistake-ridden English and caricatured personas.[110] Murdock's *The Triumph of Love; or, Happy Reconciliation* (1796) put the first scene of emancipation on a Philadelphia (or American) stage when Quaker George Friendly manumits his slave Sambo. In the follow-up, *The Politicians; or, A State of Things* (1798), the newly freed Sambo debates the pros and cons of French versus American republicanism with two slave friends, Pompey and Caesar.

Although these comic blackface slaves could voice antislavery views, the figures were malleable and had proto-minstrel traits that made it easy for cultural producers to use them in racialist cartoons and oral blackface broadsides that mocked abolition.[111] Murdock's Sambo, for example, prefigured the blackface minstrel urban dandy who wastes his freedom on frivolity and leisure.[112] After gaining his freedom, Sambo preens in front of a mirror, admiring his hair, figure, and clothing, an eroticization of the black body that would be a key trait of later blackface characters like Zip Coon and his brethren. Mungo articulated sentimental antislavery through minstrel-like buffoonery, but critics focused on the latter. The *Pennsylvania Gazette* stressed how Hallam's "sooty countenance and glaring eyes were excessively humorous."[113] Mungo, Cudjo, and Sambo—and their cousins Quashee, Pompey, and Caesar—were multivalent characters whose meaning was contingent on context and in whom cultural producers fused discourses of antislavery, racism, and partisan satire.

Indeed, even before the creators of oral blackface used Mungo as a recurring character in the 1810s, cartoonists had used him to satirize Jefferson's Democratic Republicans. A pro-Federalist 1793 print titled *A Peep into the Anti-federal Club* featured Mungo in a moblike crowd listening to Thomas Jefferson standing on a soapbox and delivering a parody of a monologue from *Hamlet* (fig. 4). The cartoon thus implicitly likened Jefferson to Hamlet, a character who sought to gain power through unlawful and bloody means and, in so doing, risked anarchy. At the same time, because Shakespeare epitomized British theatrical culture, the image of Jefferson as Hamlet served to deride the perceived Democratic Republicans' threat to established Anglophile culture—and therefore to deference —from political power gained by French-inspired Democratic-Republican plebeian supporters. The cartoon scorned a possible military alliance with France through the elegantly dressed "Citizen" Edmond Genêt, the French emissary to Philadelphia, who gleefully holds up a plan to subvert American government.[114] Popular democracy's threat to stability and order is personified in identifiably poor "citizens." The "rabble" includes, on the far left, a black man begging from David Rittenhouse, a patriot and renowned astronomer, scientist, and member of the American Philosophical Society. A black man at the far right is addressed by one of Jefferson's followers as "Citizen Mungo," whose presence encapsulated a mocking double entendre. The cartoonist used the figure to warn that the Democratic Republicans would break down deference by including propertyless laborers, mechanics, and even "mungos" as equal citizens and derided Jefferson's willingness to exploit their support to climb to power. But the two blacks also satirized the pro-slavery bias of the Democratic-Republican Party and its inconsistency with the "spirit of '76" they purported to uphold. Subsequent prints also used Mungo to critique the Democratic Republicans on similar grounds.[115] When the creators of oral blackface named their recurring characters Mungo, Cudjo, Quashee, and Sambo, they drew on immediately recognizable theatrical slaves who had already migrated from theater to print.

The first oral blackface dialogue, titled *African Tammany Society Celebration*, originally published in 1809 from the *Troy Gazette* in Bradford Country, Pennsylvania, and republished in a Philadelphia paper, *The Tickler*, later that year, depicted a fictional black Tammany society holding a meeting to celebrate American independence. The group's name referenced the all-white revolutionary group, the Sons of Saint Tammany, an offshoot of the Sons of Liberty, whose members included Benjamin Franklin, John Dickinson, Benjamin Rush, and the playwright John Leacock.[116] The aim of the piece was to pour scorn on blacks' claims to the revolutionary legacy of liberty and rights for which the Sons of

Figure 4. A Peep into the Anti-Federal Club (1793). Many historians have used this cartoon to illustrate the extreme partisanship that had developed between Federalists and Democratic-Republicans. But it also demonstrates how the theater played a crucial role in mediating these political fissures, at the heart of which was the issue of slavery: Jefferson performs a monologue from Hamlet from his soapbox, and Mungo, the blackface rebel slave from Isaac Bickerstaffe's wildly popular musical comedy *The Padlock* is a conspicuous presence. Courtesy of The Library Company of Philadelphia

Liberty had fought. The Sons of Saint Tammany had conspired for revolution by laying claim to Tammany, a Delaware Indian chief who signed a peace treaty with William Penn and became a symbol for American colonists of their claim to the New World. Leacock included a Tammany poem in his pro-revolutionary *Fall of British Tyranny*: "In freedom's bright cause, Tamm'ny plead with applause / And reason'd most justly from nature; / For this, this was his song, all, all the day long; / Liberty's the right of each creature, brave boys."[117] But Tammany society members also, like their fellow patriots at the Boston Tea Party, dressed as American Indians to represent the new ideas that freed them from Britain's rule. At their meetings they appropriated an array of indigenous symbols and rituals, such as the powwow and the peace pipe, and performed imitations of Indian oratory and ritual dances.[118] They also engaged in ritual toasts and songs, which were afterward printed.[119] They lionized the departed Chief Tammany to celebrate the arrival of a new era in which European Americans would lay claim to the New World by spurning the Old World.[120] The Tammany society members took their activities seriously as a patriotic encomium to an independent nation founded on "the broad basis of natural rights" and "indissoluble bonds of Patriotic Friend-ship."[121] So when the African Tammany dialogues linked the displacement of Na-tive Americans and the disparagement of free African Americans, they not only promoted a white body politic from which both groups were excluded but also denied them any claim to the revolutionary heritage of natural rights and bonds of indissoluble friendship shared by white patriots.

The *African Tammany* dialogues clearly also served to reinforce the recent ex-clusion of blacks from white Independence Day celebrations and, by implication, to mock blacks' own Freedom Day celebrations. The first African Tammany dia-logue was dedicated to "the amusement of our Society of white Indians" before it launched into blackface oratory to establish its characters and purpose:

> De anniversary of de American independence, who is tirty tree years old now, our Tammany Society all celebrate 'em on de fourth of July at de wigwam which we got in Second-Street. We got a nice good bower in dat place which Quasha and Cudjo fix up—We light a council fire to warm a poor negur, light a pipe a pieceby, and boil roast beef on—we hab good rum—good roast pit—good loaf and fish—good tobacco—good fiddle—good pow wow—good company, better dan de demmicrats I guess . . . De *spirit of Tammany* he was dere, and was mighty grad to see us all so merry—Sambo says he see him.[122]

Here, Quasha, Cudjo, and Sambo are imitating the Sons of Saint Tammany's civic rituals: the meeting in the wigwam, the powwow, the council fire, the toasts, and the peace pipe. But they are shown enacting these symbolic ceremonies friv-olously, after having played the fiddle, drunk some "good rum," and become "so merry." Their tipsy celebration implied that the black Tammany members un-derstood neither the significance of the Sons of Saint Tammany to the revolution nor the seriousness of civic celebrations of independence. The comment "better dan de democrats" alluded to Thomas Jefferson's Democratic-Republican Party, which claimed to be more radically democratic than the Federalists yet remained the party of most Southern slaveholders. As well as rejecting blacks' claims to the revolutionary legacy, the dialogue thus also scoffed at black participation in the "white" public sphere, be it political parties or Independence Day celebrations.

The creators of African Tammany went on to lampoon blacks' expulsion from Independence Day celebrations. In one vignette the narrator laments, "De Sachem of de toder Tammany Society didn't cum. If all our society had cum togeder, I guess we should hab one long procession . . . pity we sons of Tammany couldn't agree to be all wrap up togeder in one piece of wampum." There followed a parody of the public toasts customary at political and civic events, and a standard part of white Tammany ceremonial rituals. In another pointed reference to blacks' exclusion from civil society, one toast reads: "May all de Tammany Societies come into one society, den what a dam big society we shall hab." A later toast contains several related puns, calling for "de 4th of July" to come a "dozen times a year" so that the Sons of Tammany will have more "free days." Here, the writers jeered at blacks' desire to be a part of the all-white celebrations of July 4 while simultaneously deriding their Freedom Day counter-celebrations by suggesting blacks "free day" celebrations were merely occasions to be frivolous, drunk, and lazy.

This new genre of racial ridicule, with its free interchange between theatrical, print, visual, and civic culture, soon spread, with far-reaching implications. Indicating the immediate popularity of oral blackface in Philadelphia, the *Tickler* promptly published other African Tammany Society dialogues, as did *Poulson's Town and Country Almanac*.[123] But the genre was not limited to Philadelphia. In Boston and New York, "Bobalition" broadsides used the same Tammany Society characters and also featured toasts and civic meetings, but they added dialogues written out in the form of a play script. Like the African Tammany series, the Bobalition broadsides used the abolition of the slave trade—and blacks' celebration of it—to portray black civic participation and aspirations to political equality both threatening and laughable. To this end, the earliest extant Bobalition broadsheet, titled *Invitation, Addressed to the Marshals of the Africum Shocietee at the Commemoration of the Abolition of the Slave Trade* (Boston, 1816), explicitly derided free blacks' Freedom Day parade, as did subsequent broadsides. The development and spread of this new performative genre reflected the hardening of white racist attitudes and prefigured the increase of racial violence in Philadelphia and other Northern cities.[124] Post-abolition oral blackface dialogues and their illustrations also marked the genesis of a fully transatlantic genre of racial ridicule in the 1820s and 1830s, one that built on the template set by the African Tammany Society and Bobalition dialogues and their illustrations and relied on a free-flowing transatlantic circulation between print and theatrical performance.

The abolition of the slave trade in 1808 was thus a trigger for the articulation of citizenship as exclusively white and male and for increased expression of white racist attitudes towards blacks. Using the neoclassical lexicon, images and performance traditions developed in the revolutionary years, artists and thespians in the early republic helped create and animate ideas of exclusively white, male citizenship and embedded them both in performances of racial mockery and constructions of the whitened Columbia in her Temple of Liberty. In the 1790s, the constricted definition of liberty as a white, male, and expansionist prerogative had not yet been cemented, and it coexisted with more inclusive constructions of polity and rights. Thus, Samuel Jennings had in 1791 still been able to hold up an image of Columbia emancipating black slaves to boast of the extension of republican liberty and rights to even the lowliest members of the temple. But by the early nineteenth century, the meanings of Columbia had shifted far away from the goddess whose liberty was both political and emancipationist.

The shift had been threefold. For some—like Branagan and Edwin—the goddess in her temple became a bitter symbol of the dichotomy between republican rhetoric and reality, and they and others embedded into Columbia their desire not only to end slavery but also to banish blacks from the body politic and even the country. But other white cultural producers used visual and theatrical representations to remove the slaves from the temple in order to create a version of national harmony in which tensions over race and slavery were rendered conveniently invisible. Finally, some white satirists, reacting directly to slave-trade abolition and the perceived threat of the growing free black population and its institutions, created a genre to mock free blacks' claims to membership in the body politic as counterfeit. As Paul Goodman has argued, the idea of America as a "Herrenvolk republic" did not randomly appear. Rather, "it emerged only after the progress and demands of free blacks compelled whites to clarify and make explicit their understanding of American republicanism as the white race's exclusive gift."[125]

While Philadelphian whites expelled blacks, figuratively and literally, from Columbia's temple, they still hailed the brick and mortar Temple of Liberty, built by slaves, as a symbol that the new republic, as Pennsylvania congressman James Wilson put it in 1787, would "lay a foundation for erecting temples of Liberty in every part of the earth."[126] This formulation echoed Thomas Paine's utopian vision, from 1776, of the spread of democratic revolution. But Paine and Wilson's proud pronouncements were also prescient intimations of the new nation's imperialist ambitions: her manifest destiny to establish, in Jefferson's words, an "empire of liberty" that would stretch across the continent, displacing indigenous inhabitants. Wilson's global vision also, perhaps unwittingly, foreshadowed the nineteenth-century initiative to expunge free blacks from the new nation—as Branagan and others had recommended—and even the "repatriation" of free black Americans to an African colony with the promising name of Liberia. The nineteenth-century Temple of Liberty was an implicitly racialized and gendered metaphor for polity, a far cry from what Paine had envisioned as an enactment of the revolutionary goddess's egalitarian Temple of Liberty. As well as transforming Columbia into the symbolic mother of the white Herrenvolk republic, early Americans also began reworking her into an imperial motif—an irony, given that the figure had been forged out of opposition to imperial Britannia.

CHAPTER TWO

Abolitionist Britannia
and the Blackface Supplicant Slave

The nations not so blest as thee
Shall in their turns to tyrants fall;
While thou shalt flourish great and free,
The dread and envy of them all
Rule, Britannia! Britannia rule the waves:
Britons never will be slaves.

—James Thompson, "Rule Britannia" (1740)

James Thompson's "Rule Britannia," a poem glorifying empire, militarism, and commerce, was set to music and turned into a nationalistic anthem by Thomas Augustine Arne in 1740. The anthem took on new antislavery resonance in 1807 as Great Britain abolished the slave trade and fought Napoleon. Artists, abolitionists, pamphleteers, and thespians proudly celebrated slave-trade abolition as evidence of Britannia's commitment to liberty in language and images that had their origins in the American, French, and Haitian revolutions. Cultural interlocutors had first begun figuratively associating Britannia with antislavery in the late 1760s as a rebuttal of the American colonists' ire at Great Britain's "tyranny" and political "enslavement." Their popular reworking of the idea of British "liberty" undergirded the establishment of the London Society for the Abolition of the Slave Trade in 1787 and the first parliamentary abolition petition of 1789. After a lull in antislavery momentum in the repressive anti-Jacobin milieu of the 1790s, which associated abolitionism with the violent excesses of the French and Haitian revolutions, Britons resuscitated abolitionist Britannia in the early nineteenth century. This new version was predicated on the boast of a "great and free" nation opposing the tyrant Napoleon, who had reinstated slavery in the French colonies in 1802. When the slave-trade abolition bill passed in 1807, Britons touted the national icon as unequivocally abolitionist. Architects built monuments and sculptures to Britannia's emancipation of her slaves in her Temple of Liberty. Poets extolled Britannia's glorious decree in jubilant verses. Artists rendered Britannia freeing her supplicant slaves. And in *Furibond; or, Harlequin Negro*, according to the stage directions, the "figure of Britannia with her lion descend[ed] from the Skies" and, carrying a writ of law abolishing the slave trade, heralded Britain's "blest decree, that gives the Negro *Liberty*."[1]

This chauvinistic boast about British liberty came in the aftermath of defeat in the American war, a war that provoked great anxiety in Britons about racial, national, and imperial identity. The American revolutionary war had divided Britons, some of whom deplored it as an "unhappy and unnatural" civil war with "our friends, our brethren," as the *London Evening Post* reported.[2] The war triggered anxiety over the meaning of subjecthood—were the Americans fellow Britons or subject peoples?—and over larger questions about British imperial expansion, such as the acquisitions made by the East India Company or the incorporation into the empire of French Canadian Catholics.[3] American independence nonetheless highlighted stark contrasts between many Britons' ideas of cultural, ethnic, and political sovereignty and the nascent nationalist identity embraced by their cousins in North America. After the loss of the American colonies, one conduit into which Londoners channeled this angst over the "civil war" with America was a chauvinistic reclamation of British liberty, which tapped into "a culture of patriotism," albeit one in which many Britons had considerable unease about imperial identity. In contrast to the American transformation of Columbia from an emancipationist to an exclusionary symbol, Britons performed Britannia as triumphantly abolitionist, with slave-trade abolition serving as a potent signifier for British liberty.

Yet, like Columbia's slave-trade abolition bill, Britannia's "blest decree" freed no slaves. Pantomimes like *Furibond*, as well as images, songs, and cartoons featuring theatrical characters, played a key role in reconciling the continued practice of chattel slavery in Great Britain's Caribbean colonies with Britannia's putative liberty. Artists, poets, and thespians performed slave-trade abolition as the glorious triumph of the virtuous goddess bestowing liberty on passively grateful slaves. These enactments expunged the slaves' agency, and hence the slaves themselves, by lionizing a pantheon of white philanthropists as liberal Britannia's collective representatives. Even as they masked the reality of slavery in the British West Indies, white Britons' erasure of the slaves in theater and popular culture signified a profound anxiety about empire. Triggered by the need to reinvent national and imperial notions of "Britishness" in the face of imperial defeat in the American war, this anxiety grew out of differing American and British meanings and praxes of liberty and slavery. Slave-trade abolition marked the genesis of a self-congratulatory mythology in which this postwar anxiety, as well as national guilt over British slave-trading and slave-owning, was expiated by visual erasure of the slaves themselves from national memory.[4]

This mnemonic sleight-of-hand also had striking consequences for subsequent debates about civic subjecthood, rights, and emancipation. First, the celebration of philanthropic reform "from above" not only ignored Britain's slave population's participation in its own deliverance but also implicitly rejected the democratic, rights-based motivations of both black freedom fighters in the Caribbean *and* white plebeian protestors at home. In depicting Britannia's abolitionist decree as emblematic of a liberal, Whig state, artists and thespians helped fix a social and racial codification that denied the civic equality and rights of black subjects of the empire and of white plebeian subjects of the nation. Second, denying the slaves' agency while boasting about Britannia's governmental powers conveniently privileged an ethos of *eventual* emancipation. Gradual emancipation was promoted over immediate liberty, especially liberty won by revolutionary means. Moreover, blackface supplicant slaves in images, prose, and lyrics along with the theatrical jester, Harlequin Negro, were symbiotic counterparts to white Britannia in articulating subjecthood as white, masculine, and a prerogative of the bourgeois and elite. Blackface slaves and Harlequin Negro, with his hypersexuality and comic obsequiousness, prefigured blackface minstrel figures and revealed racialist anxiety about the threat of black emancipation to Britons' racial purity.

Britannia's Liberty, Columbia's Slaves, and Transatlantic Antislavery

Cultural producers began creating the lexicon of images and discourse they would later use to celebrate slave-trade abolition during the imperial standoff that erupted with the Stamp Act Protests of 1765 and built up into the American Revolution: British liberty as antithetical to American tyranny; abolitionist Britannia in her temple; and the blackface supplicant slave as a figure that embodied both racialist anxieties and celebration of British philanthropy. These motifs developed through circulation of theater, print, and visual culture. The revolution's rhetoric of rights and liberty stimulated a surge of antislavery sentiment and action, just as it had done across the Atlantic. For, as Linda Colley has suggested, abolitionism became a way for Britons to "reaffirm their unique commitment to liberty at a time when war with America had called it into question."[5] British cultural producers refuted the Americans' accusations of tyranny and political enslavement by castigating the colonists as slaveholders and, in so doing, rehabilitated Britannia's "liberty" as antislavery. Although not the last word in reconstituting "Britishness," cultural producers' efforts were nonetheless crucial:

slavery was at the very heart of transatlantic competition over national cultural and political identities.

Although Britannia's use as an anthropomorphic symbol of the British Isles dated back to the Roman empire and the myth of Britannia's "liberty" had been founded on the legacy of the Glorious Revolution, the figure was fully forged in the fires of the American Revolution.[6] When the crisis between Great Britain and her North American colonies exploded in the 1760s and 1770s, Britons and Americans struggled to lay claim to competing meanings of "liberty." In Great Britain, both opponents and supporters of the Americans' protest grounded their stances on the meaning of British liberty. As early as 1766, parliamentarian Edmund Burke, who was sympathetic to the colonists' fury, averred, "Without freedom [the empire] would not be the British Empire."[7] In ideological contrast, Londoner Robert Avery wrote a theatrical ballad justifying British imperial policy, *Britannia and The Gods in Council; A Dramatic Poem: Wherein the Felicity of Great Britain Is Proved and the Causes of the Present Disputes in Europe and America Are Debated* (c. 1765).

Artists also used anthropomorphic female images of Great Britain and her rebelling North American colonies like *The Female Combatants* (1776) to show contending understandings of liberty (fig. 5). Like the colonists, Britons often depicted America as Native American, but they did so to reject the colonists' claims of a "natural right" to liberty. In *The Female Combatants*, the regally dressed, neoclassical Britannia warns her rebellious colonial offspring: "I'll force you to obedience, you rebellious slut." America, depicted as a half-naked Native American, defies her "mother" with a cry of "Liberty, Liberty forever, Mother, while I exist." America's shield rests on a flourishing tree of liberty, topped with the Phrygian cap of liberty, while Britannia's unhealthy tree, labeled "for obedience," is emblematic of the ailing empire. A superficial perusal might suggest that the image supported the colonists' fight for independence. But by depicting Britannia insulting America as a "rebellious slut," the artist conflated licentiousness with rebellion and implied that American colonists could not claim *true* liberty because their actions were illegitimate and immoral.[8] The artist thus claimed Britannia's rule of law and America's obedience to it as requisite to the healthy "liberty" of empire, and chastised the colonists by portraying their accusations of Britain's imperial tyranny and enslavement as the unjust complaints of an unlawful and slatternly child bent on destroying the health of the empire.

London writers, poets, and playwrights also rebuked the colonists' allegations of metaphorical enslavement by juxtaposing them to the reality of African slavery in America, a rhetorical move famously captured in Samuel Johnson's sarcastic

Figure 5. The Female Combatants (1776). This British print epitomizes how even some Britons represented the American colonies as Native American: a bare-chested Columbia is using her fist to aggressively challenge the overdressed, bewigged, and elite Britannia. Courtesy of Lewis Walpole Library, Yale University

snipe, "How is it we hear the loudest yelps for liberty among the drivers of Negroes?"[9] Indicting North Americans as the "drivers of Negroes" allowed Britons to claim moral, and political, superiority, as in Londoner Ambrose Serle's *Americans against Liberty; or, An Essay on the Nature and Principles of True Freedom, Shewing That the Designs and Conduct of the Americans Tend Only to Tyranny and Slavery* (1776).[10] Serle was the private secretary to General William Howe from 1776 to 1778, and his main thrust was that Americans enjoyed the same "constitutional liberties" as Britons and were therefore not oppressed. But he also insisted American slaveholders were themselves guilty of the charges of "enslavement" and "tyranny" they leveled at Great Britain:

To say, that the British Constitution may become the Patroness of Tyranny, is to assert, what not only is contrary to all Fact and Experience, but what is directly opposite to Common Sense. But can they [Great Britain] not enslave America? I answer, Slavery is no Part of our Constitution. We have no Idea of it in our Law. It is not to be found in our Country. Negroes here, wherever they have been Slaves before, are emancipated in a Moment by setting Foot upon our Liberating Shores.[11]

Here Serle expediently ignored the realities of West Indian plantation slavery and British domination of the slave trade. Indeed, between 1660 and 1807, British ships carried approximately 3.4 million slaves to the Americas, more than all other slave-trading nations combined.[12] He also failed to mention that London itself was a slave-trading port. Between the late seventeenth century and slave-trade abolition in 1807, more than 2,500 ships left the port of London for Africa, delivering back to the New World approximately 750,000 slaves.[13] But when Serle cited laws rendering slaves "emancipated in a Moment by setting Foot upon our Liberating Shores," he alluded to an event that had animated abolitionist fervor and helped Britons repair British "liberty" as antislavery despite these inconvenient realities: the Mansfield ruling on the Somerset case.

The Somerset case, popularized by antislavery sympathizers as a clarion call to end the slave trade, hinged on the fate of James Somerset, a runaway slave. While docked in England, Somerset had escaped from his master, Charles Stuart, who had brought Somerset with him from Boston. Stuart reclaimed Somerset and put him on a ship to Jamaica to sell him. Abolitionist and self-trained legal advocate Granville Sharp had intervened and represented Somerset in a case tried in the Court of the King's Bench before Lord Mansfield, who ruled in 1772 that Stuart could not compel Somerset to return to a foreign country. Mansfield, who owned slaves on his West Indian plantation, tried to protect the property basis of British slavery by restricting his decision to the issue of Somerset's coerced return. Opponents of the slave trade, however, interpreted his ruling to mean that a slave became a freeman once he set foot on British soil and made full use of the case's broader implications, which permitted writers like Serle to tout it as emblematic of British "liberty" and adversative to the "tyranny" of American slavery.[14]

Thespians and poets continued the ongoing reworking of British liberty through oratorical debates, verses, and theatrical performances celebrating the Mansfield ruling in order to disparage American slavery. On June 5, 1782, the Lyceum Theatre staged a rousing oratorical debate on "Whether Slavery, as enforced by the European Nations, is to be defended on any principles?" given the precept of British constitutional "liberty."[15] That the Lyceum—a minor theater licensed only to stage dance, burletta (brief comic operas), and mimed storytelling, known as "dumbshew"—held a serious debate about slavery indicated the groundswell of popular antislavery feeling. Poet William Cowper also celebrated the Mansfield ruling in his 1785 poem *The Task*: "Slaves cannot breathe in England; if their lungs / receive our air, that moment they are free."[16] And John O'Keefe, an Irish actor and playwright who spent much of his career in London, staged the Mansfield ruling in his comedy *The Young Quaker*. His play debuted at the Smock Alley Theatre Royal in 1784 before migrating to London's Covent Garden Theatre Royal. Unlike the minor theaters, the royally patented theaters—Covent Garden, Haymarket, and Drury Lane in London and Smock Alley in Dublin—were licensed to perform narrative dramas and comedies. In *The Young Quaker*, O'Keefe promoted antislavery sentiment and pride in the Mansfield ruling by disparaging American slavery.

O'Keefe wrote the play with overt antislavery intent, as he recalled in his memoirs: "I had also a motive for wishing [the actor] Lewis to play young Sadboy, my sincere desire that my opinion of the Slave Trade, in two speeches in that comedy, might be spoken on the boards of the great winter house, particularly on Lewis's benefit night, when I knew the night would be full."[17] He communicated his message in part by poking fun at the abstemious religiosity and manners of the Quakers, or Society of Friends, through the characters of Young Reuben Sadboy and his father Old Sadboy. In one of his speeches, Young Reuben Sadboy admits to his father that instead of "transacting business for the faithful in Philadelphia" while in London, he has been among "merchants, tobacco sellers, horse-racers, and wine-bibbers."[18] After Reuben begs his father's forgiveness, the father restores the inheritance he had threatened to rescind and bequeaths to his son "my vineyard, my House, my Plantation, and my Slaves." Reuben Sadboy responds:

> I hold half your favours on a very loose tenure—while Liberty is the boast of Englishmen, why should we still make a sordid traffic of our fellow creatures? I will accept of the House and Plantations, on behalf of myself and my brethren in America; but as to Slaves, I declare that every Slave of mine shall henceforth be as free as the air he breathes. Liberty shall no longer be considered as the peculiar blessing of England; it shall be extended to America; and may him only be deprived of it, who can make a Slave of any one.[19]

O'Keefe referenced the Mansfield ruling to brag of "the peculiar blessing" of British liberty that made a slave "as free as the air he breathes" by contrasting it to American slavery, thereby scoffing at independent America as a bastion of liberty and rights. O'Keefe ignored both British West Indian slavery and the fact that the

Philadelphian Quakers were antislavery. He must surely have known that the Society of Friends in both London and Philadelphia had, by the 1780s, renounced slaveholding and begun actively working against slavery. Londoners' idealization of Britannia's antislavery liberty was possible because the reality of British plantation slavery was far away from the metropole whose air was "too pure for slaves to breath."

While O'Keefe's play did not feature a slave character, the blackface slave was integral to the reformulation of Britannia's "liberty" as antislavery. In London, as in Philadelphia, Mungo from Isaac Bickerstaffe's *The Padlock* became a ubiquitous icon of blackness in prose, theater, and print, so much so that by the late eighteenth century "mungo" was a synonym for an African slave.[20] Londoners used print and embodied performances of Mungo to negotiate questions of slavery, liberty, and race provoked by the revolutionary conflict. Mungo first appeared as a comic, albeit sympathetic, buffoon in *The Padlock*, a musical afterpiece that debuted in Drury Lane Theatre Royal in 1767. But by the 1770s, as the imperial crisis escalated, cartoonists used Mungo as a receptacle for anxieties about imperial decline, fear of miscegenation, and political corruption. Political commentators made these linkages explicit when the influx of black refugees from the American Revolution added to the indigent population of London. But this did not stop the abolitionists who formed the London Society for Effecting the Abolition of the Slave Trade from appropriating Mungo as their blackface supplicant for Britannia's liberty. Even after being coopted to make a sympathetic antislavery appeal, however, Mungo retained his comic dimensions and embodied white Londoners' discomfort with real-life blacks.

Mungo became a prototype for comic blackface servants or slaves in London (just as in Philadelphia) and prefigured later blackface minstrelsy both because of his malapropisms and his sheer popularity. As soon as it debuted, *The Padlock* was a smash hit, "a very compleat pretty piece that went off very well and was much applauded."[21] The piece ran for 54 performances that season and was performed 142 times in the next ten years.[22] The Mungo character was wildly popular with audiences; his visage showed up in prints and on tea caddies, and his name graced the title of an anthology of prose and poetry, *The Padlock Open'd; or, Mungo's Medley* (1771).[23] Masqueraders even impersonated Mungo at balls.[24] As in Philadelphia, the music from the opera caught on and his familiar lament—"Mungo here, Mungo dere, Mungo everywhere . . . me wish to de Lord me dead"—often accompanied his image.

The character of Mungo became a staple in political cartoons expressing concerns about real-life blacks in Great Britain. Journalists inveighed against the increased presence of blacks in London, and late eighteenth-century cartoons and newspaper items offer evidence of amplified anxiety about racialized human difference, national identity, and imperial prowess in relation to America, especially after British defeat in the American War.[25] By 1750, Great Britain had a black population of approximately fifteen to twenty thousand, concentrated in the major ports of London, Liverpool, and Bristol.[26] In London, blacks' increased presence elicited fears of miscegenation and calls for their expulsion. As early as 1764, one writer signing himself as "Anglicanus" complained that London blacks "fill the places of so many of our own people; we are by this means depriving so many of them the means of getting their bread, and thereby decreasing our native population in favour of a race, whose mixture with us is disgraceful." Anglicanus concluded by imploring Parliament to "totally prohibit the importation of any more of them."[27] A correspondent to the *London Chronicle* in 1773 also exhorted "Parliament [to] provide such remedies . . . by expelling [blacks] now here . . . and save the natural beauty of Britons from the Morisco tint."[28]

Some London political cartoonists began conveying this racialized xenophobia through the instantaneously recognizable figure of Mungo. Prints like *High Life below Stairs; or, Mungo Addressing My Lady's Maid* (1772) (fig. 6) targeted the black population as a symptom of societal decay and reviled interracial relations.[29] The artist, along with Anglicanus and other commentators, presented interracial relations as a contravention of the social order. In the print, Mungo is seen drinking with and embracing a white woman, while a second Mungo sits behind him, aiding his advances with a serenade on a coronet or French horn. The caption, "for Wine inspires us, and fires us, with Courage Love, and Joy," further suggests licentious eroticism. The small wigs and cocked hats worn by the two men, the open book lying on the floor, and the wine decanter and glasses all intimate and lampoon blacks' aspirations to upward mobility, epitomized by literacy, finery, and leisure. The lady's maid shares their aspirations, as is evident by her elaborate headdress, which emulates the finery of her social betters. The Mungo figures are, however, breaching *both* the social and racial order by aspiring to "high life" with the white women found "below the stairs."

As the conflict with the American colonies intensified, Londoners also perceived in the black population their own imperial decline. A series of "Mungo prints" negotiating anxiety about imperial corruption and defeat and published during the ministry of Lord North (1770–82) featured Jeremiah Dyson, the Lord of the Treasury, as Mungo.[30] North was widely viewed as having bungled colonial policy in both Ireland and North America, and he and his cabinet were ultimately blamed for the loss of the American colonies. Meanwhile, the Irish adminis-

Figure 6. High Life below Stairs (1772). The cartoon played on class and racial differences in its depiction of black "Mungo" servants flirting with white chambermaids, and it precipitated a trend in visual and performative depictions of life above and below stairs. In 1774 James Bretherton's London print, also titled *High Life below Stairs*, also depicted a black servant "below stairs" on an equal basis with a white housemaid and coachman. The following year, David Garrick's popular comedy *High Life above Stairs* flipped the perspective to lampoon upper-class Londoners. Courtesy of Lewis Walpole Library, Yale University

tration ran a huge public debt. Dyson earned the nickname "Mungo," after a Member of Parliament attacked him for being the "adviser and conductor" of North's policies and, on the grounds of his supposedly servile complicity to imperial corruption, sarcastically noted that Dyson reminded him of a song he heard at Drury Lane, "Mungo here, Mungo there, Mungo everywhere."[31] *Hibernia in Distress* (1773) was one of several satirical prints in which artists used Dyson/ Mungo to represent imperial corruption and failure.[32] The print featured Hibernia lying on the ground compromised and vulnerable, her harp—a symbol of

Ireland—broken. Running at North's heels, Dyson/Mungo is wheedling, "Don't forget poor Mungo my dear Lord North," a plea with a double meaning: Dyson is seeking Lord North's approval and patronage, but Mungo is also issuing an antislavery appeal.

When hundreds of black "loyalist" refugees from the American Revolution dramatically swelled the indigent population of London after 1784, their presence was a reminder of defeat that served to amplify the association between blackness and imperial decline. After Great Britain and the new United States formally ended hostilities in 1783, thousands of loyalist slaves were transported by the British to Nova Scotia, and hundreds found their way to London. Once there, most joined the ranks of the black penniless alongside unemployed white demobilized sailors and soldiers.[33] In response, philanthropists and abolitionists formed the Committee for the Black Poor with the initial goal of charitable aid and the later goal of resettling poor blacks in Africa. The committee included key abolitionists: several of the Society of Friends (Quakers), William Wilberforce, who was soon to lead the first parliamentary abolition campaign, and—initially—black abolitionist Olaudah Equiano.[34] In 1786, the committee founded the Sierra Leone colony based on a proposal by Henry Smeathman. Smeathman had been commissioned by the British government to determine if Sierra Leone would make a suitable penal colony. He deemed the torrid climate unsuitable for white guards and prisoners but proposed the site to the committee for a colony of "black persons and people of Colour, Refugees from America, disbanded from his Majesty's Service by sea or land, or otherwise distinguished objects of British humanity, [who] are at this time I greatest distress."[35] In 1786, the committee began sending free blacks to Sierra Leone, and in 1787, 400 people (330 black men and women, and 70 white women married to black settlers) arrived there.[36] More settlers relocated in 1792 and founded Freetown.

A 1787 print by E. Macklaw brought together the figure of Mungo and the Sierra Leone colony as converging points for anxiety over the lost war and colonies, the increasing black population, and political corruption.[37] In the print, North is "blacked up" and dressed as Mungo, and he heads toward the Brooks Club, which is pictured as a debtor's prison. The prison door is guarded by a Native American in feathered headdress, symbolizing that North will soon be paying for the loss of the American colonies. Although Macklaw pictured North on his way to pay for his imperial ineptitude, the caption read, "The Poor Blacks Going to Their Settlement," an explicit reference to the Sierra Leone colony. The Sierra Leone colony was closely linked in the press with the newly founded Botany Bay penal colony in Australia, an association compounded by Sierra Leone's history as a site first considered for a penal settlement.[38] And following the infamous anti-Catholic Gordon Riots of 1780, the press explicitly conflated the black ex-slaves with Botany Bay convicts. On June 2, 1780, Lord Gordon led a march to force the repeal of legislation that had eased the political restrictions on Roman Catholics. The marchers, a crowd of forty to sixty thousand, rioted and largely destroyed Newgate Prison. West Indian and American ex-slaves participated in the riot, lashing out at their economic privation by attacking the prison in which penurious blacks were incarcerated for petty theft and indebtedness. The press indicted the "Newgate prisoners, Botany Bay convicts and vagabond blacks" who had followed Lord Gordon's riotous lead, linking poor blacks both to the penal colony and irrational mayhem.[39] But at the same time as North was Mungo, the removal of "the Poor Blacks" to Sierra Leone also signified the removal from sight of an undesired ex-soldier-slave population that had become a symbol of potential decay through racial "admixture," in topical parlance.

The print also illustrates how Londoners reacted to the American Revolution: unease about imperial decline, disparagement of slavery, and, for some, insistence on Britishness as white. Kathleen Wilson's assertion that Macklaw's print "confirms that black Britons had no real claim in the nation" bears relation to a contentious debate about the intentions of the Sierra Leone Committee. One historian has condemned the aim of the Sierra Leone Committee as a purely racist impulse to "rid Britain of her black population and make Britain a white man's country."[40] Others have countered that the evidence suggests instead that the committee was "motivated by a sincere desire to help those in need, particularly those who had served their country in a lost cause."[41] The associations Macklaw made between blackness, corruption, and criminality certainly suggests that he rejected blacks. Yet regardless of the exact nature of the committee's intentions, the colonization effort—and Macklaw's print—should ultimately be understood in light of the dialogue that began during the American revolutionary years but was intensified by defeat: attempts to redefine Britishness, which hinged on constructing British liberty as antislavery and empire as liberal. For in *The Poor Blacks* and other prints, artists simultaneously disparaged blacks as unwanted convicts and lamented the loss of the American colonies by explicitly linking imperial decline to the stain of slavery through its most iconic representation, Mungo. Thus, rejection of blacks' subjecthood in the metropole was not antithetical to redefining British liberty as antislavery; it was, rather, its counterpart.

Because these black freedom fighters brought the tumult of the American Revolution and the vexed question of slavery close to home, their presence stimulated Londoners' first efforts at organized antislavery, for which Mungo became a spokesman. In 1787, London Quakers joined with evangelicals like Hannah More, William Wilberforce, and others who, like Granville Sharp and Thomas Clarkson, were motivated by religious and Enlightenment precepts, to found the London Society for the Abolition of the Slave Trade, which was in communication with and influenced by the Pennsylvania Abolition Society. Several London abolitionists were made signatory members of the Pennsylvania society, including Granville Sharp and Thomas Clarkson.[42] In the 1780s, to publicize the London society and the first parliamentary debates on ending the slave trade, *The Padlock* was performed with the addition of an antislavery epilogue. Written by an abolitionist and delivered by the actor Charles Dibdin as Mungo (and printed in *The Bee* in February 1793), the epilogue appealed for emancipation on the grounds of natural liberty and rights:

> Thank you, my massas! Have you laugh your fill?
> Then let me speak, nor take that freedom ill . . .
> . . . For whilst I tread the free-born British land,
> Whilst now before me crowded Britons stand;
> Vain, vain, that glorious privilege to me
> I am a slave, when all things else are free.
> Yet I was born, as you are, no man's slave,
> An heir to all that liberal Nature gave;
> My thoughts can reason, and my limbs can move
> The same as yours; like yours my heart can love;
> Comes freedom then from colour? Blush with shame
> And let strong nature's crimson mark your blame!

In asking the audience to set their laughter aside and reject slavery, Mungo animated familiar abolitionist refrains. His annunciation of universal humanity— "my thoughts can reason . . . the same as yours"—and his rhetorical question, "comes freedom then from color?" rested on precepts of natural rights. Mungo also celebrated the Mansfield judgment of 1772, calling on his listeners to rectify the legal injustice of permitting slavery in British colonies while prohibiting it in "the free-born British land." Revivals of *The Padlock* were symptomatic of a larger trend in the London Theatres Royal to restage stock slave narratives—such as George Colman's Jr.'s *Inkle and Yarico* and Thomas Southerne's *Oroonoko*—in the few years immediately preceding the 1789 debate; the piece was one of several that antislavery activists began harnessing to build sympathy for the abolition cause.

Yet Mungo's performance stirred sympathy for a romanticized abstraction of plantation slaves without necessarily fostering sympathy for the plight of real Africans.[43] Mungo's newfound antislavery appeal was contingent on Britain as a "white" land of freedom and justice, with slavery a problem associated with morally debased colonials, most especially Americans, as the American Revolution had subverted race and class alignments.[44] The audience was asked to sympathize with the plight of a household slave in the exotic setting of Salamanca, kept chained by a lecherous and tyrannical Spanish Don. Moreover, the epilogue's author cleverly underscored the theatrical nature of Mungo's "blackness." For one, by beginning the monologue in pseudo West Indian dialect—"Thank you, my massas! Have you laugh your fill?"—the author capitalized on Mungo's hilarity as a clownlike character before shifting into "white" cultured English to plead for antislavery support. The author also highlighted the imaginary nature of Mungo's slavery by reminding the audience that it contradicted the landmark Mansfield decision of 1772. On the one hand, Mungo was "tread[ing] the free-born British land," which—as audience members knew—had "air too pure for slaves to breathe in," and on the other hand, here was a slave in their midst, breathing the pure London air in front of an audience of "crowded Britions"! Both author and audience, then, were aware that Mungo, a white actor in blackface makeup, was a nonthreatening imaginary abstraction of plantation slavery. Mungo's appeal was predicated on skin color as an index to virtue and civilization.[45] White Britons' capable of "blushing with shame" were called on to feel pathos for dark-skinned slaves. To be opposed to slavery was to be proudly white, virtuous, mainland Britons, which by implication assigned the blame for the immoral and un-British wretchedness of slavery to the depravity of far-away creoles in the West Indies, East Indies, and North America.

Abolitionist Thomas Clarkson nonetheless averred that Mungo's appeal to virtuous white Britons, composed by "a worthy clergyman," "procure[d] a good deal of feeling for the unfortunate sufferers, whose cause it was intended to serve."[46] Others shared his belief. At a masquerade ball at the Opera House in May 1789 at which "1200 masks were assembled," two of the "best supported characters," the reviewer reported, were "a poor Mungo, who . . . inveighed in most pathetic terms against the slave trade; in which he was not only joined by his sable mistress Wowski [a blackface slave character in *Inkle and Yarico*], but by the whole audience."[47] Eyewitnesses' accounts of Mungo masqueraders prior to the late 1780s consistently described him either as a decoratively costumed fool or in derogatory racialist terms. A Mungo impersonator at a ball in the late 1760s, for example, was deemed "very fine in jewels and exceedingly diverting," while censorious description of a masquerade Mungo in the mid-1770s scorned the impersonator as "behaving no better than a black."[48] These masqueraders embodied mutating but overlapping performances of Mungo—clownish buffoon in the immediate afterglow of *The Padlock*'s 1767 debut; conduit for postwar racial anxieties in the mid-1770s; and abolitionist spokesman in the 1780s. Britons wove all three semiotic threads into the fabric of the emerging civic mythology of Great Britain as a white metropole and abolitionist empire of liberty. Under sway of the American Revolution, poets, thespians, artists, and abolitionists thus established a lexicon of symbols and rhetoric to animate this civic mythology, putting neoclassical Britannia in contrapuntal dialogue with print, theatrical, and masquerade blackface burlesque. Although the French Revolution, war with France, and the outbreak of a massive slave revolt in the French sugar colony of Saint Domingue would temporarily hamper antislavery efforts, Britons would eventually revive the images and discourse they created in the American revolutionary years to celebrate slave-trade abolition.

French Liberty, Anti-Jacobinism, and Britannia's Blackface Slaves

On August 5, 1789, the Royal Circus staged John Dent's *The Triumph of Liberty; or, The Destruction of the Bastille,* a runaway success that would be performed for seventy-nine consecutive nights. In it, Dent celebrated the French Revolution and the fall of the Bastille as a triumph of British-style constitutional monarchy in a scene in which "Britannia descend[ed], with liberty and reason and the Magna Charta" and "trampled on the figure of Despotism" before the chorus sang, "Hail Britannia, 'tis to thee we owe our liberty."[49] At its outset in 1789, the French Revolution was widely fêted by the London public and in the theater—not only by pro-democratic radicals but also by reform-minded moderates who, like the Royal Circus performers of Britannia, hailed it as the creation of a constitutional state along British lines. Even some conservatives rejoiced at the vaunted weakening of the absolutist Catholic state that was Britain's old enemy.[50] The public avidly followed the events in France, from the revolutionaries' formation of the National Assembly in June to their subsequent demands for a constitutional monarchy. When Parisians attacked the Bastille prison, a symbol of political oppression, on July 14, 1789, the Royal Circus capitalized on public excitement about the Bastille's fall. Astley's Ampitheatre and Sadler's Wells Theatre which, like the Royal Circus, were minor theaters not licensed to perform narrative drama, promptly staged competing versions.[51]

Dialogue-driven dramatizations of the fall of the Bastille in the major theaters had less success because discussions of democratic rights (and their obvious implications for slavery) incited the wrath of the censor, who either banned the productions or demanded significant cuts. The minor theaters did not have to submit choreography, mime, and ballads to the Lord Chamberlain for approval, but the Haymarket, Drury Lane, and Covent Garden Theatres Royal were obligated to submit their manuscripts. Both Drury Lane and Covent Garden proposed dramatizations of the fall of Bastille that the Lord Chamberlain either heavily censored or banned because of politicized dialogues. Covent Garden began rehearsing *The Bastille* by Frederick Reynolds, which favored the revolution, but the Lord Chamberlain denied it a license. He also rejected the first manuscript of John St. John's *Island of St. Marguerite*, whose hero was the famous "man in the Iron Mask" imprisoned on St. Marguerite from 1687 to his death in 1740s, when John Philip Kemble tried to produce it at Drury Lane.[52] The censor demanded that St. John excise parallels between the inhuman treatment French prisoners had received at the Bastille and that of his hero, along with the rousing musical finale, sung by an ensemble St. John described as "the mob." The finale included lyrics urging the people to "assert your Freedom [and] Vindicate the Rights of Man" and exhortations like "we once were free, shall we be Slaves?"[53] The censored version still intimated how democratic sentiments had resonance for the rights of slaves to be free, when the chorus sang, "Freedom's voice and liberty we'll crown / . . . Tyranny and torture cease."[54]

As well as inspiring democratically based arguments for natural liberty, the French Revolution also provoked oppositional reactions that ruptured the fledging British antislavery movement by intensifying existing divisions between the conservative "loyalists" and the reformers and radicals. The latter had been agitating for expanded suffrage and democratic parliamentary reforms while the opposing camp supported the status quo of traditional political hierarchies in Church and King Clubs.[55] In theaters, loyalists jeered as radicals and reformers cheered the fall of the Bastille. As playwright Frederick Reynolds observed, "The French Revolution . . . excited the public attention in a considerable degree; but it did not cause a general sensation until the memorable fourteenth of July, 1789, when the Bastile [*sic*] was destroyed. Then . . . the loyalist saw the revolution in one light, the democrat in another, and even the theatrical manager had also his view of the subject."[56] Abolitionists were split in their allegiances. Thomas Clarkson and Whig members of Parliament Charles James Fox and Richard B. Sheridan (who was also the manager of Drury Lane) were among the revolution's celebrants. In August 1789, Thomas Clarkson even went to Paris to try to persuade the newly formed French National Assembly to include slave-trade abolition in the constitutional reforms they were formulating.[57] But many conservative abolitionists like Tory member William Wilberforce, Hannah More, and the evangelical Clapham sect of the Church of England to which they belonged, opposed slavery as un-Christian yet abhorred using the ideas of domestic popular democracy and republican rights as the basis for antislavery. More, for example, decried republicanism and expressed regret that in France "the lawless rabble are so triumphant" and the revolution was being guided by a "spirit of licentiousness and insurrection."[58]

British antislavery was not only divided within but also attacked from without, especially after 1793 when the violence of the Terror, the outbreak of war with revolutionary France, and the escalation of the slave revolt on Saint Domingue ushered in a repressive anti-Jacobin milieu. Even before 1793, antislavery momentum had been ominously associated with events in Saint Domingue and France and the 1789 parliamentary debate on slavery and abolition, which began just as the Bastille fell, had resulted in defeat. Edmund Burke's *Reflections on the Revolution in France* (1790) had foreshadowed this anti-Jacobin panic, warning that the revolutionary fire in France could spread, and calling on its flames to be thoroughly doused at home: "Whenever our neighbor's house is on fire, it cannot be amiss for the engines to play a little on our own."[59] When Thomas Paine published his pro-revolutionary response, *The Rights of Man*, he was tried for sedition and sentenced to death in absentia, as he had by then fled to France.[60] In January 1793, the radical Jacobins, led by Robespierre, executed King Louis XVI and subsequently declared war on Britain. Conservatives' fears that French radical republicanism would spread at home were not altogether unfounded, as radicals had founded Corresponding Societies to agitate for democratic reform. In 1795 Prime Minister William Pitt's ministry prosecuted members of the London Corresponding Society under the Seditious Meetings and Treasonable Practices Act. In this context, proslavery agitators attacked the abolitionists as unpatriotic. Wilberforce, a foe of the French and Saint Domingue revolutions, lamented, "People connect democratical principles with the Abolition of the Slave Trade and will not hear it mentioned."[61]

Abolitionism, with its "pro-French" Jacobin connotations, was especially despised as unpatriotic when the French National Convention decreed the abolition of slavery in its colonies in 1794 and when Toussaint Louverture, the leader of the slave insurrection, joined forces with the French against the British in hopes of earning autonomy for the former slaves and *gen de coleur* on Saint Domingue. As the Earl of Abingdon fulminated in a parliamentary session held on April 11, 1793, "the idea of abolishing the slave trade is connected with the leveling system and the rights of man . . . if proofs are wanting, look at the colony of St. Domingo, and see what the rights of man have done there."[62] Britons' trepidations about the

spread of "black Jacobinism" were amplified by reports of French agents fomenting resistance to the British among Jamaican maroons.[63] Fears that the revolution in Saint Domingue would spread to the British Caribbean were fanned by
the sensationalist coverage in the London press of the Great Maroon Wars in
Jamaica from 1795 to 1796. A typically lurid account described how the "Maroons
. . . spread death and conflagration" and justified the Jamaican planters' use of
"100 blood hounds" to "hunt a race of savages ferocious and bloodthirsty."[64]

Burke and others explicitly linked the French and the Saint Domingue revolutions. While sympathetic to slave-trade abolition, Burke emphatically denied the
rights of slaves to forcibly overthrow slavery on the same grounds as he denied
the right of French revolutionaries to overthrow royal and noble hierarchies. In
Reflections, he rebutted the French revolutionaries' claims by using chattel slavery as an analog. Burke insisted the French had not been "a nation of lowborn
servile wretches until the emancipating year of 1789" and admonished them not
to behave like "a gang of Maroon slaves suddenly broke loose from the house
of bondage, and therefore to be pardoned for your abuse of the liberty to which
you were not accustomed and [are] ill fitted." For Burke, then, both Maroons and
French revolutionaries were equally "ill fitted" for the sudden liberty brought
about by revolutionary violence, and both posed a threat to customary order.[65] In
this rabidly anti-Jacobin milieu, even abolitionists who, like Thomas Clarkson,
believed the French Revolution had afforded "the Negroes [on Saint Domingue]
an opportunity . . . of endeavouring to vindicate from themselves the unalterable
Rights of Man," were confounded in their efforts by the shibboleth of abolitionism's association with the violence on the island and the Terror in France.[66]

The disastrous effect of the French and Saint Domingue revolutions in derail-
ing organized antislavery efforts was reinforced in theatrical and print culture.
After 1793, the theater—both stage productions and print editions of plays—was
much more stringently censored to eliminate political content. As playwright
Frederick Reynolds complained, the theaters were forced to stage the "trumpery
trap claps" of patriotism.[67] The Lord Chamberlain's prohibition on staging revolutionary events or themes after 1793 effectively eradicated historical tragedies
and hence helped foster forms of theater blending music, dance, and drama
that, prior to 1793, had been the province of the minor theaters.[68] Now the licensed Drury Lane, Covent Garden, and Haymarket Theatres Royal, eager to find
new material in the face of the restrictions, embraced hybrid genres: melodrama
(deriving from the Greek *melos* and with the meaning of music-drama), pantomimes, and farces.[69] In May 1797, Covent Garden staged the nationalistic *Britons
Roused!*, which was followed in October by the equally jingoistic new melodrama

England's Glory. Reynolds was not alone in his scorn of "trumpery trap claps." Theater critic George Daniels similarly bemoaned the loss of the "old and better times of the drama; before tragedy had degenerated into bombast and pantomime —and comedy into face-making and buffoonery."[70] His nostalgia was to no avail. From the mid-1790s onward, pantomime, farce, and melodrama dominated the stage.

The "face-making and buffoonery" of comedy, pantomime, and melodrama characterized much of the theatrical performance of slavery after 1793. Light-hearted apologia could certainly be found in plays written prior to 1793.[71] But after the ban, blackface clowns who shared Mungo's proto-minstrel traits but not his capacity for sentimental antislavery appeal proliferated. Exemplifying this mold were the many blackface clowns in John Cartwright Cross's melodramas and spectacles, which graced the theater boards and circus arenas alike. In his *Surrender at Trinidad; or, Safe Moor'd at Last*, for example, which opened at Covent Garden on May 11, 1797, and dramatized the English navy's defeat of a Spanish garrison in Trinidad, Cymbalo is a puerile, comic character who spoke with a pseudo-West Indian dialect. His master, Gasper, is a cruel Spanish jailer who menaces the Britons held captive in the Spanish garrison in Trinidad from whose lecherous clutches Cymbalo helps a young English woman escape. Cymbalo assures her that "me love you—me love your Countree" and makes no attempt to escape his own enslaved condition, thus sidestepping the issue of Britain's plantation slavery and slave trade. *Surrender of Trinidad*'s billing indicates it was a crowd pleaser.[72] While Mungo had appealed for freedom based on natural rights, many blackface slave characters of the mid-to-late-1790s were instead, like Cymbalo, ventriloquists of apologia.

Popular visual performances also attacked the French revolutionary credo of *liberté, egalité, fraternité* through images celebrating Britannia's liberty as superior to the Gallic Marianne's. In 1792, for example, the conservative Thomas Rowlandson compared the characteristics of British and French liberty in *The Contrast*.[73] The print shows a dignified neoclassical Britannia who exemplifies religion and morality side by side with a debauched Marianne who, in flames and trampling on bodies, represents France's deterioration into amorality and atheism. Rowlandson contrasted British loyalty, law, obedience, and justice, represented by the scales of justice and the Magna Carta held by Britannia with French rebellion, tyranny, and anarchy, represented by a decapitated head on Marianne's trident and a hanged noble swinging on the gallows in the background. British industry and national prosperity, symbolized by merchant ship in the background of the image, trumped French idleness and private ruin. Significantly, Britannia's

Figure 7. James Gillray, *Philanthropic Consolations after the Loss of the Slave Bill* (1796). By depicting Wilberforce and fellow evangelical abolitionist, Samuel Horsley (Bishop of Rochester), fondling bare-breasted African women and being served drinks by a black servant or slave, this anti-Jacobin print tarred the abolitionists—even loyalist Tories like Wilberforce and Horsley—with the brush of French debauchery by playing on pernicious perceptions of blacks as overly lascivious. Library of Congress

liberty was *not* defined by Jacobin-tainted abolitionism, even though just a few years earlier, during the American Revolution, poets, thespians, and illustrators had made this claim a proud boast.

Artists' renderings of the blackface slave to disparage abolitionism as antipatriotic, pro-Jacobin, and a taint on white British citizenship provided the discursive complement to images of no-longer-abolitionist Britannia. Wilberforce persisted in his parliamentary campaign to abolish the trade and, in March 1796, introduced another bill to abolish the trade by 1797. The bill was defeated. James Gillray's *Philanthropic Consolations after the Loss of the Slave Bill* (1796) mocked Wilberforce and fellow evangelical abolitionist Samuel Horsley (Bishop of Rochester) and linked them to French debauchery by depicting them fondling barebreasted African women and being served drinks by a black servant or slave (fig. 7). In the 1790s, Wilberforce and his conservative allies (like Horsley) were fighting for an end to the slave trade rather than slavery itself. But Gillray conveyed a palpable fear of the black freedom that might ultimately result from their efforts: miscegenation, as free blacks moved from the colonies to the metropole, and, with it, a revolutionary overturning of all social propriety and accepted hierarchies. His hypersexualized, near-grotesque African woman—the object of Wilberforce's lust—powerfully symbolized the potential of freed slaves to degrade (white) British culture. Gillray also reanimated the racialist derogation common in the Mungo cartoons of the 1780s and, other depictions of blacks, as licentious and morally inferior to white Britons. These racialist and nationalist ideas would continue to circulate freely between print, cartoons, and theater in the 1790s.

Abolitionist Britannia "Amidst the Battle's Roar"

The figure of Britannia as the patroness of antislavery and the blackface slave as an antislavery supplicant resurfaced with a chauvinistic flourish along with Napoleon's rise to power. His ascent began in 1799 when he staged a coup d'état; in 1802 he assumed solo executive power and, as Consul of France, restored slavery to the French colonies, reversing the abolition the National Convention had instituted in 1794. When he crowned himself Napoleon I, Emperor of France, in 1804, his coronation triggered a political sea change that revitalized British antislavery and precipitated the 1807 slave-trade ban. Poets and thespians celebrated abolition using the antislavery motifs from the American revolutionary years—Britannia and her supplicant blackface slave—the antislavery resonances of which were refurbished by aversion to Napoleon's despotism.

Napoleon's imperial ambitions shattered the tenuous 1802 Peace of Amiens, and Great Britain's declaration of war against France in 1803 prompted a swell of anti-Napoleonic patriotic pride in Britannia and her liberty. At the Drury Lane Theatre Royal, the resumption of war was announced in a jingoistic prologue preceding *The English Fleet* (1803), delivered "with great animation" by Charles Kemble. Urging the audience to support the war, Kemble reminded them,

> Your Daughters, fresh in bloom, mature in charm
> Doom'd (should he conquer) to the Spoiler's arms
> Your sons, who hear the Tyrant's threats with scorn
> The Joys, the Hopes of ages yet unborn,
> All, ALL endear this just, this sacred cause.

His final, heraldic call to arms, "PROTECT, PRESERVE, AVENGE your native land / For lo! Britannia cries, amidst the Battle's roar / Return victorious, or return no more!" met with "bursts of applause . . . [and] a general call for 'God Save the King,' which was sung by all the vocal Performers."[74]

This patriotic fervor coupled with Napoleon's reinstatement of slavery purged

abolitionism of the Jacobin taint that had stymied the movement through the
1790s. Even the slave revolt on Saint Domingue, which had evolved into a full-
scale fight for independence from France, took on newly positive dimensions
as Toussaint Louverture was valorized as Napoleon's foe. In this spirit, James
Stephen, who had held a government post in St. Kitts before becoming an abolitionist and later a member of Parliament (1808–15), celebrated Toussaint's
valor in *Buonaparte in the West Indies; or, The Indies*. After Toussaint's death in a
French prison, Stephen eulogized him as a "great and good man . . . who perished
under [Napoleon's] merciless oppression."[75] During the American revolutionary
era, abolitionism had symbolized the liberal antithesis of tyranny, and it did so
again after 1802, when abolitionist sympathizers reasserted Britannia's liberty
in diametric contrast to Napoleon's "merciless oppression."[76] The parliamentary
antislavery campaign was revived and local organizations remobilized massive
popular support for slave-trade abolition.[77] "Amidst the Battle's roar," as Kemble
had put it, Britannia's liberty had become a foil to the French "Tyrant's threats."

In his tract, *The Crisis of the Sugar Colonies* (1802), Stephen invoked the Saint
Domingue revolution to make a powerful argument for British slave-trade abolition.[78] Britain had acquired Essequibo, Demerara, and Berbice from the Dutch,
and Stephen adamantly opposed establishing sugar plantations on these newly
conquered territories. He also made the larger argument that establishing a
profitable empire without slaves was in Great Britain's long-term economic self-
interest, and abolishing the slave trade was one step toward that goal. Stephen
reasoned that the slaves in the British colonies, following the example of Saint
Domingue, would ultimately throw off their chains. Great Britain should, therefore, accept this eventuality as inevitable and avoid the loss of her colonies by
moving toward a system of free colonial labor. Stephen was writing before Haiti
became a free, black republic in 1804, but in his prescient view, "permanent
restitution of the slave system in the French Islands" would be impossible due
to "the change in ideas of the negroes," as the "restless desire" to throw off "the
weight of the chain" would far outweigh "their apprehensions of . . . the dangers
of resistance." This being so, he argued, it was only a matter of time until the
slaves in the British islands followed the example of "St. Domingo . . . the cradle
of liberty." Rather than perpetuating a doomed economic system, Britons should
"try to found . . . a new and happy system of colonization, which while it produces
wealth, may with an equal progress furnish free, strong and faithful hands to
defend. Let . . . our new Islands . . . become at once an example, and a protection,
a farm of experiment and a fortress to the rest of our Sugar Colonies."[79]

Stephen's arguments were key to reigniting parliamentary abolitionism, and in 1805, Prime Minister William Pitt, using Stephen's *The Crisis of the Sugar Colonies* for support, issued an order-in-council forbidding the import of slaves to Essequibo, Demerara, and Berbice.[80] Pitt, however, did not live to see the total abolition of the slave trade. His death in 1806 brought about the formation of a new ministry, led by Lord Grenville and known as the "Ministry of All the Talents." Both Grenville and Foreign Secretary Charles James Fox saw abolition as a timely reform measure that would popularize their coalition. In 1806, Parliament passed the Foreign Slave Trade Bill, prohibiting British trade in slaves to foreigners and newly conquered territories. The motion to abolish the slave trade was overwhelmingly endorsed by the House of Commons in June 1806. On March 25, 1807, the House of Commons approved the bill, making the trade illegal as of May 1, 1807. Although Fox, too, died before the trade was abolished, Grenville assured the passage of their bill in the House of Lords.

It was these white male parliamentarians—Fox, Pitt, Wilberforce, and Grenville—along with other prominent white abolitionist leaders, like Thomas Clarkson, who were credited with abolishing the slave trade, which was lauded as a huge victory of British liberty and law. Parliamentary abolitionism was, however, as much *reactive* as proactive. Black abolitionists such as the Sons of Africa, along with white British women and large numbers of plebeians all played significant roles and, in reality, the parliamentarians were responding to a groundswell of cross-class, multiethnic popular support. But it was the actions of rebel colonists and slaves that were truly pivotal. Slave-trade abolition was integral to efforts to preserve empire not only after the loss of the American colonies but also in the face of the ongoing threat of slaves' incurable and potentially revolutionary desire for freedom. The last thing the British empire wanted was a hundred more Toussaints. Abolitionist parliamentarians responded to calls for reform that they hoped would translate into a triumphal reassertion of Britain as liberty-loving metropole and "free" and virtuous empire.

Enacting Britannia's Liberty

Artists, architects, playwrights, and poets celebrated abolition as the symbolic triumph of a liberal state at home and a "free" and virtuous empire abroad, one in which slaves were recipients, not actors. A monument dedicated to Fox at Westminster Abbey showed him dying in the arms of the Goddess of Liberty. At his feet a slave knelt and looked up to him in grateful awe.[81] A tribute to Clarkson entitled "The Supplicant" was erected at his birthplace, Wisbech. These public monuments reflected political divisions: though Wilberforce, staunch abolitionist ally Edmund Burke, and William Pitt were all Tories, artists largely extolled the abolition bill as a Whig triumph. Proud well-to-do Whigs commissioned architects to build private Temples of Liberty boasting sculptures of Britannia freeing her slaves, including one at Woburn Abbey in Bedfordshire to eulogize Fox.[82] Designed by Whig architect Henry Holland, work on it began in the late eighteenth century and was completed after Fox's death in 1806, just as the legislative ban was passed.[83] The epitaph inscribed on the pedestal of his bust firmly associated the myth of "liberty" for the slaves with "patriotic zeal" for peaceful, prosperous empire:

> Here, 'midst the friends he loved, the man behold
> In Truth unshaken and in Virtue bold,
> Whose patriotic zeal, and uncorrupted mind,
> Dared to assert the Freedom of Mankind . . .
> 'Twas Fox . . . whose wisdom bade the broil of nations cease,
> And taught the world Humanity and Peace.[84]

Britannia, however, had central pride of place in the temple, and it was to her that Fox was shown appealing for the slaves' liberty. Depicted as crowning a beseeching slave with the cap of liberty, Britannia was surrounded by symbols of imperial trade, peace, and prosperity that included a dove, an olive branch, and a scepter.

While this art reached a limited and elite audience, the theater negotiated the conflict between slaveholding empire and liberal nation by festively performing the slave-trade ban for larger and more diverse audiences. James Powell's *Furibond; or, Harlequin Negro*, was one such celebratory piece. Opening at Drury Lane Theatre Royal on December 28, 1807, to a clamorous audience, *Harlequin Negro* was an allegory for the triumph of parliamentary abolitionism performed through song, mime, speech, and dance. Actors in colorful costumes and decorative masks breathed life into Britannia, her abolitionist agents, and the supplicant slave, played by a white actor in blackface makeup. Although there is no dedicatory preface stating this directly, the timing and content of the play strongly suggest that it was written to commemorate the abolition bill.[85]

Harlequin Negro's author, James Powell, was an antislavery advocate of the loyalist persuasion, à la Hannah More and William Wilberforce, and was actively involved in the suppression of radicals. He played a nefarious role in the quashing of the English and Irish democratic movements.[86] Powell was probably infiltrating radical networks when he wrote *Harlequin Negro* and may have worked as a government mole during the "OP," or Old Price, riots at Covent Garden in 1809, which broke out after the lavishly renovated theater raised its prices expressly to cultivate a more exclusively middle- and upper-class audience. Despite the government's clampdown, the radical threat, although reduced to conspiratorial whispers, had not been silenced. In fact, by making trade organization illegal, the Combination Acts of 1799 and 1800 had, paradoxically, given radicals an opportunity to harness industrial economic grievances to the underground apparatus of political reform.[87]

In the context of simmering worker discontent, the conservative Powell's choice of a Harlequin pantomime as vehicle for abolitionist liberalism is revealing, as the traditional black mask of the Harlequin figure and blackface makeup had often signified subversive, antigovernment radicalism, with plebeian radicals applying blackface as a form of protest.[88] Drawing on E. P. Thompson's *Whigs and Hunters*, John O'Brien offers the example of the "Blacks," rural gangs in Waltham and Windsor forests who in the early eighteenth century wore blackface makeup when conducting their illicit poaching and deer thieving. The Blacks, O'Brien argues, blacked up not only to disguise their identities but also to "identify themselves with Africans" in order to "stage a kind of resistance to power." They described themselves as "the Black Chief and his Sham Negroes," and in mock ceremonies they appropriated well-known blackface theatrical characters.[89] Thus blackface was associated both with Africanness and rebelliousness. And the Harlequin figure had already been utilized to discuss slavery in pantomimes like *Harlequin Mungo* (1789).

It seems hardly coincidental that the reactionary Powell chose a genre for his theatrical celebration of abolition in which the protagonist, Harlequin, could also be read as the plebeian underdog. In Harlequin's commedia del arte roots, he had often been a symbol for shifty positions and manipulations, a multivalency that allowed thespians and artists to use the Harlequin character to simultaneously symbolize conflicting stances. *Harlequin Negro* was a conservative encomium to the power of state in which abolition was a Whig governmental victory enacted "from above" by Britannia—with the implicit suggestion that plebeian rights, too, could not be *demanded*, only *bestowed* by government at the time and in the manner of its choosing. Powell followed established precedent in the representation of Africanness and slavery while using blackface and black mask as a proxy for class and subversion. Theatergoers and playwrights alike would have known that theatrical and masquerade performances were the only venues in which it was legal to "black up," rendering the blackface slave / black-masked Harlequin subject to multiple valences of race, class, and status.[90] The blackface slave who is magically transformed into the black-masked Harlequin in *Harlequin Negro* thus embodied aspects of the peasant underdog, the underground radical protestor, and the African slave.

The pantomime also would have served the interests of abolitionist Whig MP Richard Sheridan, the owner and manager of Drury Lane, as it symbolically celebrated virtuous Britannia and the pantheon of white abolitionists in her temple and, in so doing, reconciled the glaring contradiction of liberal nation and slaveholding empire. Although one scholar has suggested *Harlequin Negro* was "a baffling choice for a Christmas season entertainment,"[91] Sheridan would probably have had both political and pecuniary reasons for staging *Harlequin Negro*. The pantomime would have been an appealing choice for him as a populist vehicle through which to fête abolition as a patriotic coup of *moderate* Whig liberalism. The passage of the slave-trade bill was popular, so a theatrical celebration of it had the potential to be very well received. And Sheridan's newly renovated theater was strongly associated both with his politics and with extravagant productions, especially after he enlarged it in 1796 so that it could hold an audience of over 3,600.[92] Drury Lane was the perfect venue to perform a festive abolitionist pantomime for a largely Whig-sympathetic audience.[93]

Moreover, by 1807 an increasing proportion of Drury Lane's audience was of the middling and elite sorts. One of the purposes behind rebuilding the previously decrepit theater was to foster this more affluent audience and thus avoid the turbulent plebeian politics of the revolutionary era, which tended to spill over into the theater's galleries and pits and was why from the mid-1790s to the late nineteenth century a company of guards was kept posted at the theater.[94] In the new theater, boxes could accommodate 1,828 spectators at 6 shillings a head. The 123 boxes were elegant and spacious; according to *Thespian Magazine*, they were "lined with blue silk, and the cushion of the parapet is blue velvet. Each box holds nine persons with ease." Moreover, there were "four elegant apartments level with the lower circle of boxes and furnished with elegant silk sofas."[95] These apartments and boxes vastly expanded the seating available for the higher classes and were priced to exclude people of humbler means. Although the audience was still socioeconomically diverse, there were fewer lower-priced seats, while seats in the plush boxes and lower circle had become more numerous.[96] When abolitionist Britannia took the stage in *Harlequin Negro*, she was seen by a greater percentage of the Whig-sympathetic middling sorts and elites and a reduced percentage of potentially more radical lower classes.

The very structure of Drury Lane Theatre was a physical symbol of progressive Whig liberalism. The new playhouse was designed by Henry Holland, the same architect who had created the Woburn Temple of Liberty as a tribute to Fox. His neoclassical theater boasted iron columns that supported five tiers of galleries and a stage that was eighty-three feet wide and ninety-two feet deep. Because of its cavernous size, productions mounted at the new Drury Lane tended more toward spectacle than spoken narrative.[97] Drury Lane Harlequin pantomimes, in particular, became known for their elaborate stage machinery and spectacular processions.[98] *Harlequin Negro*, which boasted elaborate scenery and lavish costumes, was thus aesthetically, as well as politically, suitable for a Christmas extravaganza.

The fact that *Harlequin Negro* was a harlequinade only made its message of the power of state and its reconciliation of liberal nation and tyrannical empire more readily digestible, as it conformed to a standard structure of conflict resolution between authoritarian power and underdog. The genre derived from the Italian commedia dell'arte treatment of Harlequin and Columbine, made popular in Britain by fairground entrepreneurs in the early eighteenth century.[99] Typically, the harlequin pantomime had one act divided into two parts. The first part set up the conflict and featured a magical character that transfigured hero and heroine into black-masked Harlequin and Columbine. The second was the harlequinade proper, in which the evil characters were transformed into stock masked tricksters—the Clown, the Lover, and the Pantaloon—and the conflict was resolved in a series of high comedy scenes. *Harlequin Negro* used this standard two-part set-up and harlequinade denouement, but it also conformed to conventions peculiar to the Christmas harlequinade. The first part of a Christmas pantomime traditionally featured two young lovers kept apart by the oppressive older generation, often authoritarian parents. The second part invariably comprised a sequence of comic vignettes in which the Pantaloon, the Lover, and the Clown strove to keep the lovers apart but Harlequin and Columbine repeatedly outwitted their elders. The harlequinade climaxed in a "dark scene" in which the oppressive authority reasserted control and separated the lovers. The conflict was then brought to resolution in a final scene by a benevolent, magical character or characters (in *Harlequin Negro*, Britannia and her abolitionist agent, Fairy Benigna), who convened the characters in a sumptuous setting, resolved their differences, and reunited the lovers.

Harlequin Negro followed precisely the accepted Christmas harlequinade narrative form, but its celebration of the abolition of the slave trade distinguished it as more than the conventional tale of conflict between an older, authoritarian power and a pair of young lovers. The first half was set on "A Plantation in Jamaica" owned by Sir Peevish Antique, whose daughter, Columbine, is being courted by Furibond, an evil enchanter. The scene begins with Columbine's discovery that Furibond has asked for her hand in marriage; it is a match her father favors. Columbine has dramatically different romantic interests: she is in love with one of her father's slaves, named in the text only as "slave." Determined to prevent this romance, Sir Peevish and his overseer bind the slave, dubbed now "disobedient slave," to a tree to be whipped into submission. He is saved by a snake who transforms into Fairy Benigna. Britannia descends from heaven with a "blest writ" of freedom and magically converts the slave into the black-masked Harlequin. Columbine pledges her love for Harlequin in a brief tableau of "Harlequin kneeling to Columbine," and the first half closes with Columbine and Harlequin running away together.

The first half sets up the ensuing harlequinade by establishing an abolitionist allegory: the forces of evil, symbolized by the planter lobby, slavery, and the slave trade, are pitted against the forces of good, represented by the parliamentary abolitionists, British law, and benign imperialism. Sir Peevish Antique, as his name suggests, is a collector of antiquarian objects. But his name also connects him to the planter lobby, who were "peeved" that their long-profitable slave trade had been rendered legally extinct, or "antique." The moniker "antique" also implied that pro-slave-trade ideology was backward compared to the growing belief in the moral and economic superiority of free wage labor, as articulated by Adam Smith and others. Fairy Benigna's name, meanwhile, signifies "benign" empire and offers tacit reassurance that abolitionism, contrary to being a snake that would poison the empire, is instead good for it. Responsible for the slave's emancipation, Fairy Benigna represented the parliamentary abolitionists and imperial benevolence while Britannia personified British morality, law, and nation.

This parable stripped the slave—and the underdog more generally—of culture, agency, and resistance by glorifying government power and redemptive philanthropy while simultaneously promoting the falsehood of a free empire without slavery. These dual rhetorical moves begin when Fairy Benigna, after rescuing the slave from the overseer's brutality, addresses him as "son of humanity" and informs him that "a Friendly Genius of the upper air," later identified as Britannia, can relieve his distress by granting a secret wish. The slave is nameless, which renders him a generic representation with no specific identity. The anonymous slave then makes a series of requests of Fairy Benigna, and Powell embeds jingoistic ethnocultural superiority in each of these exchanges. First, the slave "by signs, complain[s] of his black complexion," and Fairy Benigna offers to make him white on the condition he abandons the "beauties of the mind" and becomes a narcissist who cares only for himself. The slave declines. This vignette echoed the lament of William Blake's *Little Black Boy* (1789), "I am black. Oh! But my soul is white," and could perhaps be construed as validating the slave's intelligence and that of Africans more generally.[100] The scene also suggested the racialist supposition that whiteness equates with greater intelligence. Next, the slave requests power. In a chauvinistic nod to anti-Napoleon patriotism, he rejects this choice "with horror" when Fairy Benigna shows him his future as "a Tyrant trampling on a subject."

Once the slave refuses to become a white narcissist or a political tyrant, Fairy Benigna offers him instead the opportunity to become a philanthropist, previewing the slave's metamorphosis in a clairvoyant view of Harlequin "dispensing comfort to the opprest with grief / Heaven's instrument of general relief." After the slave "expresse[s] raptures at the sight," Fairy Benigna transforms him into the black-masked Harlequin. One scholar describes this staging of emancipation as "a vivid moment of empowerment changing the oppressed black Caribbean slave into a gorgeously costumed comic hero."[101] But it was not the slave who was empowered; it was not even *his* idea to become "Heaven's instrument of general relief." Rather, this role was granted to him by the sage, benevolent agent of empire, Fairy Benigna. "Disobedient slave" becomes docile supplicant.

The slave's final request of Fairy Benigna comes when, as Harlequin, he "supplicate[s] for the emancipation of his fellow Slaves who appear in chains." This exchange highlights Powell's elision of continued plantation slavery, an elision that reconciled liberal nation and slaveholding empire by trumpeting slave-trade abolition as if it had ended slavery itself. The slave begs Benigna to emancipate his fellow slaves, still "driven by the slave-driver." "Poor Afric's children sigh for liberty," she concedes, but "Alas! That task was not reserv'd for me." Instead, she instructs Harlequin, the slaves' emancipation can only be effected by Britannia, thus suggesting that while the end of slavery might be empire's eventual goal, it would certainly not be immediate. Then the "figure of Britannia with her lion descended from the Skies," formally announced by Fairy Benigna, who proudly proclaims: "Listening to the Negro's cries / See, Britain's Genius from the Skies!" In a self-laudatory tone, Britannia, carrying a "writ of law," condemns slavery and champions Britain's abolition of the trade:

> She heard the toil-bled father's shrieks,
> While tears roll'd down their sable cheeks;
> Saw mothers from their children torn,
> Beneath the whip to waste and mourn.
> The lash she heard, she saw the wound,
> And human gore pollute the ground;
> Each feeling tie that nature gave,
> Sunk lost and shatter'd in the *Slave*.

Kindled with a sacred ire,
Her voice broke forth in words of fire;
England shall stamp the blest decree,
That gives the Negro *Liberty*.

As the 1807 legislation had, of course, banned only the slave trade and did not, in fact, give "the Negro liberty," the last two lines pointedly misrepresent the "blest decree." Despite the sentimental platitudes of compassion for "the toil-bled father's shrieks," the "mothers from their children torn," and the slaves suffering "beneath the whip," Liberty, as Fairy Benigna had already made clear, would have to wait. These lines thus encapsulated Britain's conflicted identity as liberty-loving nation and slave-holding empire. The moral and chaste Britannia, "Friendly Genius of the skies," abolishes the slave trade and boasts of "giv[ing] the Negro *Liberty*," yet actually frees only *one* slave on one Jamaican sugar plantation. Britannia's individual manumission was a sign of Britain's liberalism in which its subjects could take chauvinistic pride. But the sentimental antislavery rhetoric did nothing about the continued slavery in Britain's expanding empire and offered slaves only one role: that of being grateful for the "gift" of slave trade abolition.

The Drury Lane thespians' patriotic trumpeting of the 1807 abolition bill and denial of the slaves' agency or freedom reached its zenith in the final scene, which transferred the action from Jamaica to England. Following convention, the harlequinade was comprised of scenes of comic trickery in which the forces of evil—in this case, Sir Peevish, the Pantaloon, Furibond (masked as the Dandy Lover), and his evil servants, the Clown and Maligna—give chase to the lovers and try to separate them, only to be overcome by the forces of good, Fairy Benigna, Harlequin, and Britannia. Just as in the pantomime's first half, all power and agency are assigned to the metaphorical representations of the parliamentary abolitionists. The good fairy buries Furibond and Maligno beneath the surface of the earth: "She waved her wand; the earth opened. Furibond and Maligno sank." In the final scene, Fairy Benigna transports Harlequin and Columbine to her temple-like palace "composed of pillars richly set with emeralds, rubies [and] sapphires," where they are married. Finally, Fairy Benigna "bestowed her benediction" on the couple. Thus, the Fairy Benigna, representing the parliamentary abolitionists, defeats the ideological and economic forces that drive the slave trade, embodied in the evil sorcerer, Furibond, and his assistant, Maligno. The curtain falls.

The union of Harlequin/slave and Columbine, daughter of a slave owner, in

Britannia's Temple of Liberty completes the pantomime's glowing tribute to parliamentary abolitionism and the power of state, while performing reconciliation on several levels: between continued slavery but potential eventual emancipation; between the pro- and antislavery lobbies via the marriage plot; and between slaveholding empire and liberal nation. Audiences may have understood the marriage of Harlequin and Columbine as signifying a future when the slaves had been freed and reconciled with their former masters. Yet slave/Harlequin is the sole recipient of Britannia's beneficent liberty, which was magnanimously conferred on him *only* after he agreed to Fairy Benigna's terms: namely, her proposal that he become Britannia's "instrument of general relief." And that "general relief" was clearly *not* emancipation for the slaves; indeed, the kinds of relief Harlequin acts out are quite different. As Fairy Benigna's proxy, when Harlequin marries Columbine he effects a rapprochement between the parliamentary abolitionists Fairy Benigna represents and the proslavery lobby personified by Columbine's father. In uniting the pro- and antislavery forces behind the banner of "liberty," Harlequin also brings the "relief" of reconciliation between liberty-loving nation and slaveholding empire. Finally, slave/Harlequin's submission to Fairy Benigna and Britannia signifies the underdog's more general acquiescence to the authority and law of nation and empire. Harlequin and Columbine's marriage was thus less about the future freedom of slaves than it was a reconstitution of British ideas of nation and empire.

At first glance, the pantomime and its interracial union might appear to present an arrestingly progressive view of "race," yet *Harlequin Negro* also conveyed negative, hypersexualized connotations of "blackness" at variance with the implied racial reconciliation, thus exploiting Britain's anxiety about interracial unions between black men and white women. Proslavery propagandists played on this anxiety through images of bestial black men to articulate abolition's threat to the British polity.[102] Clara Reeve, for example, warned that with abolition, Africans "will flock hither from all parts, mix with the natives, and soil the breed for the common people," producing "a vile mongrel race of people, such as no friend to Britain can ever wish to inhabit it."[103] *Harlequin Negro* was an embodied metaphor of the threat to British racial purity as the white woman's body was an idealized zone of national identity, anthropomorphized in both Britannia and Columbine.

This connotation of black sexual threat would have been amplified by the fact that by the early nineteenth century, Britannia had come to represent a moral, as well as a political, construction of nation and empire. Against the backdrop of the evangelical movements of the late eighteenth and early to mid-nineteenth centuries, women's special role as the purveyors of spirituality and morality also became integral to Great Britain's imperial vision. In Georgian and Victorian culture, women were increasingly assumed to be morally superior to men, and thus more fully capable of embodying religious rectitude.[104] As scholars have noted, the "unimpeachable figure of Britannia" came to represent the moral nation and empire in opposition to representations in popular literary and visual culture of political corruption in the form of a debauched woman.[105] As woman's role was increasingly associated with her spiritual influence at home, the images of a chaste Britannia expounded a developing ideology of domestic femininity in which antislavery became a clarion call to Christian morality and chastity, a chastity that was threatened by the interracial valences of *Harlequin Negro*.

Perhaps unsurprisingly, then, the figure of Harlequin Negro and "blackness" more generally were depicted as lascivious, docile, and comical. As George Rehin has suggested, Harlequin was a cousin to later blackface minstrelsy, sharing elements of theatrical form, makeup, and costuming, and the character types—such as the hypersexed dandy—that have continuity with later minstrel characters like Zip Coon and Jim Crow.[106] In *Harlequin Negro* these associations were embedded in the very permeability of "blackness" in the pantomime. At one point, for example, the Clown assumes the role of "shoe-black" to polish his master's boots. Instead of shining Furibond's shoes, however, the Clown wipes the black polish on Furibond's stockings. During the resulting tiff, he blackens Furibond's face, clothes, and legs, transforming him into the "Buck," a caricature of a hypersexualized black man and figure of ridicule in the pantomime.

Powell's emphasis on true inner whiteness of the Harlequin, conveyed through the slave's decision to keep his black skin only because the fairy stipulates that its whitening would be contingent on the loss of his "beauties of the mind," may also have served to lessen the slave/Harlequin's blackness by depriving him of his cultural heritage. Furibond the Buck is a white man with an evil heart, while the Harlequin has a good "white" heart encased in a "black" body. The visual linkage in theater of evil with blackness and good with whiteness dates back to medieval morality plays and the Harlequin character had long been associated with diabolical magic.[107] In Powell's pantomime, these linkages were inverted: visual whiteness was associated with evil and visual blackness with good. The inversion resulted in the assigning of black magic to the white enslavers—the "enchanter" Furibond and the "evil sorcerer" Maligno—while the "black" Harlequin has no magic or culture of his own and is empowered to act as "instrument of relief" only after being "granted" that power by white governmental philanthropist, Fairy Benigna.

This assigning of sorcery to the white forces of evil (and of white magic to the powers of white government) further reinforces white over black by depriving slave/Harlequin of his magic and revolutionary potential. As is well documented, the Caribbean magical practices of voodoo and obi (or obeah)—derived from the West African practice of summoning a pantheon of ancestral spirits to one's aid through fetishes or charms—were strongly linked to slave revolt and maroon resistance.[108] The leaders of the revolution on Saint Domingue were practitioners of obeah. These black Jacobins in turn inspired a wave of revolts by slaves throughout the West Indies.[109] Powell's depiction of the white Furibond as an obeah sorcerer and of Maligno as a force of supernatural evil demonizes obeah. In so doing, Powell deprives the "good" African slave of his liberatory agency and articulates a clear mandate for *gradual* emancipation and paternalistic rule from above.

The question of how to interpret the harlequin character divided nineteenth-century contemporaries and continues to divide twenty-first century scholars. Was he a rebel performing for a radical audience or, conversely, a populist appeaser entertaining the crowd? One nineteenth-century essayist construed the Harlequin as the underdog through whom audiences vicariously fantasized about dispossessed peasants taking back their lost common land from the overlords who had enclosed it.[110] *Harlequin Negro*, however, would more likely have been read by its predominantly middle- and upper-class audience in the new, lavish Drury Lane in much the way pantomimes are read by historians J. M. Golby and A. W. Purdue. Golby and Purdue describe the genre of Harlequin pantomimes as a temporary "humbling of the mighty" that "emphasized rather than questioned the normal order of things . . . it was not authority *per se* which was derided but the *wicked* squire, the *pompous* mayor or the lord who [had] no right to his title and estate and has to hand them back to . . . the hitherto humble hero."[111] The humble hero Harlequin Negro, although celebrating slave-trade abolition, did not oppose the overall hegemony of whites over blacks. Nor did he protest the continuation of slavery in the colonies when the fairy insisted that only Britannia had the power to end it. Though the pantomime temporarily "turned the world upside down," it did so in order to assure the more permanent status quo.[112] The radical threat of the underclass was represented in Act 1, scene 1 by the "disobedient slave." But the initially rebellious slave turns supplicant recipient of the self-aggrandizing genius of Britain's beneficence. Thus, although all pantomimes allowed audiences to assign a variety of meanings, it is as a counter-revolutionary foot-solder for Britain's imperial hegemony and liberal state that the Harlequin Negro character is best understood.

Furibond; or, Harlequin Negro opened at Drury Lane on December 28, 1807, to mixed reviews. While the *Morning Herald* called the scenery "beautiful" and "sometimes splendid," the reviewer was less than enthused about the central plot, finding it uninteresting and improbable. The critic conceded that "the story might have . . . been tolerably interesting" but went on to add that it failed because the plot was "without an object" and the "tricks and drolleries therefore were . . . unmeaning."[113] The *Times* concurred, and described it as "a miserable effort in this species of composition" with "scenes [that] were tedious, languid and unconnected." The *Times* reporter also observed that the pantomime "provoked the bile of the audience, and . . . their disapprobation was vehemently expressed."[114] The playbill for December 29, however, contradicted this impression, bragging that the pantomime's opening night "was received throughout by a brilliant and overflowing audience, with universal approbation and unprecedented marks of applause." While this may have been hyperbolic advertising, the second performance did elicit better reviews. The *Times* critic wrote, for example, that the piece was performed "with much greater success than any one who witnessed the first representation could have expected" but nonetheless concluded, "the principal objections still remain . . . [and] it has not stamina for a protracted existence."[115] This conclusion was wrong, as *Harlequin Negro* had a healthy run of twenty-eight performances that season, which meant that the pantomime was seen by a staggering 840,000 people. Whatever technical problems had beset its initial production, the "bile" and "disapprobation" of the audience had given way to popular acclaim for the patriotic and spectacular animation of Britannia and her supplicant slave, the triumphal insignia of a liberal state in which abolition substituted for the enactment of domestic reform.

Contemporaries understood this substitution. Radical William Hazlitt lamented the conservative thrust of abolition in his observation that Wilberforce was passionate about fighting for the rights of African slaves abroad yet unbending in his rejection of plebeian rights at home. Hazlitt summed up the contradiction, remarking wistfully that Wilberforce's "humanity is at the horizon three thousand miles off . . . he unbinds the chains of Africa, yet helps (we trust without meaning it) to rivet those of his own country, and of Europe."[116] Powell and Sheridan did their part in crafting a conservative reformist ethos by dramatizing Britannia symbolically dispensing freedom to kneeling, grateful slaves. Because the kneeling slave was Harlequin with his multiple valences—as African slave, plebeian underdog, and tangible link to the English poacher "Blacks"—*Harlequin Negro* promoted abolitionism as central to Britannia's self-image as a benevolent empire and liberal nation. Powell's pantomime embodied the denial of domestic reform and freedom for the slaves amid anxiety that eventual emancipation (and its frightening potential for widespread miscegination) would despoil the whiteness of the nation.

Artists, poets, thespians, and antislavery advocates celebrated slave-trade abolition using characters and images born of the eighteenth-century revolutionary convulsions. In the wake of the "civil" war with America and anxiety about the meaning of class and ethnicity for national identity, Britons began defining British liberty as antislavery in opposition to the American colonists' claims of British tyranny in the 1770s and 1780s. Yet they simultaneously began denigrating blacks in the capital by associating them with imperial decay, corruption, and miscegenation. Conservatives temporarily smeared abolitionism in the 1790s, but Britons recovered abolitionist Britannia and the supplicant blackface slave in the jingoistic anti-Napoleonic milieu of 1807 and further cemented the vision of ethno-cultural superiority first articulated in the American revolutionary years. In the 1810s and 1820s, Britons and Americans, with very different motivations, would invest in their goddesses—abolitionist Britannia and Columbia, mother of the white republic—competing imperialistic fantasies of spreading redemptive liberty to Africa's shores. As American Joshua Marsden put it, Columbia's Christians would "lead the African to God."[117] British poet James Montgomery similarly prophesied the impact of British civilization and Christianity on the "dark continent" of Africa but at the same time asserted Britannia's imperial naval prowess: "Thus saith Britannia, empress of the sea / Thy chains are broken, Africa be free!"[118]

CHAPTER THREE

Spreading Liberty to Africa

Africa, so long forlorn,
Jesus now will richly bless,
With salvation's joyful morn,
Tidings of delightful grace
Every toil-degraded slave,
Bow'd beneath oppression's rod
Bleeding clemency shall save;
Lead the African to God.

—Joshua Marsden, "The Spread of the Gospel" (1810)

After slave-trade abolition, Philadelphians and Londoners developed idealizations of Britannia, abolitionist empress of the sea, and Columbia, mother of the white republic, and imagined them saving the African continent from war, paganism, and the interior slave trade. Indeed, Anglo-American redemptive liberty would also "lead the African to God," as Joshua Marsden, an American Methodist missionary, put it in his hymn, "The Spread of the Gospel." Marsden's lyrics were part of an outpouring of post-slave-trade abolition imaginary and documentary performances—poems, stage plays, missionary accounts, travel narratives, and scientific treatises—that saw Africa as a dark continent in need of salvation. Britons and Americans created visions of spreading liberty to Africa that, while different, were both intricately bound up with the way slave-trade abolition served to reconcile supposedly liberal nations with their slaveholding empires. Americans' imperial fantasy of redeeming Africa through the spread of Christianity and civilization was linked to the fear of slave insurrection and the related impulse to purge the civic polity of black citizens. Britons' urge to save Africa was, by contrast, grounded in expanding the empire's naval prowess and on the continued contradiction between abolitionist nation and slaveholding West Indian empire. The American idea of removing blacks went back to Henry Thornton's Sierra Leone scheme and Thomas Jefferson's repatriation proposals in his *Notes on*

Virginia, which Philadelphians like Thomas Branagan had revisited during the slave-trade abolition debates. In the 1810s and 1820s, Philadelphians and other Americans rephrased this impulse as a desire to spread liberty and Christianity to Africa through evangelical missions and by establishing a colony there of freed African American slaves. While the British also wanted to spread Protestantism via missions in Africa, London playwrights, poets, missionaries, and explorers focused on how British naval power could forcibly prohibit other nations from conducting the transatlantic slave trade, thus celebrating the extension of British liberty to a ravaged continent.

After slave-trade abolition, Britons and Americans extolled Britannia and Columbia in her respective Temple of Liberty in much more overtly imperial terms than before. The London-based African Institution, founded in 1807 to replace the Society for Effecting the Abolition of the Slave Trade, set as its goal the dismantling of the interior African slave trade as a means of extending Britannia's "blessings of freedom and civilization to Africa."[1] The Royal Navy, meanwhile, established the West Africa Squadron to suppress the Atlantic slave trade by patrolling the West African coastline, a strong assertion of Britannia's naval prowess as "empress of the sea," as British poet, James Montgomery, described her.[2] In the United States, the American Colonization Society (ACS) was founded in 1816 to promote and support the African colony of Liberia for freed African American slaves. One of its founders, Reverend Robert Finley, pronounced that an American colony of free blacks in Africa would "extend the empire of liberty and Christian blessings to surrounding nations."[3] Francis Scott Key, a Baltimore Presbyterian who was closely involved with the establishment of a mission to Africa, invoked the Temple of Liberty when he predicted that removing freed American blacks to Africa would spread Columbia's civilization to that continent, which would then witness "spires of temples glittering in the sun," "harbors shaded by the snowy wings of departing and returning commerce," and the "hum of industry resounding in the streets."[4] After slave-trade abolition, cultural producers on each side of the Atlantic invoked republican Columbia's and monarchical Britannia's liberty to promote the redemption of Africa in strikingly similar imperial language, albeit to different ends.

In the United States this imperial ethos was compounded by the War of 1812, which engendered a new sense of national greatness.[5] Triggered by British restraints on American naval trade neutrality during Britain's war with Napoleon's France, Americans and Britons shed blood between 1812 and 1814 over the United States' insistence on neutral shipping rights, fury over British impressment of American citizens into the Royal Navy, and desire on the part of some

Democratic-Republicans to oust the British altogether from the North American continent and to annex Canada.[6] The War of 1812 also reignited the furious competition over the meanings of slavery and liberty that had originated in the revolutionary years. To the British, America's exploitation of African slaves while promoting liberty for white men disqualified the republic as a beacon of liberty. Conversely, Americans castigated the British impressments of American sailors as white slavery.[7]

Although the war was an inglorious stalemate and the Treaty of Ghent formalizing its end left Canada under British rule and did not resolve the issues of shipping rights and impressments, Americans considered it a resounding triumph.[8] "The Star Spangled Banner," Francis Scott Key's defiant anthem celebrating the defeat of the British at Baltimore, epitomized Americans' celebration of the war's end as confirmation of the nation's political and cultural independence. White Americans also exulted in their defeat of the Native American uprising led by the Shawnee leader Tecumseh, whose confederation of Wyandots, Kickapoos, Delawares, Winebagos, Potawatomies and other tribes had allied with the British in a desperate attempt to staunch white American expansion into Indian country and to create a pan-Indian sovereign state in the Northwest.[9] With the confederation's defeat and Tecumseh's death at the Battle of the Thames, Americans felt assured of their right to move into Indian country and make it their own.[10] The question of whether or not to expand slavery into the newly "open" western territories of the defeated pan-Indian confederacy provoked, in turn, renewed calls for the removal of free blacks from the United States.

Despite the war, Britons and Americans remained in constant dialogue, with plays, travelogues, and mission reports traveling back and forth across the ocean and with a hardy stock of shared, however contested, symbology. Missionaries, explorers, poets, and thespians on both sides of the Atlantic used shared language and symbols for their post slave-trade abolition visions of imperial expansion, be it British or American. Through transatlantic exchange, they also helped create and disseminate newly racialized typologies of human difference, the key to which was a permeable interchange between philosophical and religious discourse and popular theatrical performances. In the 1810s and 1820s, London and Philadelphia anatomists, surgeons, and biologists published "scientific" theories of race that placed Europeans at the head and Africans at the foot of a hierarchy that affixed physiognomic features and skin complexion to geography and supposed strata of "civilization." These theorists of biological race drew heavily on travel narratives and mission reports, such as the wildly popular editions of Mungo Park's *Travels into the Interior of Africa* (London, 1799; Philadelphia,

1800), to substantiate their claims.[11] Poets and thespians, in turn, used travelogues like Park's, mission reports, and also "scientific" discourse on race as their
sources for literary and theatrical performances of slavery in Africa. Thespians
were instrumental in solidifying the newly imperial impulse to rescue the "dark
continent" and in animating this emergent typology because their staged performances put "expert" intellectual ideas into embodied form for popular consump-
tion and reached a far wider audience than did print. While a few playwrights
and poets imagined Africa as a natural paradise populated by innocent "noble
savages,"[12] a more common depiction was that of George Colman in his drama
The Africans; or, War, Love, and Duty (1808), which William Dunlap adapted for
the American stage (New York, 1810; Philadelphia, 1811). This vision portrayed
Africa as a wasteland despoiled by the slave trade and populated by heathens
ranked low in the new "scientific" hierarchies ordered by skin complexions and
physiognomic features determined by geography.

Missionaries, Explorers, and Columbia's and Britannia's Empires of Liberty

African missions, ethnographic expeditions, and new organizations on both
sides of the Atlantic all helped form competing imperial visions of African colonization and Christianization in Great Britain and the United States. The Sierra
Leone Company, originally established in 1786 by the London Committee for
the Black Poor but later taken over by the British crown, founded a colony in
Sierra Leone in 1788 and began "resettling" former slaves there. But the African
Institution (1807–27), which replaced the Society for Effecting the Abolition of
the Slave Trade, had a new strategy: not only did it work to persuade other European nations to abandon the slave trade and to pressure the government to use
naval power to prevent slave-trading, but it also sponsored proselytizing missions
meant to dissuade Africans from slave trading. Africa and Africans assumed a
place in the imaginary of Britannia's imperial temple as a continent of heathens
to be saved from darkness by the spread of British "liberty." Meanwhile, although
Americans also set up African missions and some Philadelphians, both black
and white, imagined Africa as a site of Christian redemption from paganism,[13]
most Americans' understanding of Africa's role was markedly different. The goal
of Christian salvation was deeply interlinked with the vision of Africa as a site to
which blacks would be "returned" after they were expatriated from Columbia's
Temple of Liberty.

In 1816, the Reverend Robert Finley, Francis Scott Key, and others formed the
American Colonization Society (ACS) with the intent of resettling free blacks in

what would eventually become Liberia. Early proponents of colonization argued that an African colony would provide a model of democracy and Christianity to the "dark continent" and that African Americans could enjoy there the rights denied to them in the United States. The ACS was thus founded on an inherent contradiction: that blacks who were seen as unqualified for assimilation into American society and its values were nevertheless eminently qualified to carry democracy, civilization, and Christianity to Africa.[14] Henry Clay, a key supporter of African colonization, summed up this paradoxical ethos when he argued that free blacks did not enjoy the freedoms and rights of white Americans. Pointing to Sierra Leone as a successful colonization project, he concluded that African colonization could not "be a nobler cause . . . [as] it proposes to rid our country of a useless and pernicious, if not dangerous portion of its population . . . contemplates the spreading of . . . civilized life, and the possible redemption of ignorance and barbarism."[15] Just as spreading liberty and civilization to Africa was intrinsic to Britannia's benevolent, post-slave-trade empire, it was also a requisite to preserving Columbia's white Temple of Liberty through deracination.

In addition to these new organizations, British and American explorations into the interior of Africa burgeoned after slave-trade abolition, which helped to popularize the cause of saving Africa. Far and away the best-known scientific exploration into the interior of Africa was that of Mungo Park, which was sponsored by abolitionist Joseph Banks, a key member of the African Institution. Park's account of his trip, *Travels into the Interior Districts of Africa*, was an instant sensation on both sides of the ocean. The first London edition sold out within a week, and the release of two more British editions was immediately followed by German, French, and American editions.[16] Abolitionists, scientists, playwrights, poets, and evangelical missionaries all cited the book.

Excitement about Park's *Travels* and other explorers' exploits in Africa tied into new evangelical zeal that led to missionary expeditions to Africa. In Great Britain, as has already been noted, the evangelical revivalism of the late eighteenth century had given birth to the Church of England's London-based Clapham sect, also known as the "Saints," to which abolitionists William Wilberforce and Hannah More both belonged. Methodism had also mushroomed in the industrializing urban centers. In the first few decades of the nineteenth century, America was swept up in the camp meetings and ecstatic evangelism of the Second Great Awakening, a reformed Congregationalism that rejected the old Calvinist idea of predestined salvation by God's grace alone and instead emphasized the need for free will to attain salvation. Amid the fervor of the Second Great Awakening, evangelicals formed new denominations, and Methodists and Baptists revived enthusiastic practices of their faiths. By the late 1820s, Charles Finney had brought to white Philadelphians his fiery brand of reformed Calvinism from the "burned-over district" of New York. Concomitantly, new black churches formed: Methodist, Baptist, and Presbyterian.[17] In both countries, this religious enthusiasm led to support for new African missions, and the missions' published reports helped disseminate the ideas of human difference in relation to physiognomy, geography, and religion.

Although depictions of Africa and Africans in travel narratives, histories, and mission accounts were not new, the late eighteenth- and early nineteenth-century mission and travel reports describing Africans differed from older reports in crucial ways. Classical writings such as those of Pliny and Ptolemy, the adventures of medieval travelers like Marco Polo in the thirteenth century, and sixteenth- and seventeenth-century travelogues supplied a mix of fact and fantasy in their ethnographic descriptions of faraway lands and peoples.[18] The Society for the Promotion of the Christian Gospel, founded in 1698, and the Society for the Propagation of the Gospel, established in 1701, also published reports of African life.[19] But unlike these earlier travel and mission reports, the late eighteenth- and early nineteenth-century scientific expeditions and Christian missions were founded specifically to explore, expand into, and convert Africa. In London in 1776, for example, the *Evangelical Magazine* devoted an entire edition to Africa, and by 1795 the ecumenical London Missionary Society and the Anglican Church Missionary Society had been founded to propagate the gospel among the African "heathen." By 1804, the Church Missionary Society had begun its work in Freetown, Sierra Leone. And back home, an eager public, whose interest in Africa was already aroused by current events, devoured the mission and exploration accounts.

For Londoners, theatrical, artistic, and political celebrations of slave-trade abolition as well as the regrouping of the African Institution, piqued interest in travel and mission reports from Africa. In Philadelphia, nineteenth-century mission reports of Africa coincided with and helped cement enthusiasm for schemes to repatriate American blacks to Africa. The ACS made spreading Christianity, commerce, and culture to the "dark continent" and thereby atoning for the slave trade their key justification for "repatriating" American blacks. While not all supporters of missions and colonization schemes viewed Africans as innately inferior, all were convinced that Africa was culturally "backward" and in need of the progressive influence of American industry and enlightened civilization. Colonizationist Edward Dorr Griffin, in a sermon entitled *A Plea for Africa*, made this clear when he condemned those "who cast the Africans into another species, and sorted them with the ape and ourang-outang" and instead contended that climate, education, and culture accounted for "racial" difference. Griffin also maintained that slavery was responsible for the "present depressed state of the African mind," which was the basis for his claim that colonization augured "a bright day arising on Africa." Repatriated American blacks, he averred, would simultaneously escape the degrading condition of slavery in America and bring cultural and economic uplift to Africans.[20] Although Griffin unequivocally rejected polygenesis—the theory that blacks and whites descended from different species—he clearly viewed western Christianity and culture as superior.

By propagating this belief that the "enlightened" Christian white man (or even the African American "civilized" by western culture) was superior to the African, many early nineteenth-century mission reports abetted the calcification of notions of race. This emergent taxonomy posited gradated positions for Africans based on both perceived cultural difference and physiognomic factors such as skin complexion. The Church of England's *Travels in South Africa* (1815) reported on its mission "of diffusing the Gospel in Heathen and other unenlightened countries" and asserted that dark-complexioned sub-Saharan Africans of the Caffraria tribe were a "tall warlike race . . . addicted to plundering." By contrast, the light-complexioned people of Madagascar who came "from the Persian and Arabian gulfs, and from Egypt" were "well shaped and . . . chiefly of an olive colour" and had a "character replete with frankness [and] they are not considered a savage people."[21] The author of *Journal of a Visit to South Africa in 1815 and 1816* enthused about the "beneficial influence of Christianity in enlightening and civilizing Heathen nations." He described the "natural indolence" of the "black or tawny" "Hottentots," who were "poor, squalid and ignorant wretches" until Christianity "gradually change[d] their dispositions, making them obedient . . . to all those moral and civil obligations which the Gospel inculcates."[22]

American mission reports similarly popularized deeply racialist visions of Africans, visions that intersected with hardening white racism toward black Americans. For these missions postdating slave-trade abolition, the goal of saving Africa was penitence for America's slave-trading past—which, in reality, was not past, as Africans were still being illicitly brought into the country as slaves long after the 1808 ban.[23] Nonetheless, American mission reports articulated this ideal of the penitential deliverance of heathen Africans. *A Compendious History of the Principal Protestant Missions to the Heathen* (1813), for example, reported on the mission to the "Foulah Country in Africa," which was sent because "the inhabitants of Africa were considered as having peculiar claims on the Christian world, on account of their having been treated so inhumanly by the slave traders." The author described the "Heathen darkness" and "forbidding wilds of Africa," where "that portion of the human race . . . had been reputed as nearly on a level with the brutes."[24] Other American missions with similar agendas soon followed.[25]

Late-eighteenth- and early-nineteenth-century explorers' accounts of interactions with specific African tribes also informed new scientific theories of biological race. In particular, Mungo Park's *Travels* became a key source for London scientists who essayed new theories of racial differences. Surgeon James Cowles Prichard, in *Researches into the Physical History of Man* (1813), quoted from Park to support his arguments for biological racial difference.[26] Prichard was a firm believer in epigenesis, the theory that all humans, no matter how physically and culturally different, stemmed from the same original species. He founded his belief in the unity of the human race on the scriptural account of Adam and Eve as the parents of all humans. Although influenced by Johann Friedrich Blumenbach, Prichard departed from his five-fold typology of human physical types—Malay, Mongolian, Caucasian, Ethiopian, and American—to propose three human types descending from Noah's three sons: black, white, and an intermediate hue.[27]

Prichard suggested that congenital hereditary racial difference was a later development, the result of both climate and culture. His work thus took into account language, customs, and belief systems in conjunction with physical anatomy to determine a typology of human difference. Prichard supported his theories with detailed descriptions of "the tribes who inhabit the countries bordering on the Senegal and Gambia rivers" from "Mr. Park, [who] divides them into four principal nations, the Mandingoes, Feloops, Jaloffs and Foulahs."[28] Prichard's work had a transatlantic reach and was cited by racial theorists like Philadelphian Samuel Morton, with whom he was in correspondence.[29] In *Crania Americana* (1839), Morton posited, based on skull size and shape, that humans could be arranged in a hierarchy of intelligence in which whites were at the apex—due to their supposedly larger and therefore more intelligent brains—and Africans at the base.

Other theorists of hereditary racial difference soon followed Prichard's lead in exploiting Park's travelogue. Anatomist William Lawrence, in *Lectures on Physiology, Zoology, and the Natural History of Mankind* (1819), cited both Prichard's earlier treatise, *De generis humani varietate* (1808), and Park's *Travels* to support his contention that, while Africans and Caucasians were of the same species, "the Negro is more like a monkey than the European." He again quoted directly from Park when he insisted that the Foulahs were "less glossy black than those of the Gold Coast . . . [with] not such flat noses or thick lips," but the much darker "Eboes from the Bight of Benin" were darker-complexioned, more Negroid in features, and hence less civilized. The Eboes, he concluded, were "the lowest and most wretched of all the nations in Africa" as "the conformation of the face . . . very much resembles that of the baboon."[30] Missionaries' and explorers' narratives, especially Park's, provided scientists with observed "evidence" to support their new racial theories.

The Performance of Scientific Racism and Britannia's Liberation of Africa

These ethnographic theories reached scientists and well-educated literati, but cultural producers transmitted "expert" knowledge on "race" and ethnography through art, prose, and theater to broader readerships and audiences. George Colman's play, *The Africans; or, War, Love, and Duty*, presented in London in 1808, drew on Park and was part of the larger fabric in which cultural producers contributed to a growing vision of imperial and "racial" British hegemony. In this vein, James Montgomery, James Grahame, and E. Benger rejoiced in slave-trade abolition as a triumph of the liberal nation and empire in *Poems on the Abolition of the Slave Trade* (1809).[31] The book was intended to "popularly commemorate" the "illustrious act of the British Legislature," as the printer's advertisement announced. The abolition bill had "vindicate[d] our religion and our laws." Not only was it evidence of "the dignity of the British Empire," but it had also "extend[ed] its influence to the . . . universal interest of mankind."[32] Dedicated to the "Society for Bettering the Condition of the Natives of Africa," the compilation of poems celebrated the spread of Britannia's liberty to desperate Africa.

The book stressed how civilized Britannia had saved heathen Africa by ending the slave trade, venerating an Anglo-American pantheon of white abolitionists and downplaying the continued horrors of West Indian plantation slavery. Indeed, the compilation celebrated the end of the trade as if it were the end of slavery itself. James Grahame's poem was even titled *Africa Delivered; or, The Slave Trade Abolished*, and it praised the "generous band, united in the cause / Of liberty to Africa restored" and their Christian "faith, which trampled Slavery underfoot." He ignored not only British West Indian slavery when he praised "Britannia's will" that had "consumed the tyrant's chain" but also American slavery. Referencing the parallel American ban on the slave trade, he praised the "joy and freedom" of "blest Columbia" who had, with Britannia, "restored to human rights" the continent of Africa. He concluded by eulogizing Philadelphian Quaker antislavery pioneer Anthony Benezet, as well as British abolitionists Sharp, Wilberforce, Clarkson, Grenville, and Fox.[33] E. Benger, in *A Poem, Occasioned by the Abolition of the Slave Trade*, memorialized "benignant Sharpe" as the "father of the cause" and praised the spread of Britannia's "royal stole" of liberty to her empire: "Lo, Britain reigns a queen! With proud control / O'er distant realms she sweeps her royal stole."[34]

In contrast to Benger and Grahame, James Montgomery's *The West Indies* explicitly condemned West Indian slavery: "Britannia shared the gain, the glory and the guilt / By her were slavery's island-altars built / And fed with human victims." But he, too, expiated Britannia's guilt by extolling her national liberty and its agents, Clarkson, Wilberforce, Fox, Pitt, and "Sharpe, [who] on proud Britannia's charter'd shore . . . taught the world, that while she rules the waves her soil is freedom to the feet of slaves." And the focus of the poem, like those of Benger and Grahame, was a lionization of Britannia's extension of liberty to her empire:

> Thy chains are broken, Africa, be free!
> Thus saith the island-empress of the sea;
> Thus saith Britannia. O, ye winds and waves!
> Waft the glad tidings to the land of slaves;
> Proclaim on Guinea's coast, by Gambia's side
> As far as Niger rolls his eastern tide,
> Through radiant realms, beneath the burning zone,
> Where Europe's curse is felt, her name unknown,
> Thus saith Britannia, empress of the sea
> Thy chains are broken, Africa, be free!

Thus, Africa was the benighted "land of slaves" and Britannia, the "empress of the sea," was the continent's savior.[35]

Moreover, in both Montgomery's poem and the accompanying image by R. Smirke (fig. 8), enslaved West Indians and Africans were again passive supplicants with no cultural agency. Unlike James Powell in *Furibond; or, Harlequin Negro*, Montgomery did not deny the rebel slave his African cultural practice. Instead, he demonized it, associating the "appalling mysteries of Obi's spell" with "wild Maroons" and "the dæmon-spectres of Domingo" and describing revolt as the "avenging thunder" and "grim delight" of "rapine and massacre."[36] In evoking the well-known association between obeah, revolt, and vengeance, Montgomery, on the one hand, agreed with abolitionist James Stephen that slavery inherently encouraged revolt. On the other hand, like *Harlequin Negro*, *The West Indies* proposed that the answer was not sudden emancipation: the transition to a post-slavery polity should come instead through civilized, gradual legislative means. Montgomery contrasted the savagery of self-liberation with the civilization and justice of Britannia's Christian Liberty, and Smirke's illustration reinforced this

Figure 8. R. Smirke, illustration for James Montgomery's *The West Indies* (1809). In this image, Smirke depicts West Indian slaves and Africans as passive supplicants. Childlike and half-naked—as if to suggest their lesser civilization—they are granted "liberty" by a fully clothed and all-powerful Britannia, her imperial lion at her side. Library of Congress

contrast, showing all-powerful Britannia, her imperial lion at her side, dispensing liberty to a group of half-naked and childlike slaves in shackles. Britannia's liberty was that of a higher civilization, handed down from the scales of justice in the sky to the Africans kneeling beneath her pedestal.

Smirke and Montgomery, however, did more than celebrate slave-trade abolition; they also depicted a continent plundered by Africans kidnapping other Africans into slavery. Montgomery detailed the violent kidnapping of Africans by other Africans to assuage the European slave market:

'Twas night: his babes around him lay at rest
Their mother slumber'd on their father's breast:
A yell of murder rang around their bed;

They woke, their cottage blazed, the victims fled;
Forth sprang the ambush'd ruffians on their prey
They caught, they bound they drove them far away
The white man bought them at the mart of blood
In pestilential barks they cross'd the flood.

And Smirke's illustration accompanying Montgomery's description of African slave traders depicted, as would Colman's play, savage Africans violently forcing more vulnerable Africans, the hapless victims of warfare, into slavery: European slave traders are nowhere in sight. Smirke's visual imaginings of savage African slave trading and of Britannia freeing her slaves with the scales of civilized justice celebrated civilized, Christian Europeans intervening to "save" benighted Africa from barbarity and heahenism.

While Montgomery, Benger, Graham, and Smirke did not directly cite Mungo Park, other poets and playwrights quoted his *Travels* to animate emergent ideas about "race" as a physiognomic category and cultural marker. Poets Robert Southey and William Wordsworth, both sympathetic to antislavery feeling, drew on Park's *Travels* in their evocation of Africa—Southey in the fourth book of *Thalaba*, and Wordsworth in book 13 of *The Prelude*. So did George Colman in *The Africans; or, War, Love, and Duty*.[37] The play was based on Jean Pierre Claris de Florian's novel, *Sélico, Nouvelle Africaine* (1788; English translation 1794), about the activities of European slave merchants and the struggles of Africans for freedom. While Colman may have been indebted to missionary materials in a general sense, he *explicitly* relied on Mungo Park. He set the play in the Foulah village of "Fatteconda in Bondou, a district of Africa situated between the rivers Senegal and Gambia," an area of West Africa Park described. "The principal of the Foulah states," Park had observed, "is that within the Serra Leona [sic] . . . Others of less note, are Bondou, with Foota-Torra, adjacent to it, lying between the rivers Gambia and Falemé . . . [and] along the upper part of the Senegal river."[38] Fotta-Torra became Fatteconda in the play, but otherwise it was all Park. The play offered a firm condemnation of slavery while at the same time it portrayed an Africa in need of enlightened Western liberty and materialized developing racialized taxonomic categories via its text, actors, sets, costume, and makeup.

Part of Colman's inspiration to dramatize *Sélico* must surely have been popular theatrical precedent. The story had already been successful on stage in French, German, and English. Its plot revolved around two noble Africans of the Foulah tribe, Selico and Berissa, separated on their wedding day when a slave-trading Mandingo tribe invades their village. The greedy Mandingo warriors want to capture Foulah villagers in order to sell them to European slave traders. Mug, a white man in domestic slavery to the Foulahs, and Selico's bride-to-be, Berissa, are among those captured. When Selico, believing Berissa to be dead, finds the Mandingo camp in order to sell himself into transatlantic slavery to feed his near-starving mother, he and Berissa are reunited. Selico's mother arrives at the Mandingo camp in time to save her son and successfully appeal for his release. *The Africans* lifted a veil on indigenous slavery and exposed the role European slave traders played as instigators of interethnic bellicosity.[39]

Colman also drew closely from Park to describe the physiognomic appearance of his characters and to establish that the pastoral and peaceful Foulahs were "ten shades lighter" complexioned than their barbarous neighbors, the plundering and "deep black" Mandingo. When Selico's brother announces her forthcoming marriage, he describes the complexion and features of the Foulah: "Last night, beneath the trabba tree, our market place, did I harangue the people on your nuptials . . . Africans, said I, Townsmen of Fatteconda, here in Bondou, between the Senegal and Gambia. We Foulahs are the prettiest of negroes; for the same sun that dyes our neighbors black (Feloops, Mandingoes, Jaloops, and the rest) has dipt us Foulahs lighter by ten shades." Colman incorporated almost verbatim descriptions in chapter 2 of *Travels* in which Park noted that "the Feloops, the Jaloffs, the Foulahs and the Mandingoes" were the "four great classes" of the "natives of the countries bordering on the Gambia." According to Park, the "Foulahs . . . are chiefly of a tawny complexion with soft silky hair, and pleasing features. They are much attached to a pastoral life."[40] In his geographical appendix he italicized for emphasis these physiological distinctions: "the Foulahs, although they partake much of the Negro form and complexion, have neither their *jetty* colour, *thick lips*, or *crisped* hair."[41] Unlike Colman, Park did not denigrate the Mandingo as savage, commenting instead that "they are, generally speaking, of a mild, sociable and obliging disposition." But Colman's attribution of warmongering and slave-trading to the Mandingo nonetheless came directly from Park, who offered a lurid description of the cruelty of the enslavement of Mandingo "captives taken in war," as well as the role played by European "slave ships on the coast" in instigating and perpetuating cyclical warfare and slave-trading.[42]

Colman not only dramatized the interethnic wars driven by the insatiable demands of the transatlantic slave trade, he also illuminated the damaging effect this perpetual strife had on the largely agrarian economies of West African communities like the Foulah village of Fatteconda, his fictive version of Foota-Torra. As far back as 1789, Wilberforce had maintained that the slave trade was the impetus for war and hardship in Africa, rendering Africa "in a worse state than that of the most barbarous and savage nation."[43] But it was not until *The Africans* that this argument was staged. Colman's villains were a group of vicious European slave traders, the pointedly named Marrowbone, Grim, Flayall, and Fetterwell. To underscore their fiendishness, when Fetterwell introduces himself and his fellow rogues to Demba, the slave-raiding king of the Mandingos, he likens their occupation to butchery:

> Let me introduce my friends and brother traders. Here's Mr. Flayall, bound to Barbadoes—Mr. Grim, going to Jamaica—young Mr. Marrowbone, once a carcass butcher in Clare-market, but an estate dropping to him in the West India Islands, he now barters for blacks, instead of bargaining for bullocks—Captain Abraham Adamant, who lost his left leg when the inhuman negroes chucked him down the hatchway, for only stowing fifteen in a hammock, in hot weather.

Colman clearly condemned as barbarous the slavers' callous treatment of the slaves as "inhuman" animals to be bartered, shipped, and slaughtered for profit.

He also exposed the role the European slave trade had played in generating war. In an exchange between the traders and the Mandingo chief's messenger in Act I, scene 2, it transpires that Demba had murdered and replaced the legitimate king of the Mandingos, an opportunist usurpation made possible when "the troubles about liberty broke out among the warriors." The "active, cruel, and cunning" Demba has deputized Mug, the literate white man captured in the Mandingo raid on the village of Fatteconda, to invite the traders to Demba's forthcoming market. Reading from "an official letter of welcome," Mug announces: "Sir, I have the honour to inform your excellency, that his majesty Demba Sego Jalla, the Mandingo king of Kassan, whose important cares of state have never afforded him leisure to learn to write, has taken many prisoners now on sale. The capture has been so great that it will be worth the English traders' while to travel up to the camp to inspect them." The audience learned from this that the Mandingo's attack on the Foulahs was motivated to supply the demands of the slave trade, and that the foray was part of a broader pattern of interethnic wars and slave raids. The scene also revealed the internal political consequences of "troubles over liberty," which had galvanized a cycle of instability expressed in factional rifts and violent coups d'états.

Colman also documented the economic and cultural losses the slave trade inflicted on indigenous pastoral life, using the disruption of Selico's and Berissa's wedding to symbolize the erosion of village culture and the figurative displacement of domestic harmony and culture. The wedding preparations under way include a lavish traditional feast composed of "kous-kous, honeycombs, yams, watermelons . . . and broil'd elephant." In the Mandingos raid, however, they destroy the Foulah crops, leaving the village without food. The hardship caused by the slave trade is personalized through Darina, Selico's aging mother. Close to starvation, Darina becomes increasingly frail, which is the motivation for her son selling himself into slavery.

Although Colman presented a sentimentalized view of the Foulahs, he acknowledged that slavery existed in their culture, too. But he used the portrayal of Foulah slavery as a vehicle to champion British "liberty" and indict the barbarity of the European traders. In one breath, Colman praised the parliamentary abolitionists through an exchange between Berissa, who was opposed to slavery on humanitarian grounds, and her father, the slave-owning Farulho. When Farulho offers to grant his daughter a wish as a wedding present, she implores him to free his slaves: "Oh, my father! There's my wish—to make men happy you must make them free!" The English Mug praises Berissa's sentiments and informs her, "That's an English sentiment: go to London, and Parliament will naturalize you directly." Berissa continues to plead with her father, begging him to "think how the slave's heart must sicken for his home," how parents are torn by slavery from their children, and "how many slaves have perish'd by despair." Farulho finally capitulates, announcing, "At dawn I will assemble all my slaves, and give them liberty forever!" Colman thus assigned sentimental humanitarianism to virtuous African characters and linked it to the abolitionist English Parliament that serves as a foil to the European villains. Even the cruel Mandingo chief, Demba, ultimately frees Berissa and Selico on sentimental grounds, declaring, "My heart was never moved 'till now."

Colman's endowing his African characters with sentimental liberatory agency was, however, tempered by the play's trumpeting of white cultural superiority. Mug's assertion that an enlightenment belief in the natural right to liberty was "an English sentiment" was but one example of the proud patriotism Colman worked into the play both overtly and tacitly. In an allusion to the recent legislation, for example, Fetterwell remarks to Mug, "We must make short work of this [purchase of slaves], as this will be our last venture; for, when I left London, a bill was passing that will kick our business to the devil." Mug replies "I am very glad to hear of it. The work begins in the natural quarter, and the stream of freedom flows from the very fountain head of true natural liberty." Thus the play espoused the rhetoric of Britannia as the all-powerful and magnanimous custodian of superior law. By emphasizing the spread of liberty to the interior of Africa, Colman avoided mentioning the persistence of slavery in the colonies and its contradiction with "true natural liberty."

Finally, Colman embedded into his characters the equation, posited by Park and theorized by Prichard, Lawrence, and other scientists, of skin color in relation to hierarchical rankings of culture, nation, and biology. He even related these rankings to a corresponding suitability for disparate types of labor. In this taxonomy, Europeans were assigned to higher rungs on the ladder than Africans in general, but darker-complexioned and more "negroid" Africans were presented as less intelligent and better suited to manual labor than lighter-complexioned Africans. Thus, when Selico tries to sell himself into slavery, the European slave traders are not interested, because as a Foulah he is a member of, as one trader put it, "a lighter breed not . . . so hardy as the black negroes." As a white man, Mug was of the lowest monetary value as a slave because, as his master, Farulho, insists, whites are unsuited to physical work yet superior in their suitability to mental and governmental labor. It was also on this basis that Demba, after acquiring Mug in conquest, appointed him "secretary of state," a position in which he performed purely administrative functions. The unstated corollary to Colman's racialized assignation of disparate work functions was the implicit absurdity of assigning intellectual and governmental positions to dark-complexioned blacks. Furthermore, there is the implication people of different skin colors should not mix. While still in bond to Farulho, Mug bemoans the fact that "all the black and yellow men are jumbled together." When Mug and Farulho envision a time when Mug will return to England, Mug tells Farulho, "When we part, we shall never meet again in this world . . . our persuasions are as different as our colour." The celebration of British abolition reflexively incorporated a colonialist philosophy of white ethnocultural superiority. In this ethos, different peoples were assigned fixed, separate, and unequal places because of inherent physiognomic, cultural, and geographical differences, even in a future beyond slavery.

When *The Africans* first opened in London, it was unpopular with audience and critics, largely because of Colman's assignation of sentimental morality to African characters. The audience was unenthusiastic on opening night, as the *Times* reported: "the third act went off very heavily, and with considerable disapprobation."[44] The *Literary Panorama* shed some light on the "disapprobation" when it thoroughly panned the play; the reviewer went so far as to question why Colman wrote the piece "unless he had written it for a wager, to shew how tamely contemptible an audience may be rendered."[45] But the *Monthly Mirror* made clear what the problem was when it questioned the "noble virtues . . . among barbarian tribes" and complained, "The sentiments, though dignified, and in human nature, were not always strictly African." Theater aficionado and reporter Henry Crabb Robinson agreed, noting scathingly that *The Africans* was "a miserable sentimental piece . . . pathetic incidents take place among a tribe of Africans in which filial and parental love are exhibited in great power, and what is much worse the refined morality and ostentatious parade of sentiment so fashionable in our age and country."[46] Dramatist Richard Brinsley Peake also deemed the eloquence and sentiment of Colman's African characters unrealistic because the characters should only have "required the utmost simplicity of diction."[47] Colman responded to his critics by explaining that he wrote *The Africans* to show that "the nobler virtues are more practiced among barbarian tribes than by civilized society; that the savage heathen, who wages war to extermination and devours his captives, not infrequently displays a glorious self-denial, a sublime magnanimity that with true believers pass for fable and romance." Yet he admitted that his characters' "nobler virtues" were exceptional, and the general rule was the cannibalistic "savage heathen" character of Africans and the superiority of Western "civilized society."[48]

Despite its inauspicious debut, the play had a successful run.[49] For thirty-one nights, the actors in *The Africans* performed for Londoners missionaries' and adventurers' visions of a desecrated Africa while making a case for Britannia's abolitionist liberty. Just how closely intertwined the theater's and the travelers' vision of Africa was with abolition was evidenced by the financial sponsorship of the first London edition of Park's *Travels* by noted abolitionists William Wilberforce and Henry Thornton, as well as thespian John Philip Kemble.[50] When the curtain rose on *The Africans*, the vast audiences of the Haymarket Theatre Royal saw a vivid performance of the abolitionist and missionary vision of spreading Britannia's liberty to Africa's shores.

The Africans, Racial Theories, and Columbia's "Empire of Liberty"

Despite its high quotient of British patriotism, *The Africans* was also vibrantly topical on Columbia's side of the Atlantic. The play's arrival in Philadelphia in 1811 after its successful New York debut coincided with the stirrings of African colonization via Paul Cuffe's voyages carrying African Americans to Africa (which predated the founding of the American Colonization Society in 1816). But the Philadelphia production also intersected with vociferous local debates about scientific theories of "race." Moreover, the contemporary relevance of *The Africans* was enhanced by the direct linkages between the colonization movement, abolitionism, and Mungo Park's travelogue. Charles Fenton Mercer, one of the founders of the ACS, was a subscriber of the first Philadelphia edition of *Travels into the Interior of Africa*, along with abolitionists Thomas Mifflin and Benjamin Rush, and actor Thomas Cooper.[51] Publisher and antislavery sympathizer Mathew Carey underwrote the edition.[52] Carey would go on to publish *The Africans* in Philadelphia in 1811. He would also later support African colonization schemes, arguing that the repatriation of free American blacks to the colony of Liberia "has commenced spreading the blessings of civilization, morals, and religion among the [African] natives."[53]

William Dunlap's decision to adapt Colman's chauvinistic British play amid mounting British-American tensions on the eve of the War of 1812 may seem surprising. After all, during the imperial crisis of the 1760s and 1770s, the Sons of Liberty, seeing theater as a form of pernicious British cultural influence, destroyed a theater house in New York and disrupted performances in Philadelphia.[54] Yet despite these protests and a war-time ban on theatrical entertainments, patriot soldiers continued to perform British-imported surreptitiously.[55] After independence, some American thespians, including Dunlap, tried to cultivate a uniquely American cultural idiom in plays like Dunlap's *The Glory of Columbia; Her Yeomanry* (1807).[56] Journalists, from the 1790s onward, called for thespians to form "an American stage" with "productions suited to our habits, manners, and nature of our [republican] government."[57] And declaration of war in the summer of 1812 brought American-penned patriotic dramas, such as *Bunker Hill* and *The American Naval Pillar*, to the stage.[58] British theatrical fare continued to be popular, however, even during and after the war, which helps explain why *The Africans*, with its British patriotic sentiments, could be staged in pre-war New York and Philadelphia.[59]

The Old Drury on Chestnut Street, in fact, depended on British plays to turn a profit, and William Wood, the theater's co-manager, went to England recruit British actors for the company.[60] Philadelphian audiences' "prejudice against any native play," Wood lamented, made it very hard to attract audiences to American-penned plays. When Wood decided to produce a play by the American playwright James Barker, he even deliberately misled audiences into believing that the production came from London. After the piece "was played with great success for six or seven nights, when believing it safe, I announced the author, and from that moment on *it ceased to attract*," Wood claimed.[61] On the eve of war Americans still looked to Britons to set the aesthetic standards.[62] Although patriotic American-penned dramas proved popular on the eve of and during the War of 1812, these co-existed in the repertory with British-imported fare that was already commercially and aesthetically tried and tested.

Dunlap likely adapted Colman's play because of its relationship to Africa, abolitionism, and African American rights and liberties. A member of the New York Manumission Society, a member of the board of trustees for the New York

African Free School, and a delegate to the abolition conventions in Philadelphia in the 1790s, Dunlap was an active abolitionist.[63] He claimed that a childhood mentor inspired him to despise slavery and to free the family slaves after his father's death.[64] Dunlap also employed at least one free black man at his New York Park Theatre.[65] Convinced, however, that the sudden emancipation "of savages who have been torn from their native country and forcibly fixed in another as servants to ignorant and selfish masters" could lead only to "devastation, misery, and murder," Dunlap promoted gradual emancipation.[66] He doubted that free blacks could acculturate into the white American republic without being readied for freedom by education, and he feared that former slaves, if suddenly emancipated, would follow the example of Saint Domingue and "inflict misery and death upon thousands" of white Americans.[67] *The Africans* must have seemed a perfect vehicle for him to express his profound dislike of slavery, as well as his doubts about the ability of African American "savages" to integrate into society. Moreover, his fervent belief that the theater was a "school for morality" must have factored into his decision to stage a play that had so much didactic potential.[68]

Dunlap may also have been drawn to the play because Colman had assimilated explorers' and missionaries' observations about perceived cultural and physiognomic difference. Dunlap articulated some derogatory views of Africans but firmly eschewed the notion of innate racial difference in favor of environmental and cultural explanations of human variation. He commented in his diary on ideas and readings pertaining to race. For instance, after reading Long's *History of Jamaica* (1774), in which Long had likened West Indian slaves to monkeys, Dunlap expressed contempt for Long as a "pious apologist for Slaveholders."[69] Dunlap concluded that Long's assertions of "Negroes" as an apelike and separate species of human were "a strange mass of absurdity in theory, and error in supposed fact."[70] Dunlap instead believed that slavery had degraded the "savage African [slaves]," whose minds should therefore be "gradually prepare[d] for emancipation" until they were "fitted to receive liberty."[71] He commented, "In Philadelphia, where the emancipation of the blacks originated there are more free people of that colour than in any other place in the union. Most of them are degraded and vicious but there are many useful and respectable."[72] Dunlap, while prejudiced, was no believer in biological racial inferiority.

Fascinated as Dunlap was with the question of race, he would no doubt have been acutely aware of seething debates about so-called racial difference that erupted in Philadelphia just as the play was opening there, as would the educated Philadelphians in the audience. Two Philadelphians, Samuel Stanhope Smith and Charles Caldwell, spearheaded a passionate dispute over the environmental versus biological nature of race. At early stages of their medical careers both Smith and Caldwell had been associated with abolitionist Benjamin Rush, who adhered to environmental explanations of human difference. Caldwell trained as a physician under Benjamin Rush and was a member of the medical faculty at the University of Pennsylvania in 1810.[73] His nemesis, Smith, trained in medicine alongside Rush at the College of New Jersey, which later became Princeton.[74]

Smith initially published his *Essay on the Causes of the Variety of Complexion and Figure in the Human Species* in 1787 as a counter to Thomas Jefferson's insistence in *Notes on the State of Virginia* (1781–82) on "the real distinctions which nature has made" between white and black.[75] Jefferson equivocated on the question of mono versus polygenesis but "suspected" the inferiority of Africans and African Americans: "I advance it as a suspicion only, that the blacks, whether originally a distinct race, or made distinct by time and circumstance, are inferior to whites, both in body and mind."[76] Smith countered Jefferson by arguing firmly for monogenesis and environmental causes of physiognomic human difference such as skin complexion. Like Dunlap, Smith indulged in denigration of blackness and Africans. In the 1787 edition of his essay he claimed, for example, that "the eye of a savage is vacant and unexpressive—the whole composition of his countenance is fixed and stupid." But he was nonetheless a devout environmentalist who insisted that the "savage countenance" of Africans was "formed by the state of society."[77] Following Buffon, Smith also posited that it was "the power of climate" that caused variations in skin complexion, hair color and type, and other physiognomic differences.[78] Thus, for Smith, the "torrid zone of Africa," which "is the hottest country on the globe," produced the dark skin and other physiognomic features of those of African descent, which, when combined with what he perceived as a lack of cultured civilization, produced a "savage" and "degenerate" disposition.[79]

The 1810 publication of a revised version of Smith's *Essay* provoked a heated rebuttal by Caldwell, who held the viewpoint that "Negroes" were a separate and innately inferior species, the viewpoint that would soon eclipse environmental understandings of "race" in the United States.[80] Caldwell's position accorded well with that previously expressed by Jefferson, that "[w]hen freed, [the black] is to be removed beyond the reach of mixture" lest he become "a blot on this country."[81] Caldwell's arguments served to legitimize convictions that African American slaves could not be assimilated into the white republic once emancipated and therefore should be expelled to Africa. In his review of Smith's *Essay*, Caldwell argued for polygenesis and for the existence of separate white and black races.[82] He would eventually become a member of the avowedly racist antebellum School of Ethnology.[83] *The Africans* opened in Philadelphia just as its literati and medical establishment were caught up in this storm of controversy over "race," which decidedly impinged on the questions of slavery and of free blacks' "repatriation" to Africa versus assimilation into America.

The play proved popular in Philadelphia, although precisely whose adaptation —Colman's or Dunlap's—was gracing the stage is not altogether certain. Dunlap's version had debuted at his own theater in New York on January 2, 1810. Dunlap listed himself as author of *The Africans* in his *History of the American Theatre*.[84] Yet he made little or no written alterations to Colman's script.[85] As a consequence, when Philadelphian printer Mathew Carey (who published the manuscripts of most of the New Theatre's productions) released *The Africans; or, War, Love, and Duty* in 1811, he explicitly advertised the edition as having been written by George Colman and "performed at the Philadelphia Theatre," and his 1811 edition is identical to the script for Colman's 1808 production in London.[86] Most likely it was Colman's version that debuted and was performed thereafter in Philadelphia.

The Africans brought the fantasy of Africa as a "dark continent" in need of redemption to the stage at the very moment black and white Philadelphians were discussing colonization of Africa by "repatriating" free black Americans. The first practical African colonization endeavor was organized by a marine merchant and ship captain of mixed Native and African American descent, Paul Cuffe, who visited Philadelphia in 1810. Cuffe drew up plans to use his ship to transport free African Americans to Sierra Leone after communicating with the African Institution in London and visiting Sierra Leone in 1811. When he returned to America, he presented his scheme to black audiences in New York, Baltimore, and Philadelphia, where the idea met with initial enthusiasm from some free black elites, including the well-to-do Philadelphia sailmaker, James Forten, as well as from white abolitionists.[87] The War of 1812 postponed the voyage, but in 1816 he took thirty-eight black Americans to Sierra Leone. He died a year later without having completed his plans for further trips.

The Africans debuted just as Cuffe was proposing his dream of African colonization and amid the escalating tensions that erupted into the War of 1812, which reignited Britons' and Americans' furious competition over the meanings of slavery and liberty. Jonathan Russell, President James Madison's chargé d'affaires in Britain, protested British impressment of American sailors by comparing it unfavorably to African slavery, arguing that while "the negro was purchased already bereft of his liberty . . . the American citizen is torn without price, at once, from all the blessings of freedom."[88] Similarly emphasizing Americans' birthright of the "blessings of freedom," a New York member of the Democratic-Republican party clamored for "the restoration of enslaved freeborn Americans . . . by the dealers in the flesh and blood of white men." In Philadelphia, the Democratic-Republican newspaper, the *Aurora*, echoed these sentiments. Calling for war, an *Aurora* journalist decried the "white slavery" of British impressment.[89] All these commentators muddied the fraught line between black slavery and white freedom upon which the United States' racialized socioeconomic hierarchy rested. Even as Americans resuscitated their revolutionary rhetoric of British enslavement, the British replayed their own tactics from the previous war, recruiting fugitive black slaves by offering them freedom, a bounty, and the promise of land in a British colony.[90] The stakes over competing precepts and praxes of liberty were high: not only were white Americans' claims to the North American continent grounded on the notion of spreading republican liberty, but so also were Great Britain's ambitions to spread monarchical "liberty" to Asia and Africa.[91]

Chauvinistic theatrical performances celebrated American republican "liberty" in opposition to the tyrannical British imperial monarchy, yet they did so using the shared British-American neoclassical symbols created in the revolutionary years. For a patriotic celebration of July 4th in 1812 by the "Old Drury" Chestnut Street Theatre of Philadelphia, which performed regularly in Washington during its off-season repertory travels, the troupe executed "a grand patriotic and appropriate olio in the Temple of Liberty, consisting of recitations, patriotic and comic songs, national dances, &c." The performance was preceded by a comedy, which was introduced by an "occasional address . . . allusive to the present state of our country."[92] In September, with the war in progress, Chestnut Street thespians opened their new season in Philadelphia, as stage manager Charles Durang recorded, "with a series of entertainments commemorative of the late brilliant naval victories" followed by a new patriotic opera entitled *The Constitution; or, American Tars Triumphant*, an obvious ode to the expectation of American victory and British withdrawal from the continent. The evening's entertainment was completed with the performance of a new patriotic naval song, "The Pride of Columbia."[93] In February 1814 when the war's end was announced, the theater ensemble performed a triumphal "Temple of Concord" at the center stage of which was an "Altar of peace," accompanied by a musical "ode to the return of peace."[94] Thespians thus eagerly participated in the nation's battle with Great Britain over language and national identity by resuscitating the revolutionary-era Temple of Liberty to celebrate naval and military success (however ambiguous in reality) and national pride in republican liberty. In the celebratory aftermath of the war's end, "the frequent patriotic [theatrical] celebrations . . . proved a welcome aid to [the] exhausted treasury," Wood recorded. Yet thespians—many of them from Great Britain—created these nationalistic performances employing British Atlantic neoclassical symbology, and this proudly patriotic fare coexisted in the repertory with British-imported fare, which continued to be popular and profitable.

Amid the jingoism, white Americans' newly confident imperialist ethos of westward expansion also raised the troubling question of whether to allow the expansion of slavery into recently acquired territories. Debates over slavery's possible expansion in turn provoked dissension over slavery itself and over the rights and citizenship of free blacks. Not coincidentally, the ACS was founded in the war's strengthened conviction in white Americans' right to displace Native Americans and expand westward to fulfill their "pilgrim" mission to spread from "sea to shining sea," as Kathryn Bates would articulate it in "America the Beautiful" in 1895.[95] Some proponents of "repatriating" free blacks to Africa argued that African colonization and the founding of Liberia would provide a pathway to gradual emancipation in the United States, as well as the uplift of Africa.

William Thomas Hamilton made this latter argument in a sermon delivered and published for the benefit of the ACS. Hamilton characterized Africa as a "vast continent enveloped in the deepest shades of idolatry" and "darkness," which he defined as "ignorance, depravity, and wretchedness." He called for the evangelizing of Africa to bring "lightness" and Christianity to the "benighted heathen" on the borders of Liberia, likening African colonization to the Puritans' "city on a hill" and John Elliot's proselytizing of Native Americans. Drawing on climate-based theories of human difference, Hamilton claimed that bringing light to Africa was the unique task of African Americans because "evangelizing Africa . . . must be effected by coloured missionaries . . . of the same race with the people they would covert: to them the climate is congenial, to whites it is destructive." Hamilton also contended, as had Henry Clay and others, that African Americans would be able to enjoy in Liberia the freedom and equality they lacked in the United States. The cost of the voyage to Liberia would therefore be "to the coloured emigrant, the price of political liberty," as well as "moral and religious improvement."

Like Dunlap, Hamilton pointed to the Haitian Revolution as evidence of the necessity both of removing free blacks from the United States and of gradually ending slavery. (Indeed, Dunlap's views were very much in accord with those of the key proponents of the ACS.) If the freedman were to remain in the United States, Hamilton declared, he would vengefully wreak "the awful hour of retribution . . . And how amply he does so, let St. Domingo testify. Look to the far famed Hispaniola! You there witness the genuine fruits of slavery! . . . Oh! It chills the heart to think of such scenes being acted over again in our own borders, among our countrymen, our brethren in the south." He then claimed that removing freed slaves and providing a safe alternative to ex-slaves wreaking revengeful violence in the United States would also encourage Southerners to manumit their slaves, thus speeding the end of plantation slavery. "Every hour is precious," Hamilton warned, because "the increase of the black population, more especially in the south, vastly exceeds that of the whites . . . something must be done."[96]

At first elite Philadelphian blacks and some white abolitionists were enamored of the ACS, but many soon turned against the idea of African colonization when they perceived that Southern planter interests had taken over the organization. Initially, elite black Philadelphians like James Forten were inspired by the promise that repatriation would guarantee them the political rights and liberty the United States government had denied. That white Philadelphian philanthropist "friends" to the black community, including Quaker abolitionist Robert Vaux and Presbyterian Richard Rush (the son of Benjamin Rush), supported African colonization probably helped shed a positive light on the scheme.[97] Meanwhile, Philadelphian blacks soon recognized the limits of the slave-trade abolition bill, as slavery continued to expand westward after the Louisiana purchase. The escalation of white racial hostility and even violence, as when white mobs drove blacks out of Independence Day celebrations, must also have lent appeal to a settlement where blacks would have liberty, rights, and self-determination. But when Forten, Absalom Jones, Richard Allen, and other community leaders called a meeting in 1817 to discuss African colonization, the three thousand blacks who thronged Mother Bethal Church overwhelmingly opposed it. As Forten wrote to Paul Cuffe, they believed "slaveholders wanted to get rid of them so as to make their property more secure."[98] Philadelphian blacks went on to take the lead in organizing a series of mass meetings to condemn colonization. In 1817, James Forten and Robert Purvis spelled out the black community's objections in a pamphlet that argued that colonization would perpetuate slavery, as masters only colonize "those among their bondmen who feel that they should be free . . . and who thus may become dangerous to the quiet of their masters," leaving enslaved "only the tame and submissive."[99]

Although many white Philadelphian abolitionists persisted in supporting colonization, some heeded the sentiments of black Philadelphians and turned against it. One of Philadelphia's most prominent white philanthropists, the physician and slave-trade abolition advocate Jesse Torrey, considered colonization before ultimately rejecting it. In his *Portraiture of Domestic Slavery in the United*

States . . . and, A Project of a Colonial Asylum for Free Persons of Colour (1817), Torrey passionately opposed the slave trade and advocated an amelioration of extant
slavery's conditions. He also discussed at length what he regarded as the lauda-
tory goal of spreading, through African colonization, "the banners of knowledge
and rational religion [to] triumph over ignorance and superstition in Africa" in
order to bring about "redemption from barbarism of a benighted quarter of the
globe." Here, Torrey drew directly on Mungo Park's *Travels*, excerpts of which he
included in his appendix.[100] But he also investigated the views of black people on
colonization. He included minutes from the Meeting of Free People of Colour in
Richmond, who, like their Philadelphia counterparts, had almost unanimously
spurned African colonization.[101] Then, after observing that some black Philadelphians had originally been drawn to Cuffe's plan, Torrey noted that they had now
turned against colonization. He concluded by quoting "a servant at the house
in which I lodge" as "expressing great repugnance" at the prospect of going to
Africa.[102]

While clearly drawn to the ideal of a Columbian "empire of liberty" on Africa's
shores, Torrey was affected by black objections to colonization and proposed that
the true solution lay in extending liberty and rights to Africans in America. He
resuscitated the abolitionist motif of the Temple of Liberty to make his case. First,
he argued for the morally deleterious effect of slavery on both slave and master
and proposed that the only way freed slaves could be properly integrated into the
temple would be if they were "morally and physically" qualified for liberty before-
hand: "Intellectual and moral improvement is the safe and permanent basis on
which the arch of eventual freedom to the enslaved Africans may be gradually
erected."[103] He then went on to use the building of Columbia's capitol as a bitter
critique of slavery in a republic of liberty. The original Temple of Liberty had been
burnt down during the War of 1812, and was being rebuilt after the war. Referring
to the "conflagration . . . of the old capital," Torrey suggested,

> The Sovereign Father of all nations permitted the perpetuation of this apparently
> execrable transaction as a *fiery* though salutary signal of his displeasure at the con-
> duct of his Columbian children, in erecting and idolizing this splendid fabric as the
> temple of freedom and at the same time oppressing with the yoke of captivity . . .
> their African *brethren* . . . making merchandize of their *blood*, and dragging their
> bodies with *iron chains*, even under its towering walls? Yet, it is a fact, that slaves are
> employed in rebuilding this sanctuary of *liberty*.[104]

Since the British troops' destruction of the Capitol was divine retribution for chattel slavery, rebuilding it with slave labor was all the more damnable. What Torrey

did not note, however, was that some of the slaves who built the original Capitol later escaped to gain their freedom by joining the British in the War of 1812 and fighting in the Redcoat regiment that burned it.[105]

Torrey did, however, illustrate the exclusion of black Americans from Columbia's white Temple of Liberty through his commentary on Alexander Lawson's engraving *View of the Capital after the Conflagration of 1814*, which served as frontispiece for his *Portraiture of Domestic Slavery*. In the print, Columbia, personified as Liberty and Humanity, is shown looking down from above on her new Temple of Liberty, with the slave laborers who rebuilt it looking forlornly at it from outside. Torrey's acerbic commentary on the image sarcastically spelled out his point:

> Alas, poor Africa . . . this solitary magnificent temple, *dedicated to liberty*, opens its portal to all other nations but *thee*, and bids their sons drink *freely* of the cup of *freedom* and happiness: but when *thy* unoffending, enslaved sons, clank their blood-smeared *chains* under its towers, it sneers at their calamity, and mocks their lamentations with the echo of contempt! Elevating my eyes . . . I imagined I discerned the geniuses of *Liberty* and *Humanity*.

Torrey immediately followed his commentary on the illustration with a reproduction of the patriotic anthem, "Hail Columbia!," completing his association of caustic antislavery sentiment with the image of Columbia in her temple. But he gave the final words of indictment to a black American when he passed along an anecdote told to him by a legislator in the House of Representatives, Mr. Adgate. "He related to me," Torrey reported, "while at Washington, the following fact: . . . during the last session of Congress (1815–1816), as several members were standing in the street, near the new capital, a drove of manacled coloured people were passing by . . . One of them elevating his manacles as high as he could reach, commenced singing the favorite national song, *Hail Columbia, Happy Land*."[106] The shackled slave, like Torrey, sarcastically intoned the ideals of Columbia's temple to point angrily at his exclusion from its rights and liberties. But, as Torrey lamented, "Domestic Slavery, however a noxious weed to the tree of liberty, has taken deep root in this highly favored country."[107]

On both sides of the ocean, the vision of spreading liberty to Africa was deeply entwined in a reconstruction of civic mythology of liberty that grew out of renewed war. The War of 1812 pitted the United States' claims to being the true arbiter of liberty against those of Britain, but the republic lost moral ground to the monarchy on the question of slavery.[108] While the United States was using slaves to rebuild its Capitol, Great Britain employed the Royal Navy to prohibit the Atlantic slave trade. Britannia's abolitionist liberty was, however, interdependent on an emerging sense of ethnocultural superiority and a newly aggressive imperial thrust into Africa. Likewise, the United States, symbolized by white Columbia, worked to reconstruct and preserve national harmony by relocating blacks to the dark continent that they were uniquely qualified to enlighten. In the 1820s and 1830s, travelers and thespians would consolidate Atlantic conventions of race and slavery when Londoners flocked in droves to the United States to observe and report back on the outcome of America's "great experiment" in democracy, as Fanny Trollope would put it. These observations would, in turn, stimulate a new theatrical variety show derived from a critique and burlesque of American slavery and race.

PART TWO

EMANCIPATION
AND POLITICAL REFORM
Burlesque, Picaresque, and the Great Experiment
(1820s–1830s)

"Although much has already been written on the great experiment . . . on the other side of the Atlantic, there appears to be still room for many interesting details on the influence which the political system of the country has produced on the principles, tastes, and manners, of its domestic life."[1] Thus wrote Fanny Trollope in her *Domestic Manners of the Americans*, a travelogue on her years in America, including Philadelphia, during the 1820s. Published in 1832, *Domestic Manners* was cited by both British reformers and conservatives in their raging battles over suffrage and slavery in the years leading up to Great Britain's 1832 Parliamentary Reform Bill and the 1833 Emancipation Bill. Trollope critiqued America's "great experiment" in democracy as having had a deleterious effect on social deference and cultural manners visible in everything from the lack of educated dinner conversation to the absence of books, pianos, and games in the drawing room. While conservatives cited these failures as stemming from American democracy, Trollope aimed her most acidic critique at the failure of America's principles of equality when it came to Native Americans, women, and—most especially—slaves: "The sight of slavery in every direction is not very agreeable, and it is not the less painfully felt from hearing upon every breeze the mocking words, 'all men are born free and equal.' "[2] Liberals seized on these observations to argue for reform: expanded suffrage at home and emancipation of the slaves in the British West Indies.

Britons' double use of Trollope's *Domestic Manners* underscores how American slavery and democracy continued to be crucial benchmarks in British debates about emancipation and democratic reform, and how slavery remained at the crux of competition between British and American political and national identities. For Trollope was not alone in her fascination with America's great experiment. After the War of 1812 had established the finality of the United States' separation from the British empire, curiosity about John Bull's cousins propelled a stream of London writers, performers, cartoonists, abolitionists, and reformers across the Atlantic. Like Trollope, many of them condemned slavery's place in the republic, and their critique of the United States inflected British debates about emancipation and parliamentary reform.

Their observations also provided fodder for two new transatlantic performance genres that developed out of a free-flowing interplay of print, cartoons, and the-ater, and their exchange between London and Philadelphia: proto-vaudeville vari-ety acts featuring blackface American characters and a form of urban picaresque in cartoons, prose, and theater. A key to the transatlantic development of these genres was the increased circulation of print and theater, owing not only to post-war British travels to America but also to an explosion in print production and distribution in the United States spurred by new developments in transportation. Not only did Philadelphia see an increase in newspapers, pamphlets, and car-toons, but also a more mature theater culture that, by the 1820s, included several new theaters, such as the Arch Street and Olympic theaters, which staged these new picaresque and burlesque works. Although sentimental antislavery of the ilk of George Colman Jr.'s *Inkle and Yarico* persisted, these new genres were the most significant developments in the British Atlantic lexicon of race and slavery of the 1820s and 1830s, producing enduring and instantly recognizable representations of slavery and freedom on both sides of the ocean, most notably the blackface urban dandy, forerunner of Zip Coon and Dandy Jim, and the Yankee slave owner Jonathan Doubikin.

The variety burlesque and urban picaresque genres had far-reaching signifi-cance for British Atlantic discourses of race and slavery. First, while both genres originated in London, they hinged on political commentary on black freedom and slavery in America and its "great experiment" in democracy. The urban pi-caresque genre began in London prose, cartoons, and a series of stage plays that offered voyeuristic glimpses of high-life and lowlife London and the white dan-dies of the new professional middle class. The genre was later racialized by a Philadelphia cartoonist in a series of *Life in Philadelphia* prints that disparaged black freedom through the figure of the black urban dandy. London cartoon-ists and thespians then borrowed this racial cartooning to negotiate anxiety over black freedom in the West Indies following the 1833 Emancipation Act; they used the urban picaresque genre and the blackface dandy primarily to disparage free blacks and slave emancipation. The proto-vaudeville variety act, concomitantly created almost single-handedly by Charles Mathews, a London comic actor, mim-icked enslaved black Americans and a Yankee slave-owner, Jonathan, in order to intervene in antislavery debates by critiquing slavery's role in America's "great experiment."

The urban picaresque's symbols and characterizations of black freedom and the variety show racial burlesques' motifs and figures of black slavery were fully transatlantic in origin and reach. Indeed, Atlantic urban picaresque and variety show burlesque developed precisely during the years in which many historians have suggested that distinctively national popular cultures and identity cohered. David Waldstreicher proposes that during this period a sense of American national identity was forged out of the public fêtes and rituals learned in the revolutionary years. British historians Linda Colley and Eric Hobsbawm, meanwhile, claim that warfare with France was pivotal to the forging of British national identity and culture in the early nineteenth century.[3] Indeed, the figures popularized by urban picaresque and variety show burlesque, like Jonathan and the blackface urban dandy, emerged as spokesmen for British and American contestation over national political and cultural identities, which hinged on confrontations over slavery: British critiques of slavery's place in the American republic and American anxiety over Great Britain's continued commercial "enslavement" of the United States, even as its citizens continued their predilection for British cultural products.[4] Although put to different ideological uses in London and Philadelphia, these characters also transcended national culture, becoming recognizable symbols of slavery and freedom on both sides of the ocean. Interestingly, the same London and Philadelphia theaters and communities where the variety show burlesque and picaresque genres gestated also fostered antislavery oratory and social reform efforts performed for plebeian audiences. The urban picaresque and proto-vaudeville variety genres were also used to critique slavery, even as their characters disparaged the idea of black freedom.

These genres also carried new ideas about race back and forth across the ocean and, in so doing, produced a British Atlantic understanding of race that merged American political discourse with British cartooning and theatrical traditions. Well into the nineteenth century, blacks in London intermarried, intermingled, and coexisted with whites, in contrast to the hostile and increasingly violent relations between black and whites in Philadelphia. Why, then, did convictions about African moral and intellectual inferiority and the separate species origins of the "white" and "black" races take equal hold in London (and Great Britain more generally) and in America? One answer is the imperial ethos of Great Britain, which placed a growing emphasis on the nation's ethnocultural superiority, due in part to reports from African mission societies and explorers. Scholars have also suggested that British ideas about race took a more pernicious turn thanks to American cultural influence.[5] This explanation of transatlantic "influence" has validity, but it accounts for only one-way cultural traffic. The variety show and urban picaresque genres originated in London's "minor" theaters and satirical cartooning traditions of the 1820s, but they matured through constant transatlantic exchange and reformulation to comment on class and racial issues peculiar to London, Philadelphia, and the British West Indies. In the process, artists and performers on both sides of the ocean developed a shared lexicon of images and performative conventions about race. These transatlantic genres of variety shows and urban picaresque set the stage for the multivalent signification of later blackface minstrelsy, as well as a more reformist discourse of race and class of the 1830s, 1840s, and beyond.

CHAPTER FOUR

Black Freedom and Blackface Picaresque
Life in London, Life in Philadelphia

In the 1820s, transatlantic exchange gave rise to a new picaresque "urban specta-tor" theatrical genre. Adapted from comic prose sketches and cartoons, William Thomas Moncrieff's play *Life in London; or, Tom and Jerry* debuted to instant acclaim at London's Adelphi Theatre in 1821 and Philadelphia's Chestnut Street Theatre in 1823. Along with Moncrieff's subsequent *Life in Paris*, and *The Death of Life in London* (as well as "sequels" by other playwrights), the play provided a satirical look at newly recognizable class divisions and emergent ideas of mascu-linity through the eyes of its roguish heroes, the eponymous Tom and Jerry, two aspiring dandies of the new English urban middle class. Included in the purview of Tom and Jerry's picaresque urban spectatorship was a parody of black and white working-class Londoners that took a keen look at the integration of blacks into both "low" and "high" life.

But the significance of the urban picaresque genre for British Atlantic dis-course on race and slavery went beyond the transatlantic popularity of *Life in London*. While the prose, cartoon, and theatrical *Life in London* satires had only limited intersection with debates about black slavery and freedom and were at heart a class-based commentary, *Life in London* became the template for a trans-atlantic racialized urban spectator genre. Philadelphia cartoonist Edward Clay played a crucial role in its development. Clay visited London in the 1820s at the height of the *Life in London* craze and then emulated the new genre in his 1828 cartoon series *Life in Philadelphia*. Clay, however, transposed the class-based divi-sions of London to race-based stratification in Philadelphia. He burlesqued free blacks' aspirations to a middle-class lifestyle and inclusion in the body politic: the urban white dandy of London was now an overdressed black American. By the 1830s, the transatlantic flow was reversed when London cartoonist George Tregear reworked Clay's racist cartoons under the title *Black Jokes* and used his new ver-sions of *Life in Philadelphia* to disparage not only America's "great experiment" but also black freedom in the British West Indies. The print-theater circulation came full circle in the 1830s when the blackface dandy stepped out of Clay's and

Tregear's prints and onto the transatlantic stage, appearing in full-length plays and comic variety acts. The urban picaresque genre, while originating in London class-based satire, intervened directly in transatlantic debates about slavery and freedom and birthed an enduring proto-minstrel figure.

High Life and Low Life London

Pierce Egan created the germinal source for the urban picaresque genre in his comic prose series *Life in London; or, The Day and Night Scenes of Jerry Hawthorn, Esq. and His Elegant Friend Corinthian Tom, and Accompanied by Bob Logic* (1821).[1] Egan may have been inspired by Rudolph Ackerman's *Microcosm of London, or London in Miniature* (1808–11), which had established a market for plates of London's parks, clubs, churches, and houses of entertainment.[2] Egan's *Life in London* prose sketches were picaresque in two senses. First, they were written in the picaresque literary form, that is, a prose fiction with a simple plot divided into episodic vignettes. Second, the plots were driven by the adventures of three urban rakes, Corinthian Tom, Jerry Hawthorne, and Bob Logic, whose exploits took them wandering among the high life and lowlife of the city, the latter of which prominently featured black Londoners. Tom, Jerry, and Bob were licentious voyeurs who offered a voyeuristic experience to readers and viewers. Egan's prose sketches promptly spawned competing illustrations, the most influential of which were George Cruikshank's narrative illustrations of "high" and "low" life London.[3] His lowlife illustrations caricatured the London working class, both black and white, as raucous and intemperate, while the high-life plates poked fun at elite dandyism and the social pretensions of the new middle class. Cruikshank's plates, in turn, were dramatized by several playwrights, with the most popular iteration that by William Thomas Moncrieff.

Egan's picaresque prototype established the episodic narrative, key lowlife and high-life characters, and all the specific London settings that Cruikshank and Moncrieff adopted in their versions. Egan's *Life in London* was first published between 1820 and 1821 in twenty monthly installments at a shilling each, and then in book form in 1821 with Cruikshank's illustrations. Corinthian Tom was a brothel-frequenting rake, and Jerry Hawthorne a visiting country cousin determined to see the sights of London. Together with Tom's friend Bob Logic, the three roved the streets of the metropolis in search of risqué adventure. The meaning of "Corinthian" is obscure today, but it was obvious to Egan's contemporaries as a synonym both of an immoral city and a brothel, colloquially known as a "Corinth." The moniker also referred to Shakespeare's "fast man" in *2 Henry IV* "I am no proud Jack, like Falstaff; but a Corinthian, a lad of mettle, a good boy."[4] The basic storyline was simple. Jerry, "the only son of an opulent esquire in the west of England," was sent by his father to London to be shown around by his cousin Tom, an Oxford-trained lawyer, because "a short residence in the metropolis [is] . . . necessary to make a finished gentleman of Jerry." Jerry "was but a short time in London ere he became initiated in all the mysteries of high and low life" by Tom and his fellow "Oxonian," Bob Logic. They cajoled Jerry into "losing his money at the gaming table, spending an evening in dissipation between wine and women . . . in short, he was a capital of the Corinthian order."[5]

In 1821, an edition of *Life in London* was published with George Cruikshank's illustrations, who easily adapted Egan's prose to cartoons that he populated with recognizable black and white Londoners who were recurring characters in the narrative. The wayward heroes of the narrative may even have been modeled on the collaborators themselves, with George Cruikshank represented by Corinthian Tom, his brother Robert Cruikshank a fictive Jerry Hawthorne, and Bob Logic synonymous with Pierce Egan.[6] The first stop for Tom and Jerry is a clothier, where Jerry is relieved of his country clothes and fitted out to "perform" as a true London "dandy" while Tom poses and primps at his side. This episode established Tom, Jerry, and Bob as self-fashioning dandies. Egan slyly inserted an "outside observation" on his heroes as "deck'd in fictions ruff and plume" and as self-conscious social posers who were "masquerading" by assuming an attitude or "mask." This commentary came in a song rendered by two "sharpers" (or petty thieves) who watch Tom and Jerry leave the tailor's shop: "All the world are masquerading / Deck'd in fictions ruff and plume / Sporting, toiling, praying, trading / All in turn the mask assume." As the sharpers' song made clear, the posing and escapades of Tom, Jerry, and Bob were highly performative. The threesome then venture to a debauched masquerade ball at the Royal Opera House; the playhouses; the Olympic Theatre café; a raucous, music-filled pub in the back slums; and an exhibit at the Royal Academy where the aspiring middling sorts in their finery are every bit as much on display as the art.

Although Egan and Cruikshank both included black Londoners as recurring characters in the storyline, neither was commenting primarily on race but rather on a society defined by hierarchical socioeconomic strata and new sensibilities about class. New workingmen's organizations, such as cooperatives and trade unions, developed in response to industrialization and urban poverty, had helped foster a new consciousness among plebeians of what well-to-do philanthropist and factory reformer Robert Owen had recently dubbed "the working classes."[7] Concomitantly, the middling sorts had developed a new awareness of class cohesion and their place between the old landed classes represented in Parliament and the propertyless majority.[8] This new middle class was a product of the urban, industrial centers and the realms of commerce, manufacturing, and the professions, but it was politically unrepresented due to property requirements for suffrage. Egan's and Cruikshank's urban dandies, as educated but propertyless professionals, were of this new "middle class."

The narrative and visuals of Tom and Jerry's trip to the clothiers also set a very influential blueprint for the Anglo-American depiction of young up-and-coming professional men as metropolitan dandies. By the early-to-mid-nineteenth century, the "dandy," described by Thomas Carlyle as "a Clothes-wearing man, a Man whose trade, office, and existence consists in the wearing of clothes," was characterized by his exhibitionist devotion to effete style and fashion. Carlyle also pointed to the strong association in the 1820s and 1830s between dandyism and "trade and office," that is, the new professional middle class of the industrialized, urban centers.[9]

In contrast to the late-nineteenth-century homoerotic, aesthete dandy infamously emblematized by Oscar Wilde, the white urban dandy of the 1820s, while homosocial, resonated with emergent heteronormative ideas about virile manliness. This new urban ideal of masculinity was linked not only to fashionable elegance but also to enthusiasm for sports and games. Egan was a well-known sportswriter who covered boxing, cockfighting, wrestling, and other manly sports for the *Weekly Dispatch* before beginning his own Sunday newspaper, *Pierce Egan's Life in London; or, The Sporting News* in 1824, in which he republished his *Life in London* series.[10] Egan explicitly described Corinthian Tom not only as "manly and elegant" and "fashionable in his apparel" but also an expert boxer.[11] In the later nineteenth century, sports and games would, on both sides of the ocean, become intertwined with masculine ideals of chivalry and moral rectitude (with femininity then complementarily defined by domesticity and subservience).[12] In the 1820s this new sporting, dandified sense of middle-class masculinity was closely linked not only to imbibing and poking fun at the urban entertainments of art, theater, and coffee shops but also to mingling with the poor in lowlife pleasure resorts like gambling dens and pawnshops. William Makepeace Thackeray said of George Cruikshank, "that he pities and loves the poor, and jokes at the follies of the great, and that he addresses all in a perfectly sincere and manly way."[13] Urban dandies Bob, Jerry, and Tom exemplified this developing construct of manliness: fashionable, sporting, men-about-town who caroused in both lowlife and highlife venues.

Cruikshank kept Bob, Jerry, and Tom in starring roles but gave a prominent place to real-life African-Britons such as Billy Waters and African Sal, whom

Cruikshank had depicted in previous cartoons to denounce immediate slave emancipation and plebeian radicalism. Cruikshank made Billy Waters (a one-legged fiddler who made his living performing outside of the Adelphi Theatre where Moncrieff's *Life in London* would open) and African Sal recurring characters. He had already featured Billy Waters, African Sal, and black radical Robert Wedderburn along with white abolitionists like Wilberforce in his antiradical *The New Union Club* (1819), which depicted a world turned upside down by plebeian Jacobinists joining forces with white abolitionists and black liberationists (fig. 9). In it, Wedderburn represented the fusion of plebeian Jacobinism and slave emancipation.

The son of a West Indian white slave master and black slave mother, Wedderburn was an ultraradical Methodist preacher who lived and preached in the working-class parish of St. Giles and authored a fiery pamphlet series, *The Axe Laid to the Root* (1817), protesting West Indian slavery.[14] A follower of Thomas Spence, Wedderburn believed in a revolutionary movement for democracy. Spence had published Paine's *Rights of Man* in 1792 and spent long periods in prison for the publication of radical and seditious pamphlets, newspapers, and broadsides. After Spence died in 1814, his followers continued to agitate for radical democratic revolution, and Wedderburn and other Spenceans believed the plight and cause of black colonial slaves and white plebeian laborers were inseparable. He protested for the rights of laborers in the metropole, as well as for African slaves in the colonies. As he put it, "I am a West-Indian, a lover of liberty, and would dishonour human nature if I did not shew myself a friend to the liberty of others."[15]

In *The New Union Club*, Cruikshank made clear the danger he believed radicals and emancipationists like Wedderburn posed to the social order. He showed Wedderburn delivering an incendiary oratory to an unruly mob of abolitionists and the plebeian underclass, which included African Sal and fiddler Billy Waters. By depicting an anarchic "world turned upside down" by black liberation, Cruikshank denounced the efforts of radicals like Wedderburn to interlink the causes of emancipation for slaves and plebeian suffrage at home. Cruikshank's print recapitulated the *Union Club* (1801), in which James Gillray had highlighted the contentious nature of the 1800 union of Ireland and England by depicting English and Irishmen in drunken and debauched celebration of the union. In the *New Union Club*, Cruikshank satirized white abolitionists Zachary Macaulay and William Wilberforce, who can be seen seated on a commode. Wilberforce and Macaulay were firmly opposed to Jacobin politics, but Cruikshank depicted them suffering humiliation from the anarchic chaos they had helped wreak through aiding emancipation. Wedderburn was, however, the leader whose impassioned

The NEW UNION-CLUB.

Being a Representation of what took place at a celebrated Dinner given by a celebrated ——— Society.——— Vide Mr. M——'s Pamphlet entitled "More Thoughts &c &c."

Figure 9. George Cruikshank, *The New Union Club* (1819). Cruikshank's print decried the dangers posed to social order by abolitionists—even conservatives like Wilberforce, shown here seated on a commode—and emancipationists, like the black radical, Robert Wedderburn, who stands on the table delivering an incendiary oratory to an unruly mob of abolitionists and black and white plebeians. Cruikshank suggests not only that black liberation will result in anarchy among the metropole's underclass but also that blacks are unfitted for freedom and will waste it in frivolity and licentiousness. Lewis Walpole Library, Yale University

table-top oratory incites the lawless anarchy Cruikshank believed would erupt after emancipation and universal suffrage: white plebeian and black Londoners are drinking, flirting, fighting, and carousing.

Cruikshank's rejection of democratic liberty for slaves and workers is focused on the potentially dangerous racial and political amity among the working classes on the left side of the print: the yellow-petticoated African Sal is among the most debauched participants of the "mob," with bottle in hand and a drunken white man in her lap. Cruikshank was probably reacting to the noticeable realities of interracial marriage, sociability, and politics among London's poor. Wedderburn, Sal, and Waters were part of a small black population, numbering approximately five thousand and predominantly male, who labored alongside poor white Londoners as sailors, crossing-sweepers, vendors, and prostitutes.[16] Baptismal and marriage records show that black Londoners were relatively well integrated with whites in working-class neighborhoods and parishes like St. Giles, Marylebone, and St. George's in the east, and St. Johns at Hackney, and there was a high rate of interracial marriage. As several scholars have noted, class interests were stronger than color lines.[17]

Although Cruikshank was conservative politically, his *Life in London* illustrations and Egan's prose also reflected concern with the problem of urban poverty. Cruikshank was actively concerned with humanitarian issues such as temperance, public health, and urban sanitation.[18] That he paid attention to the poor's plight in his images is perhaps all the more striking as his fears about plebeian and interracial radicalism would have been amplified by the Cato Street conspiracy of 1820. The plot, an attempt to overthrow the government and foment a radical democratic revolution in which Wedderburn was involved, was a response to the Peterloo Massacre of 1819, in which eleven people died after police broke up a protest for improved factory conditions and universal suffrage. Cruikshank reacted by vociferously repeating his opposition to immediate emancipation, universal suffrage, and republicanism in several prints, including his 1820 *The Radical Ladder*, in which he denounced the Cato Street conspirators and the threat of Jacobin "mob government." In *Life in London*, Cruikshank again embraced a stratified status quo, while also depicting the grinding toll of urban poverty on the black and white downtrodden of the Corinthian city.

Political conservatism and acceptance of a hierarchical class-based society was embedded in Egan's prose and was intrinsic to the allegoric frontispiece for *Life in London*, attributed jointly to George Cruikshank and his brother, Robert (fig. 10). Titled the *Corinthian Capital*, the image shows the enthroned George IV (to whom Egan had dedicated his *Life in London* prose series) holding court with the "Roses, Pinks and Tulips, the Flowers of Society." Bolstering the royal podium are the pilasters of society, the "Ups" of London: the "Noble," a "Respectable" from the merchant middle class with clerical quill behind his ear, and the fine society of an elegantly attired lady and her driver. At the center is the wheel of fortune within which Tom, Jerry, and Logic toast their Corinthian city and lifestyle with Robert Burn's verse, cited at the column's base, "How are we met, three cheery Boys . . . And many a night we've merry been, and many more we hope to be." To the left an inmate peers out of prison bars, labeled "Ins," and to the right a newly released ex-convict represents "Outs." The wheel is supported by the plebeian "Downs," an ale-drinking "mechanical" and a "tag rag and bob tail," and at its fundament a dark, dank cellar with a drinking sweep and his wife. Rural peasantry is represented by the "strings of beans" and "bunches of turnips" to

Figure 10. Robert and George Cruikshank, frontispiece to *Life in London* (1821). The image embeds political conservatism and acceptance of a monarchical and hierarchical class-based society. George IV, enthroned at the top, holds court over a columnar society in which the nobles and respectable merchant classes support the monarchy, the new urban professionals (like Tom and Jerry) support mid-level society, and mechanics and farmers form the base. Courtesy of The Library Company of Philadelphia

either side of "The Base." Cruikshank's image of a society vertically stratified by inequality in rank, opportunity, and fortune was clearly shared by Egan, as it was inherent in his categories of high and low life.

Black characters, although not featured in the frontispiece, appeared in many of Cruikshank's plates (and, less frequently, in Egan's text), but neither Cruikshank nor Egan singled out black Londoners for a specifically racialized burlesque. Rather, black Londoners were integrated as members of a given social stratum.

In one episode, captioned "Masquerading it in Among the Codgers in the Back Slums," Tom and Jerry mingle in the poor parish of St. Giles. Egan's prose—and Cruikshank's accompanying illustration—describes the "back slums" as teeming with entertainment, unrestrained exuberance, and camaraderie, and as a place in which the black community members were fully and equally participant. Neither black nor white lower sorts are depicted as in any way threatening. In fact, if Moncrieff and others were correct in believing that Egan and the Cruikshank brothers were the alter egos of Tom, Jerry, and Bob and visited the high-life and lowlife settings in person, then it is also apparent that Cruikshank and Egan themselves were neither uncomfortable nor callous toward London's white and black poor.

These same observations can be made of any number of Egan's vignettes and Cruikshank's illustrations, many of which show Tom, Jerry, and Logic "masquerading it" in lowlife sites of pleasure that feature black Londoners comfortably intermingling with white Londoners of the same class stratum. When Tom and Jerry stop off at a coffee shop near the Olympic Theatre, for example, their voyeuristic perspective on the jollity and lasciviousness of the scene is one of bemused enjoyment rather than disdain (fig. 11). As Egan wrote of the episode, "Tom and Jerry have just dropped in, by way of a finish to the evening . . . quite prime for a lark." But in contrast to the pub in the back slums, Egan and Cruikshank used the Olympic café episode to issue a pointed social commentary. As Egan explained of the plate, "This group . . . displays a complete picture of what is termed 'LOW LIFE' in the Metropolis: drunkenness, beggary, lewdness, and carelessness being its prominent features." The group's behavior is not, however, attributed to any intrinsic immorality but rather to desperate economic straits born of endemic urban poverty.

Egan made this clear in his comments on the down-on-her-luck black prostitute, "Mahogany Bet, so termed for her never-fading color," seen seated in front of the fire, toasting crumpets and keeping company with a white fellow prostitute. "Mahogany Bet," Egan sympathetically remarked, "has braved the wind and weather, night after night, under some gateway, for succeeding winters, but quite done up as to matters of trade . . . is now glad to singe a muffin . . . to prevent total starvation."[19] Unlike the celebratory glee of the flamboyant back slums pub crowd, the poor customers at the Olympic Café, among them Bet and her companion, appear viscerally downtrodden by their lot, their faces drawn, features distorted, and bodies hunched over. Yet despite the evidence of harsher lifestyle and the more marked contrast, therefore, between Tom and Jerry's affluence, social standing, and dandified appearances and that of the café's regulars, London's underbelly is portrayed as an exhilarating rather than menacing zone of pleasure.

I.R.& G. Cruikshank.

MIDNIGHT.   TOM & JERRY, AT A COFFEE SHOP NEAR THE OLYMPIC.

Figure 11. George Cruikshank, *Midnight. Tom and Jerry at a Coffee Shop Near the Olympic* from *Life in London* (1821). The print shows the protagonists enjoying their voyeuristic foray into London's underworld rather than recoiling from it, offering visual evidence that London's black and white poor socialized with each other on an even footing. The setting also demonstrates the importance of the theater for London's new urban professionals. Courtesy of The Library Company of Philadelphia

Given that London's predominantly poor black population intermarried with whites and was integrated into London's working-class neighborhoods and recreational life, the appearance of black Londoners in Egan's and Cruikshank's lowlife scenes was perhaps less surprising than that they also appeared, albeit less frequently, in depictions of high life. One such vignette had the threesome attending an art show at the Royal Academy, and in Cruikshank's illustration a top-hatted and coattailed black man mingles easily with the well-dressed high society crowd. Egan offers no specific commentary on the well-heeled black man's presence at such a gathering, and his casual inclusion suggests the existence of at least a few black Londoners who were not mired in poverty. Moreover, the print confirms again that for Egan and Cruikshank, regardless of any sense of ethnocultural superiority they might have imbibed from early nineteenth-century British culture and its growing sense of empire, the crucial division in the metropolis was class.

Stage adaptations of Egan and Cruikshank's *Life in London* were phenomenally successful at the "minor" unlicensed theaters that lacked a royal patent to perform narrative dramas, including the Adelphi (where *Life in London* debuted) and the Olympic and Surrey, where competing versions were staged. The popularity of Tom, Bob, and Jerry's forays into low life London was surely at least partially because the audience personally identified with lowlife Londoners and propertyless men of the middling sorts and enjoyed this celebration of young professional men of this class as cultured dandies. In contrast to the Drury Lane, Covent Garden, and Haymarket Theatres Royal, at the minor theaters audiences were largely (although not exclusively) male and female plebeian and "white-collar" lower and middling sorts. In fact, the royally patented theaters discouraged attendance by the working classes and tried to foster more "respectable" bourgeois and elite audiences. When Drury Lane and Covent Garden were rebuilt in 1796, they raised prices and converted the "public" spaces of gallery and pit into private boxes. The reduction of lower-priced seating pushed the lower sorts to the minor theaters, which by the 1820s had, as a consequence, proliferated. The Surrey's audience, for example, was composed of working men and women such as costermongers, sweeps, and trade journeymen, while that of the Adelphi was more "respectable" yet still humble, typified by the lowly clerk.[20]

No less than six successful dramatic adaptations of *Life in London* (including one by Egan himself) took the stage at the Adelphi, the Olympic, and the Surrey (or Royal Opera House), but it was Moncrieff's adaptation at the Adelphi that was the most successful, enjoying a run of ninety-three nights after its debut on November 26, 1821.[21] Moncrieff's show was so wildly fashionable that young men began to pose as Corinthian Tom and imitated his "flash," from his dandy clothes to the slang of his speech.[22] At least sixty-five imitative and plagiarized books and serials contributed to the Tom and Jerry craze between 1820 and 1824. The production gained even more attention when evangelicals protested the play's vulgarity and lewdness by distributing their tracts outside the theater door. They appealed to the theatrical censor, the Lord Chamberlain, to close down the production. After seeing the piece, he instead returned the following night with his wife.[23] The following two seasons the play was no less a phenomenon and even two years later seats for the play were booked two weeks in advance.[24]

While Egan and Cruikshank had not singled out high-life or lowlife black Londoners for explicitly racialized burlesque, the theatrical *Life in London* did, helping to establish performative conventions of later blackface minstrelsy. Moncrieff adapted Egan and Cruikshank's picaresque genre by, as he explained, putting "the matchless series of plates . . . into dramatic motion, running a connecting story through the whole."[25] Moncrieff took into account the popular taste for

burletta by including parlor songs, dance tunes, and airs from *Don Giovanni* and
the John Gay's *Beggars Opera*.²⁶ The playbill for the premiere suggested *Life in
London's* variety when it bragged that the piece was "a "Classic, Comic, Operatic,
Didactic, Aristophanic, Localic, Analytic, Panoramic, Camera-Obscura-ic, Extravaganza Burletta of Fun, Frolic, Fashion, and Flash in three acts."²⁷ Moreover,
it incorporated elements of racial mimicry of real-life black Londoners Dusty
Bob, Flashy Nance, African Sal, and the fiddler Billy Waters, whose roles the
playwright greatly expanded. In so doing, Moncrieff established blackface conventions that would become significant features of minstrel performance in the
1830s and 1840, most notably, that of having males in drag perform female roles.
Although the early-nineteenth-century pantomime clown Joseph Grimaldi had
popularized female impersonations—a tradition that dated back to Restoration-
era breeches roles—Moncrieff made cross-dressing explicitly racial. He singled
out black female characters for cross-dressing, which served to desexualize them,
in contradistinction to Cruikshank's prints, in which black and white female
characters were equally degraded by poverty.

Although Moncrieff's "fun, frolic, fashion, and flash" resonated with the
"lower sorts" in the Adelphi's audience and also drew middle and upper-class
spectators, the piece garnered mixed responses tinged by class differences. Over-
night, the play made the Adelphi London's chicest theater and, as Moncrieff
delightedly noted, peers competed with plebeians and dukes with doormen for
tickets to the show.²⁸ As a young man, William Makepeace Thackeray, who would
become famous for his novels satirizing British society, thought *Life in London's*
heroes "to be types of the most elegant, fashionable young fellows the town afforded."²⁹ But while some of the more prestigious visitors to the Adelphi clearly
could not get enough of the uproarious gin houses and lusty theater café scenes,
not all were as entertained as Thackeray and the Lord Chamberlain and his wife.
Harriet Arbuthnot, granddaughter of the eighth earl of Westmoreland and wife
of the Tory joint secretary to the Treasury, loathed the show and her evening at
the Adelphi Theatre, which, she complained was "crowded to an overflow, [and]
the people were hollowing and talking to each other from the pit to the gallery,
and fighting and throwing oranges at each other." She was no less disgusted by
the play's forays into lowlife London than by the rowdy behavior of the lowlife
Londoners in the pits and galleries. "The play itself," she noted with disdain,
"was a representation of all the low scenes in London, such as the Watch House,
sponging and gaming houses and the rendezvous of beggars. In short, it was
a sort of very low Beggars' Opera, but it is impossible to describe the sort of
enthousiasm with which it was received by the people, who seemed to enjoy a

representation of scenes in which, from their appearance, one might infer they frequently shared."[30]

Despite the misgivings of some refined visitors to the suddenly fashionable Adelphi and the heated criticism of the religiously upright, the play and its sequels had lasting theatrical influence even after the Tom and Jerry craze subsided. Well into the 1830s and 1840s playwrights used Egan and Cruikshank's *Life in London* as inspiration for new theatrical permutations, such as *Tom, Jerry, and Logick's Hop at Brighton* in 1834 and *Life in Dublin; or, Tom, Jerry, and Logic on Their Travels*, produced in 1842 at the Royal Opera House.[31] Moreover, the high-life scenarios resonated with a growing consciousness of metropolitan fashion and inspired related plays at the legitimate patented West End theaters, such as *High Life in London*, presented at Covent Garden Theatre Royal in 1826.[32]

The Flash Man in Philadelphia

The dandy fashions, urban spectatorship, and class-based parody of *Life in London* were key contributors to the transatlantic circulation of print and theater that produced a genre of distinctively British Atlantic burlesque of black freedom. Moncrieff's *Life in London*, with its insights into London race and class dynamics, almost immediately migrated to Philadelphia, where it premiered at the New Theatre on Chestnut Street in 1823 and was an immediate success. After four April performances at the end of the theater's season netted a healthy nightly average of $420, *Life in London* migrated to the Olympic Theatre, which catered to audiences dominated by the working classes. It was a smash hit there, remaining on the stage for the entire month of May.[33] Its sequel, *Tom and Jerry; or, The Death of Life in London* debuted in London in 1824 and was performed in Philadelphia theaters later that year. *Life in London* also migrated to other northern cities, including New York, where the all-black ensemble at the African Grove Theatre produced their own version that included a vignette titled "Life at the Slave Market."[34]

Much as in Britain, one reason for *Life in London*'s popularity was that newly mobile young urbanites could identify with its rakish heroes. Dramatic innovations in transportation—roads, canals, and steamships—had facilitated an influx of young men into the major seaboard cities of Philadelphia, New York, Boston, and Baltimore, whose populations had also increased due to immigration. In the context of single youth-oriented city life, the "flash man," in the parlance of the time, had become a recognizable figure. Unlike the distinctly middle-class professional urban dandy of London, the flash man of America's northern cities had the connotation of being a bit of a con man: a dandy with no obvious means of making a living who was "fast," or deceptive. But he had in common with his London counterpart the habits of dressing in "flash" clothing and of engaging in sporting and urban leisure entertainments of both the respectable and under-world varieties. Advances in transportation had also spurred a massive explosion of newspapers, pamphlets, and cartoons, and by the late 1830s the urban flash man had inspired a genre of scandalous papers, variously titled *The Flash, The Libertine,* and *The Rake.* Filled with gossip about sports, prostitutes, and theatrical denizens, they were sold in saloons and barbershops and on steamboats.[35] Small wonder, then, that Tom's, Jerry's, and Bob's forays into London brothels, theatrical entertainments, public houses, and gaming houses were wildly popular. In Philadelphia, much as in London, *Life in London* helped popularize its heroes' sartorial choices. Comic actor Francis Wemyss, for example, was seen on the street in full dandy regalia, wearing a "Bob Logic hat," a "green Bond street prom-enading coat, rounded at the skirts," and a "red waistcoat, with pocket flaps and bell buttons, [with] salmon-colored stockinet pantaloons, fitting to the skin, [and] Cossack polished boots."[36]

Life in London also resonated with the radicalized Jacksonian workingmen who became the mainstay of the audiences at the Olympic, where *Tom and Jerry* enjoyed its extended run. Andrew Jackson had campaigned for the presidency in 1828 on a platform of expanding democracy and reforming the government, which he presented as a necessary curative for the corrupt and aristocratic ad-ministration of John Quincy Adams (1825–29). In reality, Jackson's presidency (1829–37) did not bring about greater democracy. A slave owner and defender of slavery, he was integral to the forcible removal of southeastern Indians (in contravention of treaties) and did not oversee a redistribution of wealth or expan-sion of social mobility. But his presidency did usher in a new system of competi-tive parties: Jackson's Democratic Party, which harked back to the Democratic-Republican tradition of Jefferson and Madison, and its nemesis, the Whig Party of Henry Clay, Daniel Webster, and John Quincy Adams, whose roots were in the Federalist Party. Moreover, these parties did not base their power on the old elite networks of their predecessors but on voter support. In consequence, Jackson and the Democratic Party stirred up plebeian radicals who in the late 1820s re-newed their demands for universal manhood suffrage. These Jacksonian Demo-cratic working men were the ones filling the audience at the play about the three dandies' exploits in lowlife London and the transvestite blackface Nance and Sal running at the Olympic Theatre for over a month.

Shifting audience composition and theatrical tastes in Philadelphia in the early 1820s also played a role in the success of *Life in London.* Public taste for "legitimate drama was in temporary decline" as a journalist for *Poulson's Daily Advertiser* sniffed regretfully. Popular instead were equestrian spectacles, circus acts, and burletta, as well as narrative melodramas and farces, often staged at the Arch Street and Olympic theaters, which would soon stage blackface minstrelsy.[37] Faced with new competition and changing public tastes, the New Theatre on Chestnut Street sought to distinguish itself as the site for legitimate drama and respectable audiences. Despite the newfound sense of national confidence after the War of 1812 and the lingering resentment of Great Britain's commercial and naval prowess, legitimacy and respectability were still measured by British cultural standards. This "anglophilia" also had a class dimension; British taste was considered genteel. In the continued postcolonial American "culture of insecurity," as one scholar has dubbed it, the managers began marketing the theater as the "Old Drury" of Philadelphia, in order to evoke the reputation of London's Drury Lane Theatre Royal.[38] They further tried to maintain the theater's respectability by emulating the similarly motivated renovations of London's Drury Lane and Covent Garden theaters. After a fire burnt the theater down in 1820, its managers rebuilt it with entrances and exits stratified by the price and prestige of seating areas. As manager William Wood explained, "Much attention had been bestowed on the . . . comforts of the audience, by large doors of exit and entrance from the boxes. A convenient and handsome entrance had been provided to the pit from Sixth Street . . . the gallery entrance was from the rear of the house, on Carpenter Street."[39]

But these efforts to refine the theater and its fare by emulating the London theaters stirred class-based protest, as the plebeian audience members raised "serious objections . . . to the pit entrance" and issued, as an irritated Woods put it, an "inflammatory hand-bill."[40] Titled "Equality, or the New Theatre as It Should Be," the bill objected to the "citizens . . . whose inclination, taste, or means may lead to the Pit or Gallery" being "subject[ed] to an entrance comparatively less respectable than what has been assigned to those whose assumed superiority has led to distinctions wherein no distinctions are at all justifiable."[41] The managers were forced to concede and provide the pit and gallery viewers with a door on Chestnut Street. They also continued catering to popular taste for burletta from London's minor theaters, like *Life in London*, in order to compete with the Arch Street and Olympic theaters.

Burlesquing Life in Philadelphia

While there is little indication that *Life in London* stirred commentary on race in Philadelphia among either its elite or its vocal plebeian audience members, it provided a prototype for peculiarly Philadelphian racial burlesque that did. In particular, Cruikshank's illustrations, which spectacularly visualized the "urban spectator" genre of burlesque essayed by Egan in prose and adapted to stage by Moncrieff and others, were the inspiration for Edward W. Clay. Clay was a Philadelphia cartoonist who transposed the class taxonomy of *Tom and Jerry* onto local race relations in a series of cartoons titled *Life in Philadelphia*. This series set the mold for the American version of the blackface stage dandy, who would appear in both variety minstrel acts and stage plays. Although Clay incorporated varied social and political commentary, his overriding purpose was to lampoon free blacks' aspirations to upward social mobility by painting them as ridiculous and ill-behaved in high-life settings. Despite the contrasts between class delineation in London and the Philadelphian emphasis on race, the sketches, cartoons, and plays featuring a voyeur's slice of life in the two cities were conceptually interrelated constituents of a fully transatlantic genre.

Clay etched his original *Life in Philadelphia* series after returning from a three-year tour of Europe that included time spent in London at the height of the *Life in London*'s popularity. He may well have seen Moncrieff's *Life in London* at the Adelphi, as he had a demonstrable interest in the popular theater.[42] Clay worked as a theatrical illustrator, and, perhaps inspired by Cruikshank's high-life fashion plates and/or *High Life in London* at Covent Garden in 1826, he later produced a sheet of "Theatrical Portraits" illustrating dress and fashion both onstage and off. And, as scholars have noted, Clay's 1828 *Life in Philadelphia* cartoons resemble scenes in a play.[43] Many of the prints in *Life in Philadelphia* depict blacks performing a variety of high-life activities, such as attending dances, fancy-dress balls, tea parties, and shopping in fashionable stores. Under titles such as *Fancy Ball, How You Like de Waltz Mr. Lorenzo?*, and *Shall I Hab de Honour to Dance de Next Quadrille*, the prints included malapropistic dialogue that functioned as a form of oral blackface built on the exclusionary motifs established between 1810 and 1820 in oral blackface that reacted to slave-trade abolition. Clay also frequented London print shops during his sojourn in the metropolis.[44] There he would likely have seen not only Cruikshank's plates for *Life in London* but also Rudolph Ackerman's *Microcosm of London; or, London in Miniature*, images of architectural and leisure sites of the city.[45] Clay's cartoon, *A Dead Cut*, from his *Life in Philadelphia* series, provides evidence that he perused London print shops, as it is clearly modeled after London cartoonist M. Egerton's *The Cut Direct!* (1827), one of three that Egerton etched of urban white dandies (fig. 12).[46] Egerton depicted an aspiring urban dandy of the new middle class taking on airs by snobbishly "cutting" the less fashionably attired fellow young professional across the street.

Figure 12. M. Egerton, *The Cut Direct!* (1827). This class-based satirical print featuring an urban dandy of the new middle-class offers suggestive evidence that Edward Clay's racialized *Life in Philadelphia* prints were inspired by the picaresque trend of London's cartoon and theater culture. Clay borrowed this class-based joke and transposed it to his race-based cartoon by the same title. Courtesy Lewis Walpole Library, Yale University

"Who the Devil are you," the dandy sniffs, after accusing the lower-class pedestrian of being "impudent."

Clay's 1829 version, retitled *A Dead Cut*, borrowed the title and basic premise of Egerton's class-based joke but racialized it to mock free blacks' "pretensions" in aspiring to middle-class status in Philadelphia. The cartoon features a well-heeled couple who cross paths with a still-poor and shabbily dressed old friend, a boot-shiner. When the boot-shiner exclaims at his friend's visible newfound success—saying, "Lord a' marcy, why Caesar, is dis you? Why, when you 'rive from New York?"—Caesar "cuts" him by pretending not to recognize him,

Figure 13. W. H. Isaacs, *The Cut Direct; or, Getting Up in the World* (ca. 1832). Both Edward Clay's *Life in Philadelphia* engraving, *A Dead Cut* (1829) and Isaacs's London knock-off repeat Egerton's joke about the snobbery of white professional Londoners on the make but racialize it. Clay used the joke to mock newly affluent Philadelphia blacks' aspirations to upward mobility and transmogrified the original dialogue into malapropistic "black" speech. Isaacs exaggerated the malapropisms and the characters' physiognomic features even further to disparage black freedom as the debates about slave emancipation in the British West Indies were under way. Courtesy of The Library Company of Philadelphia

claiming, "You must be mistaking in de person, Black man." Caesar's female companion, fancily attired with an oversized plumed bonnet, believes Caesar's assertion of mistaken identity, and—echoing the dialogue of Egerton's London class-based cartoon—asks, "What does the imperdent nigger mean, my love?" Caesar's use of "Black man" to reject his old friend and his companion's descriptive, "imperdent nigger," reinforced Clay's mockery of "impudent" blacks aspiring to "white" middle-class standing. In 1832 Londoner W. H. Isaacs repeated Clay's racial joke under the title, *The Cut Direct; or, Getting Up in the World* (fig. 13). Isaacs's reclaiming of the title of Egerton's original nonracial, class-based satire further corroborates the print as Clay's original inspiration, although Isaacs altered the dialogue to make it even more malapropistic than Clay's: Caesar's female companion now comments, "To be sure he is my Lub, we are Guinea People, you imperdent nigger." Reproduced amid heated British debates about slave emancipation, Isaacs disparages black freedom by darkening the complexion of all three figures, exaggerating their physiognomic features, and pointedly noting their African "Guinea" origins.

In contrast to Egan's, Moncrieff's, and Cruikshank's voyeuristic view of the class-based hierarchy of the Corinthian capital, Clay embedded in all his *Life in Philadelphia* cartoons a racial taxonomy of quotidian life. The cartoons were so popular that the term "Life in Philadelphia" became a standard phrase to refer to fashions, trends, and—most especially—black Philadelphians' social practices and sartorial choices.[47] Unlike the *Life in London* series, Clay never depicted whites and blacks in the same cartoon. Out of a total of fourteen plates, only four were of white Philadelphians. In one, for example, he mocked white socialites as foppish dandies, while another depicted a Quaker couple in traditional dress and poked fun at their speech and austere lifestyle under the title *Behold, thou art fair, Deborah*.[48] The remaining ten plates depicted free blacks, and the humor consistently rested on scorning blacks' aspirations to the high life of fashion, culture, and civic affairs as an absurd contravention of the "natural" racial hierarchy of white social and political hegemony.

While Egan, Cruikshank, and Moncrieff had not portrayed either poor black Londoners or more affluent blacks as a threat, Clay made clear that the much larger black middle class in Philadelphia was just that. In London, class trumped race and racism: poor blacks were integrated into "low life" and the tiny number of more well-heeled blacks milled easily with the white middling and upper sorts in "high life" settings like the Royal Academy. But in Philadelphia, even the most educated and affluent blacks were excluded from civic festivities, educational institutions, churches, and community entities, and forced, therefore, to start separate organizations. Clay was reacting to the growth of a black community that by the 1820s was almost entirely free, and to that community's development of a wealth of social and philanthropic institutions, including churches, charitable societies, and freemasonry lodges. In one print Clay depicted black freemasons as buffoonlike and ignorant.[49] He also portrayed blacks as comical and out-of-place in high-life situations by exaggerating features, gestures, and apparel so that black subjects appeared to be wearing fancy dress costumes in order to suggest they were playing in unseemly masquerades rather than simply living their lives. The perceived threat of the free black community to the political and social order of the city underlay Clay's derision of blacks' social and civic aspirations, just as it had for the creators of the African Tammany and Bobalition dialogues and their illustrations (see chap. 1).

Clay built upon these earlier creations by besmirching free black Philadel-

Figure 14. Edward Clay, *Back to Back*, from *Life in Philadelphia* (ca. 1829). Clay suggests free Philadelphian blacks had put their freedom to poor use by depicting the couple in exaggeratedly fancy dress and suggesting they donned it to frivolously celebrate slave-trade abolition on Freedom Day—a suggestion that puts Clay's print squarely in the tradition of racialist Bobalition broadsides and links it to contemporaries' critiques of middle-class blacks' sartorial self-fashioning. Courtesy of The Library Company of Philadelphia

phians' celebration of Freedom Day, the civic counter-theater free blacks developed after being violently ousted from Independence Day parades in 1805 (and the "white" festive public sphere more generally). In *Back to Back*, Clay suggested that free Philadelphian blacks had put their freedom to poor use, engaging in frivolity and putting on airs above their place instead of applying themselves to sober industry (fig. 14). A foppish dandy preens for his overdressed female companion and asks, "How you like de new fashion shirt, Miss Florinda." She responds by reminding him that he wore this finery to participate in the free black community's January 1st Freedom Day celebration marking the 1808 slave-trade abolition: "I tink dey mighty elegum—I see you on New Year day when you carry de colour on de Abolition 'siety—you look just like Pluto de God of War." In keeping with the Bobalition broadsides, Clay used the blackface urban dandy to heap contempt on free blacks' civic participation, and through the absurd "Pluto de God of War" compliment even targeted blacks' use of neoclassical motifs in civic celebrations such as the motif of Columbia in her temple to celebrate Independence Day.

Other eminent white Philadelphians used the black urban dandy to disparage free blacks' institutions. In 1828, the same year Clay issued his *Life in Philadelphia* series, local annalist John Fanning Watson sneeringly wrote, "In the olden time, dressy blacks and dandy coloured beaux and belles, as we now see them issuing from their proper churches, were quite unknown. Their aspirings and little vanities have been rapidly growing since they got those separate churches, and have received their entire exemption from slavery." Watson went on to bemoan that blacks no longer knew their proper, humble place in the social order: "Once they submitted to the appellation of servants, blacks, or negroes, but now they require to be called coloured people, and among themselves, their common call of salutation is—gentlemen and ladies." "Thirty to forty years ago," Watson longingly noted, blacks "were much humbler, more esteemed in their place, and more useful to themselves and others." He then lambasted free blacks' aspirations to be part of "white" fashionable society and cast their civic participation as a laughable imitation of civilized whites: "As a whole they show an overweening fondness for display and vainglory—fondly imitating the whites in processions and banners, and in the pomp and pageantry of Masonic and Washington societies etc." Like Clay, Watson concluded that blacks had put their freedom to idle and unwise use: "With the kindest feelings for their race, judicious men wish them wiser conduct, and a better use of the benevolent feelings which induced their emancipation among us."[50]

Watson's and Clay's sentiments were shared by antislavery sympathizers like Fanny Kemble, an actress who began her career in London before moving to Philadelphia. Kemble also ridiculed the appearance of elite free blacks, but her racialist repugnance coexisted with a deep aversion to slavery. Indeed, after a bitter divorce from her Georgia planter husband, Pierce Butler, she published an unsparing critique of Southern slavery in her *Journal of a Residence on a Georgian Plantation*.[51] Yet in the journal she kept during her Philadelphia residence in the 1820s and 1830s, she cast aspersions on free blacks' donning of fashionable attire by derogating the "grotesque" contrast between brightly colored fashion garments and dark skin: "After dinner [we] sat looking at the blacks parading up and down; most of them in the height of the fashion, with every colour in the rainbow about them. Several of the black women I saw pass had very fine figures, but the contrast of a bright blue or pink crape bonnet, with the black face, white teeth and glaring blue whites of the eyes, is beyond description grotesque."[52]

While Watson's and Kemble's observations were clearly skewed by racism, they were nonetheless a reflection of cultural realities of the emergent black middle class in Philadelphia. Even for slaves with limited material assets, dress and fashion had been "practically and symbolically important to a slave's sense of individuality and liberty," and runaway slaves were often described in advertisements as "remarkably fond of dress": slaves' sartorial choices were a form of resistance.[53] This opposition style was taken up by free African Americans, too. Similarly, "stylin'," to borrow another scholar's term, was a way for free blacks' to assert their freedom, autonomy, and belonging through self-consciously oppositional choices of dandified dress and affect.[54] But black dandies did not merely mimic white dandy dress styles; they also creatively reinterpreted these styles to subvert and destabilize white cultural and racial hegemony. Thus, racial and class cross-dressing, as practiced by enslaved blacks in eighteenth- and nineteenth-century festivals like Negro Election Day, which entailed electing a "king," and later Freedom Day festivities celebrated by free Northern blacks, subverted and parodied white authority.[55] In this light, Clay's cartoons can be construed as a parody of blacks' parody of white hegemony.[56] Like the white writers, etchers, and printers who created Mungo onstage and in cartoon iterations and the African Tammany dialogues, and Bobalition broadsides, Clay regarded African American civic activities and aspirations to civic participation as important enough to satirize—honing in on free blacks' wardrobe as a reflection of their upwardly mobile aspirations. While Clay's intent was to deride and disenfranchise Philadelphian blacks, he was (albeit unwittingly) participating in a parody of an oppositional parody of white institutions.[57]

Clay's etchings not only mirrored Kemble's disgust with dark skin and Watson's disparagement of "dressy blacks . . . and dandy beaux and belles" but also put into vividly accessible form newly pernicious theories of race that placed those of African descent at the bottom of a taxonomic racial order based on skeleton and skull size and shape. One of most outspoken theorists of this new pseudoscience of phrenology or "craniology" was an eminent Philadelphian, the physician and natural scientist Samuel George Morton of the prestigious Academy of Natural Sciences of Philadelphia.[58] Morton claimed he could judge the innate intellectual and moral capacity of a race by skull size and shape, with larger skulls the repository of larger, superior brains and smaller cavities indicative of smaller brains and inferior intellect. On this basis, he categorized and defined as distinctly separate the Asian, Native American, Caucasian, and Negroid "races." For Morton, the Negroid race was measurably inferior in intellectual and moral capacity because the typical Negroid skull was characterized by a low forehead and jutting jaw and thus a smaller skull cavity. To support his theories, Morton collected hundreds of skulls from all over the world and used them to supposedly delineate precisely the craniometric differences between Caucasian and Negroid peoples.

Using skeletal anatomy as the index for racial gradation was not new, but unlike eighteenth-century theories, nineteenth-century craniology rested on the assumption of a gradation of races with different innate intellectual capacities. As early as 1794, Anglo-American artists had had access to translations of the work of Dutch anatomist Pieter Camper, who had suggested a hierarchical gradation of different skull types, "an arrangement of these [skulls], placed in a regular succession: apes, orangutans, negroes, the skull of an Hottentot, Madagascar, Celebese, Chinese, Moguller, Calmuck, and diverse Europeans."[59] Camper's gradations were based on facial angle, or the degree to which the jaw protrudes from the rest of the face. Although an anatomist and surgeon by profession, Camper was also an artist and sculptor, and his explicit intent was to provide guidelines for correct anatomical illustration, as he believed that artists too often transposed European facial bone structure onto their representations of other races.

For Camper, the neoclassical, and hence the European, was most beautiful, while he perceived a "striking resemblance between the race of Monkies and that of Blacks."[60] But Camper was reluctant to definitively commit to a polygenetic explanation of racial variety because it contradicted the biblical account of creation. He was convinced of monogenetic racial origin and adamant that physiognomy bore no relation to intellect or moral worth; like Buffon and Blumenbach, he believed instead that racial varieties were a product of climate and environment. Nevertheless, his followers from the 1820s used his work to support and promote polygenesis, culminating in Josiah C. Nott's and George Gliddon's tribute to Morton's work, *Types of Mankind* (1854).

Morton's craniology and ideas of polygenesis were gaining ground in 1820s Philadelphia, and Clay's depictions of "black" features and anatomical structure in the *Life in Philadelphia* cartoons realized these ideas in popular form. Clay's drawings portrayed African Americans with exaggerated, almost apelike features such as jutting jaws, low foreheads, and large posteriors. In some of his cartoons, Clay vilified black skin complexion and physiognomy to deepen his burlesque of black subjects as ridiculously out of place in high-life settings. In one print, a dark complexioned African American woman asks a white stocking-store attendant, the shades and hues of whose wares were geared to the skin complexions of his white customers, "Have you any flesh coloured silk stockings?"[61] By implication, the etchings supported the contention of Morton and others that those of African descent were intellectually and morally inferior, in that Clay assumed free blacks' aspirations to middle-class culture—balls, tea parties, fashion, and the like—were a breach of the city's socioracial hierarchy. The cartoons, of course, also depicted black organizations, activities, and dress as a laughable aping of the superior white culture.

Although Clay's racial burlesque was predominantly social rather than political, one print addressed the conflicted place of slavery in the brewing ferment of early Jacksonian politics in Philadelphia. Radical Jacksonian wage-earners favored expanded (male) suffrage and touted a mantra of equal democratic rights, but they had a complicated relationship to antislavery ideas. Some joined antislavery organizations while others sympathized with a gradualist approach to ending slavery. Still others, however, were downright hostile both toward antislavery beliefs and to African Americans.[62] Indeed, in the Northern cities with sizeable free black populations—New York, Philadelphia, Boston, and elsewhere—many radical Jacksonians not only opposed abolition but also resisted, sometimes violently, the entry of black workers into trades.[63] In Philadelphia, racial hostility was exacerbated by the decade-long economic slump after the War of 1812. During this time, Richard Allen's African Methodist Episcopal Church and other black churches became targets of racist violence. And when free black men tried to form an African Fire Association, the fire companies, which were hubs of the white working-class democratic impulse, refused to permit it.[64]

It was in this context of deteriorating race relations, economic hard times for wage earners, and the fraught relationship of radical Jacksonian Democratic workingmen to antislavery activity that Clay drew *What de debil you hurrah for General Jackson for?* in 1828.[65] Visible in the background are an aroused group of Jacksonian democratic rabble, a group that a young black would-be Jacksonian appears to have just left before his run-in with an older African American man who grabs the boy by the scruff of his neck and demands why he is "hurrahing" for the Southerner, Jackson, and the party of slave owners. At the boy's feet lies an issue of the *Democratic Press*, a radical organ representing the Jeffersonian and later Jacksonian workingman's interests. The *Democratic Press* also stood for virulently racist opposition to black citizenship. It was in this paper that congressman Tench Coxe published a series of virulently racist essays, "Considerations Respecting the Helots of the United States, African and Indian, Native and

Alien, and Their Descendants of the Whole and Mixed Blood" (1820). The essays denied the eligibility of free blacks for citizenship on the grounds that they were descended from "uncivilized and wild men . . . not capable of genuine modern civilization."[66] Coxe's views of African Americans' innate inferiority were emblematic of the *Democratic Press*. Clay thus used this plate to mock free blacks' hopes that the democratic impulse of Jackson's Democratic Party would include them.

Clay wielded the urban picaresque to disparage the extension of the "great experiment" of democracy to black Philadelphians (and, by extension, to free blacks in other northern cities). In the 1830s, Clay's etchings became an influential prototype for stage performers and cartoonists in both London and Philadelphia whose work was a conduit through which to comment on black slavery and freedom. Clay's blackface urban dandy would soon appear onstage in plays and minstrel acts in both cities, and his prints would be reproduced and reworked by several London publishers to comment on emancipation in the British West Indies. The blackface urban dandy became not only a popular mainstay on the transatlantic stage but also freely moved between the permeable media of theater, print, and civic rhetoric.

The "Black Jokes" of Emancipation

In the 1830s, several London artists refashioned Clay's cartoons to respond to the Emancipation Bill of 1833, which began a drawn-out process of freeing the slaves in the British West Indies. Two dramatic events precipitated the passage of emancipation legislation. The first was a massive slave rebellion in Jamaica in 1831 to 1832, the so-called Baptist War. Jamaica was the most lucrative of Britain's sugar-colonies, and this slave revolt was the largest of all the many British West Indian insurrections, involving sixty thousand slaves and causing the deaths of 540 slaves and 14 whites.[67] Jamaican planters blamed Christian missionaries, especially the Baptists, for inciting the revolt, and they retaliated by vandalizing churches and jailing then expelling the missionaries.[68] After their return to England, the exiled missionaries were invaluable abolitionist propagandists who helped reignite popular antislavery enthusiasm. Seizing the moment, Thomas Buxton proposed to Parliament in 1832 that a committee be appointed "for the purpose of effecting the extinction of slavery throughout the earliest period compatible with the safety of all classes in the colonies."[69] Consensus on the terms of the slaves' emancipation was elusive, and the ultimate legislation was a compromise that promised freedom to slaves after serving a six-year "apprenticeship" of compulsory labor to financially compensate their masters' loss. The law took effect on August 1, 1834.

While the terms of the emancipation bill were contested, what made its passage possible was the Parliamentary Reform Act of 1832. Throughout the 1820s, radicals and reformers had been engaged in increasingly well-organized agitation for extended suffrage and parliamentary reform. Resurgence of democratic revolution in France in 1830 heightened the expectation of reform, and the death of the authoritarian George IV and accession of William IV to the throne that year gave the liberal Whigs an opportunity to oust the Tories. Parliamentary reform was the central issue of the campaigns for these elections, which the Whigs won. Under Lord Grey, they began working on a parliamentary reform proposal in 1831 and 1832.[70] Meanwhile, eruptions of popular agitation lent the bill's passage urgency. London theatergoers in the lower-cost pits and the "gods" in the galleries hollered and sang for reform. The Christmas pantomime for 1831, *The World Turned Upside Down; or, Harlequin Reformer*, incorporated advocacy for the bill, which was greeted with "tremendous rounds of applause from the gods."[71] Political unions submitted thousands of reform petitions to Parliament and held mass meetings. In London, pro-reform demonstrators smashed the windows of the houses of prominent reform opponents, and riots broke out in several major cities. Union leaders and other middle-class reformers exploited the threat of plebeian revolution to further their cause.[72]

With plebeian popular agitation as the menacing undertone of reformers' demands, Parliament passed the Reform Bill in 1832. The working classes, however, viewed the bill as a "great betrayal." The act granted seats in the House of Commons to large cities that had burgeoned as a result of industrialization and took away seats from the overrepresented "rotten boroughs" with very small populations. But while the act expanded suffrage, allowing a total of one out of six adult males to vote, it retained property qualifications. The vote was extended to urban householders who earned ten pounds a year, which did not enfranchise all the middling folk, much less the working classes. The denial of universal manhood suffrage angered many plebeians who had played a key role in agitating for reform and supporting the middle-class politicians leading the charge for the bill's passage.

Abolitionists, however, made good use of working-class agitation for reform in their fight for emancipation. In a persuasive parliamentary speech, Thomas Buxton played on the radicalized politics of the working poor to advocate emancipation:

> Is it certain that the colonies would remain to the country if we were resolved to retain slavery? . . . How was the government prepared to act in case of a general insur-

rection of the negroes? . . . a war against a people struggling for their rights would be the falsest position in which it was possible for England to be placed. And did the noble Lords think that the people out of doors would be content to see their resources exhausted for the purpose of crushing the inalienable rights of mankind?[73]

Buxton powerfully tied the question of emancipation to the inevitability of revolt, which he posited as a struggle for the democratic "inalienable right of man" to liberty. At the same time, Buxton invoked the specter of working-class radical discontent when he suggested that the ire of the "people out of doors" (i.e., the poor and indigent) would be provoked by governmental "crushing" of the "inalienable" rights of the slaves to liberty.

It was precisely this tie between the urban democratic impulse and slave emancipation that framed London artists' and engravers' refashioning of *Life in Philadelphia* following the Reform and Emancipation Acts. William Summers began the craze of redrawing Clay's prints in the early 1830s, and in 1833 W. H. Isaacs continued the series, utilizing the etchings of Charles Hunt to reproduce many of Clay's cartoons, including the version of *A Dead Cut*.[74] All but three of Clay's prints were reprinted in London, the exceptions being two prints of white Philadelphians and one print making fun of black freemasons.[75] As black freemasons in London attended the same lodges as whites, this particular joke might have been less humorous there.[76] New prints, such as engraver I. Harris's *Grand Celebration ob de Bobalition ob African Slabery* (published in versions by engraver Gabriel Shire Tregear and W. H. Isaacs), were added to the London series. Tregear reworked Clay's prints and added six new images to make a set of twenty, which he published in 1834 as *Tregear's Black Jokes*.[77] While the successful transfer of Clay's cartoons was attributable in part to the shared cultural background and common understandings of London and Philadelphia, the London cartoons took on new meanings and form. London artists like Isaacs, Summers, Hunt, and Tregear made changes that signposted shifts in the cartoons' meanings, exaggerating the features of Philadelphian blacks even more grotesquely than had Clay, rendering them more bestial in anatomy and features.[78]

Tregear's Black Jokes best demonstrates this greater viciousness of style. In his hand-colored aquatints, the subjects are colored more deeply black than in Clay's originals, have grossly large posteriors, low foreheads, and jutting jaws. Additionally, Tregear added racialized "jokes" that emphasized skin color, such as in *The Christening*, which depicted a black pastor dunking a baby in the christening font as the mother comments, "Oh dear . . . I fraid you'll wash all him complexion away and gib him de water on de Brain." Similarly, an illustration of a group playing cards was titled *The Card Party: They Certainly Are Blacklegs,* while another print was titled *Cinderrella [sic] and her Black Prince* and depicted an ugly Cinderella with huge gnarled nose and crooked, toothy grin on a theatrical proscenium with her dark-complexioned prince. While these racialized stylistic changes can be partially explained as conformity with the well-developed conventions of British print satire from William Hogarth to George Cruikshank, which depended on exaggerated caricature of its subjects, they also indicate a shift in signification.

Most obviously, *Tregear's Black Jokes* exploited the supposed foibles of free black Philadelphians to denigrate black freedom in the British West Indies and its threat to British imperial hegemony. Not just the timing but also the substantive content suggest that Tregear intended his *Black Jokes* to illustrate the negative consequences of the British Emancipation Act of 1833. Tregear included prints in which the setting of the joke evoked Caribbean instead of urban metropolitan locales. *Blackberrying,* for example, depicted a tropical slave funeral. In it, a barefooted old man is reading from a book as a corpse on a bamboo stretcher is laid in a grave and a monkey and a serpent in a palm tree wave goodbye. The "black joke" is issued by the pallbearers, the first of whom comments, "how precious pale he look in de face," to which the second replies, "Aye, aye, him be no Moor."

But Tregear's most explicit commentary on emancipation was *Grand Celebration ob de Bobalition ob African Slabery* (1833), which mocked blacks' celebration of their freedom (fig. 15). The London iteration of the *Grand Celebration* was a transatlantic creation that fused American racial satire with Atlantic performative tropes to comment on the British emancipation law. Unlike *Blackberrying,* the *Grand Celebration* was firmly set in the American context and its politicized dialogue came directly out of Bobalition broadsides of the 1810s and 1820s such as *Africum Shocietee: Grand Bobalition of Slavery* (Boston, 1818), which had mocked black Freedom Day celebrations in a series of malapropistic toasts to "bobalition."[79] Tregear not only borrowed the conceptual premise of the Bobalition genre but also the dialogue's comic reproach. The third speaker from the left, for example, references the American Colonization Society in his lament that "White Man, mighty anxious to send nigger to de place dey stole him from, now he got no further use for him," while another speaker refers to Columbia, "de Genius ob Merica." In this print, Tregear thus took a direct slap at the American Colonization Society and sarcastically alluded to the failure of Columbia to extend her republican principles of equality for all to African Americans. Tregear simultaneously used this American topical dialogue to make black Philadelphians targets of ridicule but, as is evident from his transposition of some "jokes" to the Carib-

Figure 15. I. Harris, *Grand Celebration ob de Bobalition ob African Slabery,* from *Life in Philadelphia* in *Tregear's Black Jokes* (1833–34). This London iteration, inspired by Edward Clay's mockery of black freedom, was a thoroughly transatlantic creation that fused American racial satire with Atlantic performative tropes to comment on British emancipation. Courtesy of The Library Company of Philadelphia

bean, his larger discursive political context was the meaning of British freedom in the West Indies.

Additionally, the meaning of British freedom in the metropole may have been part of the illustration's discursive subtext. Jan Marsh has suggested that the *Grand Celebration* and the other prints in *Tregear's Black Jokes* are a discourse on white Englishness, with the black body serving as a mediating contrast. Tregear's prints, Marsh asserts, "encourage an orthodoxy of race through skin colour that is more compelling than Clay" and "a most persuasive visual example of what Englishness is not."[80] While Marsh is correct about Tregear's transatlantic merging of discourses, his purpose was also to delimit the meaning of British freedom in a larger political sense. The two issues—slave emancipation and democratic rights at home—could not be separated, as both were founded on a notion of British liberty. This interrelatedness lay at the heart of Thomas Buxton's appeal to Parliament. The London versions of the *Life in Philadelphia* prints, including Tregear's, were issued *after* the Reform Bill and hence amid plebeian anger over the "great betrayal" and its concomitant danger of renewed radical unrest. Tregear and other Londoners retooled *Life in Philadelphia* not only to parody black freedom but also to denigrate the political participation of the lower classes, of which blacks were a visible and integrated part.

The London iterations of Clay's cartoons also helped solidify the transatlantic blackface minstrel character. Indeed, one of *Tregear's Black Jokes* became the blueprint for illustrated advertisements of Dandy Jim or Zip Coon. Clay's urban "dandy Negro" was already becoming a trademark figure on the transatlantic stage, appearing regularly in London and Philadelphia. James Hackett's *The Times; or, Life in New York* (1829), which debuted at Philadelphia's Old Drury in the 1830–31 season, featured "Mr. Pompey, A dandy Negro Waiter, leader of the Broadway fashions in sabledom."[81] W. B. Bernard's *The Kentuckian; or, A Trip to New York*, meanwhile, featured a free urban black dandy character and helped popularize the type. A phenomenal success, *The Kentuckian* debuted in New York in 1831 and in Philadelphia in 1834, crossing the ocean that same year and playing first at Covent Garden and later the Haymarket Theatre Royal for a six week engagement. And on September 11, 1833, a play titled *Life in Philadelphia* debuted at the Chestnut Street Theatre. While no script or reviews are extant, one might surmise from the title and timing that thespians brought to life Clay's jokes and blackface dandies in the show, listed as a farce in the theater's daybook.[82]

But it was one of Tregear's new jokes, rather than one of Clay's prints, that served as the template not only for the stage black dandy in *The Kentuckian, Life in New York*, and other plays, but also for the blackface minstrel act. When Bernard Flaherty, an Irishman born in Cork, immigrated to the United States and began performing "negro songs" on the northern seaboard theatrica circuit under his stage name of Barney Williams, he achieved celebrity in his Dandy Jim character (fig. 16).[83] The illustration of Dandy Jim used to advertise Williams's "negro songs" was an adaptation of Tregear's *An Unfair Reflection*, in which the dandy admires himself in front of a mirror (fig. 17). By the time George Washington Dixon essayed Zip Coon in 1834, the urban dandy, born in print cartoons, was already a regular between-the-acts minstrel number on the stages of London and Philadelphia and a frequent character in full-length stage plays.

Egan and Cruikshank's class-based *Life in London* prose and images had fea-

BARNEY WILLIAMS IN "DANDY JIM."

Figure 16. Barney Williams in "Dandy Jim," playbill illustration (1844). When viewed in conjunction with fig. 17, the influence of cartoon prints on the development of blackface minstrelsy on the stage is clear: this playbill reveals that Clay's cartoons of black dandies provided the template for blackface dandy stage characters and their ephemeral illustration. Courtesy Picture Collection, The New York Public Library, Astor, Lenox and Tilden Foundations

tured real-life black Londoners—the fiddler Billy Waters; African Sal; and Mahogany Bet, a prostitute—whom they portrayed sympathetically. When Moncrieff created his theatrical adaptation full of "fun, frolic, fashion, and flash," he built on preexisting blackface performance traditions such as the stock black underclass female, like Wowski, the lisping, "dingy," dark-complexioned, desexualized female servant to the noble Yarico in Colman's *Inkle and Yarico.* But Moncrieff took one step further in desexualizing black females by casting these roles with white men in blackface makeup. In doing so he helped establish a prototype for how blackface females were portrayed on stage and in cartoons. The transatlantic

Figure 17. G. S. Tregear, *An Unfair Reflection*, from *Life in Philadelphia* in *Tregear's Black Jokes* (1833). The black dandy preening himself in front of a mirror was part of a set of prints Tregear produced using Edward Clay's characters and themes, but with even more exaggerated physiognomic features. Courtesy of The Library Company of Philadelphia

interactions between the *Life in London* prose, cartoons, and stage plays, Clay's *Life in Philadelphia* adaptations, and Tregear's more extremely racist reiterations went on to birth the blackface urban dandy.

Thus, the quintessential figures of blackface minstrelsy emerged on the transatlantic stage from the London "black jokes" against emancipation and radicalism that used as their blueprint Philadelphian "jokes" about the dangers of black freedom and of extending democratic rights and citizenship to African Americans. These jokes had, in turn, borrowed the urban spectator genre of the London burletta houses but took the white urban dandy, the embodiment of the new middle class and flash-man masculinity of 1820s industrial London and Philadelphia, and racialized him. This genre corporealized theories of biologically based black and white "races" originating from different species, negative commentary on black freedom, and rejection of black citizenship and subjecthood. Transatlantic circulation between print and theater in the 1820s and 1830s would also birth a new variety act. This proto-vaudeville genre developed by Charles Mathews, among others, featured stock American character "types," some of them borrowed from Clay's cartoons. But Mathews was focused not on denigrating black freedom but rather on disparaging black slavery as inconsistent with America's "great experiment" in democracy and antithetical to British liberty. The creators and performers of this new variety genre would thus fuse Clay's derogatory burlesque of black freedom to a critique of black slavery.

CHAPTER FIVE

Transatlantic Travelers, Slavery, and Charles Mathews's "Black Fun"

At almost exactly the same time that William Thomas Moncrieff's *Life in London* play and Edward Clay's *Life in Philadelphia* series took London and Philadelphia by storm, Charles Mathews was pioneering a proto-vaudeville genre on the 1820s transatlantic stage. A London comic actor and mime, Mathews developed a one-man variety show of burlesque, comic sketches, and musical comedy after touring America, titled, fittingly, *Trip to America*. His time in Philadelphia was especially influential. "I shall be rich in black fun," he wrote home from Philadelphia in 1823 to his friend and collaborator, James Smith, "as I have studied their broken English carefully. It is a pity I dare not touch upon a preacher. I know its danger, but perhaps the absurdity might give a *colour* to it—a *black* Methodist!" Mathews then gave Smith a foretaste of the black preacher "talk" he went on to incorporate into *Trip to America*:

> My wordy bredren, it a no use to come to do meeum-house to ear de most hellygunt orashions if a no put a de cent into de plate; de spiritable man cannot get a on widout de temporalities; twelve 'postles must hab de candle to burn. You dress a self up in de fine blue a cot, and a bandalore breechum, and tink a look like a gemman, but no more like a gemman dan put a finger in de fire, and take him out again, widout you put a de money in a de plate . . . My sister in a de gallery too dress em up wid de poke a de bonnet, and de furbelow-tippet, and look in de glass and say, "Pretty Miss Phyllis, how bell I look! . . . Twix you and I, no see what de white folk make so much fun of us."[1]

Mathews revealed his awareness of the oral blackface genre that "de white folk" of Philadelphia and other Northern cities had developed: the malapropism-filled Bobalition and African Tammany dialogues mocking Freedom Day celebrations and free blacks' institutions, such as freemason lodges, charitable societies, and churches. By focusing on the Methodist church and its well-dressed congregants' supposedly mistake-ridden dialogue, Mathews adapted white Americans' burlesque of free blacks, their institutions, and their efforts toward civic belonging.

Mathews's shows, sensationally popular in both London and Philadelphia, represented the development of a transatlantic theatrical form that could function both to critique American slavery and to burlesque black freedom, depending on its context. His genre also functioned in dialectic with his perceptions of real-life African American culture, which other British travelers had found worthy of commentary in print. Actor William Macready, for example, recalled that in Southern plantations "negroes sang in their wild, fantastic yet harmonious chorus . . . to the accompaniment of guitar or banjo."[2] Fanny Trollope also commented on the "constant musical intercourse between the slave and white society" in "the chants of Negro boatmen [with] their offbeats of African origin."[3] Mathews, however, portrayed African Americans on the London stage for the first time (previous blackface characters having delineated Africans, West Indians, and, in the case of Moncrieff's *Life in London*, African-Britons).[4] And he did so through the fiddle-playing Agamemnon, apparently just as struck as Macready and Trollope by his perceptions of African American musicality. Moreover, he used characters like the Yankee Jonathan, Agamemnon's owner, to censure slavery's blemish on American democracy and praise the superiority of British liberty. Yet his comments about the dandylike dress of the would-be "gemman" in his "fine blue a cot" and his sister, vainly admiring her "poke a de bonnet, and de furbelow-tippet" in the mirror, were also closely related to Clay's *Life in Philadelphia* cartoons. Like Fanny Kemble, John Fanning Watson, and Edward Clay, Matthews acknowledged black Philadelphians' assertion, through their dress, of their freedom and middle-class status. And when Clay's cartoons were at the height of their popularity in early-1830s London, Mathews made them the basis for his annual *Comic Annual* revue, which he performed in London in 1831 before it appeared in print in serial form in Philadelphia in 1832.

But the same theaters where Mathews's shows were the most popular—the Adelphi and Surrey in London, and the Walnut Street and Arch Street theaters in Philadelphia, which all catered to audiences of predominantly the lower sorts—also staged radical oratorical performances. The British activist Fanny Wright emblematized the efforts of radicals to use the theatrical stage to proselytize for antislavery, democratic, and feminist causes. Like her friend Fanny Trollope, Wright crossed the ocean in the 1820s to tour America and investigate the "great experiment" of American democracy. She also shared Trollope's disgust with American slavery. But unlike the conservative, antidemocratic Trollope, Wright undertook an oratory tour in the United States in which she appealed not only for the immediate end of slavery but also for a truly universal suffrage that included all men and women, black or white. In Philadelphia, she gave impassioned and well-attended speeches at the Walnut Street Theatre, which was where audiences cheered Charles Mathews's send-up of black Philadelphians in *Trip to America*.

That Wright performed her radical oratory, which was later published as a political tract, on the same stages that Mathews performed his racial burlesque indicates the fluid interchange between civic rhetoric, print, and theater. The two performances also reveal, in contrasting ways, a streak of British anti-Americanism that both performers directed toward slavery. While the radical Wright castigated slavery as a horrible contradiction to democratic ideals, the more conservative Mathews held up African slavery in America as proof positive of the superiority of the British monarchy and empire. Transatlantic commentary on the "great experiment," which perpetuated revolutionary-era contestation over the meanings of polity and liberty, fueled the precursors to both blackface minstrelsy and fiery utopian radicalism.

Mathews's *Trip to America* and American Slavery

In 1823, Charles Mathews toured the United States and performed comic roles in various stage plays and his own variety entertainments in the theaters of Baltimore, New York, and Philadelphia. His Philadelphia engagement began on February 12, 1823, and ended just nights before the debut of Moncrieff's *Life in London*. Mathews delighted the audiences with the comic imitations that he would make a key component in his variety "entertainments." In Philadelphia on March 7, 1823, for example, he performed as Jack Rover in *Wild Oats* "with imitations."[5] While on tour, he also developed his *Trip to America* revue, which was a big hit when he performed it at the Adelphi and Surrey theaters after returning to London.

Mathews's mimicry of black Philadelphians in dialogue, song, and dance significantly contributed to the development of the genre that would come to be epitomized by the transatlantic popularity of T. Daddy Rice's blackface performances of Jim Crow, a singing and dancing Southern slave. Clay had borrowed from British theatrical and picaresque conventions to lampoon American blacks' freedom in his cartoons. Matthews reversed the flow, using white and black Americans as source material.[6] But in contrast to the blackface urban dandy who emerged from *Life in London* and *Life in Philadelphia* plays and cartoons, Charles Mathews's racial burlesque disparaged American *slavery* rather than black freedom. And unlike *Life in London* and *Life in Philadelphia*, Mathews's performances also intervened directly in antislavery discourse of the 1820s.

Mathews first introduced his comic impressions of Americans in *Trip to America* at London's Surrey Theatre in 1824, but the characters outlived the piece. Their first step toward longevity was in *Jonathan in England; or, Americans Abroad* (1824), a full-length farce Mathews co-wrote with Richard Brinsley Peake, in which the collaborators sublimated a satire of American democratic rights and liberties into the characters of Jonathan Doubikin, an "authentic" slave-owning white Kentuckian, and the blackface characters Maximilian and Agamemnon. Mathews also made Jonathan and Agamemnon regular characters in his "comic annuals" through the 1820s and the 1830s, advertised as *At Home and Abroad with Charles Mathews*. The annuals were one-man, vaudeville-like shows of songs, skits, and monologues that lampooned the peculiarities of various nationalities—among them Scots, Irish, German, Dutch, and, after his 1822 and 1823 tour, Americans.[7]

One reason Mathews's variety revue took off was the growth of the minor theaters, which provided the perfect venue for his comic impersonations and politicized satire. Increased censorship of royally patented theaters during the 1790s anti-Jacobin panic, including an outright ban on historical tragedies, meant that by the 1820s the Theatres Royal were regularly staging hybrid forms such as pantomime, music-dances, and mimed narrative known as "dumbshew," previously confined to the minor unpatented theaters. Conversely, the minor theaters were fusing narrative to music and dance. After the mixing of dance, music, mime, and narrative became the purview of the patented as well as unpatented theaters, the censor had increasing difficulty making strict separations between the fare of the minor theaters and that of the Theatres Royal. Moreover, the minor theaters were less rigorously censored and hence permitted more risqué innovations. Because they were forbidden to perform narrative dramas, whatever they presented was, theoretically, nonnarrative and thus did not require approval from the Lord Chamberlain. In actuality, however, the minor theaters were surreptitiously performing narrative dramas by the 1820s. As the Adelphi managers stated, their policy was to perform "as near the regular drama as the exclusive privileges of the great theaters will permit."[8]

The increased popularity of hybrid music-dance-drama entertainment, combined with the exclusionary efforts of the Theatre Royal managers to foster "respectable" audiences by refurbishing the theaters and making cheap seating less available, fostered a proliferation in minor theaters. By the early nineteenth century, twenty new minor theaters had sprung up in London.[9] More theaters meant more opportunity for both *Life in London* and Mathews's "variety" performances of the 1820s (as well the blackface minstrel troupes and vaudeville of the mid-nineteenth-century music halls). The Surrey, with its audience of South London costermongers, sweeps, and trade journeymen, and the Adelphi, whose audiences were composed of "respectable" yet still humble women and men, typified by the clerk, were home to Mathews's *Trip to America, Jonathan in England,* and *Comic Annuals.* These theaters were, of course, also host to the innovative urban picaresque of *Life in London,* with its burletta, mime, and flash. Mathews's performances, however, included overtly political commentary. In his 1820s and 1830s heyday, he could engage in rights-based political commentary onstage without necessarily incurring the censor's wrath. With no complete script and much improvisation, the full content of his act could not be submitted to scrutiny.

To be sure, when Mathews satirized American slavery and democracy in his *Trip to America,* he played to resurgent popular antislavery feeling, which was part of a wider debate about political reform. In London, organized agitation for parliamentary reform appeared, on the surface, to have been dulled in the 1820s.[10] While the most radical antigovernment foment was, however, foiled with the crushing of the Cato Street plot to assassinate the British cabinet, the reform impulse still simmered below the surface. Key plebeian issues were shortening factory hours and improving work conditions; alleviating property restrictions on suffrage; reforming the draconian Poor Laws that limited mobility by restricting aid to home parishes and the workhouse; and establishing popular education. The issue of implementing free trade by repealing the Corn Laws (which regulated the prices of grain), was the subject of heated contention. Another response to the ills of industrialization and poverty was the utopian experiments of artisan trading cooperatives and communities, including the communitarian schemes of well-to-do capitalist and philanthropist Robert Owen. Trade Unionists, republicans, and factory reformers all began agitating and organizing in the 1820s.

Catholic emancipation, the battle to repeal laws that deprived Catholics of their political rights, added an Irish dimension to the growing spirit of reform and offered inspiration and new tactics both to plebeian political reformers and antislavery advocates. The Irish nationalist and abolitionist Daniel O'Connell, himself of the middling sorts, led the quest for Catholic emancipation. The campaign culminated in victory when O'Connell won a by-election in 1828 to become a member of Parliament, an office from which he, as a Catholic, was legally barred. Rather than risk civil insurrection in Ireland by refusing O'Connell his seat, Parliament pushed through a law in 1829 repealing most political restrictions on Catholics and lesser restrictions on Protestant dissidents. Political reformers in the late 1820s followed O'Connell's example by forming political associations with varied agendas: radical demands for universal manhood suffrage, the more moderate proposal of extending the franchise to small property owners, the goal of reapportioning parliamentary seats, and antislavery agitation.[11]

This wide-ranging debate about and campaigning for human rights and political reform was under way among the newly defined working class when Mathews brought his *Trip to America* home to the Surrey Theatre in 1824. Indeed, the issue of black slavery and freedom pervaded these larger arguments about democratic and human rights. London Owenists, along with some republicans in the Painite-Jacobin mold, had an antislavery position as a function of larger humanitarian and democratic principles.[12] Catholic emancipation, meanwhile, by its very name invoked the cause of black freedom. It is unlikely to have been a coincidence that O'Connell founded his Catholic Association, aimed at mobilizing Irish opinion in favor of political emancipation from anti-Catholic laws, in the same year that the London based Anti-Slavery Society was established with the goal of emancipating slaves in the British West Indies. Above all, antislavery sentiment was central to reform dialogues because organized antislavery activism had provided an inspirational model for successful enactment of humanitarian reform. Reformers and radicals sought to emulate the antislavery movement's mobilization of public opinion through pamphleteering, mass meetings, and national organizations with local chapters.[13] For all these reasons, antislavery ideas were unavoidable in debates among reformers, radicals, and plebeians in 1820s London.

The antislavery movement regained popular fervor after the Congress of Vienna, a meeting of European leaders to redraw the map of post-Napoleonic Europe, renewed French slave-trading rights in 1815. In response, abolitionists succeeded in effecting a registration of slaves. When the slave census unequivocally demonstrated that the abolition of the trade in 1807 had not led to the hoped-for decline in slavery, popular support for emancipation increased. The resolve of the parliamentary emancipationists (led now by Thomas Fowell Buxton, who had replaced the aged and ailing Wilberforce) was only stiffened when slaves, yet again demonstrating their burning desire for freedom, revolted in 1824 in Demerara, Jamaica, and elsewhere in the West Indies.[14] Shortly thereafter, the *Anti-Slavery Monthly Reporter* was established in London and began publishing polemical emancipation appeals. By the mid-1820s, massive crowds of both genders and all socioeconomic classes regularly attended antislavery rallies in the cities and provinces.[15] Mathews's burlesque of black Americans and critique of American slavery was thus performed for plebeian audiences stirred up by popular antislavery and the larger program of human rights and political reform to which the cause belonged.

Moreover, Mathews may well have been performing for racially mixed audiences, the white members of which were part of a working-class culture in which prejudice against and identification with nonwhite Londoners could coexist. This is not to suggest that working-class Londoners harbored no color prejudices and xenophobic impulses. The growing ethos of ethnocultural superiority toward the "African" was certainly evident in British culture by the early nineteenth century. This prejudice had been on display in the pageantry surrounding the 1807 slave-trade abolition bill, including James Powell's pantomime *Furibond; or, Harlequin Negro* (1807) and George Colman's *The Africans; or, War, Love and Duty* (1808) (see chap. 3). Some of the Surrey and Adelphi's lowly attendees may even have seen these pieces performed from the vantage of the lower-cost seats in the more exclusive Theatres Royal. Yet when Mathews performed at the Surrey and Adelphi in 1823, it was for audiences that, while predominantly white, coexisted harmoniously with black neighbors and were roused by the tenets of reform and human rights that underlay the campaign for slave emancipation.

Just as Moncrieff's *Life in London* dramatized real-life Londoners, Charles Mathews based his characters and critique of slavery in *Trip to America* on real Americans he met while on tour. No script is extant for *Trip to America*; there may never have been a full one, as Mathews's performance was heavily improvised. Much of the entertainment's content can, however, be deduced from reviews, which provide detailed accounts of performances. Mathews's own commentary on its creation and content illuminates his intention to satirize American democracy and its inconsistencies, with particular regard to slavery. His published treatments of the most popular skits, his memoir (ghostwritten by his second wife), and the letters he wrote while traveling through America to his wife and his literary friend, James Smith, who later helped him prepare *Trip to America*, show his intentions.[16] Both the memoir and the letters are filled with Mathews's musings on American slavery, liberty, and quotidian life, as well as on how he intended to translate these impressions into performance.

Trip to America burlesqued events and people from the main stops of Mathews's American tour and included several impressions of black Americans, both slave and free. His tour took him through the Northern seaboard cities with sizeable free black populations: New York, Boston, Baltimore, and, via a steamboat manned by an Irish and African American crew, Philadelphia.[17] He embarked on his American odyssey to gather new source "material in America for a plentiful harvest" following the phenomenal success of his travelogue variety show *Trip to Paris*, the form of which he replicated in *Trip to America*.[18] Both were rather like a lecture tour, in which Mathews kept the stage bare but for an armchair and a lamp intended to suggest an evening "At Home with Charles Mathews," as the *Trips* were billed. Mathews was the sole performer, recounting his adventures through mimicry, anecdote, song, and dance and assuming a wide variety of characters, each with his own distinct dialect and costume.[19]

One common element, however, in *Trip to America* was Mathews's disparaging view of American democracy, as recorded in his letters to James Smith. He conceded that in the Northern cities the "upper orders of people . . . are well informed, hospitable, unaffected . . . [and do not] differ . . . from the polished people of the same rank in England," but he echoed Fanny Trollope in his indignation at what he perceived as the lack of deference among the white "lower sorts," which he believed resulted in "all the menial situations [being] filled by negroes, and Irish and Scotch."[20] "The servants, waiters, porters, etc. are nearly all 'niggars'; the hackney-coachmen nearly all Irish and Scotch," he complained, while the lower-class white "American is too proud and independent to accept a menial situation."[21] Mathews claimed that "liberty and independence" had produced only "one effect, which is, to render the rich and educated slaves to their inferiors; at least to their absurd notions" of social equality.[22] He concluded that "the [white American] lower orders . . . prevent a European from being comfortable, if he has not made up his mind very resolutely to look, laugh, and thoroughly despise. If this be the effect of a Republic form of government, give me a monarch even if he be a despot."[23]

Mathews had indeed "made up his mind . . . to look, laugh, and thoroughly despise" the white American "lower sorts," as well as to satirize the inconsistency of slavery with republican government. What made his ridicule especially notable was its strong element of smug British chauvinism. This nationalism was also reflected in his decidedly unrepublican discomfort with American democracy's loss, in his eyes, of customary deference among its "lower sorts." Mathews's critique of American slavery thus stemmed more from his contempt for Americans' "absurd notions" of social equality than from any principled aversion to slavery. His burlesque of slavery was part of a patriotic boast about British monarchal "liberty" in comparison to American republican "liberty." Nonetheless, he performed a rejection of slavery through his impersonation of Jonathan W. Doubikin, "a real Yankee," and his relationship to his "poor, runaway Negro," Agamemnon, a character Mathews portrayed comically but sympathetically.[24]

The inspiration for Jonathan and Agamemnon stemmed from real people Mathews met on his tour, reimagined to suit his satirical ends. He based Agamemnon on a free black he encountered in Philadelphia, "a very fat Negro, whom I met, driving a stage-coach, and urging his horse by different tunes on a fiddle, while he ingeniously fastened the reins around his neck." Mathews mod-

Figure 18. Mathews in America (1824). The print depicts the six ethnic "types" Mathews portrayed in his one-man show, *Trip to America. From left to right:* Col. Hiram Pegler, a Kentuckian peddler and accordion player; the French exile, Monsieur Capot; Agamemnon, an overweight and ragged black fiddler slave; his master, the Yankee Jonathan Doubikin in a long coat and brimmed hat, with rifle over his shoulder; the Pennsylvania Dutch Miss Mangelwürzel; and Mr. O'Sullivan, an Irish immigrant. Jonathan and Agamemnon were the centerpieces of Mathews's variety act and his critique of American democracy. Courtesy of The Library Company of Philadelphia

eled Jonathan, meanwhile, on a New England farmer he spied on his steamboat travels, costuming him in a large straw hat, sealskin waistcoat, and long, ankle-length brownish coat (fig. 18).[25] The character's name was clearly a pun on Americans' British heritage: Jonathan for John Bull, and Doubikin a pun on the fraternal British-American relationship: "do be kin."[26] Mathews poked fun at American speech and manners by perpetually spicing Jonathan's drawl with American idioms and colloquialisms, such as "I guess," "I reckon," "I calculate," and "pretty considerable."[27] But the country bumpkin, Jonathan, was no longer a New England farmer, nor was Agamemnon a Philadelphia coach driver. Instead, in his "monopologue" on daily life in Natchitoches, the oldest permanent settlement in the Louisiana Purchase territory where the Kentuckian Jonathan had supposedly moved with Agamemnon, Mathews transmogrified them into a slave master and his slave.[28] Mathews's tour was confined to the Northern seaboard cities and he had, therefore, been neither to the Louisiana territory nor to a plantation. The Natchitoches setting was pure invention and can only have been chosen to highlight his disdain for slavery.

That Jonathan and Agamemnon were two of only six "Yankee" characters in *Trip to America* makes clear the importance of Mathews's views of white slave-holders and enslaved blacks to his disparagement of American democracy.[29] A taste of how Mathews used these comic characters to pour scorn on American slavery and democratic liberty can be found in the published version of the Natchitoches "monopologue," an abbreviation of the lengthier performance piece. In one sequence, Jonathan relates a story about his Uncle Ben trying to sell him a slave:

> "Uncle Ben," says I, "I calculate you have a Nigger to sell?" "Yes, I have a Nigger, I guess. Will you buy the Nigger?" "Oh, yes! If he is a good Nigger, I will, I reckon; but this is a Land of liberty and freedom, and as every man has a right to buy a Nigger, what do you want for your Nigger?" "Why, as you say, Jonathan," says Uncle Ben, "this is a land of freedom and independence, and as every man has a right to sell his Niggers, I want sixty dollars and twenty-five cents."[30]

Mathews repeats "land of liberty and freedom" and "land of freedom and independence" to pointedly make fun of American democracy on the grounds that it was fundamentally undermined by slavery. And, in choosing to make Jonathan a slave owner and Agamemnon an escaped slave and set their narratives in Louisiana, Mathews aimed a conscious jibe at American slavery as inconsistent with the rights of "every man" in a republican "land of liberty and freedom." He must have expected the barb to have a supportive audience. He would certainly have been attuned to the political sympathies of his London audiences, as he had performed his *Trip to Paris* at the Surrey all through 1822 before embarking on his tour of America. Jonathan's anecdote about Uncle Ben's slave sale, along with other vignettes involving Jonathan and Agamemnon, embedded a patriotic critique of slavery into comic burlesque.

Trip to America was extremely popular, so much so that it drew the interest of reviewers who did not ordinarily write about shows at minor theaters like the Surrey. William Hazlitt, for instance, proclaimed Mathews to be a talented impersonator who had captured accurately "the loutish stare of rustic simplicity" and "the artful leer of vulgar cunning" in his characters of the lower sorts.[31] The reviewer for the *Literary Gazette* also stressed the comedic qualities of Mathews's performance, especially his Jonathan character's "Yankee" dialect: "The way in which the assent of 'O Yes,' and the dissent of 'O No' were given by genu-ine Yankees . . . and the being 'pretty particular considerable damned' over every-thing, never failed to excite . . . bursts of laughter."[32] Later, Mathews would take the slave-owning Yankee from this lighthearted farce and use him to offer a more biting critique of slavery and American democracy.

Yankee Jonathan and America's Great Experiment

Mathews's chauvinistic aversion to the United States was on even more blatant display in *Jonathan in England; or, Americans Abroad*. This performance also grew out of Mathews's American tour, but it enacted a far more caustic critique of the incongruity between American slavery and liberty. Mathews co-wrote *Jonathan in England* with Richard Brinsley Peake, and it debuted at the Surrey on September 2, 1824. The play reprised the characters of Jonathan and Agamemnon as the basis of the dialogue and some of the incidents. The presumption of both the farce and its antislavery commentary was to bring the bumbling Jonathan and his slave, Agamemnon, across the ocean and thereby contrast American slavery with British liberty. Jonathan and Agamemnon arrive in Liverpool, where Mr. Ledger, a merchant long acquainted with Jonathan's plantation-owning Uncle Ben, provides Jonathan with a letter of recommendation to Sir Leatherlip Grossfeeder, a councilman in London. But the night before Jonathan and Agamemnon set off for London, two postilions rob Jonathan, taking the introduction letter and leaving in its place one recommending them as stable boys. When the two arrive in London, Sir Leatherlip mistakes Jonathan for a servant and finds his pretensions to socialize with him an insolent breech of social hierarchy. Before the truth is finally discovered, Jonathan's mistaken identity makes for shenanigans and jokes about the American lack of class-based deference and manners.

Antislavery sentiment was, however, embedded in the plot, driven by the conceit that Jonathan was in Great Britain to write a book that he would publish in Philadelphia and New York upon his return. The intended travelogue was presented as a rebuttal of *Trip to America*, as Jonathan made clear: "I've done the Title page already—'Remarks on the state of the British Nation, by Jonathan W. Doubikin, United States.' I'll touch 'em up in an atarnal manner that's what I will . . . I'm pretty considerably darn'd mad about that Mathews, who I hear has taken me off at the playhouse, but I'll make the whole kingdom smart for it when my book is published."[33] Inherent in this fictive revenge was an ironic antislavery commentary. Mathews had toured America and brought home to Great Britain his satire of American slavery and liberty. By contrast, Jonathan brought American slavery—in the person of his slave, Agamemnon—with him to Great Britain and in so doing provided a favorable commentary on British liberty.

In Act I, scene 2, for example, Jonathan tries to sell Agamemnon to Tidy, a waiter at Mr. Ledger's Liverpool Hotel, in exchange for a horse. Jonathan informs Tidy, "Couldn't get any fool to buy him [Agamemnon] in America, so my Uncle Ben told me I'd better go try and sell him in England," but Tidy scoffs at Jonathan's ignorance of British liberty and law: "Sell him in England sir! Ha!" After Jonathan strikes Agamemnon and threatens to cane him, Ledger and Tiny threaten to throw Jonathan out of the hotel. Jonathan indignantly responds to their threat with a succinct comparison between British and American "liberty": "Do you call this a land of liberty where I cannot cane my own nigger without being ordered out of the house—do explain to me the principles of the British constitution!" The scene ends with Tidy expelling both master and slave and describing Jonathan as "quite a stranger to our customs." American slavery, for Peake and Mathews, had no place in the land of British liberty, not even in Liverpool, formerly Great Britain's largest slave-trading port.

In Act II, Jonathan arrives in London and again tries to sell Agamemnon, this time to the butler of Sir Leatherlip's household. The butler's huffy refusal and sympathy for Agamemnon underlined yet again the crudeness of the American "lower sorts" in comparison to the British servant class. Peake and Mathews also used the contrast between Jonathan and the butler to deride American racism. The butler still believes Jonathan to be a stablehand and so instructs him to take tea alongside Agamemnon with the household's servants, including Blanche, a "negro maid." Jonathan vehemently protests this interracial tea break: "Mr. Butler, I don't pretend to know much about the decorum of the British constitution, but there's one thing I don't approve in your arrangement and economy at this moment of consideration—keeping company with your niggers." The butler responds, "What does it matter if the face is black, so that the heart is in its right place." The scene reinforced the notion that Americans' "great experiment" in democratic "liberty" had birthed a society that not only lacked any sense of class manners but also was built on an objectionable race-based hierarchy.

The attack on American slavery culminates in a scene between Blanche and Agamemnon, in which Jonathan receives his comeuppance. Blanche befriends Agamemnon after giving him a halfpenny for singing a rendition of "Opossum up a Gum Tree," a song Mathews popularized in the 1830s that went on to become standard blackface minstrel fare. When Agamemnon explains to her that he is a slave, Blanche, in a reference to the Mansfield decision in the Somerset case, responds "My good man, dere be no slave in dis country—moment you put your foot on shore here, in England, you free!" Agamemnon initially does not believe her: "Free? Free? What is dat? We hear de name in America, but we don't know what it is." Mathews and Peake reiterated their sardonic commentary on the inconsistency of slavery with American democratic "freedom." The playwrights followed their taunt by having the American slave deliver a eulogy to the goddess of British liberty: in ecstasy over his unexpected and newfound freedom, Agamemnon cries out, "Oh nice country England . . . Rule Britannia!"

Mathews's sublimation of antislavery into the comic burlesque "Yankee" characters set a lasting precedent, but the initial response to *Jonathan in England* did not indicate the longevity the characters would acquire. The play proved far less popular at London's Surrey Theatre than the more good-natured burlesque of *Trip to America*. Mathews withdrew *Jonathan in England* shortly after its debut and did not perform it in London again. And in America, not surprisingly, his send-ups of American democracy earned the ire of Philadelphians, who, according to one critic, found *Trip to America* "stupid and tedious."[34] In 1834, Mathews found himself defending his work when performing in Philadelphia during his second tour of America. As theater manager Charles Durang explained, "Mathews . . . after eleven years' absence . . . appeared again in Philadelphia. On his second visit to our soil, he felt exceedingly anxious to remove a false impression, which the American public had received in consequence of his . . . satirical drawings of or peculiar notions and ideas upon our social system, as given in a piece or monologue, called his *Trip to America*. This he was determined to give on our boards, word for word, in order to refute the calumny, which he did most amply . . . He played his "men and manners' with his usual éclat for several evenings."[35] Irritation with Mathews had even provoked American stage star James Hackett to borrow the title and rework the piece as a satire of the British.[36] Hackett's 1831 rebuttal marked the emergence of a coterie of America thespian stars that included Hackett, Edwin Forrest, and Robert Montgomery Bird and was symptomatic of a turn toward the creation and celebration of a uniquely American theatrical idiom.

Although Mathews's impersonations were a plastic medium that could accommodate political satire, audiences appreciated them more when the political commentary was a function of the humor rather than becoming more pronounced than it. Londoners spurned the more acidic antislavery of *Jonathan in England*, while Philadelphians seemingly forgave Mathews his parody of American democracy and freedom in *Trip to America*. Mathews thus set a double precedent for the Atlantic performative lexicon of race and slavery. The enduringly popular Jonathan would become a form of theatrical shorthand for a slaveholding American, a character British playwrights used from then on as a mouthpiece for antislavery sentiments.[37] At the same time, Mathews's burlesque of American slavery and freedom, like his impersonation of a black Philadelphian Methodist preacher, helped popularize American-derived racist oral blackface in embodied performances on the London stage. The variety genre Mathews pioneered thus merged slavery and antislavery discourses and embedded them in printed and theatrical racial burlesque.

Transatlantic Radicalism and the Great Experiment

Printed and theatrical racial burlesque were not separate from political rhetoric, something that Fanny Wright's oratorical performances made evident. On July 4, 1829, Wright took the stage at the Walnut Theatre, one of several Philadelphia appearances she made on her North American speaking tour. Head uncovered and dressed simply in a white muslin gown, she made a passionate appeal for the United States to live up the promise of its Declaration of Independence by extending "universal suffrage to all of humankind." She was known to some as a popular travel writer, to others as the founder of an experimental community for freed blacks, and to still others as an infamous pariah who rudely breeched all ideals of feminine decency in her public and highly political performances. The thirty-four-year-old Wright, at five feet ten inches, had an imposing stage presence and commanded large audiences composed of the curious, the critical, fellow radicals, and many women.

On the surface, Wright's utopian oratory seems far removed from Mathews's racialized burlesque and the *Life in London* and *Life in Philadelphia* craze, yet she performed in exactly the same time period, on the same stages, and to the same radicalized and enthusiastic audiences. Antidemocratic travel writer Fanny Trollope, comic actor and upholder of British liberty Charles Mathews, and feminist and democrat Fanny Wright were all part of a discourse in which American slavery and democracy were integral to Atlantic visions of polity—a discourse that encompassed not only variety skits and political oratory but also travelogues and cartoons that focused on American slavery as the persistent indicator of the superior state of British liberty. Yet unlike Mathews in his variety shows or William Moncrieff in *Life in London*, Fanny Wright offered utopian political prescriptions for universal suffrage, women's rights, and the end of slavery.

The Scottish-born Wright was a friend of Fanny Trollope, and shared Trollope's and Mathews's curiosity about the "great experiment" of American democracy. But Wright did not see American democracy as a failure. Instead, she believed its only shortcoming was that it had not gone far enough. While both Wright and Trollope opposed slavery, Trollope had couched her antislavery arguments in a fundamental critique of America's republican political system, which, as she saw it, was corrupted by the hypocritical contradiction "Of whips and charters, manacles and rights / Of slaving blacks, and democratic whites."[38] For Wright, however, the solution was not to reject democracy but rather to radically reform

America in order to realize its founding promises of freedom and equality. After traveling in the United States, Trollope took her critique of American slavery and democracy back to London. Conversely, Wright brought her protosocialist and antislavery attitudes from England to America, performing staged lectures in theaters in New York, Baltimore, Boston, and Philadelphia.

As a playwright, Wright was at home in the theater and likely had connections with the managers, as her new play, *Altorf*, had just been successfully staged at the Park Theatre in New York.[39] More importantly, Wright would have known that the stage offered the best chance of reaching large cross-class audiences. In 1828 and 1829, she performed lectures at the Walnut and Arch Street theaters in Philadelphia, probably knowing that their audience base was predominantly of the lower sorts. While the New Theatre had earned its "Old Drury" moniker primarily for its star ensemble and the plays it imported from the patented London theaters, the Walnut had its roots in the circus and showed varied fare. The new Arch Street Theatre, where Wright spoke in 1829, was to become the city's major playhouse. Designed by John Haviland, a leading architect of his day, it seated two thousand, with six hundred of those seats in the plebeian-dominated pit. The theater also had a sizeable lower-priced gallery in addition to its three tiers of more expensive boxes.[40] Wright thus preached her utopian vision to a Philadelphia audience with a significant number of working people.

And she spoke in an atmosphere of heightened radicalism and ferment in the early Jackson years. Not only had Jackson's presidential campaign raised hopes for democratic reform, but there was also growing enthusiasm for new socialist ideas, in particular the communitarian vision of Robert Owen, founder of New Harmony, a model industrial community in Indiana intended to be free of the harsh working conditions and poverty associated with British industrialism. In 1824, Owen had come to Philadelphia, where he gave a series of speeches and met with leading reformers like Richard Rush (the son of abolitionist Benjamin Rush) and Mathew Carey. On this and subsequent visits in the late 1820s, Owen met with an enthusiastic reception. His ideas were indirectly highly influential on Philadelphia's working class through the work of English socialist economist John Gray, who favored remaking the American market economy into a small-artisan producer economy and redistributing wealth from the merchant distributors to the laboring "producers."[41]

Wright's democratic vision was also concordant with noted American utopian thinkers such as Ralph Waldo Emerson and Margaret Fuller. Dubbed Transcendentalists for their belief that truth existed intuitively beyond material existence, Emerson, Fuller, and their fellow travelers believed self-reflection and the inner divinity of each individual should manifest itself in social reform, particularly political rights for women and the abolition of slavery. In 1826, Emerson issued a plea for transnational antislavery action. "To stop the slave traffic," he implored, "the nations should league themselves in indissoluble bands, should link the thunderbolts of national power to demolish this debtor of all Justice human and divine."[42] Just a few years later, at the very same moment Clay was burlesquing black Philadelphians' democratic aspirations in his *Life in Philadelphia* cartoons, Fanny Wright crossed the Atlantic with Lafayette in 1824 in the hope of creating "indissoluble bands" of antislavery activity, and continued these efforts after permanently relocating to the United States.

Born in 1795, Wright, the daughter of an English gentry-class mother and Scottish father, was orphaned at an early age and sent to live with her great uncle, a professor of moral philosophy at Glasgow University.[43] In Glasgow, Wright was exposed to deistic precepts and Enlightenment philosophies of natural law and equality and became fascinated by the American Revolution, the outcome of which she likened in her autobiography to the suspense of a theatrical performance: "Life was full of promise; the world a theater . . . There existed a country consecrated to freedom, and in which man might wake to the full knowledge and full exercise of his powers. To see that country was now, at the age of sixteen [a] fixed but secret determination."[44] Wright realized her "secret determination" in 1818, when she and her sister made their first two-year trip to America, during which time she came to abhor slavery.

A utopian socialist, Wright's aversion to slavery was part of her larger vision of social change, and like Emerson and Fuller, she believed that thought must be translated into action. She championed liberalization of divorce laws, birth control, free state-run secular education, the political organization of laborers, equal rights for women, and an to end slavery. After her first trip to America, Wright published her *Views of Society and Manners in America* (1821), which was highly critical of slavery on the grounds that it contradicted American republican ideals. "The sight of slavery," Wright asserted, "is revolting everywhere, but to inhale the impure breath of its pestilence in the free winds of America is odious beyond all that imagination can conceive."[45] Widely read in Great Britain, France, and the United States, her travelogue earned her friendships with reformers on both sides of the ocean. After permanently settling in America in 1824 after her brief return to Great Britain, these associations nurtured her mission to be a social reformer, a mission readily on display in her *A Plan for the Gradual Abolition of Slavery in the United States without Danger of Loss to the Citizens of the South* (1825), in which she urged Congress to end slavery through purchase and compensation to slave owners. Wright rejected the ethos of immediate and uncompensated emancipation, which she believed would be "a pretext for the fomenting of disorder and the breeding of disunion."[46]

Along with Glasgow Enlightenment thought, the other major influence on Wright was Robert Owen, whom she met just as he was setting up New Harmony, which he envisioned as a secular communal town. After visiting New Harmony, Wright determined to apply Owen's principles to a project of slave emancipation. In 1826 she purchased slaves and 640 acres near Memphis, then emancipated the slaves and settled them on the land, which she named Nashoba.[47] Her aim, as her friend Trollope (who visited Wright at Nashoba) would later note, was "to shew that nature had made no difference between backs and whites, excepting in complexion; and this she expected to prove by giving an education perfectly equal to a class of white and black children. Could this fact be once established, she conceived that the Negro cause would stand on firmer ground than it had yet done, and the degraded rank which they have ever held amongst civilized nations would be proved to be a gross injustice."[48]

Following Owen, who condemned not only private property but also marriage, Wright intended Nashoba as a model of a radical brand of communitarian secularism that encompassed the possibility of extramarital sexual relations between black and white community members. She envisioned Nashoba as an "establishment where affection shall form the only marriage, kind feeling and kind action the only religion, respect for the feelings and liberties of others the only restraint, and union of interest the bond of peace and security."[49] But she executed her scheme poorly, and by 1828 Nashoba had failed due to disease, poor harvests, and financial loss. In 1829 Wright took the freed slaves from Nashoba to Haiti, and her community was no more.[50] After Nashoba's demise, she became co-editor with Owen of the *New Harmony Gazette*. She embarked on her career as a public lecturer when she gave the July Fourth Address at New Harmony Hall in 1828, and continued it the following year in Philadelphia.

In June 1829, Wright gave a rousing pro-democratic lecture titled "Of Existing Evils and Their Remedy" at Philadelphia's Arch Street Theatre. She spoke passionately of the threat of pauperism to social peace, calling for state education funded by graduated property taxes.[51] Trollope, who attended the lecture, reported that Wright "came on the stage surrounded by a body guard of Quaker ladies . . . She was, as she always is, startling in her theories, but powerfully eloquent, and, on the whole, was much applauded."[52] But Trollope also added that Wright's claims that "Washington was not a Christian" but a deist, and her celebration of Washington's supposed rejection of Christianity provoked "great emotion and some hissing." Trollope also observed that Wright was heckled as a female public speaker, but that the house was nonetheless packed and that there were more women than she had ever observed in an American theater audience.[53]

Wright's oratory at the Walnut Street Theatre on July 4 the following month was even more provocative. She used the "festival of freedom and anniversary of human independence" to hark back to the "glorious declaration—all men are free and equal" and to ask, "Free born citizens of independent republics . . . have ye fulfilled it?" She went on to point out all the ways in which the republic fell short of its founding principles and to call for "universal enfranchisement of humankind." Railing against the inequality she saw in America, she chastised her audience by asking, "Was it to crush down the sons and daughters of your country's industry under the accumulated and accumulating evils of neglect, poverty, vice, starvation, and disease, that your fathers bought your independence with their blood, and decreed, by this charter, your equality as citizens, and your liberty as men? . . . I would tell ye, I say, to let the same walls which echoed the first cry of 'liberty and Equality' give back, ere they totter to decay, the last hollow murmurs of a deceiving sound." She ended by reminding her audience that the Declaration of Independence made them "free to choose between liberty and slavery."[54]

Wright's July 4th speech proved so controversial that it was her last performance at the Walnut Street Theatre. When she came back to Philadelphia a few months later, the theater's stockholders defied the manager's booking and canceled her contract. When her backers then tried to rent Washington Hall, the wife of the proprietor was threatened with arrest and loss of patronage to her husband. Wright released Washington Hall from the agreement and announced she would speak at a given time near Military Hall, outside and for free. A huge crowd gathered to hear her speak briefly from her carriage to urge her supporters to fight for a hall of their own, then she departed the city.[55] Thus the city's reaction to Wright was split along class lines: she garnered enormous popular support from the audiences in the Walnut and Arch Street theaters that catered to the tastes of Jacksonian plebeians, while earning the ire of the elite, including the powerful theater stockholders.

Wright also provoked a mixed response because she flagrantly flouted gender strictures. As Fanny Trollope noted, "That a lady of fortune, family, and education . . . should present herself to the people in this capacity would naturally excite surprise anywhere . . . but in America, where women are guarded by a seven-fold shield of habitual insignificance, it has caused an effect which can scarcely be described."[56] Here, Trollope alluded to the expectations that American women in the 1820s be pious, virtuous wives and mothers whose realm of influence was domestic, and who were "shielded" "seven-fold" from the public sphere that was the prerogative of males. This model of femininity had its seeds in the post-revolutionary notion of expansion of female education grounded on the belief that "republican mothers" should be educated in order to instill public and civic virtue in their sons.

By the 1820s, however, ideals of femininity and masculinity had shifted to emphasize women's moral virtuousness and domestic skills. This shift was linked to the revivalism of the Second Great Awakening and the social ills the revivalists sought to address. Since the problems of poverty, violence, drinking, consumerism, and a decline in religiosity were associated with male behavior, women needed to be protected by staying in the domestic sphere. Women—especially the white, Northern "middling sorts"—played special roles in the reform efforts that grew out of revivalism such as the temperance movement and rehabilitation of "fallen women," activities that were viewed as an extension of female domestic virtue. Prescriptive sermons, pamphlets, and ladies magazines reinforced these new ideas of "true womanhood." As *Godey's Magazine* put it, "[A]ll True Women are urged in the strongest possible terms, to maintain their virtue, although men, being by nature more sensual than they, will try to assault it."[57] Philadelphian Thomas Branagan weighed in to assert that while men could not keep themselves from being sinful and sensual, women were stronger and purer and must not let men "take liberties" incompatible with their "delicacy."[58]

Fanny Wright's behavior contravened these emergent gender mores in the most extreme ways imaginable, from her speeches delivered to mixed male and female audiences to her repudiation of conventional Christianity, her rejection of marriage as tyranny, and her condoning of interracial sexual relations. Unsurprisingly, Wright was vilified in print and from the pulpit by revivalist luminaries like Lyman Beecher, who described her as "the female apostle of atheistic liberty" and vented his outrage that "her lectures were thronged, not only by men, but even by females," both the "low and vicious" and "females of education and refinement . . . of respectable standing in society . . . who advocated her sentiments."[59] Wright was not just bad in herself; she was a bad influence on female audience members. Her onstage and in-print performances, with their brazen upending of social mores, illustrate how the media of racial burlesque and radical oratory shared the same stages and grappled with the same issues of race and rights.[60]

Charles Mathews's *Comic Annual*, Emancipation, and the Great Experiment

Mathews, Wright's political opposite, also dispersed his ideas in multiple media: cartooning, theater, and politics. In the 1830s, against the backdrop of debates about the Parliamentary Reform and Emancipation Bills, Mathews, despite his earlier criticisms of American slavery, used the theatrical stage to inveigh against immediate emancipation in the British West Indies. In his 1831 *Comic Annual* variety show, in a story of a West Indian slave master who freed his slaves and then sent them to Philadelphia, he used London iterations of the *Life in Philadelphia* cartoons to reject a radical remaking of British "liberty," be it in the form of workers' suffrage at home or slaves' immediate freedom in the colonies, in favor of more moderate reforms that offered less of a threat to imperial and domestic order.[61] In so doing, Mathews issued a British moderate's contest of American polity and national identity: a rejection of democracy and affirmation of a reformist constitutional monarchy.

The *Comic Annual* was an extravaganza that Mathews had developed in collaboration with Richard Brinsley Peake. Every year since the mid-1820s, Mathews had performed a brand new *Comic Annual* of skits, burletta, and impressions of topical events and topics. He usually presented it in April to end the London theatrical season before taking off to tour the provincial theaters.[62] He also published an illustrated prose version of the *Comic Annual* show. His *New Comic Annual for 1831* included dialogues that incorporated Clay's captions verbatim and were illustrated by woodcuts of Londoners' versions of Clay's most popular *Life in Philadelphia* prints, including *The Cut Direct* (see fig. 13 on p. 136) and *Back to Back* (see fig. 14 on p. 138). Clay had engaged with Mathews's work in his theatrically oriented cartoons three years earlier. When James Hackett wrote and starred in *John Bull; or, Jonathan in England* (1828), a send-up of Mathews and Peake's *Jonathan in England*, Clay drew a lithograph of Hackett as the protagonist.[63] Now Mathews was using Clay's *Life in Philadelphia* cartoons as the basis for his own show.

The 1831 *Annual* was performed amid the raging debates surrounding the run-up to the Parliamentary Reform Bill of 1832 and Emancipation Act of 1833. The original objective of the Anti-Slavery Society, founded in 1823, had not been immediate emancipation. As Sir Thomas Fowell Buxton explained, the group's aim "was not the sudden emancipation of the Negro; but such preparatory steps, such measures of precaution, as by slow degrees, and in a course of years, first fitting and qualifying the slaves for freedom, shall gently conduct us to the annihilation of slavery."[64] But after government attempts to compel the planters to reform slavery failed, the Anti-Slavery Society began to abandon gradualism; by 1830 it was forthrightly committed to immediate emancipation.[65] "Towards the end of 1830," as the society's annual report for 1832 noted, "an unusual degree of excitement upon the question of Negro Slavery obviously pervaded the public mind" and convinced the abolitionists they had the public behind their cause.[66]

The "unusual degree of excitement" about slave emancipation was intertwined with popular enthusiasm for political reform and the passage of the Reform Bill in 1832. An itinerant abolitionist made this connection clear in his report to the London Anti-Slavery Society in 1831: "I was quite amazed to see the interest which our cause excites, seeing the intensity of feeling of the fate of the reform bill. Though under great temptation, I am strictly obedient to my instructions not to mingle [parliamentary reform] politics with my advocacy of Negro freedom, and yet I observe an ardour equal to political enthusiasm."[67] By 1832, however, the Anti-Slavery Society had replaced this earlier caution about associating the cause of emancipation with that of political reform with explicit instructions to exploit the linkage between emancipation and the general election. To this end, the *Anti-Slavery Reporter* warned members not to promise "suffrages to any candidate until they will support total emancipation."[68] When Mathews performed and published his *Life in Philadelphia* skits in 1831, he did so as the interlinked causes of emancipation and the proposed Reform Bill had gained momentum.

Mathews's live performance of the cartoon characters must be deduced primarily from the published *Comic Annual for 1831*, as no manuscript is extant and other evidence is scant. Clues, however, can be found in his wife's *Memoir of Charles Mathews*, in which she reproduced the playbill for the *Comic Annual of 1831* along with excerpts of critical commentary.[69] A playbill for the *Comic Review for 1830*, also reprinted in in the *Memoir*, also listed a sketch about West Indian slavery. That Mathews took on the topic in both 1830 and 1831 suggests that he was attuned to the emancipation debates and believed the question to be of interest to his audience at the Adelphi Theatre, of which he became a part owner in 1831. The playbill for the *Comic Annual for 1831* hints that he performed at least some of his adaptations of *Life in Philadelphia* characters in the final "novel entertainment," the dramatis personae for which listed "Mr. Capsicum, a Trinidad merchant," "Cleopatra, his Negro nurse," and "Mr. Caesar le Blond, a black Adonis."[70] Mr. Capsicum and Cleopatra may have been Mathews's creations, but Caesar was a recurring character in Clay's prints. Mathew's description of Caesar as "le Blond, a black Adonis," referenced the archetypal young man of beauty in Greek mythology, implying that the character was a hypersexed black fancy-man.

The printed version of *Comic Annual for 1831* provides more substantive documentation about the onstage narrative. The story was of a West Indies planter, Mr. Bacchus, who frees his slaves and sends them to New York and Philadelphia. He later checks up on them, because, as he explains, "I was curious to know, after the lapse of a few years, the result of my experiment."[71] He finds them engaged in all the frivolity and frippery of Clay's cartoons. In one vignette, for instance, Mr. Bacchus "met with Caesar . . . who was in company with Florinda, A Negress, both also covered in fashionable finery." As Mr. Bacchus looks on, Caesar the black Adonis preens for Florinda and asks her, "How you like de new fashion shirt, Miss Florinda," which was the dialogue of Clay's original print, *Back to Back* (see fig. 14 on p. 138). In a later scene Mr. Bacchus encounters the fashionably dressed Caesar, who had many times escaped a severe flogging for "malversation in the field," and observes him indulging in "pride" and "vices" by snubbing a shabbily dressed old friend as too far beneath him to associate with. The accompanying woodcut version of Clay's *A Dead Cut* showed the well-heeled couple crossing paths with the former acquaintance. Mathews copied Clay's captions for the characters' dialogue, as when the friend exclaims, "Lord a' marcy, why Caesar, is dis you?"[72] By using Clay's cartoons, Mathews suggested that freedom would be squandered on West Indian slaves, who would use it only to put on airs and indulge in ridiculous fashions.

Just as London cartoonists' renderings of *Life in Philadelphia* were more viciously racist than the originals, the *Comic Annual For 1831* was much more vituperative in tone than *Jonathan in England* or *Trip to America*, in which antislavery opinion was superseded by the humor of blackface burlesque. In the earlier efforts, Mathews's criticisms of slavery were firmly grounded in its incompatibility with American democratic "liberty," which formed the crux of a broader hostility toward, and critique of, the United States. In the early 1830s, by contrast, the focus was on the potential effects of emancipation on a slave in the British West Indies. At stake now was the question of how *British* (West Indian) slavery was to be reconciled with liberty in her colonies and at home.

The key to Mathews's seemingly changed views can be found in in a didactic dialogue on the meaning of liberty that began and ended the script for the *Life in Philadelphia* sketches. The dialogue takes place between Mr. Tomson, an abolitionist who in 1807 had "signed a petition to the Commons, to abolish the diabolical traffic in human beings," and Mr. Bacchus, the West Indies planter. Bacchus was, of course, the Roman god of wine and intoxication, and therefore associated with freedom through ecstasy and madness. These associations take an ironic turn when Mathews uses Mr. Bacchus to assert that men's popular passions or "liberty" must be contained by laws for the good of society. Intrinsic to the argument was a redefinition of liberty as a moral state of mind rather than a state of political or physical freedom: "Liberty," Bacchus declares, "dwells only in the mind, regulated by a just observance of the laws and circumstances that surround it." Therefore, "Liberty . . . may be as generally found with the Negroes in the plantations of our West India colonies, as amongst ourselves. Slavery may enchain the body, but cannot control the mind."

Sudden freedom is a threat, Bacchus argues, because it turns the social world upside down: "Let a man [undergo] a sudden turn of fortune . . . he will instantly load himself with the fetters of carriage, horses, and servants." Give sudden liberty to anyone and it would produce these results because "human nature is everywhere the same."[73] Here, Mathews and Peake seemed to issue an almost Hobbesian argument against both democratic reform and immediate emancipation. Bacchus asserts that his experiment demonstrated that giving liberty to "slaves" or "swine" is socially detrimental because simian-like barbarians must be gradually fitted for liberty: "This mock farce proved a perfect antidote to all my speculations of giving liberty to a slave; or, in other words, pearl to a swine,—a bust by Canova, to a Goth, an inkstand and snowy white paper to a monkey, a sharp-edged tool to a baby."[74] The equation of "liberty to a slave" with "pearl to a swine" also evoked Edmund Burke's dismissive conclusion that the lower sorts were "swinish multitudes" unqualified for full democratic "liberty." But Mathews gives Tomson the abolitionist the last word: "All this may be true, and more, but [it] is not our province to sit in judgment nor our duty to prosecute a whole race for the failings of a thousand; nay, were ninety and nine to misuses the precious gift of liberty, as instruments in the hand of heaven, we should do the deed of mercy."[75] The *Life in Philadelphia* sketches animated Bacchus's viewpoint rather than Tomson's, and their performative effect may have diluted the efficacy of Tomson's emancipationist appeal. Indeed, the dialectic of oppositional voices in the *Comic Annual for 1831* suggests that Mathews and Peake used the storyline to stake out claims for merely incremental political reforms and gradual abolition.

Thus Mathews's rejection of "sudden" democratic liberty was not necessarily a rejection of his earlier patriotic derision of American slavery and republicanism, nor of the moderate political reforms of the Reform Bill of 1832. Rather, his 1830s performances were in keeping with *Trip to America* and *Jonathan in England* because they fused racial burlesque to a reconstruction of British liberty that, while at heart conservative, nonetheless cannily played to his audience's reformist political sympathies. While Mathews clearly rejected the more radical democratic impulse and anger over the "great betrayal" of some of his working-class audience at the Surrey, he celebrated the moderate British political "liberty" of the recent parliamentary reforms. To be sure, Mathews benefited from these reforms; as part-proprietor of the Adelphi, he met the new property requirements for suffrage. When he testified in front of the House of Commons in 1832 for the Select Committee on Dramatic Literature for an investigation held to determine the efficacy of the theatrical licensing and censorship laws, he reported having purchased his share of the Adelphi for 10,000 pounds, which qualified him for the vote per the terms of the 1832 Reform Bill.[76]

In his later works, including the *Comic Annual for 1833*, Mathews showed more clear-cut support for the moderate Reform Bill. Perhaps he did so in recognition of the benefits he had personally accrued from it. But more likely he did so because its passage dampened the threat of a more radical political overhaul. A "comic song descriptive of the wonders of Reform" extolling the recent legislation elicited a chorus of "hear, hears" from the audience.[77] Mathews also performed a skit about the reform debates in the House of Commons, in which he "affect[ed] to consider his audience as members of another assembly . . . and took occasion to congratulate himself on the fact that . . . he sees very few on the 'opposition benches' [those opposed to reform], albeit there is a full muster of Pittites [a reference to the conservative Tories and their former prime minister, William Pitt]." The skit closed when Mathews announced "the ayes had it" and "the bill do pass." Mathews found a way to entertain the plebeian and lower-middling Adelphi audiences who were enthusiastic about political reform while at the same time repudiating democracy and nationalistically castigating the United States. His apparent shift in tone on black slavery from the 1820s suggests that his denigration of outright slave emancipation in the 1830s was based not only on racialist fears of black freedom but also on a more fundamental rejection of radical democratic "liberty" and the American republican version of it.

In his performances, Mathews helped develop an emergent British Atlantic popular culture in which ideas about the place of slavery and freedom in America's "great experiment" were pivotal. In the 1820s and early 1830s, British transatlantic travelers of all stripes—from the conservative Trollope to the moderate Mathews to the radical Wright—critiqued slavery's incongruity with American democracy to promote their larger visions of polity and, in so doing, helped establish an Atlantic discourse of slavery and freedom. But this developing Atlantic popular culture was not merely a product of British interlocutors and their responses to America's "great experiment." Wright's radicalism was shaped by Glasgow Enlightenment thought and socialist ideas bred in the British industrial context, ideas she then connected to her calls for universal suffrage and freedom.

Similarly, the most significant new genres and conventions for performing race, slavery, and black freedom—emblematized both by the urban picaresque of *Life in Philadelphia* and *Life in London* and Mathews'. proto-vaudeville variety shows— originated in the London print and burletta houses. But the maturation of this emerging lexicon relied on a free-flowing transatlantic circulation between print, cartoons, and theater and the sublimation of American burlesque of black freedom into British performances of race and critique of American slavery.

The British critique of American democracy and slavery were crucial to both the utopian discourse and racial burlesque that developed in tandem in the 1820s. The burlesque, the picaresque, and the "great experiment" of American democracy were fundamentally intertwined elements of the Atlantic lexicon of race, rights, and slavery. The transatlantic circulation of cartoons, theater, and politics increased after the War of 1812, in part because of the establishment of new theaters, the increased print industry, and developments in transportation in the United States, but also because war's end lent finality to the breach between Great Britain and the United States, which motivated numerous Britons to cross the ocean and investigate their estranged cousin, Jonathan. The interchange paved the way for Jim Crow, emancipationist appeals, and renewed revolutionary fervor on the Atlantic stages of the mid- to late 1830s. In the 1830s and 1840s, a wave of slave revolts in North America and the British West Indies, as well as revolutions in Europe, intensified the battle lines over slavery and stirred discontented industrial workers to clamor anew for political and economic reforms. In both London and Philadelphia, radicalized playwrights and writers resuscitated eighteenth-century revolutionary events and rhetoric to protest in one breath factory conditions, lack of plebeian suffrage, and the plight of chattel slaves in plays and lecture performances that, building as they did on the burlesque and picaresque genres, often featured blackface characters.

PART THREE

RADICAL ABOLITIONISM, REVOLT, AND REVOLUTION

Spartacus and the Blackface Minstrel

(1830s–1850s)

"We are not merely Britons, but cosmopolites. We go to the east and to the west, to the north and to the south, to seek for misery and to endeavour to relieve it."[1] So declared a delegate at the first ever World Anti-Slavery Convention, held in London in 1840. The spokesman's proud boast echoed Paine's 1776 poem extolling the Atlantic Goddess whose Temple of Liberty drew a "fraternity of brothers . . . unmindful of names of distinctions . . . from the east to the west" to found a republic on natural and equal rights to life and liberty, and to call for the spread of those rights throughout the Atlantic world.[2] Unlike Paine, the delegate was not advocating republican government. But he nonetheless evoked Paine's vision by making explicit both the transatlantic reach and cosmopolitan, utopian purpose of the convention, which was attended by prominent American and British abolitionist men. An apex of transatlantic antislavery cooperation, the World Anti-Slavery Convention aimed to bring together American and British abolitionists to work for the demise of slavery in North America, Brazil, Cuba, and throughout the Atlantic world.

But this moment of cosmopolitan antislavery activity was actually less harmonious than it seemed, as the discourse on race, slavery, and freedom in London and Philadelphia was rife with conflict, ambiguity, and seemingly contradictory impulses. For one, the transnational antislavery movement whose utopian goal was to reconstruct the entire Atlantic world into slave-free economies was birthed in the same decade in which scientific theories of polygenetic, biologically innate, separate races became widely accepted and were used to bolster arguments for the continuation of American slavery. Performers of the 1830s and 1840s, building on the racial burlesque that had matured in the 1820s, animated these ideas of biologically separate races with different origins in their caricatures of black slavery, most famously epitomized by T. Daddy Rice's impersonation of a Southern black slave, Jim Crow. Rice began performing this solo blackface minstrel act in 1829, and it was all the rage on the transatlantic stage in the 1830s and 1840s. Atlantic enthusiasm for Jim Crow spawned a plethora of "Ethiopian operas," brief supporting acts in larger variety shows. The synchronicity of cosmopolitan emancipation endeavors, on the one hand, and full-blown scientific racism embedded in mockery of black slavery, on the other, represented a dialogue between the burlesque and the utopian.

It was only one facet of the dialogue. The 1830s and 1840s witnessed severe economic distress, renewed revolution in Europe, and slave revolts in the United States and British Jamaica; the turbulence produced both a violent backlash against abolitionism and a utopian, racially inclusive discourse from radicals demanding freedom, economic justice, and political rights for a "universal brotherhood" of white "wage" slaves and black chattel slaves. The deteriorating economic conditions of industrial workers fostered the Chartist movement and demands for suffrage in London, as well as the first stirrings of organized labor in Philadelphia. In London, some Chartists were also abolitionists who called for industrial workers and African slaves to fight against oppression. In Philadelphia, by contrast, abolitionists and labor leaders were less likely to see shared interests between slaves and laborers because of the economic competition between the city's large free black population and poor whites. Nevertheless, a minority voice still articulated the utopian vision of "brotherhood" even as racial friction and violent anti-abolitionism escalated, culminating in the 1838 burning of the abolitionists' meeting place, Pennsylvania Hall.

The near-synchronous emergence of blackface minstrelsy and racially inclusive utopianism in both Great Britain and the United States merits transatlantic analysis, but most of the scholarship on minstrelsy examines it in only one national context. Scholarship since the 1990s has demonstrated that minstrelsy had a satirical force and function in American class as well as race relations.[3] Such explanations render the genre more ambiguous than the unmitigated racist subjugation proposed by earlier scholars.[4] Scholars of blackface minstrelsy in the British context, meanwhile, have explained its popularity in terms of the self-fashioning of the working-class in relation to imperialist expansion, and as a carnival-like inversion of Victorian ideals of moral rectitude, probity and reserve.[5] Some work since 2000 has treated minstrelsy as a transatlantic genre.[6] Most minstrelsy scholarship is, however, confined to *either* the British *or* the American context—some even interpreting the medium as quintessentially American.[7] But Jim Crow grew out of picaresque and burlesque conventions developed through transatlantic circulation in the 1810s and 1820s. Blackface minstrel variety acts (and their descendants, the main-act "tambo and bones" minstrel troupes) were popularized by English, Irish, and Scottish, as well as American, performers who drew on an array of transatlantic performance traditions. The genre had continuity with British and continental Harlequin and clowning traditions.[8] Blackface minstrelsy's musical sources drew in part on Scottish and Irish melodies.[9] And, strikingly, a high proportion of blackface performers were not Americans; instead they were British and Irish actors who perfected their craft first in Great Britain before migrating to the United States.[10]

Moreover, while offering sophisticated analyses, scholars have tended to focus on American or British minstrelsy as a problematic unto itself, bifurcated from the period's coexisting utopian impulse. Blackface minstrelsy, utopian radicalism, and antislavery were imbricated threads of a transatlantic discourse. Lawrence Levine pointed out in 1988 that performances of Shakespeare and blackface minstrel parodies of Shakespeare were part of the same cultural fabric.[11] Indeed, blackface minstrel lyrics regularly relied on burlesquing Shakespearian classics such as *Romeo and Juliet, Hamlet,* and *Macbeth.*[12] Rather than reifying a bifurcation between "high" and "low" culture, however, chapters 6 and 7 demonstrate a circulatory flow between utopian tracts, novels, lectures, and plays produced by radicals who consciously sought to challenge racial and social hierarchies yet used the language and conventions of blackface minstrelsy to do so.

Playwrights and performers helped craft this discursive co-emergence of racially inclusive universal brotherhood alongside full-blown racism, anti-abolitionism, and racial hostilities. Indeed, Jim Crow could take on antislavery valences, and utopian radicalism could be in tension and in sympathy with antislavery. In the 1830s, London and Philadelphian theaters were venues both for blackface minstrelsy and neoclassical performances of resistance to universal oppression such as adaptations of the story of Spartacus, which resonated with Polish and French uprisings as well as slave revolts in the United States and the Caribbean. When a wave of socialist uprisings swept Europe in 1848, thespians and activists in both Philadelphia and London resuscitated eighteenth-century revolutionary events and rhetoric to protest in one breath factory conditions, lack of plebeian suffrage, and the plight of chattel slaves.

But blackface minstrelsy and revolutionary utopianism did not merely take the stage side by side; rather, blackface minstrels became *part* of the performance of revolutionary utopianism. The blackface picaresque in theater and cartoons and the blackface vaudeville essayed by Charles Mathews in the 1820s and early 1830s had laid the groundwork for this union. In the 1830s, playwrights and performers like T. Daddy Rice built on this preexisting fusion to exploit the period's preoccupation with revolt and revolution. In the 1840s, radical-leaning playwrights and performers combined their retellings of the American, French, and Haitian Revolutions with blackface minstrelsy in their depiction of black revolutionary heroes. The myriad stage adaptations in both cities of Harriet Beecher Stowe's *Uncle Tom's Cabin*—which ranged from comedic minstrel versions to sentimental antislavery dramatizations—would consummate this marriage of antislavery and blackface burlesque and the fully transatlantic nature of the antislavery movement.

CHAPTER SIX

Spartacus, Jim Crow,
and the Black Jokes of Revolt

"Where will it end? Revolution on the back of Revolution for a century yet?"
Thomas Carlyle despaired in 1830 as the aftershocks of another revolution in
France reverberated throughout Europe.[1] His anguished question was not rhetorical. The July Revolution in France had brought down the would-be absolutist Bourbon monarchy of Charles X, who had been restored to the throne after
the fall of Napoleon in 1814, establishing a constitutional monarchy with Louis-
Phillipe, the Duc d'Orléans at its head. The revolution precipitated demonstrations and clashes between reformers and troops in several German states, including Brunswick, where insurgents overturned their authoritarian monarch for a
more liberal one. Secret societies and street demonstrations produced a series
of revolutionary regimes in southern Italy. That same year there was an unsuc-
cessful Polish insurgency against Russia, which had subjugated Poland since
the late eighteenth century, and whose annexation was formalized in 1814 by the
Congress of Vienna.[2] News of the revolution in Paris also reinvigorated radicals
in London and Philadelphia. In August 1831, Nat Turner led a bloody slave rebellion in the state of Virginia, and in December of the same year a massive slave
revolt broke out in British Jamaica.

This surge of political revolutions and slave revolts in the early 1830s galvanized a sequence of political changes in Great Britain that also reverberated in the
United States. The European political revolutions precipitated the Parliamentary
Reform Bill of 1832, which extended suffrage to the new middle class, while the
revolt in Jamaica helped push through the Emancipation Act of 1833 and set in
motion the liberation of the slaves in the British West Indies. The Emancipation
Act stimulated new abolitionist vigor in the United States where an ethos of immediate abolition and social reform crystallized under William Lloyd Garrison's
leadership and that of black leaders including Frederick Douglass, James Forten,
and Robert Purvis. Garrisonian abolitionism would, in time, shift the epicenter of
the American antislavery movement to Boston, but the changes in Great Britain
were more immediately felt in Philadelphia, where the British Emancipation Act

inspired abolitionists to found the first national American Anti-Slavery Society, modeled on the National Anti-Slavery Society of Great Britain.³ The American society held its first convention in Philadelphia in 1833 amid ever more desperately contested sectional battles over slavery and violent opposition to abolitionism aroused by Turner's 1831 insurrection.

In the mid- to late 1830s, playwrights and performers turned their preoccupations with the period's larger dramas of class conflict, slave revolt, and Atlantic revolution into stories that used slavery as a universal symbol of oppression and slave revolt and emancipation as emblems of universal liberation and democracy. To this end, Londoner Jacob Jones and Philadelphian Robert Montgomery Bird dramatized the story of Spartacus, leader of one of the greatest slave rebellions of antiquity, making the classical hero an exemplar of the universal struggle for freedom from oppression. Meanwhile, T. Daddy Rice, blackface minstrel performer and originator of Jim Crow, drew on beliefs in the innate inferiority of blacks for racial burlesque that rebutted Garrisonian abolitionism and advocated the South's proslavery agenda. As the specter of civil war began to haunt American politics, revolt and revolution composed a contrapuntal fugue between the blackface minstrel and Spartacus's utopian discourse of universal liberty.

Spartacus in the Atlantic Arena of Revolt

Jacob Jones and Robert Bird were just two of many playwrights who exploited the story of Spartacus's slave revolt as a topical message of universal resistance to slavery and oppression. Jones's *Spartacus; or, The Roman Gladiator* (1827) adapted the Spartacus story to arouse sympathy for the Poles' failed 1830 rebellion against Russian rule and to convey empathy for British radicals disappointed with the "great betrayal" of the 1832 Reform Bill, which had extended suffrage to the middle-class leaders of reform but not to the plebeians whose support had ensured its passage. Bird's *The Gladiator* (1831) was far more widely known than Jones's work and was one of the first American plays to be a hit in London. *The Gladiator* marks a significant turning point in transatlantic theatrical exchange, which hitherto had been dominated by British fare coming to the United States. Bird imbued the Spartacus story with antislavery sentiments that resonated in Philadelphia, since the antislavery discourse then prevalent drew on Greco-Roman precedent to indict slavery. His language of slavery, liberty, and rights also strongly appealed to Jacksonian Democratic workingmen, as he no doubt knew. What Bird did not expect, however, was that *The Gladiator* would debut (in New York in September 1831 and in Philadelphia in October 1831) immediately after

Nat Turner's slave revolt and that the play would thus have topical allusions to the "black Spartacus" of Virginia.

Turner's revolt struck fear into white Southerners and deeply shocked ardent opponents of slavery: both sides feared it presaged a massive uprising against slavery. Actress and Philadelphia resident Fanny Kemble prophesied, "Oh! What a breaking asunder of old manacles there will be . . . what a fearful rising of the black flood; what a sweeping away, as by a torrent, of oppressions and tyrannies, what a fierce and horrible retaliation and revenge for wrong so long endured, so wickedly inflicted."[4] She and others were reacting to the scale and bloodshed of the revolt, which Turner, following a prophetic vision, launched in Southampton County, Virginia. Turner and more than seventy followers, both slaves and free blacks, moved from plantation to plantation and killed fifty-seven white men, women, and children over a few days. Militias from surrounding counties joined in torturing and killing at least one hundred blacks for information and to suppress the revolt.[5] Forty rebels were tried on charges of insurrection, treason, and conspiracy, and eighteen were convicted and executed, including Turner, who was hung in November 1831. Before his hanging, Turner made a supposedly voluntary confession, which was published as *The Confessions of Nat Turner, the Leader of the Late Insurrection in Southampton, Va.* (1831) and sold as many as forty or fifty thousand copies.[6]

In the rebellion's aftermath, the sectional furor over slavery and abolition that dated back to the constitutional debates roared back to life.[7] Heated dissension shook the Virginia legislature and other Southern states in 1831. The revolt further inflamed the argument over African colonization. Supporters and members of the American Colonization Society in Virginia and other Southern states made demands in newspapers and petitions for state aid for the colonization of free blacks to Liberia.[8] Laws governing slave behavior were tightened, making it illegal, for example, to teach slaves, free blacks, or mulattoes to read or write and outlawing the circulation of incendiary materials.[9] As Kemble wrote, "To teach a slave to read or write is [now] to incur a penalty either of fine or imprisonment. They form a larger proportion of the [Southern] population by far; and so great is the dread of insurrection on the part of white inhabitants that they are kept in the most brutish ignorance . . . to insure their subjection."[10] From Kemble's perspective, and that of Northern abolitionists, such clampdowns and enforcing of "brutish ignorance" only confirmed the oppressiveness of the system Turner and his band had tried to overthrow.

For white Southerners, however, who assumed that the revolt had been incited by Northern agitators, these new laws were imperative. In particular, Southerners blamed David Walker for inspiring the revolt. In 1829, Walker, a free black who had settled in Boston, published a pamphlet, titled *Appeal in Four Articles, With a Preamble to the Colored Citizens of the World*, calling for the forceful overthrow of slavery. The *Appeal* castigated whites as an "unjust, avaricious and blood thirsty set of beings, always seeking after power and authority." Even before Turner's revolt, Walker's *Appeal* had been linked to the threat of slave insurrection because of his ominous predictions of black reprisals: "The whites want slaves, and want us for their slaves, but some of them will curse the day they ever saw us. As true as the sun ever shone in its meridian splendor, my Colour will root some of them out of the very face of the earth."[11]

Southerners also singled out for blame William Lloyd Garrison and the new, radical abolitionism for which he stood. Garrison's emergence as a leader had critical support from black Philadelphian abolitionists. In January 1831, wealthy black sailmaker James Forten underwrote the first editions of Garrison's antislavery newspaper, the *Liberator*. Forten, Robert Purvis, and other members of Philadelphia's black elite also promoted the paper and secured subscriptions for it.[12] In the first issue, Garrison called aggressively for immediate emancipation: "Urge me not to moderation . . . I will not equivocate . . . And I will be heard."[13] Although a pacifist committed to moral persuasion rather than armed overthrow of slavery, Garrison's demands for immediate emancipation marked the beginning of a reenergized American antislavery movement. He and his followers had no use for the legalistic gradualism that had characterized earlier abolitionism, like that of the Quaker-dominated Pennsylvania Abolition Society (PAS). Unlike the all-white PAS, some of whose members were active in the American Colonization Society, the new immediatism brought white and black abolitionists together and was against colonization.[14] Infused with Garrisonian fervor, the antislavery activity of the 1830s onward espoused political action rather than physical force to bring about immediate emancipation and a broader program of civic rights for blacks and women.[15]

Robert Bird had completed the script for *The Gladiator* in April 1831 and therefore did not write it with Turner's August rebellion in mind.[16] But on August 27, 1831, prior to the play's debut, Bird commented on the relationship of his play to Nat Turner's rebellion in his diary:

> Consider the freedom of an American author. If *The Gladiator* were produced in a slave state, the managers, players, and perhaps myself into the bargain, would be rewarded with the Penitentiary! Happy States! At this moment there are 6 or

800 armed negroes marching through Southampton County, Virginia, murdering, ravishing, and burning those whom the Grace of God has made their owners—70 killed, principally women and children. If they had but a Spartacus among them—to organize the half million of Virginia, the hundreds of thousands of the states, and lead them on in the Crusade of Massacre, what a blessed example might they not give to the world of the excellence of slavery! What a field of interest to playwriters of posterity.

Bird's exaggeration of the extent of the Virginia insurrection—"6 to 800 armed negroes"—and his apocalyptic description of slave revolt as a "Crusade of Massacre" culminated in his warning that the "violence" of slavery would "some day" be "repaid" by the violence and blood of a full-scale rebellion led by a black Spartacus, like Toussaint Louverture's leadership of the Haitian Revolution: "Some day we shall have it, and future generations will perhaps remember the horrors of Haiti as a farce compared with the tragedies of our own happy land! The *vis et amor sceleratus habendi* [force and the base love of gain] will be repaid, violence with violence, and avarice with blood. I had sooner live among bedbugs than negroes," Bird concluded, in a tone of racialist fear and disdain.[17]

Yet Bird did not altogether dissociate the black American rebels from the nobler virtues of the Thracian gladiators. Bird seemed to call for better leadership, "a Spartacus," to lead a large-scale revolt against oppression that would make a mockery of Southerners' claims of the benevolence of plantation slavery. He nonetheless infused this sentiment with horrified repugnance at the bloodshed, portraying the perpetrators as savage murderers, worse than bedbugs, parasitic insects that feast on human blood. Bird's diary entry reveals him to be profoundly conflicted about Turner's revolt and confused about its implications for slavery and the republic.

Bird remained deeply affected by Turner's revolt, as his 1836 novel, *Shepard Lee*, shows.[18] In *Shepard Lee*, the dissemination among semiliterate Southern plantation slaves of an abolitionist pamphlet, *An Address to the Owners of Slaves*, incites them to insurrection, with tragic consequences for slaves and master alike. Obviously, the story was inspired by David Walker's *Appeal* and its purported circulation among Southern slaves and influence on Turner and his rebels. Bird may also have either read or heard about the sensationally popular account of the uprising in *The Confessions of Nat Turner*, in which Turner—in the account mediated by his "confessor" and lawyer Edward Gray—revealed he had had a kind master.[19] In *Shepard Lee*, Bird depicted the rebel slaves as wrongly turning against a "good" master and his innocent family. Bird thus presented both slave revolt and polemical antislavery activity as threats to social and national harmony. Turner's revolt, a frightening preview for a large-scale "Crusade of Massacre," had clearly shaken Bird, who by 1836 was equivocating on slavery in a mixture of racist repugnance, tolerance for "good" masters, and fear of the threats posed by radical abolitionism and emancipation.

Bird's pre-Turner stance on slavery was, however, less conflicted, and evidence suggests that antislavery sympathy had contributed to his decision to retell the story of Spartacus's slave revolt.[20] His preliminary sketches for *The Gladiator* from the summer of 1831 convey that he intended the play as an antislavery statement. Of a scene in which Spartacus begs his new owner to also buy his wife and son, Bird noted that his intention was "an impassioned and strong dialogue about slavery."[21] He also suggested that if performed for Southern audiences, "the managers, actors, and author . . . would probably be rewarded with the penitentiary," a comment that suggests he saw his play as directly relevant to American debates about African slavery. Also, he wrote the play to debut in his home, Philadelphia, a city that, while divided on the question of slavery, had been a nexus of abolitionism ever since the American Revolution. Bird's choice of a classical analogy and hero was in keeping with prevailing antislavery discourse in Philadelphia.

Thespians, abolitionists, and polemicists had been invoking Spartacus ever since Abbé Raynal had predicted that a black "chief, sufficiently courageous . . . will shew himself . . . [to] lift the sacred standard of liberty [and] restore the rights of the human species," a prediction seemingly borne out by the massive slave revolt turned full-scale revolution led by Toussaint Louverture, which triggered a wave of slave insurrections throughout the Caribbean.[22] In 1800, in Richmond, Virginia, Gabriel, the slave of Thomas Henry Prosser, plotted an armed insurrection to overthrow Southern plantation slavery with the anticipated aid of the French.[23] Although the plot was betrayed and the rebellion forestalled, press coverage of the conspiracy convinced many that Gabriel's failed insurrection was a harbinger for the appearance in the United States of, as one Baltimore journalist put it, another "Spartacus or L'Ouverture" who would fulfill Raynal's prediction.[24] Similarly, Philadelphia newspaper coverage of the conspirators' trials repeatedly referred to both Gabriel and Toussaint as the "Black Spartacus."[25] Bird would have been aware of the linkage between Spartacus and the black slave revolts, and the common rhetorical use of Roman slave revolt as an antislavery analogy.

But even before Turner's revolt incited panic and political division, there were good reasons for Bird to opt for a neoclassical antislavery metaphor in preference to staging a direct critique of black American slavery. The heroics of a gladiator rebelling against a Roman empire in which slavery was a social but not a racial caste sidestepped an explicit invocation of America's racial slavery. The Roman story also bypassed the fraught question of whether to integrate freed black slaves into America or "repatriate" them to Africa. Jefferson had played on precisely this difference in *Notes on Virginia*: "Among the Romans emancipation required but one effort . . . The slave, when made free, might mix with, without staining the blood of his master. But with us a second [step] is necessary, unknown to history. When freed, he is to be removed beyond the reach of mixture."[26] Championing the cause of liberty in Ancient Rome allowed Bird to denounce slavery as a universal and abstract wrong, without bringing the touchy issue of colonization onto the stage. To be sure, if Bird *had* written an antislavery tragedy about Haiti or about a black American Spartacus, theater managers would have been unlikely to have allowed it to debut in October 1831, as Turner was still at large when *The Gladiator* opened in Philadelphia.

As a struggling American playwright writing for a theater still dominated by British theatrical fare, Bird would have been particularly loath to address sensitive political topics. His sarcastic opening remark in his diary entry on Turner's revolt, "Consider the freedom of an American author," alludes to this situation. When he wrote *The Gladiator*, he was little known as a playwright, having only recently abandoned a medical practice to become a writer of plays, novels, and verse and prose tales for the *Philadelphia Monthly Magazine*.[27] He wrote *The Gladiator* to be a commercially viable piece with a starring role for Edwin Forrest, a friend of his.[28] Edwin Forrest and *The Gladiator*'s shared success marked a turning point in the reception of American dramas on the early American stage. Forrest explicitly set out to promote "native" dramas, running national dramatic writing competitions with substantial cash prizes along with his commitment to produce and star in the winning entry.[29] Bird's *Pelopidas*, based on Plutarch's account of the revolt of the Greek Thebans against the Spartans, won first prize in 1830. In 1831, Forrest again awarded Bird first prize for *The Gladiator*, and playing Spartacus made Forrest an American celebrity.[30]

Forrest and Bird challenged the cultural authority of British-imported fare and actors.[31] As theater manager Charles Durang observed, *The Gladiator* set a remarkable precedent, given that "the sky of prejudice had not yet been cleared as against native pretension to dramatic literature."[32] William Wood, the manager of the Chestnut Street Theatre who produced *The Gladiator* and other American dramas, thought it was important to encourage American writers. "A Matter which I think that every American manager should aim at is the encouragement of *Native Genius*," he averred. He was aware, however, that though the Philadelphia, Boston, and New York theaters were well established and boasted celebrity American performers like Forrest, audiences and critics still disdained the works of "native" playwrights as second-rate.[33]

In Philadelphia, *The Gladiator* became a staple of the repertoire of all the the-aters—Northern Liberties, Arch Street, Walnut Street, and Chestnut Street—and was performed almost every season from its debut in 1831 until well into the mid-1850s. But Bird, Forrest, and the theater managers could not have predicted this successful outcome of a "native" drama. Producing American dramas was com-mercially risky. As one contemporary explained, "The writers of America have no encouragement whatever to venture upon the drama. The managers of the theaters . . . cannot afford, of course, to give an American author anything for a play when they can get a better one, by every arrival, *for nothing*—after it has been cast for the London stage and passed the ordeal."[34] Had Bird risked a direct ap-peal against black slavery for an audience predisposed to shun American-penned drama, it would have jeopardized the already slim chances that his play would be produced. His belief that the story of a black American Spartacus could only be staged by American "playwriters of posterity" was probably all too true.

Spartacus also afforded Bird a nonracialized vehicle through which to espouse the universal right to liberty for audiences whose taste was for blackface bur-lesque of slavery and freedom. The vaudeville and racial burlesque developed in the 1820s by Charles Mathews was dominant at the Arch Street and Walnut Street theaters, which critics had taken to calling minor. But in 1831, in an effort to compete, blackface burlesque variety shows were also staged even by the so-called Old Drury on Chestnut Street, where *The Gladiator* made its Philadelphia debut. The Old Drury season of 1830–31 featured not only dramas like *The Gladi-ator* but also blackface variety acts like that of William Kelly, whose song "Coal Black Rose" became a staple of minstrel performers. According to Durang, Kelly was one of the "first successful delineators of that species of negro . . . the Ethio-pian vocalist of this day should erect a memorial to Kelly."[35] James Hackett's "na-tional comedy in three acts," *The Travelers in America*, also came to the Chestnut in 1831, featuring characters inspired by Charles Mathews and Edward Clay, such as "Pompey, a dandy Negro of the comb and razor, leader of Broadway fashions in sabledom, played by Mr. McDougal."[36] Spartacus could be cheered on as a dramatic hero at a time when blackface slave protagonists were played for laughs.

Bird imbued *The Gladiator* with appeals to sentimental antislavery feelings. The five-act tragedy retold the story of Phasarius and Spartacus, two enslaved Thracian gladiators in Rome, 73 BC, who were assigned to fight each other to the death. In Act I, scene 1, Spartacus refuses to fight "in cold blood . . . for the diversion of Rome's rabble," even after being threatened with a whipping. He is adamant that he will not fight a fellow Thracian. But he agrees to do so after being promised his wife's and child's freedom by Bracchius, master of the gladiators. When Spartacus meets Phasarius in the arena, however, they throw down their arms after discovering they are brothers. Spartacus then organizes the gladiators in a revolt against Rome. A speech at the end of Act II, scene 3 presages Bird's description of a "Crusade of Massacre" as the bloody cost for slaves' right to liberty and "a blessed example" of the horrific consequences of American slavery's injustice. Spartacus incites his fellow gladiators to join his rebellion: "Ho, slaves, arise! It is your hour to kill! / Kill and spare not—for wrath and liberty! Freedom for bondmen—freedom and revenge."[37]

Despite the cries for "freedom and revenge," Bird's antislavery message was consonant with pre-Garrisonian abolitionist rhetoric. The scene in which Spartacus agrees to fight, in exchange for his wife and children's freedom, takes place in a slave market. Separation of families, itself, was a theme abolitionists frequently used to illustrate the evils of slavery. Repeated references throughout the play to the whippings and beatings of slaves echoed gradualist abolitionists' calls for the amelioration of the harsh conditions of plantation slavery. And toward the play's end, Bird evoked the laws against harboring Southern fugitive slaves, depicting fugitive Roman slaves being hunted down and killed. Spartacus's owner, Lentulus, after killing Spartacus's wife and children, unrepentantly declares, "I am not sorry; They were my slaves, punish'd as fugitives" (V.5). The play ends with the capture and killing of Spartacus, a hunted fugitive now "alone upon the flinty earth," by the slave-owning Crassus.

Bird's portrait of slavery in Rome was also a rebuttal of Southern arguments that used the precedent of Roman slavery to justify the American version. Nineteenth-century Southern propagandists, like Jefferson before them, evoked Roman legal theorists' sanctioning of slavery. Some even argued that Ancient Greece and Rome owed their success to the slave system.[38] Edmund Ruffin, for example, claimed, "Slavery has existed from as early time as historical records furnish," and "there was no country, in the most ancient time of its history, of which the people had made any considerable advances in industry or refinement, in which slavery had not been previously and long established."[39] Although Bird depicted his sympathetic hero as fighting for individual liberty rather than an end to slavery as an institution, he portrayed Roman slavery not only as unjust but also as symptomatic of the moral and economic decay that would bring down the empire. In Act I, scene 1, when Spartacus is asked by Bracchius what he thinks of Rome, he decries the "greatness [that] comes from the miseries of subjugated nations," and claims "there is not a palace upon these hills that cost not the lives of a thousand innocent men . . . its ingredients are blood and tears."

Bird used the character Crassus, the slave-trading praetor, to paint a picture of a decadent Rome dependent on slavery for its wealth and "palaces." First introduced in a scene in which the gladiators are plotting their revolt, Crassus is described as a "miserable rich man, the patrician monger that, by traffic in human flesh, has turned a patrimony of an hundred talents into an hundred thousand!" "Traffic in human flesh" was a clear echo of the language of Northern abolitionists, as was his reference to slave breeding. In another scene, Crassus threatens to whip an artificer for not paying the rent on one of his hired-out slaves: "Breed I then servants for the good of knaves? Find me the money, or I'll have thee whipped" (II.2).

Bird was not the only author at the time to reject Southern claims that Roman slavery was a legitimating precedent for American slavery. Several other works devoted to the topic of slavery in antiquity were published in the early 1830s. William Blair claimed that slavery had been "a main cause of the decay of the Roman Empire" in *An Inquiry into the State of Slavery amongst the Romans* (1833).[40] In 1834, in an article in the *North America Review*, George Bancroft claimed that Spartacus was "a man of genius and courage" and that "slavery made [Rome] a waste land."[41] By positing slavery as intrinsic to Rome's downfall, these works all spelled out clear analogies for the fate of the slaveholding American republic.

While Bird had intended *The Gladiator* to be "a strong and impassioned dialogue about slavery," whether or not Philadelphian audiences interpreted it an indictment of slavery is more ambiguous. In the 1840s Walt Whitman, who opposed slavery, claimed that the play was "full of Abolitionism" and "running o'er with sentiments of liberty." He pointed to the "eloquent disclaimers of the right of the Romans to hold human beings in bondage" and determined that "it is a play—this *Gladiator*, calculated to make the hearts of the masses swell responsibly to all those nobler manlier aspirations in behalf of moral freedom."[42] Responses to the play after it opened at New York's Park Theatre in September 1831, however, were nearly silent on the fraught question of slavery. A review in the *Evening Post* commented instead on the prologue lauding the Polish revolutionary uprising against Russia, which elicited "warm applause."[43] Whether or not the play was performed with this topical prologue in Philadelphia is not recorded. One of the few extant printed linkages between the play and antislavery was a poem, "The Crucifixion of Gladiators," published in *The Liberator* in October 1831, just prior to Turner's execution.[44] The poem referenced Bird's play and lamented the torture and execution of the Roman slaves in graphic images that evoked reports of Southern slaveholders inflicting recriminatory violence on their slaves in the wake of Turner's rebellion.

In Philadelphia, *The Gladiator* was an immediate success when it opened in October 1831. The play made actor Edwin Forrest a superstar and was performed over a thousand times during Bird's lifetime.[45] According to theater manager Charles Durang, its debut was "received with huzzas and thundering acclamations . . . I never saw in my experience any theatrical applause so wildly and impulsively given"[46] Durang attributed the audiences' approbation to *The Gladiator*'s "beautiful poetry," "valiant deeds," "tenderness and pathos," and Forrest's "splendid performance" as Spartacus. But he never mentioned slavery, only disparaging the "Roman barbarism [that] forced brother to murder brother."[47] A Philadelphia reviewer even suggested that the play was appealing precisely because it did *not* have topical allusions when he noted, "we are not disgusted by detecting the modern masquerading in an ancient garb."[48] Despite *The Liberator*'s fiery poem and Whitman's later interpretation, it is unclear whether audiences' enthusiasm for the play, which was performed in Philadelphia and other Northern cities to great acclaim throughout the 1830s and 1840s, was for its antislavery potential.[49]

Edwin Forrest's own politics, however, may have imbued *The Gladiator* with some "modern" signification as a critique of both "wage" and chattel slavery. The actor became closely linked with the role of Spartacus. As Wood noted in the mid-1840s, "a high estimate was placed upon Forrest's Spartacus, which at this day never fails to attract crowds at any theater."[50] And although Forrest was never actively involved in organized abolitionism, he was closely allied with the radical left-wing of the Democratic Party, in particular with the democratic egalitarian lobby, the Locofocos. Although primarily committed to emancipating Northern "wage slaves" by putting government and economy in the hands of the small producers, the movement's leaders were also opposed to slavery.[51]

Forrest was publicly associated with his close friend and Locofoco leader, William Leggett, so much so that Forrest's theatrical fans were referred to as "Loco Focos."[52] Leggett's championing of black liberty matched his advocacy of democratic egalitarianism for the Northern worker. He had publicly expressed outrage that following the Nat Turner revolt proslavery advocates were insisting that "slavery is not an evil, and that to indulge a hope that the poor bondman may be eventually enfranchised is no less heinous than to desire his immediate emancipation."[53] More radically, Leggett proposed that the federal government withhold constitutional recognition of slavery as a property right. The Constitution, he argued, "Nowhere give[s] any countenance to the idea that slaves are considered *property.*"[54] In his newspaper, the *Plaindealer*, he denounced slavery as a socioeconomic evil that "withers what it touches" and linked emancipation of the slaves to a larger vision of radical democratic transformation. Until the slaves were freed and their "enfranchised spirit" allowed "to roam on the illimitable plain of equal liberty," he proclaimed, America was failing to live up to its republican founding principles.[55] The Democratic Party eventually expelled Leggett, but the party's radicals still lionized him.[56] *The Gladiator's* popularity with plebeians in the gallery and pit may well have been boosted by Forrest's politics and his friendship with Leggett.[57]

Finally, the play's themes of slavery, tyranny, revolt, and freedom must surely have prompted some audience members to view Spartacus's struggle for liberty as analogous to the American Revolution. As Jeffrey Richards has posited, American audiences could easily have seen Rome as Britain and Spartacus as leader of the colonial slaves.[58] The trial of Gabriel, the "black Spartacus" of 1800, revealed that he had planned to march with his men under a banner proclaiming "liberty or death." Made famous by Patrick Henry, this rallying cry of 1776 actually derived from the last line of Joseph Addison's popular neoclassical tragedy *Cato.* When Cato, rebelling against Caesar's tyranny, sees that his defeat is sure, he commits suicide in preference to surrendering to imperial rule, proclaiming: "Chains or conquest, liberty or death" (II.2). The long-standing association between Addison's *Cato* and the American struggle for independence could have suggested a similar way to look at Bird's Roman revolt epic. And if audiences likened Spartacus's quest for liberty to the American Revolution, such an interpretation would similarly have impinged on debates about black liberty and slavery in America's republic.

Spartacus in London

In London, *The Gladiator* does not appear to have been seen as a critique of slavery. The play did not arrive in London until 1836, by which time British West Indian slavery was already in the process of being dismantled. Bird's drama therefore did not serve as a protest of slavery in the British empire in the manner it might have done a few years earlier. The play did, however, resonate with the political revolutions of 1830s Europe. And it helped foster a new transatlantic theatrical trend. To be sure, *The Gladiator* was the production that would open the London theater to American imports, despite a strong initial prejudice against Yankee actors and plays.

After its debut, American plays and actors began making a splash in the West End patented theaters. James Hackett, Junius and Edwin Booth, and James

O'Neill (father of the more famous Eugene) would soon follow in Forrest's foot-steps. But when Forrest and *The Gladiator* arrived in London, there was little expectation that the show would be a success. Alfred Bunn, the manager at the Drury Lane Theatre Royal, where the play opened on October 17, 1836, tried to avert prejudice against American actors and fare by redecorating the theater "in the most costly manner" to give a proper welcome to the "principal tragedian of the United States." And prior to the opening, Thomas Jones, Forrest's American negotiator with Bunn, planted a series of stories in London's *Morning Post* de-scribing the tragedian's triumphs in the Philadelphia and New York theaters.[59]

Yet Britons' resentment toward cousin Jonathan still lingered, at least on the dramatic front. London's preeminent actor, William Macready, called on Forrest before the play's opening out of a sense of professional obligation. Although he found his American colleague to have a "manly, mild and interesting demeanor" he disapproved in his diary of Forrest's acting as rough-edged and bombastic.[60] The two thespians would eventually develop a bitter enmity. British umbrage at American cultural incursions was on full display in reviews of *The Gladiator*. Both playwright and star received condescending scorn. Reviewers noted both the playwright's and actor's supposed lack of polish, a judgment that would be re-peatedly applied thereafter to castigate the American acting style as overly robust and rough hewn.[61] The *Times* noted, "Mr. Forrest made a powerful impression on the audience" and that the play had "some scenes of stirring interest," but went on to criticize the drama as "powerful rather than polished" and to claim the writing was "characterized by a rough, passionate strain in which gracefulness is sacrificed to force."[62] Charles Rice was far less equivocal. Forrest he deemed "second rate," calling his movement and vocal tactics "extremely awkward." "I never saw any man aspiring to the position of a first tragedian on a public stage possessed of so few capabilities for so arduous an undertaking," he declared. His judgment of *The Gladiator* was no kinder. He proclaimed it "one of the worst productions pretending to that title which has been brought forward at either of our metropolitan theaters for some years" and attacked its language as overly melodramatic, "full of sound and fury, signifying nothing."[63]

Despite the bad reviews, Bird's *The Gladiator* had topical resonance, evident in Rice's reference to "other productions pretending to that title." His allusion to other dramatic retellings of the Spartacus in the 1830s suggests that the epic struggle for freedom had contemporary relevance to London audiences and read-ers. Jacob Jones first wrote and published his tragedy *Spartacus; or, The Roman Gladiator* in 1827, with the intent of rousing support for Polish resistance to Rus-sian rule.[64] Although performed only at the Bath Theatre, two editions of the play were published in London. As Jones stated in the preface to the second edition, from 1837: "*Spartacus; or, The Roman Gladiator*, a Tragedy in five Acts, was written more than ten years since, and is now published . . . in consequence of The War of Spartacus having been just familiarized to the British public, through the representation, etc. of Dr. Bird's American Tragedy, *The Gladiator*." Jones also noted that the lyrics for his "Gladiator's Hymn" for the new edition had been "converted into a Lyric for the Polish Cause."[65]

Jones's purpose in publishing the second edition of *Spartacus* was probably not only to exploit the notoriety of *The Gladiator* but also to express sympathy for the 1830 rebellion in Poland. That year, as news of the July Revolution in France spread through Europe, Polish officers in the Tsar's army staged a coup intended to overthrow Russian rule. The insurrection gained momentum when the conspirators seized the army's arsenal and distributed thirty thousand rifles to the lower classes of Warsaw.[66] The armed insurgents then drove the Russian authorities out of the city and formed a government. After the urban revolutionaries failed to gain the support of the massive underclass of rural serfs—who were more interested in overthrowing the Polish landed nobility than the Russians—the Tsar's officers suppressed the insurgency and regained control.[67]

That Jones felt free to openly advocate the revolutionary Polish cause in 1837 can only have been due to the passage of the so-called Great Reform Bill in 1832, through which England arguably had staved off the revolutionary tumult that gripped much of Europe. Nevertheless, it was still bold of Jones to dedicate a play about revolt to the Polish revolutionary cause. His dedication to the second edition in particular suggests sympathy with radicals at home. It was in 1837 that radicals disappointed by the "great betrayal" of 1832 reorganized and forcefully articulated an agenda for further democratic reform. They drew up the "People's Charter," which demanded universal manhood suffrage, a ten-hour factory workday, and improved industrial conditions. These demands were the foundation of the Chartist movement. In the aftermath of slave revolt and political revolutions and amid near-revolutionary unrest, the transatlantic dramatizations in the late 1830s of Spartacus's doomed revolt reverberated with the still unresolved issues and mandates of the eighteenth-century revolutions: slavery, liberty, and democracy.

The "Black Jokes" of Revolt

Like the Spartacus story, new print adaptations of the *Life in Philadelphia* stories took on heated topical meanings in the wake of the Nat Turner slave revolt. When the London "black jokes" about emancipation and British democratic liberty—

theatrical and print adaptations of Edward Clay's 1828 *Life in Philadelphia* cartoon series—traveled back to Philadelphia in print form, they were retranslated as commentary on the seething sectional crisis of the early 1830s. Charles Mathews's *New Comic Annual for 1831* was republished in serial form, complete with London woodcuts of Clay's cartoons, in *Atkinson's Saturday Evening Post and Philadelphia Saturday News* in 1832.[68] The series responded to the anxiety caused by Turner's insurrection and conflict over the question of the Southern slave states' threat to "nullify" federal tariffs and revolt against the Union.

Atkinson's Saturday Evening Post began its publication of the *New Comic Annual* in January, just as free black Virginians were flooding into Philadelphia in the wake of the recriminatory aftermath of Turner's rebellion. Some whites feared the black migrants would disrupt the socio-racial order of Philadelphia. The Pennsylvania legislature even debated a bill to prohibit black migrants from entering the state and to repeal the fugitive slave laws of 1820 and 1826 that protected free blacks there from being kidnapped into Southern slavery.[69] In the January 21, 1832, issue of *Atkinson's Saturday Evening Post*, the editor (probably Samuel Coates Atkinson, the paper's proprietor) commented on the potential disruption of the new arrivals and noted with approval the discriminatory legislation under consideration:

> A communication in the daily papers of Thursday, in relation to the migration of a number of blacks from Southampton to this city, has created considerable anxiety. The writer asserts, on respectable authority, that within the last two months, about five hundred blacks have arrived here, direct from the seat of insurrection in Virginia. He thinks it probable that others are following, and about to follow, and that this influx of refuse population from the Southern states is alarming, and should be met by some effort on the part of our citizens to prevent danger, and secure domestic tranquility . . . Already our black population is troublesome, and the addition [of black migrants from the South] is well calculated to produce uneasiness. The matter is, we are informed, now before our state Legislature.[70]

That Atkinson chose to run the *Comic Annual* series lampooning Philadelphia's "troublesome" free black population just as the "alarming" influx of the "refuse population from the Southern states" endangered "domestic tranquility" was not coincidence. His alarmist commentary on the Southampton refugees appeared in the same issue as, and directly adjacent to, one of the earliest installments of Mathews's *Life in Philadelphia*.

Atkinson's publication of the *Comic Annual* series was also a response to the sectional nullification crisis, in which the issues of black slavery and freedom loomed large. The crisis began in 1828, after Congress passed protective tariffs on manufactured goods from New England and Middle Atlantic states. Southerners opposed the federal tariffs on economic and constitutional grounds and threatened to nullify them. Not only did the tariffs make it more expensive for Southerners to purchase manufactured goods from the North, but also Southerners feared the tariffs would result in a reduction in foreign trade that would impair the export of slave-grown cotton and tobacco. South Carolinians were especially averse to the tariffs, which they blamed for their state's depression. While Southerners' constitutional objections focused on states' rights, it was slavery that was at the heart of their contention; they feared federal economic intervention might eventually be used to legitimate intervention into slavery. And, of course, the newly militant Northern abolitionism and the reverberations of the Nat Turner insurrection further intensified sectional tensions.

It was not only black slavery but also black freedom that shaped the mounting conflict between North and South. Southerners defended their slave economy and simultaneously attacked the Northern manufacturing economies by drawing attention to the plight of the predominantly poor free black populations of Philadelphia and other Atlantic seaboard cities. In a heated congressional debate on nullification in 1830, South Carolinian senator Robert V. Hayne placed the defense of slavery and its expansion at the heart of his attack on the tariffs, arguing that free blacks in Northern cities lived far worse lives than southern slaves: "There does not exist on the face of the earth, a population so poor, so wretched, so vile, so loathsome, so utterly destitute of all the comforts, conveniences, and decencies of life, as the unfortunate blacks of Philadelphia, New York, and Boston . . . Liberty has been to them the greatest of calamities, the heaviest of curses."[71]

The nullification crisis raised the specter of civil war. After heated congressional debate, Andrew Jackson's administration attempted to find a middle way with the Tariff Act of 1832, which kept high protective duties on wool, woolens, iron, and hemp but lowered the rates on other goods. In response, South Carolina adopted an Ordinance of Nullification proclaiming the 1828 and 1832 tariffs null and void, raised funds for a volunteer army, and threatened forceful secession. Jackson countered by threatening armed suppression of the rebellion to preserve the Union. Henry Clay, the Whig senator from Kentucky, helped forge a compromise in 1833 that stipulated reductions in tariffs over a ten-year period. South Carolina repealed its nullification, and armed struggle between North and South was averted.

Atkinson's reprints of the *Comic Annual* were a satirical commentary on the nullification crisis and the threat of sectional revolt, as well as on the potentially disruptive effect of the Virginian immigrant blacks in Philadelphia. But at the same time, by lampooning Philadelphia's black elite, the prints also proved their existence, thereby rebutting Southern proslavery claims of the ubiquitously downtrodden condition of free Northern blacks. And Atkinson's small but significant changes to the sketches and captions demonstrate his intention to articulate a pro-Northern perspective on the sectional crisis. In the March 10, 1832, installment, for example, the narrator disparages the "follies of these poor ignorant blacks" and their propensities to violence and "inflammatory notions," which he pointedly concludes they had learned from "the example set by the white population." In the aftermath of the Turner revolt and the death of fifty-seven whites, suggesting that black violence imitated white was sectional provocation.

But the most striking of Atkinson's changes came in the installment of February 18, 1832, in which Atkinson reprinted *What de debil you hurrah for General Jackson for?* Clay's original illustration had scorned the hopes of free blacks that the radical democratic impulse of Jackson's Democratic Party would include them. The joke then hinged on the paradox of a Democratic Party that stood for the extension of democratic rights and liberties, yet was led by proslavery Southerners. Atkinson's new caption to the London woodcut version of the print—*What de debil you hurrah for Henry Clay for?*—completely altered the joke. Now the joke was the notion that free blacks would vote for Clay, whose efforts to avert a schism in the Union had quelled sectional conflicts over slavery. Atkinson's translation of London "black jokes" of slave emancipation in this print, as well as in his other reprints of Mathews's *Life in Philadelphia* woodcuts, thus not only articulated a Northern perspective on sectional conflict but also epitomized American whites' usage of the transatlantic blackface underdog to agitate for larger issues of suffrage and justice.

Jim Crow and Transatlantic Anti-Slavery

Even as sectional tensions over Nat Turner's revolt and nullification reached a fever pitch in the United States and as news of renewed European revolution and slave revolt in British Jamaica undergirded the swell of British support for parliamentary reform and slave emancipation, Thomas Dartmouth Rice—billed as T. Daddy Rice—was cavorting across the transatlantic stages as Jim Crow. His character, like the "black jokes" of revolt, was an avowedly political creature through which Rice delivered a steady stream of commentary on the politics of slavery and revolt to the same radicalized audiences who had cheered Spartacus. Jim Crow built on the blackface picaresque and burlesque created in the 1810s and 1820s, but the act was also a startlingly new phenomenon. For one, the figure so sensationally popularized minstrelsy that it moved from being a bit part in a variety show or an intermission interlude to become the main show. Also, Rice's Jim Crow, like Forrest's and Bird's Spartacus, reversed the pattern of London performers and fare migrating to American cities. For the first time, an American blackface act was wildly popular in London (and Great Britain). One British historian has suggested that "the influence from America," which Rice crystallized and focused, also "altered the tendency of English racial attitudes and beliefs" by inaugurating a new conception of the black individual as a comic black American slave.[72] Jim Crow launched main-act minstrelsy on both sides of the ocean, but with disparate meanings.

Rice's Jim Crow was not only transatlantic in popularity but also in genesis. His act was grounded in mimicry of American slaves that bore a clear lineage to Bobalition dialogues and Clay's cartoons lampooning free blacks, but it was also heavily indebted to earlier folkloric clowning conventions founded in British theatrical and circus traditions. The black-masked Harlequin, for instance, with his Calibanesque qualities, prefigured and even converged with the blackface minstrel.[73] The "Harlequin Negro" of James Powell's *Furibond; or, Harlequin Negro* had taken the stage as a grateful, supplicant African slave and as a lascivious, good-for-nothing "Buck" with carnal intentions toward the white Columbine: docility, laziness, and hypersexuality were also key traits of Jim Crow.

Jim Crow also had longstanding precedents in the British circus, which had popularized minstrel songs and dances. In London, this trend was epitomized by the blackface slaves in John Cartwright Cross's plays, first staged at the Royal Circus but later performed as afterpieces in the royally patented theaters. By the 1790s, these servile blackface circus clowns had been exported to Philadelphia, where they performed "negro melodies" and "Ethiopian dances" in the city's first circus, originally a riding school, established by John Bill Ricketts in 1792. By 1795 Ricketts had opened a new custom-built circus, the Art Pantheon and Amphitheatre, which regularly featured blackface importations from London, like the song of the "Poor Negro Boy" of 1797:

> Me be one poor slave, brought into Barbados
> Ven one pickaninny, such de cruel trade
> How me fetch and carry, now go here and dere
> Dey no let me rest, dey for black man no care
> Fol de rol, de rol.[74]

For audiences, there was no missing the allusion to Mungo, of Isaac Bickerstaffe's *The Padlock*, with his lament of "Mungo here, Mungo dere, Mungo everywhere."

Rice's blackface clown was a larger-than-life imitation of a shabby, Southern plantation slave that he based, according to most accounts, on an old and crippled stablehand who performed a shuffling, hopping sort of jig accompanied by a humorous song. Rice supposedly copied both the man's raggedy attire and his song and dance,[75] although other accounts have Rice taking his act from "a Pittsburg negro stevedore by the name of Jim Cuff."[76] Regardless of his original inspiration, however, his Jim Crow was a recognizable parody of a Southern slave. The centerpiece of the routine, originally developed as a "between-the-acts" number, was the "Jim Crow song" which Rice sang while dancing a jig. One of the earliest versions of the song introduced Jim Crow and his Kentucky origins in the first verse:

> Come listen all you galls and boys,
> I's jist from Tuckyhoe,
> I'm going to sing a little song,
> My name is Jim Crow.

Rice wrote and performed many different versions of the song verses, but the chorus always went, "For he wheel about, he jump about, he do just so / And every time he jump about, he Jump Jim Crow."

Rice's act bore debts both to Charles Mathews's variety burlesque and to the urban picaresque craze of the 1820s and early 1830s. One Jim Crow song was based on Clay's *A Dead Cut*, from *Life in Philadelphia*:

> I met a Philadelphia Niggar
> Dress'd up quite nice and clean
> But de way he 'bused de Yorkers
> I thought was berry mean.[77]

Whereas in Edward Clay's original cartoon, Caesar, the New York dandy snubs his old friend, whom his female companion refers to as "an imperdent nigger," in Rice's rendition the Philadelphian is the dandy and is "berry mean" to the New Yorker. By 1836, when Rice's act had become so popular that he began regularly performing Jim Crow in full-length burletta plays, farces, and even pantomimes, he incorporated stories and idioms from earlier racial burlesque. Rice wrote *Jim Crow in London* (1837), a farce capitalizing on the success of his Jim Crow skits and "operas," as a take-off of William Thomas Moncrieff's *Tom and Jerry*.[78] And in 1834, he performed as Jim Crow in a play titled *Life in Philadelphia*. Rice also penned, and appeared as Jim Crow in, *Virginia Mummy* (1835) and *Bone Squash Diavolo* (1836). The latter featured an all-blackface cast (except for one white character who was the Devil) and reconstructed *A Dead Cut* utilizing the dialogue and story Mathews had adapted for his *New Comic Annual of 1831.*[79]

Rice's send-up of a rural Southern slave marked a whole new chapter of transatlantic performance of race and slavery because he performed Jim Crow in reaction to radically new transatlantic political and intellectual realities. At this time, scientific theories of race as rigidly hierarchic and polygenetic—the idea that inferior Africans and superior Europeans descended from different species— were gaining widespread transatlantic acceptance. While earlier blackface performances, such as those in George Colman's *The Africans; or War, Love, and Duty,* had conveyed a racial taxonomy marked by skin complexion and physiognomy, these performances had portrayed these differences as based on geographical and cultural factors, rather than on separate species origins. T. Daddy Rice embraced polygenetic racist ideology and self-consciously sought to convey these beliefs in his Jim Crow persona.

Yet Rice's and the audiences' signification of the figure was more complex than mere racism. Rice was performing for radicalized plebeians on both sides of the ocean, and they could identify with, as well as ridicule, Jim Crow as an oppressed underdog. Jim Crow, as one scholar has succinctly put it, had "the allure of the low."[80] He was a very slippery character: Rice shifted his political commentary on slavery to suit different audiences, performing proslavery and anti-abolitionism in the South, playing on Northern opposition to nullification in Philadelphia, and courting British antislavery enthusiasm by expressing support for the British Emancipation Act when performing in London. Indeed, after Rice's return to the United States, one reviewer claimed his success as Jim Crow in Great Britain had made him "too anxious to mix *dignatum cum* 'darkey.'" Dignity and racial burlesque "won't mix," the critic claimed, "not even with *rice* as a basis."[81]

Jim Crow stormed the transatlantic stage just as the British Emancipation Act of 1833 galvanized the transnational antislavery movement and a nationally based American antislavery movement coalesced. The legislation was a lightning rod for transnational and interracial antislavery activism that was committed to immediate emancipation. Black Philadelphians celebrated that abolitionists had "removed from the British dominions the corroding stain of domestic slavery," as William Whipper opined in a December 1833 sermon at the African Presbyterian Church in Philadelphia.[82] Even prior to the act, Philadelphian abolitionists distributed a circular advocating the formation of an American antislavery society modeled on the British London-based Anti-Slavery Society: "In Great Britain, the efforts of benevolent individuals, associated in the form, and designated by the title of Anti-slavery Societies, have exerted so powerful an influence on the public mind, that the people of England appear almost unanimous in their demand for the abolition of slavery in the colonies."[83] In actuality, the British Emancipation Act of 1833 did not free any slaves, as it had been accomplished through a settlement whereby slave owners would be allowed to keep their slaves for an unpaid "apprenticeship" of twelve more years. Britons and Americans nonetheless touted the act as a huge success, and it led American abolitionists to found the first national American Anti-Slavery Society, as the appeal for the society's first meeting made clear.[84]

Spearheaded by William Lloyd Garrison, the American Anti-Slavery Society issued its mandate in a forceful Declaration of Sentiments that read, in part, "The slaves ought instantly to be set free, and brought under the protection of law" and "no compensation should be given to the planters emancipating their slave, because it would be a surrender of the great fundamental principle, that man cannot hold property in man." The declaration also spurned colonization schemes, proclaimed slavery to be unconstitutional, and called for "moral and political action" to end it.[85] The American Anti-Slavery Society also strove to involve Philadelphian black leaders like Whipper, James Forten, and Robert Purvis. While their role in decision-making may have been minimal, they nonetheless threw their support behind the society's goal of immediate emancipation through the tactic of moral "suasion."[86]

Precisely at this moment of cosmopolitan antislavery action, Rice essayed Jim Crow, who quickly became the most notorious burlesque of a rural Southern slave, taking his place alongside the "black jokesters" and urban dandy caricatures of free, Northern blacks. Like these blackface cousins, Jim Crow took on a variety of stances and meanings, a malleability facilitated by substituting song verses with widely changing narratives. Part of why Jim Crow's performance of Southern slavery was sensational was that both London and Philadelphia were vortexes of political pressure in the volatile 1830s. Philadelphia was racked by the mounting pressure of newly radical American abolitionism on sectional tempers already inflamed by the Turner revolt and the nullification crisis, and by the agitation of economically distressed radical plebeians. In London, post-emancipation British antislavery activists struggled to free the West Indian slaves from "apprenticeship" while Jim Crow's working-class audiences in the minor London theaters were torn between enthusiasm for British antislavery "liberty" and bitterness that democratic "liberty" had been denied them at home. By targeting the most vulnerable of all targets—the enslaved black—Jim Crow could safely advocate democratic liberty and rebellion for his plebeian audiences in London and Philadelphia.

Despite Rice's claims that his Jim Crow was an authentic "representation of the great body of our slaves" and that the "faithfulness" of his "delineation" was the key to his success,[87] his blackface impression delighted audiences precisely because it was not realistic: Jim Crow was a caricature. Just as his urban dandy alter ego was an overly stylish Lothario, Jim Crow was an exaggeratedly rustic, loping, yet hypersexed parody of a plantation slave. Bent on shirking work and having a good time, the perpetually single character was lecherous and had many illegitimate "pickanninies" for whom he took no responsibility. Jim Crow and his urban dandy cousin were "invented black folks" and, as such, could safely be objects of laughter.[88] When voiced by a buffoonlike plantation slave, Rice's commentary on acutely sensitive sectional conflicts were both funnier and more polemical.

When Rice introduced his Jim Crow act to Philadelphia at the Walnut Theatre in the summer season of 1832, it was an instant hit. He had already essayed the character in Kentucky sometime between 1828 and 1831, performing it to great acclaim throughout the South.[89] By the time of his Philadelphia debut, Rice's Jim Crow song and act were well developed, and audiences in Philadelphia (as well as New York, Washington, and Baltimore) awaited his show eagerly.[90] He did not disappoint, and was "received with wild enthusiasm, and nightly afterwards with shouts of applause," according to Charles Durang.[91] The following season Rice was booked at the Arch and Walnut Street theaters and, according to a playbill, again was "received with great applause."[92] The calamities of nullification and Turner's revolt featured prominently in his act that year. A Walnut Street Theatre playbill for March 1, 1833, announced that "Mr. Rice . . . will for the last time give in Lyric style, Jim's Fantastics, Ole Virginy Touches [and] Massa Clay's Bill," the last a direct reference to Henry Clay's compromise tariff.[93] And in one song lyric from 1833, the womanizing Jim proclaimed,

> I'm for union to a gal,
> An dis is a stubborn fact,
> But if I marry an don't like it,
> I'll nullify the act.[94]

Presumably part of what the predominantly white audience found humorous and what made the lyric facetiously pro-Union was the absurdity of hearing a blackface Southern slave character flippantly advocate the pro-South doctrine of nullification.

But other lyrics from 1832 and 1833 dealt with nullification far less frivolously, situating it in an alarming scene of looming civil war and slave revolt:

De great Nullification,
And fuss in de South,
Is now before Congress
To be tried by worth ob mouth.

. . . .

Should dey get to fighting,
Perhaps de blacks will rise,
For deir wish for freedom,
Is shining in their eyes.
And if de blacks should get free,
I guess dey'll see some bigger,
An I shall concider it,
A bold stroke for de niggar.
I'm for freedom
An for the Union altogether,
Aldough I'm a black man,
De white is call'd my broder.[95]

Here Jim Crow visualized a massive slave uprising erupting out of civil war be- tween the South and "the Union." Slave revolt was depicted as a "bold stroke" for black freedom, which Jim Crow declared himself to be for. Clearly opposed to nullification and adopting the position of a Jacksonian Union man, the lyric concluded on an even more radical note when Jim Crow asserted that "de white is call'd my broder."

Jim Crow's advocacy of a brotherhood of black slaves and white workers was arresting in its interracial implications, notwithstanding that it was performed as racial burlesque. This universalist appeal to black and white men to fight "for freedom" was addressed to working-class audience members who had been radi- calized from the late 1820s onward by protests of industrialization and its delete- rious effect on the small-producer artisan economy. In 1828, factory workers at Schuylkill had gone on strike, in the early 1830s Philadelphia's handloom weav- ers burned mills and broke machines, and growing numbers joined trade unions. By 1832 workingmen had thrown their support behind the Jacksonian platform of popular democracy.[96] Rice evidently knew exactly for whom he was performing and reflected their views in the topics he chose for his Philadelphia performances. Thus, one of his many songs from 1833 champions Jackson and spurns the Whig politics of Henry Clay, whom Jackson defeated in the presidential election of 1832:

> But Jackson he's de President,
> As ebry body knows;
> He always goes de hole Hog,
> And puts on de wee-toes [vetoes],
> Old Hick'ry, never mind de boys,
> But hold up your head,
> For people never turn to Clay,
> Till arter dey be dead.[97]

Similarly, one of Rice's recurring Philadelphia segments was "De Philidelphi Firemen against de world," which referenced the working-class volunteer fire companies; these companies functioned as hubs of working-class social and political solidarity.[98] When Jim Crow sang about fighting "for freedom," his audience would have identified with the song's appeal to the workers' struggle against "wage slavery" and political oppression.

But these same songs and skits were also a source of racialist mirth to his largely white audiences. When Jim Crow championed the fire companies there was a satirical and racist subtext, as the companies were exclusively white and had actively prevented African Americans from participating or forming their own fire company.[99] Similarly, when Rice performed skits on the "Benefit of Temperance Societies" and the subsequent "Reformation of Jim Crow," they played on racialist discourse about blacks' supposed inclination to drink heavily and their resulting unreadiness for freedom. In Philadelphian popular culture, this association had a long history, exemplified both by the African Tammany dialogues of the 1810s in which the blackface characters mimicked revolutionary-era civic rituals while drunk and in Edward Clay's cartoons. The abolitionist corollary was just as deep seated: following Philadelphia's 1780 gradual abolition bill, the all-white Pennsylvania Abolition Society implored emancipated blacks "to reflect it is by your good conduct alone, that you can refute the objections which have been made against you as rational and moral creatures" and offered free blacks rules of conduct that included churchgoing, temperance, and avoidance of "frolicking and amusements."[100] Rice invited his white working-class audiences to laugh at Jim Crow as the target of racial ridicule, even as he encouraged them to sympathize with Jim Crow as a surrogate underdog of economic and political oppression, like Forrest's Spartacus.

In this politically fraught moment of sectional and class conflict, the polysemous Jim Crow touched on conflicted radical impulses with his notion of brotherhood of white wage and black chattel slaves. While some Jacksonian Democrats —like the radical Leggett and some of his Locofoco followers—opposed slavery, others were vehemently opposed to abolitionism. And racial violence was on the rise. Escalating impoverishment of free blacks and concomitant deterioration of economic opportunities for Irish and other poor white laborers put free blacks and poor whites in direct economic competition for menial jobs. In 1832 this tension exploded into race riots in Southwark and Schuylkill.[101] And in 1834, just a year after Rice sang of slave revolt as a freedom struggle and of black and white brotherhood, violence again broke out between downtrodden working-class whites and blacks, a deadly riot in which two blacks died, and two black churches and thirty black homes were destroyed.[102] When Jim Crow performed the nullification crisis in Philadelphia in 1832 and 1833 and asked poor whites to align themselves with blacks, the caper embodied multivalent meanings: to cheer on Jim Crow was to identify with the blackened lumpenproletariat, yet the figure was also one of ridicule in the context of increasingly violent and even murderous race relations.

Jim Crow was no less a coded figure of contested meanings in his London performances, which were every bit as popular as in Philadelphia. Rice debuted the character to boisterous acclaim at the Surrey Theatre in London in 1836.[103] Shortly thereafter, however, he was hired away by the Adelphi to perform as Jim Crow in W. L. Rede's *Flight to America*. By this point, not only did Rice write his own Jim Crow plays to great acclaim but London playwrights were also writing full-length farces featuring Rice, among them *Jim Crow in His New Place*, *Otello the Moor of Bond Street*, and *Cowardy, Cowardy Custard; or, Harlequin Jim Crow and the Magic Mustard Pot*.[104] Many other Jim Crow plays would follow. Jim Crow became a ubiquitous blackface underdog in London popular culture; by the mid-nineteenth century he had become a stock figure in the Punch and Judy puppet shows, themselves adapted from the ribald Italian commedia dell'arte. In these shows, Punch regularly refers to Jim Crow as "nigger" and uses him as a punching bag, and the Jim Crow puppet responds by singing lyrics replete with what were by then well-known minstrel characters and artifacts, such as Sambo and his banjo: "Oh, lubly Rosa, Sambo come; Don't you hear the banjo?"[105]

When Rice performed Jim Crow for London's Adelphi and Surrey theaters, he tailored his politics to suit audiences accustomed to Mathews's brand of blackface burlesque, with its multifaceted dimensions of racialism in tandem with chauvinistic championing of British antislavery "liberty." Just a year after Rice debuted in London, the Adelphi temporarily merged with the Surrey, which brought the Adelphi's lower-middle class clerks together with the Surrey's rougher-hewn workers.[106] Rice, performing for audiences that included the plebeians disappointed by the "great betrayal" of the Reform Bill yet favorable toward antislavery activity, did not simply transport American race and class issues to the London stage. Instead, he adapted his blackface material to comment humorously but provocatively on British issues of slavery and democracy, his shifts in political discourse evident both in plays and song lyrics.

W. L. Rede's *Flight to America*, a play in which Jim Crow appeared as a fugitive slave from Kentucky working as a New York dockhand alongside other blackface porters and greeting British immigrants fresh off the boat, provides a good example of the British-inflected discourse on slavery. The farce incorporated American-derived racial burlesque, with Jim Crow at one point throwing a "Bobalition ball" for his fellow black dockworkers. The "ball" is foreshadowed by a Bobalition song performed by Jim Crow and the chorus:

> Strike de bango, dance and play
> Freedom reigns o'ver the plains
> Bobalition for de nigger
> Beat big drum—tambourine strum
> On dis happy day
> Fifth July.

Here, the British Rede, in incorrectly citing the fifth of July, seems to have been poking fun both at Americans' Fourth of July Independence Day celebrations and free Northern blacks' January 1st Freedom Day celebrations. Jim Crow then opens the ball with a speech to "celebrate dis de day of our Bobalition" (II.4).[107] But most of the commentary on slavery and liberty was a critique of the place of slavery in America's "great experiment" of democratic government, by now a well-worn phrase in British antislavery literature. The disembarking British immigrants engage in sarcastic commentary on slavery in the "land of liberty." Jim Crow then delivers an abolitionist speech and determines to flee to England to escape Southern fugitive hunters who have advertised in the newspaper for his capture, which Jim Crow indicts as "dis abuse ob de liberality of de press" (III.1).

A glance at the lyrics and song titles Rice brought to his London performances tells a similar tale. Many of the titles reference specifically British events, politics, and places, such as "Jim Crow's Description of the Lord Mayor's Show" and "Jim

Crow's Trip to Greenwich."[108] "Jim Crow's Trip to Greenwich" has the character traveling on a steamboat through America, France, Switzerland, Germany, and England, comparing each nation's cultural manners and politics of slavery along the way. When he embarks for England, emancipation and the Mansfield decision of 1772 that declared the air of Great Britain "too pure for slaves to breathe in" are obliquely referenced:

> Den I jump aboard de big ship
> And cum across the sea
> And landed in old England
> Where de nigger be free
> Wheel about etc.

But the reference becomes more direct as the song progresses. When Jim Crow shares a stage coach with a Frenchman, a "Yanky," an Irishman, and an Englishman, he explains:

> Dey gin to talk of pollytics
> And which country was de best
> And I gib'd my opinions dar
> Along with all the rest
> Wheel about etc.

And it is Jim Crow who had the final word on the debate:

> Now I says, look ere white folks
> De country for me
> Is de country what de people
> Habe make poor nigger free
> Wheel about etc.

That Jim Crow "jump[s] aboard de big ship and cum[s] across the sea" implies that he was a fugitive slave, not a trait Rice gave the character in his Philadelphian performances. On the surface, the song was thus a chauvinistic approbation of the Emancipation Act. His comic routine also sounded an ironic, caustic note to his politically agitated audiences about the state of British "pollytics" as "de best" for "poor nigger" in the West Indies, but not for unenfranchised plebeians in the metropole. The mercurial figure's meaning for London audiences was contradictory: both a champion and a critic of British liberty, he was an antislavery spokesman through a racial burlesque that disparaged blacks in the British West Indies, whose freedom the act had set in motion.

Rice's Jim Crow also spoke to growing white convictions of innate black in-feriority. His meteoric rise coincided with a growing transatlantic acceptance of phrenology, the idea that intelligence and moral capacity could be measured by skull size and shape. Phrenology had been promoted in the late 1820s by Phila-delphian Samuel Morton, who used skull size and shape to rank from bottom to top the Negroid, Native American, Asian, and Caucasian "races." In London in 1829, James Montgomery published *An Essay on the Phrenology of the Hindoos and Negroes*.[109] By the late 1830s, however, these ideas had become significantly more important. In 1839, Morton's *Crania Americana* was published and widely read and cited both in Philadelphia and London.[110] The following year French natural-ist Georges Cuvier's *La rège animal* [The Animal Kingdom] (first published in Paris in 1817, London in 1827, and New York in 1831) was republished in London. Cuvier posited Caucasian, Mongolian and Negro "races" identifiable by stable, unchanging physical traits and classified blacks as uncivilized and apelike: "[The negro's] colour is black, its hair crisped, the cranium compressed, and nose flat-tened. The projecting muzzle and thick lips evidently approximate it to the Apes: the hordes of which it is composed have always continued barbarous." Others had made similar assessments, but Cuvier's striking use of the neuter pronoun, "its" suggested that the "negro" was non-human.

Cuvier was not along in his inference. As phrenology gained wider traction there was also a marked shift toward polygenesis. Cuvier, a devout Christian, embraced scriptural accounts of creation and hence rejected polygenetic explana-tions of racial difference stemming from different species origins. Morton equiv-ocated on this question. But other racial theorists such as American Josiah Clark Nott, French Joseph-Arthur Comte de Gobineau, and British Robert Knox built on Morton's and Cuvier's work (and their suggestions that Africans were ape-like) to promote polygenetic explanations of white racial superiority and blacks' inferiority.[111]

Jim Crow arrived just as this shift in racial discourse was taking place and was part of the print, theater, and circus performances that popularly disseminated ideas of phrenology and polygenesis in the British Atlantic. Edward Clay had integrated skull size and shape into his *Life in Philadelphia* cartoons as early as 1828. In London, George Cruikshank had satirized the craniological theories of Franz Joseph Gall and Johann Caspar Spurzheim in his 1826 scrapbook, *Phre-nological Illustrations*.[112] Gall had developed "craniscopy," a method to determine personality traits and mental and moral faculties based on the shape of the skull, which his follower Spurzheim renamed "phrenology." Cruikshank's plates, di-vided between the categories of "Propensities, Sentiments, Knowing Faculties, and Reflecting Faculties," were a spoof of these theories and were not explicitly racial. But they were widely imitated by those who took racialized phrenology seriously. Philadelphian David Claypoole Johnston's *Phrenology Exemplified and Illustrated being* SCRAPS *for the year 1837*, for example, included apelike blackface characters.[113] That Jim Crow could animate scientific racist theories that placed blacks next to simians at the bottom of a hierarchical scale of humanity can be illustrated by one of his many incarnations, a circus act featuring a flag-bearing monkey called Jim Crow riding a pony in a circus ring for an excited white crowd. This act may have been the one advertised in the *Albany Microscope* for the circus of Gregory, Crane, Waring, Tufts and Co., which toured Philadelphia and other Northern cities with a "Traveling Menagerie . . . [of] Jim Crow and his pony, with a great variety of Monkies, Apes, etc."[114]

Moreover, Rice consciously sought to promote a Southern racist, proslavery ideology, suggesting that his provocative flirtation with radical political language in Philadelphia and his British tinged antislavery burlesque in London was a showman's savvy exploitation of his local audiences' political persuasions. He certainly played to his largely white audiences' prejudices. Racial prejudice and burlesque in North American cities in the 1830s and 1840s, as Eric Lott, Noel Ignatiev, and others have suggested, was an ingredient in the self-fashioning of the white laboring classes in an increasingly industrialized economy.[115] In Great Britain, meanwhile, imperialist expansion had helped foster a growing ethos of ethnocultural superiority, even among the working class.[116] This growing racism showed in the ludic spaces of the transatlantic theaters. In the London theaters, black Londoners could still share the cheaper seating areas with whites, but by the 1820s and 1830s, theaters in Philadelphia, Baltimore, New York, and Boston increasingly relegated black patrons to segregated sections of the inexpensive gallery (as did the Southern theaters in which Rice got his start).[117]

On some occasions Rice performed for these mixed-race yet segregated audiences his transparently Southern pro-slavery and racist politics. On December 1837, for example, a theatrical critic for *The Colored American* was in the audience for a Jim Crow performance in Baltimore. Rice prefaced his clowning routine with a speech arguing that the inferiority of the African race made them uniquely suited for slavery, which incensed the presumably African American critic, who included the speech along with descriptions of the audience's enthusiastic responses. According to the reviewer, Rice had claimed,

> Before I went to England, the British people . . . were under the impression that
> negroes were naturally equal to the whites, and their degraded condition was con-

sequent entirely upon our "institutions"; but I effectually proved that negroes are essentially an inferior species of the human family, and they ought to remain slaves. (Some murmurs of disapprobation from the boxes, which was quickly put down by the plaudits of the pit.) You will never again hear of an abolitionist crossing the Atlantic to interfere in our affairs. (Tremendous applause.) I have studied the negro character upon the southern plantations. The British people acknowledged that I was a fair representative of the great body of our slaves, and [actor] Charles Kemble attested the faithfulness of my delineations. (Three Cheers.) It will ever be a source of pride to me that, in my humble line, I have been of such signal service to my country.[118]

The critic was so outraged by Rice's speech and the audience's enthusiasm for Jim Crow that, at least momentarily, he lost faith in the transatlantic antislavery movement. In his bitter commentary, he denounced Rice's racial ridicule as well as the theaters that hosted it:

There ought to be but one sentiment concerning those theaters, where plays are presented which hold up to ridicule the foibles or peculiarities of an already too much oppressed people, and but one feeling of disgust towards these actors who represent such characters, in their most ridiculous light, and pretend that they are the characteristics of the whole people. I have been led to those remarks by reading [a] speech from the *Baltimore Sun* of that most contemptible of all Buffoons, Thomas D. Rice, alias "Jim Crow," who has completely put down abolitionism in England and silenced the Thompsons, Buxtons, and O'Connells, so much so that not an abolitionist will ever again "cross the Atlantic."[119]

It was not only Rice's "ridicule" of "an already oppressed people" that dismayed the critic but also his phenomenal transatlantic success. Rice had just returned to the United States to perform in Baltimore, Boston, and Philadelphia after a smash hit tour of Great Britain. His proud boast about ridding America of the interference of British abolitionists and protecting the Southern plantocracy made it clear for posterity the insidiously powerful way that blackface minstrelsy intervened in debates about slavery and emancipation within a transatlantic context.

By the late 1830s, debates over ideologies of biological race, by both foes and defenders of slavery, were clearly no longer confined to the literate intelligentsia but had become part of popular public discourse. Although the reviewer was mistaken to believe Rice's minstrelsy would dampen transnational antislavery work, his unease about deepening racism and anti-abolitionism at all levels of American society was nonetheless well founded. Even at the first convention of the

American Anti-Slavery Society, in Philadelphia in December 1833, delegates were verbally assaulted as they walked to the meeting. Animus against the antislavery movement and blacks flared again in August 1834 with a full-scale race riot. [120] Several hundred white men attacked a building that housed a carousel popular with both blacks and whites. As the *Philadelphia Gazette* reported, "At one time . . . four or five hundred persons were engaged in the conflict, [armed] with clubs, brickbats, paving stones."[121] The rioters then swarmed into Moyamensing, an extremely poor neighborhood with many black residents, and began vandalizing and looting churches and residences. Two more nights of rioting left one black man dead and several injured, and a church and several houses demolished.

The following year, angry white militants threw abolitionist literature into the Delaware River, an event that drew large crowds who cheered on what one witness described as the "enraged mob." In 1838, several thousand whites, with city officials looking on, burned to the ground the newly erected Pennsylvania Hall, which abolitionists had built as their meeting place.[122] Overall, between 1829 and 1842 Philadelphia experienced six race riots.[123] Black Philadelphians responded to these events with renewed abolitionist vigor, yet their leaders shared the *Colored American* critic's fears that white hostility would derail their cause. James Forten feared anti-abolitionist pressure would put down all discussion of the question and that "Parents would again be torn from their children,"[124] while Robert Purvis despaired of "the wantonness, brutality and murderous spirit of the Actors, in the late riots [and] the Apathy and inhumanity of the Whole [white] community in regard to the matter." He bitterly concluded that "Press, Church, Magistrates, Clergymen and Devils are against us."[125]

The *Colored American*'s review shows how Jim Crow could wear different faces to appeal to different audiences. At a time when racist proslavery and anti-abolition sentiments were escalating in America, Rice adapted his act to play to the crowd. The artisan audiences of the Adelphi Theatre in London had applauded British "liberty" and antislavery sentiment, even as their disappointment over the "great betrayal" of reform simmered and the Chartist movement burgeoned. By contrast, in Philadelphia and other northern seaboard cities Jim Crow, while remaining an underdog spokesman for radical democratic cries for liberty from oppression, also symbolized growing white racial hostility and anti-abolitionism. Like the "black jokes" of emancipation and revolt, Jim Crow presumed a range of polemics about race, slavery, and democracy; the blackface Southern fugitive slave character had, simultaneously, a range of ambiguous and contested meanings.

The blackface minstrel used the same language of democratic rights and liberty British and American playwrights had adapted to reanimate the neoclassical Spartacus. Both performed for plebeian audiences the same questions of revolt and freedom that preoccupied them. In London, Forrest debuted as Spartacus and Rice introduced Britons to Jim Crow in the Surrey Theatre during the same season.[126] In the 1830s, the revolutions and revolts, the stirrings of emancipation, and cosmopolitan antislavery agitation brought dramatic changes to the Anglo-American Atlantic. The blackface minstrel, on the one hand, and Spartacus's message of a universal brotherhood struggling against oppression, on the other, were two symbiotic halves of the discursive negotiations of Atlantic slavery, liberty, and democracy. In the 1840s and 1850s, these issues would be reinterpreted with the impetus of socialist revolutions that swept Europe in 1848 and the escalation of bitter sectional crisis in the United States.

CHAPTER SEVEN

Revolutionary Brotherhood
Black Spartacus, Black Hercules, and the Wage Slave

In the tumultuous 1840s and 1850s, the antislavery and democratic forces first unleashed in the Atlantic world by the American, French, and Haitian revolutions of the late eighteenth century were further inflamed by radical agitation and sociopolitical unrest. Labor conflicts and economic hardship convulsed London and Philadelphia during these years. Philadelphian white plebeians organized into labor unions and vented their distress into ever-intensifying anti-abolitionist sentiment and violence against the free blacks with whom they competed for jobs. London plebeians continued to channel their discontent into the Chartist movement, which demanded universal suffrage and factory reforms. In 1848, the unrest of the "hungry forties" culminated in a wave of pan-European socialist revolutions that reverberated in near-revolutionary tremors in the urban centers of Great Britain and the United States.

Stirred by resurgent revolutionary zeal, radicals in London and Philadelphia resuscitated the rhetoric of the eighteenth-century revolutions to demand fulfillment of their democratic promises for plebeians and slaves. Debates about slavery escalated into transatlantic ferocity with the passage of the United States' Fugitive Slave Bill in 1850, which mandated the return of escaped slaves to their owners, regardless of where they were captured. The bill enraged American abolitionists and reignited many Britons' antislavery passions. As these events combined to inflame debates about slavery, liberty, and rights, figurative blacks became the symbolic embodiment of the crises of industrialization, poverty, and labor unrest.[1] Writers, playwrights, and politicians analogized and contrasted the rights of industrial "wage slaves" and African chattel slaves. Scholars have tended to emphasize the way prominent nineteenth-century Britons and Americans argued that white "wage slaves" of the factories were far worse off than either the freed former slaves in the British West Indies or the still-enslaved African Americans in the southern United States.[2] Those promoting this argument were typically hostile to transatlantic antislavery efforts, which they saw as directing philanthropy away from impoverished industrial workers and needed factory reform.

The analogy between wage slaves and chattel slaves, however, could go both ways, as some radical labor leaders, writers, and playwrights in both cities used it to plead for a "universal brotherhood" of industrial workers and enslaved blacks. These radicals, echoing Thomas Paine's 1775 call for a "fraternity of brothers . . . unmindful of distinction" to found an egalitarian republic whose "Temple was Liberty," called on industrial wage slaves, feudal serfs, and African chattel slaves to rise up together in a movement that would be simultaneously antifeudal, anticapitalist, and antislavery.[3] Radical-leaning writers and playwrights in London and Philadelphia argued for this universal brotherhood by retelling stories of the eighteenth-century revolutions to emphasize what they failed to accomplish and demand the revolutionary promise of the "inalienable right" to liberty for the poor and the enslaved.

London playwright George Dibdin Pitt and Philadelphian novelist, playwright, lecturer, and labor activist George Lippard were among those who interlinked the causes of white industrial workers and enslaved blacks in imaginative performances of the eighteenth-century revolutions. Pitt's drama *Toussaint L'Ouverture; or, The Black Spartacus* (1846), held up its title character as a universalist icon of resistance. And between 1846 and 1848, Lippard performed and published *Washington and His Generals; or, Legends of the Revolution*, his fictionalized lectures on the American Revolution. The lectures, like his novel, *Blanche at Brandywine*, which was dramatized at Charles Willson Peale's Philadelphia Museum in 1847, valorized blacks as revolutionary heroes of a class-based struggle against oppression. While Pitt and Lippard incorporated minstrel-like traits into their blackface revolutionary heroes, they used them to call for radical and racially inclusive social and economic regeneration instead of exploiting them for racial ridicule.

The Black Spartacus: Universalist Hero of Revolutionary Brotherhood

George Dibdin Pitt brought together the causes of the urban poor and the enslaved black in *Toussaint L'Ouverture; or, the Black Spartacus*, which debuted against the backdrop of Chartist agitation for universal male suffrage and renewed antislavery efforts to dismantle slavery in the Americas. Pitt, in-house playwright for the Britannia Theatre in the impoverished East End neighborhood of Hoxton, was a frequent ventriloquist for the urban poor through his politicized dramas, which included *The White Slave; or, Murder and Misery* (1845), *Terry Tyrone* (1846)—about the United Irishmen's revolt of 1798—and *Revolution in Paris* (1848). The intense class conflict of this era, coupled with economic and political turbulence, fostered a sense of class cohesion that superseded white London-ers' racial prejudices and xenophobia. By the mid-nineteenth century, London's black population was so small it posed no direct threat to the economic interests of the white poor.[4] As in the first two decades of the nineteenth century, black Londoners continued to be relatively well integrated into the working class in the 1840s.[5] Nineteenth-century contemporaries confirm the prevalence of inter-racial relations and sociability among the poor. The London City Mission, for example, reported, "It would surprise many people to see how extensively these dark classes are tincturing the colour of the race of children in the lowest haunts of this locality: and many of the young fallen females have a visible infusion of Asiatic and African blood in their veins. They form a peculiar class, but mingle freely with the others."[6]

The Black Spartacus, which debuted at the Britannia Theatre in June 1846 for radicalized plebeian audiences, resonated both with antislavery and working-class political discourse. The black Jacobins' revolution of almost a half-century earlier remained relevant to antislavery debates; it also evoked the specter of class-based revolt. Even the outspokenly racist Thomas Carlyle made these link-ages explicit in his 1840 essay on Chartism: "Society, it is understood, does not in any age, prevent a man from being what he *can be*. A sooty African can become a Toussaint L'Ouverture."[7] Carlyle in no way in sympathized with the democratic rhetoric of rights on which the Chartist movement was founded, much less with a Jacobin-inspired revolt. On the contrary, he was arguing for a restoration of au-thoritarian, feudal order. Nonetheless, by alluding to black revolutionary leaders while commenting on the Chartist movement's potential, he rhetorically linked the rights of black slaves and of white urban workers.

The Black Spartacus has largely escaped scholarly analysis, but it merits atten-tion because it was arguably the first English-language play to directly dramatize the Haitian Revolution, and it did so at a moment of great political unrest.[8] Many historical accounts of the Haitian Revolution had been written by the mid-1840s, and the life of Toussaint Louverture had been the source of prolific literary cre-ativity. But Pitt's was the first serious theatrical treatment. Although French abo-litionist Alphonse de Lamartine's *Toussaint L'Ouverture, poëme dramatique en cinq actes* was written about the same time as *The Black Spartacus*, it was not staged until 1850.

By 1846, the Emancipation Act of 1833 had freed the British West Indian slaves, but Britons maintained a keen awareness both of slavery in the United States, Brazil, and Cuba and of the impact of emancipation in the British West Indies. In 1839 British abolitionists had formed the British and Foreign Anti-

Slavery Society (BFASS), which had an international mandate and aimed to end American slavery. Shortly thereafter, the first World Anti-Slavery Convention met in London, in 1840, with key American abolitionists in attendance. And in 1846 William Lloyd Garrison and Frederick Douglass traveled all over Great Britain on lecture tours railing against North and South American slavery.[9] Their tours were part of an expanding transatlantic exchange of British and American abolitionists, but Douglass's tour took him abroad just as the publication of his autobiography put him at jeopardy of being reenslaved in the United States. Douglass, who became famous in Great Britain and controversially purchased his freedom with donated funds, drew renewed public scrutiny to the problem of American slavery.[10]

But the British debate about slavery in the Americas was also linked to the passing of the Sugar Duties Act in 1846. The Emancipation Act of 1833 had been accomplished through a settlement whereby slave owners would be compensated and allowed to keep their slaves for an unpaid so-called apprenticeship of twelve years. When the plantation owners began moving to ensure the continued dependency of ex-slaves beyond the twelve-year tenure, abolitionists pushed for an immediate end to the sham of apprenticeship. In 1838, a new agreement was reached whereby, in exchange for ending apprenticeship, the plantation owners would gain a preferential sugar tariff to enable them to compete with Cuba and Brazil, which still used slave labor. So when the act repealed the tariff protection on sugar in the British colonies, plantation owners were furious. Many abolitionists also opposed removal of protective tariffs. They feared the new free trade policy would strengthen the institution of slavery by redirecting trade toward cheaper—slave-produced—sugar from the Americas. As one antislavery sympathizer warned in *The Spectator*, "Free trade in sugar must . . . act as an encouragement of the slave-trade—there is no doubt of it."[11] *The Anti-Slavery Reporter* echoed this foreboding and decried the Sugar Duties Act as supporting the entry of "blood-stained sugars of Brazil and Cuba."[12]

The question of slavery also converged with contestation over suffrage and industrial workers in the metropole. In 1846, the goals of the Chartists—a ten-hour work day and universal male suffrage—had still not been met. Parliament that year debated a factory bill proposing a ten-hour workday but left it unresolved and postponed action to 1847.[13] Some Chartists' radical rhetoric was predicated on a belief in the rights of white "wage slaves" and their brotherhood with feudal serfs and black chattel slaves. A pamphlet written in 1845 argued for "the universal brotherhood of man [to fight for the rights of] our *brethren* in perpetual bondage . . . condemned to be mere human property, the millions mere toiling serfs yet starving while they toil, and *our brethren* by whose skill and labour our cities have been raised."[14] Workers were prominent in the Anti-Slavery League founded in 1846 under the presidency of London Chartist George Thompson. Other reformers, like the London Unitarian minister Henry Solly, were also both Chartist and abolitionist leaders.[15] From his pulpit, Solly attacked industrial "wage slavery" and American chattel slavery in the same breath. Both, he thundered, were "the miserable victims of oppression, whether of a white skin or a dark, whether pining under tyranny in the old world or the new."[16]

Pitt and his working-class audience were familiar with these debates. Just the year before, he had written and staged at the Britannia Theatre a gothic crime melodrama titled *The White Slave; or, Murder and Misery*, which, like many of his plays, had a bleak view of urban industrial society.[17] In it, poverty-stricken George March is condemned for murder on circumstantial evidence but reprieved at the last minute. The play exposes the inequities of the judicial and penal system and their biases against the working class. As house playwright at the lowly Britannia, Pitt himself was poor, churning out plays prolifically but making little from their sales.[18] Despite his relation by marriage to the well-established sons of Charles Dibdin, who had so famously essayed the perennially popular blackface slave character, Mungo, in Isaac Bickerstaffe's *The Padlock*, he lived among the working-class in Shoreditch, an area dominated by mill-weavers.[19] In 1855, at the age of fifty-six, he died destitute and addicted to laudanum, which he supposedly used to soothe the pain from the unnamed disease that had cost him his employment at the Britannia.

Like Pitt, most Britannia employees lived in or near Hoxton, and the theater had strong ties to the local community, serving as a site for local political meetings, wakes, and inquests.[20] It staged benefit performances to raise money for political clubs, such as the performance of two plays in November 1841 to raise money for the Friends of Unity,[21] an offshoot of the National Union of the Working Classes, which was formed in 1831 with the goal of agitating for universal suffrage.[22] By the 1840s, the National Union and Friends of Unity were linked with the Chartists National Association.[23] The Britannia's audience was large, numbering roughly one thousand a night.[24] The audience included, at least once, Charles Dickens, who reported that Hoxton locals who frequented the theater were "mechanics, dock labourers, costermongers, petty tradesmen, small clerks, milliners, staymakers, shoe-binders, slop-workers, poor workers in a hundred highways, and by-ways."[25]

When *The Black Spartacus* debuted in 1846, these Hoxton laborers were especially penniless and politicized. During Pitt's tenure at the Britannia, Hoxton was in a state of social upheaval. By the mid-nineteenth century, the family-owned mills that had thrived in seventeenth- and eighteenth-century Spitalfields and Shoreditch were struggling due to the introduction of factory production and new manufacturing techniques. An increase in Far Eastern trade had also contributed to a drastic decline in the weaving trade and related crafts—including the manufacture of furniture—that had hitherto been Hoxton's economic lifeblood. Of the employed Hoxtonites who came to see Pitt's plays, many toiled in large-scale manufacturers and suffered the crowding, harsh work conditions, and poverty of industrialization.[26] In the "hungry 40s," even those East End workers not directly involved in Chartism were intensely aware of Chartist demands for universal male suffrage and factory reform. On the evidence of a ballad written to be sung at the annual dinner of the local Hackney Debating Society in 1842, East Enders understood the revolutionary heritage of this radical discourse on rights. The ballad offered this quick recap of the year's debate topics: "We've dwelt on the 'Corn Law,' on 'Trade' and 'Finance' / We've discussed 'Revolutions in England' and 'Revolutions in France.' "[27] London's urban poor clearly saw economic fairness and the rhetoric of rights, first unleashed in the eighteenth century, as intertwined.

Some evidence intimates that the proprietor of the Britannia, Sam Lane, was active in Chartism. Documents pertaining to Lane's troubles with the Lord Chamberlain's office in the early 1840s suggest Lane's Chartist sympathies. Prior to the Licensing Act of 1843, only the West End theaters with a royal patent were officially permitted to perform narrative drama, while all other venues—so-called illegitimate theaters like the Britannia—were restricted to music and dance. In practice, proprietors of nonlicensed theaters often flagrantly ignored this law. After taking the Britannia over in 1840, Sam Lane regularly produced dramas there. In the face of Chartist agitation, however, the censors at the Lord Chamberlain's office sought increased control over performances at the illegitimate theaters and became intolerant of licensing violations. Actors caught performing narrative dramas at the minor theatres were arrested and imprisoned. In 1839, for example, "Edward Richards, John Welsly, Ann Ramsay and Ellen Brown, performers at a Penny Theatre in the Mint, Southwark, [were] charged with playing the 'regular drama' in an unlicensed theatre," *The Chartist* reported.[28]

This increasingly draconian oversight made the Britannia the target of repeated police raids. In 1841 the Lord Chamberlain revoked Lane's music and dance license on the basis of police reports complaining that the theater was "attended by the lowest class—prostitutes and thieves," and its entertainment was "calculated to corrupt the morals in that thickly populated neighborhood."[29]

According to Lane's biographer, marchers in a Chartist demonstration—egged on by Lane—demanded reinstatement of his license, carrying banners bearing slogans such as "Workers want Theatres" and "Freedom for the People's Amusements."[30] This political tenor is also evident in playbills. On some, Lane advertised the Britannia under the heading "The People's Theatre;" on others, "UNITY brotherhood," perhaps a reference to the Chartist-affiliated Friends of Unity.[31]

The Black Spartacus, a story of democratic revolution by an underclass of forced labor, took the stage in this populist milieu. Pitt's play, billed as "a military drama in two acts," is largely faithful to the events and personalities of the Haitian Revolution.[32] Perhaps the immediate inspiration was Frederick Douglass's highly visible 1846 tour of England, during which he had drawn frequent comparisons to Toussaint Louverture.[33] Indeed, Pitt may have sought to exploit the linkage because black antislavery speakers provided a form of popular entertainment for British audiences.[34] Pitt's play also coincided with and mirrored the narrative of Harriet Martineau's enormously popular novel about Toussaint Louverture, *The Hour and the Man*, published in 1840. Like Martineau, Pitt depicted Toussaint as a sentimental hero of royal African parentage but also as a quintessentially Western hero shaped by French revolutionary principles. And in both accounts, Toussaint initially wanted nothing to do with the rebellion until French treachery prompted him to take on the revolution's leadership.

Marcus Rainsford's sympathetic portrayal of the Haitian Revolution was, however, most likely Pitt's main source. The title page of *The Black Spartacus* simply states, "Taken from the historical account of Hayti," an attribution closely resembling the title of Marcus Rainsford's *An Historical Account of the Black Empire of Haiti* (1805), one of the first positive accounts of the Haitian Revolution. Pitt also quotes verbatim from Rainsford when he describes Toussaint as "the Spartacus, foretold by Raynal, whose destiny it was to avenge the wrongs of his race."[35] Moreover, Pitt's crude hand-drawn sketch of Toussaint (fig. 19) bears a remarkable similarity to Marcus Rainsford's iconic portrait (fig. 20). In both, Toussaint is in uniform and wields a sword in his right hand. In Rainsford's image, Toussaint holds a map of Haiti in his left hand, while in Pitt's sketch his empty left hand forcefully points to unseen action, suggesting his military authority. Pitt's handwritten description of Toussaint's "blue and red" uniform also suggests that in his play the character was dressed in the colors of the French Revolution—evoking republican principles rather than the supposed bloodthirst of vengeful slaves, which was in keeping with Rainsford's depiction of the revolutionaries as rational political actors.

The play begins on the eve of the revolution, which is established immediately

Figure 19. George Dibdin Pitt, sketch of Toussaint Louverture (1846). Pitt's drawing was the second page of the handwritten play manuscript he submitted to the Lord Chamberlain for pre-performance censorship. He depicted Toussaint as an authoritative leader with a sword in his right hand, and his left hand decisively ordering unseen underlings to battle. The visual similarity to Marcus Rainsford's portrait (fig. 20) confirms that Rainsford's *Historical Account of the Black Empire of Hayti* was likely Pitt's main source for his play *The Black Spartacus.* © The British Library Board, used with permission

by the opening dialogue of the first scene, set on the plantation where Toussaint is an overseer. Monsieur Bayou, the wealthy proprietor, informs the newly arrived French commissioner that "news of the French Revolution has imbued the whole Black population with a desire for liberty and equality." The scene also establishes Toussaint's ethical character and intellectual acuity. Monsieur Bayou assures the commissioner that "my confidence and hope is in one Toussaint, a man possessing a superior mind and great energy. That he will ultimately decide in favour of the cause of liberty I doubt not, but as one possessing great influence with his black brethren, I know that he will even with his life oppose the massacre of the Whites."

Figure 20. Marcus Rainsford, *Toussaint L'Ouverture* (1805). This is the earliest known image of Toussaint, taken from sketches Marcus Rainsford made. It appeared as an illustration in Rainsford's *An Historical Account of the Black Empire of Hayti*. Toussaint is represented as a dignified military leader with a sword in one hand and a battle map in the other. Courtesy of The Library Company of Philadelphia

Immediately following this ringing endorsement of Toussaint's intellect and integrity, Pitt introduces the American Jonathan Jungle, Monsieur Bayou's other overseer. One of the few fictional characters in the play, Jonathan Jungle is first shown threatening to whip a slave whom he berates as "wooly-headed [and] cheeky as a pig's head." He relents only at Monsieur Bayou's insistence. Jonathan Jungle's brutal tendencies and racist language, in contrast to Toussaint's alleged tolerance and self-sacrificing humanity, represent an early stab by Pitt at the institution of American slavery.

Although the French and Haitian Revolutions are the overt narrative context of Pitt's politicized drama, his play also reveals the striking extent to which—even in the mid-nineteenth-century—the American Revolution remained a yardstick by which Great Britain's enlightened "liberty" was measured. Pitt used the character of Jonathan Jungle to challenge essentialist notions of race. The moniker "Jungle," of course, connotes uncivilized savagery, and in assigning it to a white character, Pitt turned racialist conceptions on their head. And ever since Charles Mathews had first introduced Jonathan Doubikin in his wildly popular *Trip to America*, where he used the racist slave owner to point a satirical barb at American democracy, "Jonathan" had been a stock American character on the transatlantic stage. Pitt's Jonathan was played for laughs, but the satire had a serious point to make. By transplanting him to the site of the Haitian Revolution, Pitt showed the parallels between the slave revolutionaries and their fight for personal emancipation and liberation from French imperial rule and the failures of the American revolutionaries, whose call to arms was the "natural right" to liberty from the "enslavement" of British imperial rule but who did not end African slavery in America.

After Jonathan Jungle exits, Pitt resumes his "historical account" of phases of the revolution (such as the alliance between the mulattoes and the white planters and the arrival of French troops) while constructing his antislavery edifice and lionizing Toussaint as the valiant but compassionate champion of democratic rights. The initial efforts of insurgents Jean François and Dessalines to recruit Toussaint flounder, as he declares, "I will have no hand in massacre and spoliation." Only when the French betray him and join forces with the mulattoes to imprison him does Toussaint decide to take up Jean François's challenge to "go down in posterity as the Black Spartacus predicted by Raynal to avenge the wrongs of our race." Later Toussaint helps his former master Monsieur Bayou to safety, allowing Pitt to drive home his rejection of racialist images of slave rebels as vengeful brutes and simultaneously restate his antislavery sympathies: Toussaint proclaims, "I am no villain and murderer," and vows to keep fighting until "the mighty work is consummated because the whites made me a slave. For why?—I am black, God, as if all men were not alike in the sights of heaven. Proud as the lordly white . . . the unlettered Negro has a right to say I am a Man and a Brother."

Act I climaxes with the black revolutionaries' defeat of French troops and Toussaint's admonition to his fellow revolutionaries to refrain from retributive violence. The first act is crowned with Toussaint's solemn declaration, "We are republicans, [and] this is the banner of liberty, not of murder and massacre." The play ends with Toussaint's heroic battlefield death—poetic license, as Toussaint was captured by Napoleon and died in a French prison in 1803. This fiction, however, permitted Pitt to further glorify Toussaint by making his dying words those of a martyred hero. He exhorts his troops to continue fighting "for liberty and never forget our Independence."

Pitt challenged prevailing mid-nineteenth-century notions of white racial supremacy at a time when racial categories, legitimated by scientific theories, had hardened, yet he did so for audiences accustomed to antislavery oratory and blackface minstrel performances coexisting on the same stage. In England, racist theories had gained widespread sway, perhaps epitomized by the work of anatomist Dr. Robert Knox, who claimed "race is everything: literature, science, art—in a word, civilization depends on it."[36] Perhaps Pitt's rebuttal of this white supremacy would have been mitigated by white actors performing Toussaint, Jean François, and Dessalines, presumably in blackface makeup, at a time when blackface minstrelsy was all the rage at the Britannia.[37] But this supposition is not as obvious as it might seem. For the Britannia also regularly hired the African American Shakespearian actor Ira Aldridge, whose antislavery oratory and roles were popular with the audiences.[38]

To be sure, the Britannia and other minor theaters, like the Surrey, received Aldridge warmly after he was spurned by a hostile West End. After emigrating from New York to London in 1825, Aldridge worked very little in the legitimate theaters after his debut that year at a West End theater, the Royal Coburg, garnered racist-tinged mixed reviews. The *Times* reviewer, for example, insisted that Aldridge's thick lips made it impossible for him to correctly pronounce English.[39] By contrast, the Surrey, home turf of Charles Mathews and, later, T. Daddy Rice as Jim Crow, proudly advertised Aldridge's appearance by boasting, "The circumstances of a MAN OF COLOUR performing Othello is indeed an epoch in the history of Theatricals," a claim that interpolated the era's prevailing racism, ideals of humanitarian universalism, and the commercialism of promoting the spectacle of black performance.[40]

The popularity of Charles Mathews's variety shows in the working-class theaters of London helps explain why the Britannia (and other unlicensed theaters) engaged Aldridge even as he was rejected by the West End. Mathews had already made Aldridge famous by claiming to mimic him in an "Ethiopian opera," "Opossum up a Gum Tree."[41] In his skit, Mathews alleged he had first heard this popular blackface minstrel song performed by Aldridge at the African Grove Theatre in New York (although the African American actor he purported to be imitating was actually James Hewlett, another African Grove ensemble member).[42] Aldridge capitalized on the popularity of Mathews's skit by regularly performing

"Opossum up a Gum Tree." In performing this minstrel fare, Aldridge may have been wearing "the mask that grins and lies / it hides our cheeks and shades our eyes" as Paul Lawrence Dunbar despaired in his 1896 poem about blacks' racial double-consciousness in their everyday "performances" for whites.[43] But he was also doing a send-up of Mathews's send-up: Aldridge had the last laugh.

Among the minor London theatres, the Britannia employed Aldridge the most regularly. On this East End stage, he performed *Othello* and also a melodramatic adaptation of *Titus Andronicus* written especially for him. Some spectators may have considered Aldridge's Shakespearian performances a burlesque of the bard and enjoyed his performances in a spirit of ridicule, yet Aldridge's frequent presence on the Britannia stage suggests otherwise. Audiences who found blackface minstrel troupes palatable also apparently appreciated an African American actor's antislavery efforts. In addition to Shakespeare, Aldridge performed pieces with antislavery connotations such as a version of John Fawcett's pantomime about slave revolt, *Obi; or, Three Finger'd Jack*, and Isaac Bickerstaffe's *The Padlock*, in which Aldridge played the rebellious domestic slave, Mungo. Moreover, Aldridge frequently prefaced and concluded his night's work with antislavery songs and oratories.[44]

That Aldridge combined antislavery oratory, blackface minstrel songs, and well-known pantomimes and musical comedies featuring blackface slave characters is unsurprising, given the British public's fascination with blackface minstrelsy and black abolitionists as a form of related spectacle. The British press conflated impressions of blacks in "Ethiopian operas" with antislavery sentiment. Thus, a *Daily News* journalist worried that performances by Ethiopian Serenaders were "making light of the miseries of the slave populations in the United States" before concluding their performances were "innocuous, as regards the poor helpless would beings they represent, but calculated from its force, truthfulness, and the mixture of the ludicrous with sentiment, to raise feelings which may . . . produce results which every friend of negro emancipation would hail with satisfaction."[45] Unlike Philadelphia, where the audience for blackface minstrelsy was largely rowdy workingmen, this troupe (and other blackface acts) appealed both to Hoxton laborers and London's emergent lower-middle class (some of whom frequented the Britannia) in part by offering a contemptuous portrayal of Americans and their customs.[46] Not only were blackface minstrels successful in the same towns and locations as visiting black American abolitionists like Douglass were, but they were also seen by some as fostering antislavery and anti-American sentiment, of which Aldridge was no doubt aware.[47]

When *The Black Spartacus* debuted, the Britannia's audiences had thus already been exposed to serious dramas featuring black characters, antislavery rhetoric, and blackface minstrel performances, all of which featured in Pitt's play. The majority of the black characters are historical figures, and the primary comic relief was provided by invented white characters like Jonathan Jungle. But Pitt also punctuated the drama with comic appearances by a minstrel-like blackface character, Cuffee. The humor in these scenes rested on Cuffee's interchanges with Peter Pobs and Loo Eggleston, white cockney characters on the make, whom Pitt lampooned for their efforts to assert their superiority to Cuffee. Thus these scenes permitted multiple possible readings: the laughs of racial burlesque, certainly, but also a metropolitan's satire of white plebeian' pretensions to upward mobility and racial superiority in the colonial periphery.

By the mid-1840s, Pitt had clearly become cynical about the possibility of reforming industrial urban inequities, as he was increasingly drawn to visions of revolutionary change. Indeed, *The Black Spartacus* was one of three plays Pitt wrote about democratic revolutions; it was, however, the only one to be staged, as *Terry Tyrone* (1845) and *The Revolution in Paris* (1848) did not survive the scrutiny of the Lord Chamberlain's censorship. *Terry Tyrone* sympathetically recounted the story of Irish rebel Robert Emmet, one of several republicans who, inspired by the French Revolution, led the 1792 United Irishmen's rebellion against British rule. Emmet was executed for his complicity in the uprising. After the experience of having *Terry Tyrone* rejected, Pitt submitted *Revolution in Paris* to the Lord Chamberlain in 1848 with a prefatory note claiming the play did "not in any way touch upon the present crises [as it was] a stage revolution, not that of Paris 1848." The plot, in which city workers joined forces with the middle class to revolt against the heavy taxes imposed by the government, was, he asserted, based on "the Italian revolution of 1659."[48]

Pitt's protestations were disingenuous. Perhaps he was referring in error to the revolt of Masaniello at Naples in 1647, with which he may have been familiar through novels and plays.[49] It seems more likely, however, that Pitt was simply trying to mislead the Lord Chamberlain, as his *Revolution in Paris* was a very thinly veiled fusion of Paris in 1848 and 1789. His pro-republican play is replete with references to recognizable French revolutionary events and rhetoric, such as the storming of the Bastille, the "Tricolour flag—the Symbol of Liberty," and the guillotining of moderate revolutionaries by their rivals in the radical faction. And while Pitt cautioned against the dangers of zealotry and terror in *The Revolution in Paris*, he concluded the play by overtly lauding "the principles of liberty born in France . . . Vive la Republicque [*sic*]."[50]

Given the fate of Pitt's other revolutionary plays, staging *The Black Spartacus* in a working-class theater at a time fraught with class tensions was a risky choice for him and for the Britannia. Just two years later, as the 1848 revolutions swept the continent, the play would doubtless have met the same fate as *The Revolution in Paris*, especially as the theaters of the East End were by then censored more rigorously than their West End counterparts.[51] Ironically, *The Black Spartacus* probably survived the censorship process precisely *because* of the censor's exclusive focus on topical events. In an 1832 parliamentary report, the Lord Chamberlain's office had narrowly defined unacceptable political references in drama as "anything that may be so allusive to the times as to be applied to the existing moment and which is likely to be inflammatory."[52] The Lord Chamberlain banned *Terry Tyrone* and *The Revolution in Paris* on these grounds.[53] He also banned the two-act drama, *The Chartists; or, a Dream of Every-day Life*, forbidding its performance against the backdrop of a massive Chartist petition in London in 1848.[54]

On the surface, a play staging a slave revolt was not "so topically allusive as to be inflammatory" in 1846, as slavery had already ended in the British West Indies. But, as playwright Thomas Morton noted in his testimony to the 1832 Parliamentary Committee on Dramatic Literature, no censor could predict the audience's process of reading topical political meaning into a play, as there was "a tendency in the audience to force passages . . . into political meaning" precisely *because* explicit political commentary was prohibited.[55] In the context, therefore, of its working-class venue and the prominent rhetorical conflation of racial and wage slavery, the depiction of democratic overthrow of political order in *The Black Spartacus* was not merely suggestive: it was close to seditious.

Britannia, "the Negro Question," and Telescopic Philanthropy

Pitt's 1846 parody of American "liberty" through the character of Jonathan Jungle turned out to be very topical, as novelists, cartoonists, and political commentators soon joined in a chorus of protest against American slavery following the passage of the 1850 Fugitive Slave Act. The bill was part of a congressional attempt to quell heated sectional conflict over whether or not to permit slavery in the lands newly acquired from the Mexican-American War (1846–48). The resulting compromise permitted the inhabitants of most of the new territories to decide the issue by popular sovereignty, banned the slave trade (but not slavery itself) in the District of Columbia per the demands of antislavery leaders, and bowed to Southern demands by including fugitive slave laws, which mandated that Northerners return escaped slaves to their Southern owners. This bandage on the cancer of sectionalism pleased nobody. Southerners were infuriated that they were not guaranteed the right to take their human "property" into the western territories, and Northern "free soilers" and abolitionists who wanted slavery prohibited in new territories were equally irate. The bill was just as despised in Great Britain, provoking British abolitionists' outrage that the slave-free Northern states would be forced into complicity with the Southern slave states.

As transatlantic abolitionist fervor over the Fugitive Slave Act escalated, some Londoners set the needs of the urban poor against those of black American slaves, rather than bringing the two causes together, as Pitt or Henry Solly had done. Among them were Charles Dickens, in his novel *Bleak House*; cartoonist Sir John Tenniel; and essayist and political commentator Thomas Carlyle. Dickens, Tenniel, and Carlyle each lambasted British abolitionists' reinvigorated mission to free the slaves in the United States as coming at the expense of the Great Britain's urban "wage slaves." Carlyle and John Stuart Mill sparred in a series of essays, with Mill issuing an impassioned appeal for an immediate end to American slavery. Their heated and well-publicized exchange was read in both London and Philadelphia and epitomized the way British and American commentators could either pit the plight of "wage slaves" against chattel slaves or bring the two together.

Mill and Carlyle focused their disputes over labor and race on both the free blacks in the British West Indies and the larger reality of American slavery in order to redefine Britannia's constitutional and national identity. In "Occasional Discourse on the Negro Question," which was published in 1849 in *Fraser's Magazine* of London and later revised into a provocatively retitled 1853 pamphlet, *Occasional Discourse on the Nigger Question*, Carlyle pronounced, "The [emancipated] Negroes [in the West Indies] are all very happy and doing well," while by contrast "the British whites [at home] are rather badly off."[56] Carlyle feared that the "natural" national and racial hierarchies had been reversed by emancipation of chattel slaves, on the one hand, and the economic hardships of industrial "wage slaves," on the other. In rabidly racist language, Carlyle called free blacks lazy and jeeringly dismissed their rights: "I never thought the 'rights of negroes' worth much discussing . . . the grand point . . . is the *might* of men."[57]

Carlyle proposed a return to feudal serfdom to subordinate the physical labor —the "mights"—of black former slaves, white industrial workers, and Irish "potato people" as an antidote to their "idle pauperism," which he blamed on the "dismal science" of free trade economics, the industrial "cash nexus," and abolitionists. For Carlyle, "rage against the poor negro's slavery" was *not* integral to Britannia's conscience, and the nation's well-being would be better assured by resubjugating free blacks with a "beneficient whip." In a searing rebuttal titled "The Negro Question," published in *Fraser's Magazine for Town and Country* in

1850, Mill condemned "my anti-philanthropic opponent" for misunderstanding "the great national revolt of the conscience of this country against slavery and the slave-trade . . . [as] an affair of sentiment," when it was instead a fight against the "crime and sin" of Africans being "seized by force and carried off . . . to be worked to death, literally to death."[58]

Both Carlyle and Mill made American slavery the linchpin of their closing arguments. "If the English cannot find the method . . . to command black men and produce West Indian fruitfulness," Carlyle concluded, "they may rest assured that another will come: Brother Jonathan or still another."[59] Thus, Carlyle rested his case—against free and equal labor in a free-trade economy and for a reinstatement of slavery's hierarchies—explicitly on the need to compete with the plantocracy of the southern United States. And thanks to Charles Mathews's popular character, "Brother Jonathan" was a handy stand-in for slaveholding Americans that Carlyle (like Pitt) could invoke and assume his readers understood. Mill, too, concluded his response in terms of the Southern plantocracy: not the need to economically compete with it, but rather, the moral imperative to fight the "iniquity" of American slavery.[60]

Carlyle's virulent anti-abolitionism was not the only expression of dismissal of U.S. chattel slavery and the Fugitive Slave Act of 1850 as relevant problems for Great Britain. In 1853, a journalist for London's *Reynolds Newspaper* vented his antipathy to transatlantic antislavery agitation:

> The truth is that the workers in factories are as much slaves to the money-power as the negroes in the United States are the lash and the law; and yet there is an abundance of sympathy expended upon the latter, while little enough is bestowed from the same quarter upon the former. When we contemplate the horrors of our factory system, we experience the deepest disgust for the conduct of the Duchess of Sutherland [an antislavery advocate] and her [antislavery] rose-water clique . . . in sending their maudlin sympathies traveling so many miles across the Atlantic, while they exhibit not the slightest evidence of compassion for the slaves whom the money-power rules with a rod of iron in their own native land.[61]

Were not London's urban poor, those suffering under the industrial "rod of iron," more deserving of compassion than black American slaves, asked the critic. No longer was Britannia feted as an emancipatory benefactress of the slave's liberty. Rather, antislavery philanthropy was now a detriment to Britannia's industrialized nation and its attendant problems.

Charles Dickens also took sides with Carlyle in powerfully fictive form in *Bleak House*, a novel published in monthly installments between March 1852 and September 1853. In chapter 4, titled "Telescopic Philanthropy," he indicted Mrs. Jellyby as a character "who devotes herself entirely to . . . the subject of Africa, with a view to the general cultivation of the coffee berry—*and* the natives" at the expense both of maternal concern for her own children and philanthropic concern for London's poor. Here, Dickens adopted a phrase and charge earlier coined by Richard Oastler, who wrote, "What are the ministers of religion doing? They are using the telescope—they are prying into sins and sorrows of other and far distant nations."[62] Dickens thus built upon an already established critique of British abolitionists. Yet he did not share Carlyle's proslavery sympathies. Indeed, in his *American Notes for General Circulation*, a commentary on his 1842 tour of the United States, Dickens denounced slavery and graphically detailed its violence. He lambasted republican Americans "who, when they speak of Freedom, mean the Freedom to oppress their kind, and to be savage, merciless and cruel" and "whose inalienable rights can only have their growth in negro wrongs."[63] But Dickens combined his indictment of American slavery with his attack on British abolitionists who neglected the industrial poor at home.

Bleak House popularized "telescopic philanthropy" as a cultural shorthand in visual and prose attacks on abolitionists for purportedly aiming their philanthropic telescope on Africa, freed blacks in the British Caribbean, and enslaved blacks in the southern United States while neglecting the plight of white British "wage slaves." One indication of the contagious appeal of Dickens's concept of "telescopic philanthropy" was that in March 1865 *Punch Magazine* published a cartoon that assumed the viewers' familiarity with the phrase. As the U.S. Civil War still wreaked its deadly carnage, the cartoon castigated abolitionist support for freeing all the slaves in the Confederate states. Lincoln's Emancipation Proclamation of January 1, 1863, had declared only partial abolition, stipulating that slaves in rebellious areas were, in the eyes of the Union, free, but leaving slavery in place in the border states loyal to the Union. The cartoon by Sir John Tenniel, titled *Telescopic Philanthropy*, addressed the issue of "foreign" versus "domestic" philanthropy by depicting Britannia, her industrial workers, and the black slaves in the Confederate South (fig. 21).

In the image, Britannia, with trident and shield at her side, looks through a telescope at enslaved Africans on the distant North American shores while impoverished London urchins desperately tug at her imperial robes. The subtitle reads, "Little London Arab. "PLEASE 'M, AIN'T WE BLACK ENOUGH TO BE CARED FOR?" and finishes by announcing "With Mr. Punch's compliments to Lord Stanley." Lord Stanley had, the week before, argued in Parliament that Great Britain should disband the African squadron, a naval unit formed to police the

TELESCOPIC PHILANTHROPY.

Little London Arab. " PLEASE 'M, AIN'T WE BLACK ENOUGH TO BE CARED FOR ?"

(*With* Mr. Punch's *Compliments to* Lord Stanley.)

Figure 21. Sir John Tenniel, *Telescopic Philanthropy* (1856). Tenniel's cartoon features Britannia viewing the black slaves in America through her telescope. She is so preoccupied that she ignores London's poor children pulling at her sleeves for attention. The print criticizes abolitionists for being oblivious to the urban poor at home. From from *Punch Magazine*, Mar. 4, 1856, p. 86, © Punch Limited, used with permission

West African coast and prevent slave trading. Stanley insisted that Great Britain "owed nothing to Africa" and should instead focus on "civilizing savages" in the "population within five miles of the House of Commons" that had been "neglected."[64] Both Stanley and Tenniel had adopted the categories proposed by Henry Mayhew, an English social researcher, journalist, and reform advocate, who had distinguished between savage "nomadic" and settled "civilized" tribes and designated London's poor as "urban nomads."[65] Hence, Tenniel depicted urban nomad children as dark-complexioned "little Arabs," savages in need of civilizing philanthropy.

The image also highlights how, amid the crisis of industrial poverty in the1840s and 1850s, some contemporaries rejected the idea of Britannia's liberty as predicated on opposition to slavery, a chauvinistic boast harking back to the American revolutionary years. Dickens, Stanley, and Tenniel no longer heralded Britannia as intrinsically antislavery. They did, however, persist in using the United States as the yardstick against which they measured the nation and empire's well-being. Each did so by holding up the condition of London's predominantly white poor as more dire than that of black American slaves and more worthy of charitable attention.

With near-revolutionary tumult in the 1840s and raging sectionalism across the ocean in the 1850s and 1860s, Britons persisted in using American slavery and republican liberty to gauge British reform, polity, and empire. They did so by invoking the figurative American black slave to make radically different claims. As Carlyle, Dickens, and Tenniel would have it, Britannia's antislavery philanthropy was telescopic in its greater concern with African slaves across the Atlantic than with wage slaves at home. For Mill, Britannia's "liberty" instead rested on the moral imperative to fight American slavery. Chartist and abolitionist Henry Solly, along with playwright George Dibdin Pitt, presented the plights of black American slaves and white urban "wage slave" as interlinked because both were suffering brutally crushing oppression. Even Pitt's staging of the Haitian Revolution pointedly decried American slavery by highlighting its inconsistency with the American revolutionary heritage.

George Lippard, Black Hercules, and Revolutionary Brotherhood

In Philadelphia, too, there were radicals who, like Pitt, resuscitated the eighteenth-century revolutions to call for an end to the oppression of both industrial workers and chattel slaves. George Lippard was among them. From a family of humble means, Lippard was orphaned early in his life and, while a young man, spent time destitute and homeless, experiences that shaped his lifelong sympathy for the poor and oppressed. In his brief, colorful life, Lippard was a sensational author of twenty-three gothic novels, a popular lecturer-performer, playwright, journalist, literary critic, newspaper publisher, and labor organizer who in 1848 founded the Brotherhood of the Union, a secret society of artisans and mechanics.[66] In his fictionalized lectures, *Legends of the American Revolution; or, Washington and His General* (performed and published serially between 1845 and 1848) and his 1846 novel, *Blanche of Brandywine*, adapted for theatrical performance in 1847 that told of an American revolutionary battle, black revolutionary heroes fight valiantly alongside white mechanics and artisans. By retelling

American revolutionary events, Lippard made a class-based and racially inclusive argument that harked back to the radical Thomas Paine, for the extension of liberty and equality to wage workers and black slaves alike.

Like Pitt and Solly, Lippard espoused an inclusive utopianism that ran counter to a prevalent exclusionary discourse of working-class advocates more concerned with reform for northern "white slaves" than ending black slavery in the South. Mill and Carlyle were widely read in America, as their articles were reprinted in American journals, both Northern and Southern, and used to spar over slavery and the reviled Compromise of 1850.[67] Antislavery Northerners hailed Mill as the voice of economic and moral reason, while proslavery Southerners touted Carlyle's rejection of slave emancipation in the West Indies as economically disastrous to bolster their case for expanding slavery to the Western territories. And there were home-grown American discussions of wage and chattel slavery as well. George Henry Evans, a labor leader and printer, had helped popularize the language of "white slavery" and "wage slavery" in the 1840s, declaring, "Stealing the man away from his land or his land away from the man alike produces slavery."[68] While Evans saw landless industrial workers and Southern chattel slaves as equally brutalized, some Northern wage workers and their advocates cast industrial workers as worse off than black slaves and rejected abolitionist efforts, fearing emancipation's impact on the economic fate of "white slaves." Southerners also defended slavery by castigating the impoverished conditions of Northern wage laborers. George Fitzhugh, for example, cited Carlyle to claim that Southern slaveholders were benevolently paternalistic, caring more for their slaves than Northern industrialists did for their unskilled workers.[69]

Although the analogy between wage and chattel slaves was a transatlantic discourse—indeed, early uses of "white slavery" in the United States often referenced British female and child factory workers[70]—the racial dimensions meant different things in the two nations. Scholars generally agree that by the 1840s working-class consciousness in the Northern states was predicated on the racial solidarity of whiteness.[71] Hence, in Philadelphia, with its huge population of working-class free blacks, the term "white slave" was exclusionary in a way that had far harsher real consequences than in London, where the black population was so minute that workers were predominantly white. Racial animosities in Philadelphia, which recurrently erupted into race riots, were further inflamed by the influx of huge numbers of Irish immigrants. While initially disparaged by native-born whites as ethnically inferior, they secured their place in Philadelphian society by laying claim to their whiteness.[72] Despite the heritage of the United Irishmen who, inspired by the French Revolution, were opposed both to British rule and to slavery, Irish immigrants were hostile to abolitionism and black Philadelphians.[73] A bloody riot in 1844 driven by nativist, anti-abolitionist, and antiblack virulence led Frederick Douglass to claim, "There is not perhaps anywhere to be found a city in which prejudice against color is more rampant than in Philadelphia."[74] Unsurprisingly, then, in Philadelphia (and the United States more generally), "white slavery" was used more commonly than the more inclusive "wage slavery" in the 1840s and 1850s.[75]

It is all the more remarkable, therefore, that throughout his oeuvre Lippard is strikingly racially inclusive. He sometimes juxtaposes the oppression of Northern "white slaves" to that of Southern "black slaves," but more often he uses the inclusive phrase "wage slave." Lippard also includes women in this category because "Wage Slavery . . . in the large cities of the North, crushed woman into a life of shame—of hopeless want—or into an untimely grave."[76] For Lippard the world was divided into "only two nations—the OPPRESSED and the OPPRESSORS," and the oppressed were black and white, male and female.[77] Lippard's conflation of class and race was crucial for his vision of an alliance between multiethnic white workers and black slaves.[78] In his revolutionary fiction Lippard includes sympathetic black and mixed-race characters to suggest that both wage slaves and black slaves were equally in need of liberation from oppression.[79] He did not, however, participate in the organized abolition movement, which he believed posed a threat to the Union's harmony and was focused too narrowly on the plight of black slaves.[80] Lippard also criticized white Americans' displacement of Native Americans, in keeping with his conviction that "every human creature hath a right to Life, Liberty, Land, and Home," as he put it in the oath required to join his Brotherhood of the Union, which he led from 1848 until his death in 1854, at age thirty-two, from tuberculosis.[81]

Lippard's aesthetics and commitment to working-class reform were transatlantically inspired. He modeled his early gothic novel *The Ladye Annabel* on *The Mysteries of Paris*, by the French socialist Eugène Sol.[82] Like Karl Marx (and Walt Whitman), Lippard envisaged an international revolution of the oppressed against the capitalist industrial hegemony, which he expressed in his lecture performances, plays, and novels, as well as in the Brotherhood.[83] He was also an admirer of both Charles Dickens and Charles Brockden Brown as writers of the people, believing that writers should commit their literature to challenging the capitalist system.[84] For Lippard, Thomas Paine epitomized the author-as-revolutionary. He tried to repair Paine's reputation, tarnished by his *Age of Reason* (published in three parts in 1794, 1795, and 1807), which had been castigated by Britons and Americans alike as atheistic. Lippard rehabilitated Paine as "an

author-hero of the Revolution" and "a virtuous supporter of the rights of mankind" in a lecture he delivered at the City Institute in 1852 and later published as
a pamphlet.[85] In it, he praised Paine's critical role in the American Revolution as
a pamphleteer and his support of the French Revolution, calling his work part of
"the first great effort of man to free himself from the lash and chain."[86] Nowhere
is Lippard's embracing of Paine's "fraternity of brothers" and use of literature as
a vehicle for radical social transformation more blatant than in his revolutionary
re-creations, with their black and white underdog heroes.

In *Blanche of Brandywine* (1846) and *Legends of the Revolution* (1845–48), Lippard featured white mechanic and black slave heroes and celebrated multiethnic
working-class revolutionary agency. *Blanche of Brandywine; or, September the Eighth
to Eleventh, 1777: A Romance of the American Revolution* features Ben Sampson, a
black character he had performed the previous year in his popular lectures.[87] Did
Lippard wear blackface makeup to portray his black hero? Did he give the figure
minstrel-like "black" dialect and play Sampson for laughs? Or did he perform the
character as a heroic protagonist? These questions are not answerable, as reviews
of these performances are not extant. But Lippard's biographer, John Bell Bouton,
writing in 1855, claimed Lippard "would have made a capital actor. He had an active figure, a face full of expression, and a power of mimicry rarely equaled upon
the stage. He would have been successful either in tragedy or comedy."[88] Bouton
is, however, silent about Lippard's performance of Sampson.

The Sampson character was clearly popular, for Lippard includes him in both
Blanche of Brandywine, originally published serially for the *Saturday Courier* in
1845 and as a book in 1846, and in his *Legends of the American Revolution*. Lippard's fiction offers clues that he exploited the popularity of blackface minstrelsy
yet also challenged racism in his portrayal of Sampson. In both works, Sampson's dialogue is the mistake-ridden "black" dialect associated with blackface
minstrelsy. Yet Lippard repeatedly described him as a "black Hercules," a moniker that subverts minstrel tropes by making the character a brave, neoclassical
hero.

Blanche of Brandywine is a complex story of romantic betrayal fused with
the revolutionary heroics of plebeian patriots. Echoing Charles Mathews, Lip-
pard's heroes were identifiable American ethnic "types": black Sampson, Irish-
American Blacksmith Tom O'Dilworth, Pennsylvania Dutch Hirpley Hawson,
German-immigrant Gottlieb Hoff, Scottish Jacobite exile Captain Frazier, and a
Polish soldier, Pulaski. The overarching plot tells the tale of Lord Percy George of
Monthoner, a British officer who, despite being betrothed to a British countess,
Lady Isidore, falls in love with Blanche Walford, a simple farm girl and Captain

Frazier's niece. Disguised as a British officer, Lady Isidore comes to America to find her fiancé and kills herself after discovering his love for Blanche. A variety of gothic subplots culminate in the British killing Sampson's master, Jacob, by burning him alive. Jacob's gruesome death spurs the plebeian characters to join the patriot cause. The novel culminates in the Battle of Brandywine, where Sampson, Gottlieb Hof, Blacksmith Tom and others rally under George Washington to fight the British and their loyalist supporters.

Lippard's inclusive definition of the oppressed extends to Native Americans, which he expresses through an improbable subplot. Lord Percy Monthoner takes his commission as aide-de-camp of Lord Cornwallis because his dying father, the Earl of Monthoner, asks him to go to America on a secret mission to deliver a letter. The letter is to his son, Randulh, the progeny of a relationship with Randulh's Native American mother, whom the Earl abandoned when he returned to England and married Percy's English mother. On his deathbed, the Earl wants to right this wrong by legally recognizing Randulh as his heir. But rather than telling a rosy story of reconciliation, Lippard uses this subplot to protest the unjust displacement of Native Americans. After reading the letter, Randulh—who until then has been passing as white and fighting with the patriots—rejects both the patriot cause and his English descent. He breaks his sword and flings the broken pieces at George Washington's feet before announcing, "With that broken sword, every tie that bound me to your race is rent asunder . . . accursed be my hand, if I ever draw a sword in your quarrels again." Aghast, Washington pushes him to clarify: "Your quarrels? . . . do you not belong to the white race? Are you not an American?" Randulph replies, "I am an Indian! . . . Yes I am one of that race whom it has been a policy of your European adventurers to despoil of their lands, to trample under foot, to kill by nations . . . If there is a drop of white blood in my veins, I disown and curse it from this hour!" Randulph then reclaims his Indian name of Wyamoke and rejects his newly inherited title.[89]

While Lippard protested Native American displacement through Randulph's rejection of the patriot cause, he underscored the plight of African American slaves by animating Sampson's championing of the revolution. Lippard introduced Ben Sampson early on as of African heritage, Herculean strength, and a supporter of George Washington. Sampson first appears in a scene in the schoolmaster's house in which he interrupts a conversation between his master and the Quaker Gilbert Gates, challenging Gates's loyalist sympathies. Lippard describes Sampson as "seated a little aside from the group." Yet rather than connoting lower status, positioning Sampson separately from the group permits Lippard to use him as an authoritative commentator on Washington's worth. Sampson has no qualms about offering his opinion. Indeed, after flexing "his muscular arms in the cotton garment that clothed his Herculean form," he proclaims himself to be on an equal footing with George Washington, a "berry good man. Better not say he haint, Massa Gates," based on his royal ancestry. "Ben Sampson's fader prince in he own country—Wash'ton prince in his own country."[90]

Already sympathetic to the patriots, Sampson soon plays a pivotal role in rallying the plebeian characters to their cause after his master's murder. Until then, Blacksmith Tom, Hirpley Hawson, and Gottlieb Hoff are ambivalent about the patriot cause for reasons epitomized by Tom's explanation that he has a wife and child and "the British haven't stepped on my toes."[91] Here, Lippard clearly differentiated between "the British" and the American colonists. Sampson's bravery galvanizes their conversion. When British and Hessian troops abduct Jacob's daughter, Polly, Sampson singlehandedly tries to prevent their entry into the cellar where she is hiding: "Ye must walk over dis niggah's dead body fust! . . . you no pass dis door!" he proclaims. Although he "fought like an enraged tiger, bravely beating his foes aside," Sampson incurs a "fearful sword gash" and is unable to prevent British soldiers from abducting Polly after they murder her father. After the British leave, Sampson, wielding a scythe, cuts his right arm and drops the blood from the wound onto Jacob's skull while swearing that the British "shall die by this scythe . . . Sampson mingle he blood with the blood ob de dead. Revenge for his murder!" When Blacksmith Tom shouts, "What, will ye suffer the negro to be ahead of you in the good work?" the white plebeian "men of Brandywine" join Sampson in swearing a blood oath to fight with the patriots "for Vengeance, for Washington, and for Right."[92]

Sampson, aided by his pure white dog, Debbil, plays a strikingly sentimental yet fiercely brave hero as a guardian of the vulnerable. Sampson's emotional sensitivity rebutted theories of African moral and emotional inferiority first espoused by Jefferson. As an acolyte of the Revolution, Lippard may well have read Jefferson's *Notes on Virginia*, in which he posited that black Americans' emotions were hidden by a "veil of black" that rendered them incapable of experiencing or showing the same range of feelings as whites. One way antislavery sympathizers made their case in print and theater was by countering this prejudice with sentimental blackface heroes.[93] In some ways, Sampson fits this antislavery mold. After his failed attempt to prevent Polly Mayland's abduction, he later tries to save her after she has been brutally raped. Sampson and Debbil "Finds dis gal, ravin' mad, by de roadside," as he explains to Gottlieb Hoff, who is in love with Polly, and "ax her who had done her harm; she answer, 'Cap'n Howard!'" "As tears rolled down Sampson's cheeks," he describes how he carried her to a local tavern and how she died in his arms. When his master "wept like a child," the loyal Debbil, "with a look almost human in its consciousness . . . uttered a prolonged and dismal howl." Yet in contrast to docile Sambos, lascivious Jim Crows, and dandified Zip Coons, Sampson combines sentiment with assertive bravery. In one instance, Sampson, Debbil, and Gottlieb Hoff together save the patriot Captain Frazier from being hung by Tories: "Two brave men and the dog . . . plunged into [their] midst. Like an enraged tiger, the Giant Negro dashed the Tories to the ground; knife and rifle were no defense against the sweep of that terrible scythe."[94]

Sampson is also a military savior in the climactic 1777 Battle of Brandywine between Lord Cornwallis and the patriots serving George Washington, which plays out in the heroics of the plebeian "men of Brandywine." Although Gottlieb Hoff, Hirpley Hawson, and the Polish Pulaski all fight valiantly, Lippard gives "Negro Sampson" and Debbil special credit for bravery:

> And there, striding forward with immense paces, foaming like some chafed tiger, suddenly let loose from his cage, the Negro Sampson came on and the white dog came yelling by his side. The negro's . . . glittering scythe swung aloft, guided by . . . his giant strength. He rushed forward, A Black Hercules, his aquiline nose with its quivering nostrils, his thick lips whitened with foam, his massive forehead topped by short wooly hair, all turned to lurid red by flashes of Battle-light.[95]

Not only does Lippard highlight Sampson's fearlessness, but he also singles him out for his patriot loyalty, for which George Washington personally rewards him. When Sampson and Debbil rescue Colonel Frazier from the murderous designs of a band of loyalists, Sampson kills loyalist sympathizer Gilbert Gates, and confiscates the British intelligence papers he was carrying. At the Battle of Brandywine, he hands over the packet to a grateful Washington. The real-life Washington had only lifted a ban on enlisting black soldiers in 1776. He did so reluctantly, to counter British recruitment of thousands of black soldiers after British officials like Lord Dunmore, the governor of Virginia, promised them their freedom in exchange for fighting. In Lippard's retelling, however, Washington lauds Sampson and invites him to join the army: "Come my good fellow," he urges, "follow me to the Continental Army; I will reward you for this deed." Sampson accepts the invitation and pledges his and Debbil's loyalty.[96]

Despite Lippard's inclusive rewriting of revolutionary events, several critics have argued that his black characters, with their minstrel-like traits, actually serve to *affirm* an exclusive white working-class identity, in Sampson's case on the grounds of the character's loyalty to his master, his pidgin English, and physical brawn.[97] To be sure, Lippard emphasizes Sampson's physicality over his intelligence by depicting him repeatedly as "a tiger, suddenly let loose from his cage" and by racialized descriptions of his "wooly hair" and "thick lips."[98] Sampson's loyalty to his deceased master and determination to avenge him also evoke the obsequious blackface "Sambo" stereotype, expressed in his pledge to join the patriots because Jacob was "kind to Sampson" and "feed his old moder when she dyin!"[99] Lippard's assignation of Sampson's African royal heritage is another sentimental convention, dating back to Aphra Behn's *Oroonoko; or, The Royal Slave* (1688), the story of a noble African prince tricked into slavery and taken to British Surinam. When adapted for the eighteenth-century stage, the story's suitability for antislavery promotion was arguably enhanced because Oroonoko, the "oxymoronic *royal* slave" was a rare and superior exception to the general, and by implication inferior, black slave population.[100]

Yet for all Lippard's gestures toward accepted modalities of sentimental and comic blackface performances, his rendering of Sampson stakes radical claims for African Americans' revolutionary agency and inclusion in a multiracial working class. Lippard shows Sampson's loyalty and physical brawn in a positive rather than denigrative light. Moreover, while it is true that the black Hercules speaks the minstrel's dialect, Lippard also assigns other plebeian characters' speech patterns inflected by their ethnic origins, in keeping with contemporary theatrical conventions. From the smash hit of Charles Mathews's variety act onward, comic performers used dialect to represent Frenchmen, Irishmen, Yankees, and frontiersmen, as well as black slaves and freemen.[101] Gottlieb Hoff, for example, speaks accented English punctuated by German phrases, such as "Mein Gott" and "de" instead of "the," "kilt" instead of "killed," and "mit out," using the German "mit" instead of the English "with."[102] Dialect signifies the multiethnic nature of his working-class German, Irish, Scottish, Polish, and African American patriots and thus explicitly counters the nativism of the 1840s epitomized by the anti-German, anti-Irish, anti-black Know Nothings.

In several instances, Lippard explicitly reversed racial stereotypes. For example, Sampson's relationship to the loyal, sentient Debbil evokes a master-slave relationship, but the dark-complexioned Sampson and his pure-white dog turn the color markers of race on their head. Sampson's attempts to save Polly from abduction and death and his grief at her rape also ran counter to the stereotype of blacks as hypersexed and lascivious toward white women. Indeed, in Lippard's novel, only white British soldiers and loyalists violate white women. Even more revealingly, Lippard includes an episode of sexual abuse when a band of white loyalists led by the vicious David Walford *black up* to attack Rose Frazier and her "sable damsel" maidservant Phillis.[103] All these plot devices subvert accepted conventions of "black" and "white" figurative performances. Lastly, but crucially, Sampson is the first plebeian character to exhort "death or liberty," and his bravery rallies white plebeians—Gottlieb Hoff, Blacksmith Tom, and Hirpley Hawson—to the republican cause. Lippard ascribes heroic bravery, sympathetic emotions, and republican principles to Black Hercules and, in so doing, claims the revolutionary mantle of "life, liberty, and the pursuit of happiness" for black as well as white Americans.

Lippard's radical racial inclusivity did not, however, make its way into Mrs. H. M. Ward's stage adaptation of *Blanche of Brandywine*, which opened at Peale's Museum in Philadelphia in 1847.[104] Founded by painter Charles Willson Peale in 1786, Peale's Philadelphia Museum and Gallery of Fine Arts on Chestnut Street stayed in operation well after his 1827 death.[105] In 1847 it was a venue for popular dramas, farces, vaudevilles, concerts, scientific exhibits, and lectures.[106] Like Lippard, Ward was an admirer of Dickens, adapting his domestic drama, *Cricket on the Hearth*, which in 1846 played at Peale's Museum to "overflowing houses . . . and the loudest Acclamations of delight."[107] She also shared Lippard's passion for revolutionary history. Her *Blanche of Brandywine* was glowingly advertised as having "the most decided success" as "the first Domestic Drama on the Revolution ever played in this country" (pure hyperbole, as revolutionary-era playwrights like John Leacock and William Dunlap had already staged the Revolution).[108]

Possibly Ward knew Lippard, as according to a review of her *Blanche of Brandywine*, she also intended to "embody in dramatic form" Lippard's *Legends of the American Revolution* (although there is no evidence that she did so).[109] Moreover, Lippard was also connected to Peale's Museum; he staged his successful political drama, *The Sons of Temperance*, there in 1847, the same year Ward dramatized *Blanche of Brandwyine*.[110] He would go on to be a regular lecturer-performer at Peale's on varied topics, including "The French Revolution" and "Christianity of the Past and Present Time."[111] But if Ward and Lippard were acquainted, she certainly did not mirror his radical ideas of racial inclusion in the American revolutionary dream in her play. She condensed his long novel into a two-act romantic drama revolving around the tragic relationship between Lord Percy Monthoner, "willing to break his British sword and join the army of Washington for the love of Blanche," and his fiancée, Lady Isidore, who poisons herself after discovering his love for Blanche.[112] Of the plebeian characters, Ward retained only Blacksmith

Tom, omitting Sampson, who plays such a pivotal role in the novel, as well as Randulph/Wyamoke and his bitter critique of European-Americans' conduct toward Native Americans.

Even as Mrs. Ward erased the Black Hercules onstage, Lippard resurrected him in his *Legends of the American Revolution*. He first published *Legends* serially in Philadelphia's *Saturday Courier* between 1846 and 1848 in 110 stories subdivided into six books (published in two bound volumes in 1847 and 1848). His intentions, as he told *Saturday Courier* editor, Andrew M'Makin, were "to fill up old [historical] outlines with newly-discovered truths,—in one word, *to embody the traditions of the Revolution in a series of Historical Pictures . . . [and] fill up those pictures of the past with details from my own fancy, always keeping the general outline in severe accordance of known historical truth.*"[113] Lippard freely admitted that his chronicles were fanciful retellings "of known historical truth" but claimed they embodied the true spirit and "traditions of the Revolution" and would illuminate "newly discovered truths": the role of black revolutionaries, symbolized by Sampson, and the agency of everyman plebeians. For Lippard, these embroidered truths revealed a larger "newly discovered" real truth of the revolutionary traditions. In "Book the Fourth: The Battle of Brandywine," Lippard retells stories from his novel, including Randulph's rejection of the patriot cause; "The Mechanic Hero of Brandywine" starring Blacksmith Tom; "The Son of the Hunter-Spy," featuring Quaker loyalist Gilbert Gates and Sampson; and "Black Sampson," a separate story devoted to the character.[114]

In "The Son of the Hunter-Spy," Lippard altered Sampson's biography and some basic plot elements. The installment revisits the story of Jacob Mayland's murder at the hands of Tories, Gilbert Gates's complicity, and Sampson's vow to avenge Jacob's death, but with new twists. Lippard recasts Gates as an imposter who poses as a Quaker with, as Polly Mayland makes clear, "assumed dress" and an "awkward attempt at the Quaker dialect" in order to persuade her to marry him.[115] Her refusal, along with the fact that Jacob was in part responsible for the hanging of Gilbert's father, (the "hunter-spy" of the title) motivates his betrayal of the family and the resulting abduction of Polly and murder of Jacob. Sampson is still the "black Hercules" who vainly tries to fight off the Tories' attack out of loyalty to Jacob because "De ole man kind to Sampson!" but now he is an African who renders his oath of vengeance "not in English—but in his wild Ashantee tongue."[116]

In the next installment, "Black Sampson," Lippard used these biographical and plot changes to make explicit his antislavery sympathies and to enhance Sampson's revolutionary heroism. He still describes Sampson as a "Herculean outline of iron strength," who continues to be assisted by Debbil, "a noble animal, in shape something like the kingly dogs of St. Bernard, yet white as the driven snow."[117] But now Sampson is a fugitive "slave from the far south" taken in by Jacob, whom Lippard now depicts as a Quaker, playing on the long-time Quaker antislavery views.[118] Sampson's loyalty is thus no longer explained as the loyalty of a slave to his "good" master but rather that of an appreciative but proud freeman. Moreover, now Sampson speaks fragmented English because he is newly arrived and "could not speak ten clear words of our English tongue." Lippard leaves some of Sampson's dialect in pidgin English but opts to "translate" many of Sampson's thoughts "into English, because when he *thought*, it was in the musical syllables of his native Ashantee." In this "translated" voice, Sampson's thoughts—of being stolen into slavery from his Ashantee king father, of missing his native land, and of the "horrible torture" of slavery—become fluid, articulate and more emotionally sophisticated than those of the Sampson of *Blanche of Brandywine*.[119] By giving an African slave character clear thoughts in standard English, Lippard departed from the blackface conventions then prevalent.

Rewriting Sampson as a fugitive slave of recent African origin and Jacob as a Quaker who shelters him allowed Lippard to champion the universal "rights of man" and Sampson's membership in a revolutionary brotherhood. Lippard first extolls Sampson as a revolutionary hero in race-neutral class-inflected terms as "a very humble man who had toiled from dawn until dusk, with the axe or spade." He then revealed Sampson's ethnicity to his readers: "Start not when I tell you, that this hero was—a Negro! His hair crisped into wool, his skin blackened to the hue of ink, by the fiery sun of his clime and race, his hands harsh and bony with iron toil." By continuing to stress Sampson's "iron toil," Lippard includes him in the manual working classes even while differentiating him by race.

But Lippard adamantly distanced himself from abolitionism as a threat to the Union. Switching out of his storytelling and into a didactic voice, Lippard told his readers: "Do not mistake me. I am no factionist . . . I have no sympathy . . . for those miserably deluded men, who in order to free the African race, would lay unholy hands upon the American Union."[120] Even though the Union sheltered "black slavery in the south and white slavery in the north," it should not be destroyed by dissension, as it was founded on "an eternal bond of brotherhood for innumerable millions, an altar forever sacred to the Rights of Man."[121] Dividing it would solve neither industrial oppression nor African slavery. Lippard completed his "protest against . . . feverish philanthropy" by announcing "let me turn now to my hero" and launching into the brave deeds of Sampson, who "reminds you at once of Appolo and Hercules, hewn from . . . anthracite."[122] Despite having created Sampson as a member of the revolutionary vanguard and lauding Jacob for sheltering him, as well as decrying "black slavery in the south, and white slavery in the north," he disparaged abolitionism as "feverish philanthropy." Yet he failed to offer an alternative prescription for slavery's demise.

Lippard was, however, inspired anew to indict slavery in the wake of the 1848 socialist revolutions of Europe, which had pervasive ripple effects in American politics and culture. Rooted in the post-Napoleonic treaty forged by Klemens Metternich (an Austrian Prince who served as foreign minister for the Habsburg Empire), which reinstated monarchical rule by four families—Hanover, Bourbon, Habsburg and Romanoff—over almost all of Europe, the treaty galvanized independence movements in Europe and in Latin America in the 1820s and 1830s. These independence movements drew American sympathy, as did the 1848 pan-European uprisings they precipitated.[123] Like George Dibdin Pitt in London, whose *Revolution in Paris* was banned from the stage, American dramatists staged plays set in France and dramatizing aspects of the 1848 revolutions, such as *The Insurrection of Paris; or, The People's Triumph* at the Bowery Theatre in New York in March 1848 and *The Barricades*, which opened in October 1848 at the Park Theatre, also in New York.[124]

While Lippard did not write a French revolutionary story, he did pen a socialist historical fiction set in America, *Adonai: The Pilgrim of Eternity* (1849), which again critiqued slavery and oppression. In the novel, the spirit of an early Christian persecuted in Nero's Rome travels in time and observes that all the horrors of Nero's tyranny persist through the ages, including in 1848 America, his final destination. Expecting to find "the Gospel of Nazareth . . . preached unto the Poor," he encounters instead slave auctioneers in "America, the Land of the Free and Home of the Brave," specifically in the "Slave-Pen of the City of Washington"; a factory (which he first mistakes for a prison) where women and children perform grueling labor alongside men; and everywhere wealth and exemplary governmental ideals but also "poverty," "splendid crime," and "unfathomable misery."[125] Lippard called on his readers to "look to Europe," "struggling in the throes of her Last Revolution," for the "future of the human race" and of America, "the last altar of human Brotherhood."[126]

Lippard also reacted to the 1848 revolutions by trying to implement his vision of "human Brotherhood" into a secret organization devoted to labor. After reading the writings of French socialists and reformers like Charles Fourier and Louis Blanc, he founded the Brotherhood of the Union to "espouse the cause of the Masses" and reform the capitalist system that sheltered "corrupt Bankers," "land Monopolists," and "Monied Oppressors." Striking a newly militant tone, Lippard also proposed that if peaceful approaches to reform failed, then "Labor [should] go to War . . . with the Rifle, Sword and Knife."[127] Lippard's Brotherhood, which by 1850 had 142 chartered circles in nineteen states, did not make good this militant threat, but it did foster anticapitalism grounded in what its members regarded as American revolutionary principles. The Brotherhood named its democratically elected offices after Jefferson, Franklin, Washington, and other "founding fathers," with Lippard holding the top office of Supreme Washington until his death in 1854.[128] Prior to that, he was also involved in the radical Daughters and Sons of Toil, a cooperative group that supported women's suffrage, civil rights for blacks and Native Americans, and a utopian vision of the overthrow of the capitalist system.[129] In 1854, when Lippard died, Brotherhood of the Union member O. L. Drake, who held the second-in-command position of Supreme Jefferson, wrote a moving eulogy for "Brother Lippard," after which he—per an incongruously undemocratic clause in the Brotherhood's constitution—inherited the title of Supreme Washington. He aptly characterized Lippard's life mission as "friend of the oppressed," not only in his political actions but also because "throughout all his writings is breathed a spirit of brotherhood, showing that this was the *idea* of his life."[130]

Operating in markedly disparate geopolitical settings, Philadelphian George Lippard, in his depictions of Sampson, the black Hercules, in *Blanche of Brandywine* and *Legends of the American Revolution*, and Londoner George Dibdin Pitt, in his *Toussaint L'Ouverture; or, the Black Spartacus*, used their writings and dramatizations to extol what Drake would describe as a "spirit of brotherhood." Both Pitt and Lippard looked back to the promises of the eighteenth-century revolutions and called for their fulfillment to benefit the brotherhood of industrial wage slaves and African chattel slaves. Pitt, who dramatized the Haitian Revolution after slavery had ended in the distant British West Indies and in a city with a tiny black population, used his blackface Toussaint as a universalist hero of the downtrodden East End workers and his slave-driving Jonathan Jungle as a comical yet acerbic critique of American slavery's contradiction with the nation's revolutionary principles. Lippard, in contrast, was writing and performing in a city with an enormous free black population and violent race relations, and a country deeply divided on sectional lines and containing an estimated four million black slaves. In this context, Lippard, while repeatedly expressing his disgust with slavery and its contradiction to American republican principles, was also disdainful of abolitionists, whom he feared would tear the Union he revered asunder. He nonetheless claimed Paine's principles of the "Rights of Man" for African Americans and used his character, Sampson, to make a radical argument for blacks' inclusion in the revolutionary spirit of '76.

The similarities of Pitt's and Lippard's claims are in many ways more arresting than their differences. Both pointed to American slavery's inconsistency with its revolutionary heritage as a blot on progressive polity and inclusive citizenship. In both cities, they were swimming against the tide of virulent racism. They were also both countering a prevalent discourse pitting the conditions of industrial "wage slaves" as more dire and worthy of urgent attention than those of black chattel slaves. In London, the racist and proslavery Thomas Carlyle made this argument, but so too did cultural interlocutors, like Charles Dickens, who were sympathetic to the plight of American slaves yet adamant that Great Britain's industrial poor should take precedence. Philadelphians, for their part, were aware not only of proslavery Southern contentions that their treatment of slaves was more benevolent than Northern factory owners' treatment of wage laborers (like the arguments made by George Fitzhugh), but also of the cries of Northern labor leaders that white factory "slaves" were in worse straits than African plantation slaves. Pitt and Lippard both responded by dramatizing the eighteenth-century revolutions to posit a "spirit of brotherhood" and champion the rights of chattel slaves and wage slaves to economic justice and liberty. In the early 1850s, Lippard and Pitt, along with other Britons and Americans, wedded minstrelsy to antislavery reform sentiment in protest of the Fugitive Slave Act, a marriage epitomized by Pitt's dramatic adaptation of Harriet Beecher Stowe's novel, retitled *Uncle Tom's Cabin: A Nigger Drama in Two Acts*, in October 1852. On the eve of the bloody carnage of the U.S. Civil War, Britons still defined their liberty and rights in opposition to American slavery, and both Britons and Americans highlighted its contradiction to American revolutionary ideals. Slavery was still at the crux of the British and American national identities London and Philadelphian artists, thespians, abolitionists, essayists, novelists, poets, and cartoonists had helped forge through the transatlantic competition and exchange they began in the American revolutionary years.

Uncle Tom,
the Eighteenth-Century Revolutionary
Legacy, and Historical Memory

In 1853, British abolition societies solicited popular support and raised £1,930 for the American emancipationist cause through the "Uncle Tom Penny Offering," the collection of one penny from every reader of Harriet Beecher Stowe's *Uncle Tom's Cabin*.[1] Initially published in the United States in serial form in the *National Era* in 1851 and 1852 before the spectacular success of its first bound edition, prose versions of Stowe's novel soon proliferated in Great Britain and the United States.[2] Concomitantly, dramatizations of *Uncle Tom's Cabin* were sensationally popular in the theaters of Philadelphia and other Northern seaboard cities.[3] A plethora of British theatrical adaptations drew enthusiastic crowds to West End and East End theaters throughout 1852 to 1853, including Eliza Vincent's *Uncle Tom's Cabin; or, The Fugitive Slave*, Mark Lemon's consciously abolitionist *A Slave Life*, several blackface minstrel versions, and F. Neale's pantomime, *Harlequin Uncle Tom; or, Britannia the Pride of the Ocean and Guardian Genius of the Slave*, a patriotic boast of British abolitionist "liberty."[4] Small wonder, then, that British abolitionists believed the story to be synonymous with their cause and exploited its phenomenal popularity to rally support for the fight to end American slavery.

Yet Britons' passions were furiously divided over *Uncle Tom's Cabin*, divisions already ignited by the United States' Fugitive Slave Act of 1850, which had inspired Stowe's novel. The act had inflamed the crossfire between Thomas Carlyle and John Stuart Mill, and spurred Carlyle's, Charles Dickens's, and John Tenniel's contention that Britannia's "liberty" should be defined not by "telescopic philanthropy" directed toward freeing American slaves but rather toward aiding London's poor. Moreover, while some abolitionists, thespians, and writers rushed to adapt and promote *Uncle Tom's Cabin* for its condemnation of slavery and the Fugitive Slave Act, other Britons repudiated it as an incendiary novel that, by provoking Southerners' passions, would make emancipation of American slaves harder, not easier. In this vein, a *London Times* reviewer averred that Stowe was so filled with "the rightful warfare of the crusader" that she had rendered in her novel an overly harsh view of slavery that would anger Southerners. Therefore, he claimed, "the gravest fault of the book . . . will be to render slavery more difficult than ever of abolishment [because] it will keep ill-blood at boiling point, and irritate instead of pacifying those whose proceedings Mrs. Stowe is anxious to influence on behalf of humanity." No fan of slavery, the journalist pointed out its contradiction of American republican principles yet cautioned against North-South confrontation: "If the people of the United States, who fought and bled for their liberty and nobly won it are to remove the disgrace that attaches to them for forging chains for others which they will not tolerate on their own limbs, *the work of enfranchisement must be a movement, not forced upon slaveowners, but voluntarily undertaken.*"[5]

The *London Times* writer was absolutely right that *Uncle Tom's Cabin* would "keep ill-blood at boiling point, and irritate instead of pacifying" Southern slave owners: the novel and its many dramatic adaptations caused an even greater furor in the United States, already embroiled in seething sectional crisis. The *New York Herald* review of the National Theatre's dramatization of Stowe's novel is worth quoting in length, as it captures both the controversy and also the tremendous influence of the work on debates about slavery:

> The novel of *Uncle Tom's Cabin* is at present our nine days' literary wonder. It has sold by thousands, and ten, and hundreds of thousands . . . because of the widely extended sympathy, in all of the North, with the pernicious abolition sympathies and "higher law" moral of this ingenious and cunningly devised abolition fable. The *furore* which it has thus created, has brought out quite a number of catchpenny imitators, pro and con, desirous of filling their sails while yet the breeze is blowing . . . The success of *Uncle Tom's Cabin* as a novel, has naturally suggested its success upon the stage; but . . . any such representation must be an insult to the South— an exaggerated mockery of Southern institutions—and calculated, more than any other expedient of agitation to poison the minds of our youth with the pestilent principles of abolitionism.[6]

The reviewer was unsympathetic to the "pestilent principles of abolitionism" and to the novel, as he believed both incited sectional strife. Indeed, many Southerners, as the critic asserted, found the representation of slavery in *Uncle Tom's Cabin* "an insult" and "an exaggerated mockery" and denounced the work as slanderous.

Northern antislavery sympathizers, by contrast, generally praised the work's " 'higher law' moral" and hailed the influential "abolition fable" with approval. True, some black theater critics and abolitionists were dismayed at the submissive traits of Uncle Tom and the fact that Beecher Stowe had her central black characters emigrate to Liberia. But many were enthusiastic about the story's antislavery appeal. Frederick Douglass, for example, who had elsewhere castigated blackface minstrel performers and fans as "the filthy scum of white society, who . . . pander to the corrupt taste of their white fellow citizens" claimed Stowe's novel "could light a million camp fires in front of the imbattled hosts of Slavery."[7] Many white Philadelphians, like John Penington, were also enamored of Stowe's story and its dramatizations, gushing about "this far-famed production" and dismissing "the objection to it from niggerdom [and] northern lick-spittles," by which latter term he presumably meant Northern opponents of abolitionism like the *New York Herald* reporter.[8]

But did the novel hail "a new epoch . . . of abolition authorship"? The *New York Herald* reviewer scathingly concluded that the novel and its dramatic adaptations marked: "a new epoch and a new field of abolition authorship—a new field of fiction, humbug and deception, for a more extended agitation of the slavery question—than any that as heretofore imperiled the peace and safety of the Union."[9] But in many ways, the "abolition authorship" of *Uncle Tom's Cabin* was not new; it was instead the inheritor of sentimental antislavery performances such as eighteenth-century dramatic adaptations of Aphra Behn's *Oroonoko*, which featured an enslaved African prince who foments a rebellion; George Colman's *Inkle and Yarico*, with its pathetic enslaved heroine; and Isaac Bickerstaffe's *The Padlock*, with its comic Mungo, the blackface rebel slave. Modern critics write of the novel and its dramatizations in terms of its as having birthed racist caricatures, hence the well-worn use of "Uncle Tom" as a synonym for a black "sell-out" to white racism. But Stowe built on eighteenth-century forebears by embedding antislavery appeal into minstrel-like characters such as the puerile Topsy and meek Uncle Tom.[10]

Linkages between antislavery reform efforts and blackface burlesque were not obvious, however, to nineteenth-century critics and abolitionists in London and Philadelphia who, tellingly, insisted that the play's abolitionist sentiments were in *opposition* to the conventions of minstrelsy. In London, for example, dramatic adaptations of the novel earned widespread praise for their antislavery sentiment and for bringing to the stage heroic black characters instead of minstrel "niggers." The *London Times* critic, for example, extolled a stage version because "The *Uncle Tom* of Drury [Lane] is not the silly and absurd 'nigger' we have seen represented elsewhere, but one of those natural creations which powerfully enlist our feelings."[11] When another critic similarly praised a production of *Uncle Tom's Cabin*, he averred that "the slang of 'Ethiopian Serenaders' for once gives place to thoughts and language racy of the soil, and we need not say how refreshing it is to be separated for a season from the conventional Sambo of the modern stage."[12] British and American critics in the 1850s thus differentiated between minstrelsy and *Uncle Tom's* antislavery depictions. Yet the reviews unwittingly reveal the depth to which abolitionist sentiment had become so fused with blackface burlesque by the 1850s that contemporaries accepted Topsy, Uncle Tom, and even minstrel versions of the story as a form of antislavery protest.

This fusion had its origins in the American Revolution, which ushered in an enduring contestation over British and American national identities that hinged on contrasting views of slavery and liberty. These competing discourses were crucial to the development of the British Atlantic lexicon of race, slavery, and antislavery that reached maturation in *Uncle Tom's Cabin*. Through transatlantic circulation, thespians, poets, artists, cartoonists, and pamphleteers in the American revolutionary era established foundational symbols, motifs, and characters: the neoclassical Goddess in her Temple of Liberty as a powerful metaphor of polity in which slaves had a contested place, the Sambo-like blackface supplicant slave, and a good-for-nothing, lascivious, and oft-drunk free black undeserving of liberty or civic inclusion. Londoners claimed Britannia's abolitionist "liberty" to rebut American patriots' claims of British imperial tyranny by depicting their goddess in art, pantomimes, architecture, and poetry bestowing freedom on a grateful blackface supplicant slave. At the same time, London cartoonists used theatrical blackface characters like Mungo to depict blacks as lascivious and associate them with imperial and ethnic decay in reaction to the influx of penurious African American demobilized "loyalist" ex-slaves. In revolutionary America, images of Columbia emancipating the slaves soon gave way in the early republic to artistic, prose, and theatrical performances that removed the slaves from these settings, and implicitly erased their rights to liberty. Philadelphians and other Northerners also developed an ugly genre of oral blackface satire to deliver the same message of a Herrenvolk republic. By depicting blacks as drunken and ignorant, broadside creators mocked their attempts at civic participation in reaction against slave-trade abolition and the mirage of black freedom it evoked.

Emerging from the American revolutionary years, the Sambo-like blackface supplicant slave, the oral blackface freeman speaking in the minstrel's malapropisms, and the neoclassical Temple of Liberty as a symbol of contested polity were instantly recognizable on both sides of the ocean by the time of slave-trade abolition (1807 in Great Britain and 1808 in the United States). Revolutionary-era philosophical and political protest of slavery and neoclassical models of polity were thus inextricably interlinked with the popular entertainment of blackface burlesque. These linkages would be further cemented in the 1810s and 1820s with imperial ventures into Africa—the American Colonization Society's mission to "repatriate" African Americans to Liberia and Great Britain's impetus to civilize and Christianize Africa. Britons and Americans both visualized these ventures as spreading the liberty of their respective temples, while blackface theatrical visions of colonizing Africa also embedded emergent scientific and philosophical theories of race that fixed skin complexion and geography to hierarchically organized levels of civilization.

Thespians, cartoonists, and writers continued to use and elaborate on these images, conventions, and characters in the 1820s in picaresque stage plays, racialist cartoons, and proto-vaudeville blackface burlesque. These genres were potent conduits for continued competition over British and American ideas of nation and polity hinging on the meanings of slavery and liberty. The transatlantic cross-pollination of perspectives on race and slavery was amplified by the free-flowing circulation of prose, visual, and theatrical media. Out of this cartoon-theater circulation of the "black jokes" of freedom, the bestial, lascivious, and frivolous free black dandy emerged, as did the burlesque of black slavery that paved the way for Jim Crow. Cartoonists' "black jokes"—Edward Clay's *Life in Philadelphia* series and its subsequent London knock-offs—also adapted the newly pernicious ideas of race offered by craniologists who defined superior or inferior intellectual and morality as a function of skull size and physiognomic features and placed Africans at the bottom rung of this taxonomy. When the black dandy stepped out of the cartoon and onto the stage, these racial theories were viscerally embodied in figures like Dandy Jim, close cousin to Zip Coon. These images and characters were interlinked with still simmering opposition to slavery and political reform impetus: Charles Mathews used his send-up of an American slave—replete with the "black fun" of minstrel speech—to criticize American slavery's contradiction of republican principles and to support moderate parliamentary reform in Great Britain. To be sure, cartoonists, thespians, and writers were performing these racialized picaresque and burlesque genres within a larger political framework of radical agitation for political reform and on the same stages from which radical orators, such as Fanny Wright, spoke.

The 1830s and 1840s cemented the dialectic between the burlesque and the utopian performances of race, antislavery, and rights. Against the backdrop of massive slave revolts and the Emancipation Act of 1833, blackface minstrel Jim Crow strutted across the same transatlantic stages as Spartacus, the Thracian gladiator who led a slave revolt against Rome. Yet Jim Crow was a slippery figure. Depending on geopolitical context and his audiences, T. Daddy Rice might perform the character he created as an underdog spokesman for reform and even antislavery. Yet the figure also animated a racist caricature of Southern slaves as lustful, irresponsible, and lazy, and T. Daddy Rice consciously sought to animate prevalent racist theories of African inferiority in his Jim Crow performances. In the "hungry forties," amid labor unrest and industrial poverty, the radical-leaning London playwright George Dibdin Pitt and Philadelphian performer and writer George Lippard amalgamated blackface minstrelsy and revolutionary utopianism when they dramatized the events of the eighteenth-century revolutions to demand the fulfillment of their democratic promises not only for the urban industrial poor but also for the enslaved black. Lippard incorporated minstrel traits into his revolutionary hero Sampson the Black Hercules, whom he included recurrently in his lectures and novels about the American Revolution to promote a racially inclusive revolutionary brotherhood. Similarly, Pitt included blackface minstrel characters alongside Toussaint Louverture, the Black Spartacus, his iconic hero of resistance to oppression for enslaved blacks and downtrodden white workers in the London slums. Blackface minstrels became *part* of the performance of antislavery and utopian reformism, using the ideals of democratic rights first unleashed by the American Revolution.

When the United States' controversial Fugitive Slave Act passed in 1850, both Pitt and Lippard were nearing the ends of their lives. Yet up until his last breath, Lippard attacked the ills of slavery. In his unfinished novel, *Eleanor; or, Slave Catching in the Quaker City*, installments of which were published in the *Philadelphia Sunday Mercury* before his death in 1854, Lippard condemned the Fugitive Slave Act. George Dibdin Pitt, meanwhile, who outlived Lippard by just a year, dramatized Harriet Beecher Stowe's novel under the title *Uncle Tom's Cabin: A Nigger Drama in Two Acts* in October 1852 for the Royal Pavilion Theatre (after being let go from the Britannia).[13] Pitt retained Stowe's critique of slavery and of the Fugitive Slave Act. That he staged it under a title using a racial pejorative linked to blackface minstrelsy is, however, emblematic of how radical and reformist sentiments had become inextricable from racialist satire by the mid-nineteenth century. Lippard's and Pitt's protests of the Fugitive Slave Act, as well as the multiple renditions of *Uncle Tom's Cabin*, were beneficiaries of both the language of rights and blackface burlesque set in motion by the American Revolution. For it was the American war that first made slavery crucial to British or American national self-identity: a glaring aberration in Columbia's Temple of Liberty and a marker of monarchical Britannia's abolitionist principles.

After the Civil War ended and African Americans in the South were finally free, commentators were still using the British Atlantic popular lexicon of neoclassical motifs and blackface burlesque created by the decades of transatlantic exchange of images, theatrical performances, and broadsides begun in the American revolutionary contest. In July 1870, after the Reconstruction Act of

OUR GODDESS OF LIBERTY.
WHAT IS SHE TO BE? TO WHAT COMPLEXION ARE WE TO COME AT LAST?

Figure 22. Our Goddess of Liberty (1870). This print illustrates the enduring usage and co-mingling of the neoclassical motifs and blackface burlesque that originated in the American revolutionary years. It also suggests a fearful vision of a future polity in which bestial Africans hold the reins of power. From *Frank Leslie's Illustrated Newspaper*, July 16, 1870, courtesy Library of Congress

1867 had begun extending political rights to free black men and women in the South, an artist (unidentified but presumably white) published in *Frank Leslie's Illustrated Newspaper* a racialized commentary on the past, present, and future of the United States' polity through multiple depictions of Columbia, with the words, "Our Goddess of Liberty—what is she to be? To what complexion are we to come at last?" (fig. 22). The engraving featured caricatures of five female heads, each a version of Liberty defined by race. At the lower left of the image, the artist harks back to the revolutionary-era Columbia as a Native American princess with a feathered headdress, who on the right has "evolved" into a more "civilized" visage in Euro-American attire but still noticeably indigenous. The designer placed the white, neoclassical Columbia in the center of the print, suggesting her status as present-day matriarch of the nation and her continued desirability as the ideal. At the upper right is an African American Liberty with grossly disproportioned and apelike features, reminiscent of Edward Clay's *Life in Philadelphia* caricatures and craniology studies; to its left image is Liberty as an ape. These figures seem to suggest the artist's fearful vision of a postemancipation future polity in which miscegenation despoils white Columbia and bestial Africans rule.

The print points to how the synthesis of radical and reformist thought with fully rigidified constructs of race in blackface burlesque has had lasting implications for modern popular culture and intellectual discourse. In 1918, American theater historian Montrose Moses recognized this merger of abolitionist sentiment and minstrel motifs, and its origins. In his introduction to George Akien's 1852 adaptation of *Uncle Tom's Cabin*, which debuted at Troy Museum in New York on November 15, 1852, and ran for one hundred nights, Moses wrote:

> Everywhere it was regarded a typical negro play and students became interested in the question of the negro as a stage character. They . . . discussed Thomas Southerne's *Oronooko* in comparison with Mrs. Behn's *Oroonoko; or, The Royal Slave*. They had not seriously considered the development of the Ethiopian drama in America, which had begun years before the advent of "Uncle Tom," nor had they realized that long before [actor] Joseph Jefferson appeared in this play, he had, as a little fellow, blackened up and made his stage debut with "Jim Crow" Rice in dance and song.[14]

To be sure, one cannot draw a tidy, uncomplicated line between the lexicon of race, slavery, and antislavery spawned in the revolutionary era and that of the nineteenth century. But Moses articulated a crucial idea: the blending of reform politics and racial mockery in blackface performance. He recognized the links between *Uncle Tom's Cabin*, T. Daddy Rice's Jim Crow, and the sentimental antislavery of Southerne's theatrical adaptation of *Oroonoko*, popular in 1780s London as antislavery fervor was gaining sway in the aftershocks of the American Revolution.

Some of Moses's contemporaries built on these blackface conventions to make racist arguments in both popular culture and intellectual discourse. In 1904, Alfred Rosenthal lent his collection of ten Edward Clay *Life in Philadelphia* prints to be hung in Independence Hall, where they remained for twenty years, suggesting that white officialdom responsible for preserving the city's historical memory considered this racist material appropriate for public display (with no regard for how black Philadelphians might feel about it).[15] D. W. Griffith's disturbing white supremacist fantasy, *The Birth of a Nation* (1915), based on Thomas Dixon Jr.'s novel and play *The Clansman*, depicted a postemancipation race war in which vengeful black freedmen raped white women and the Ku Klux Klan emerged as victorious heroes. The film, featuring white actors in blackface makeup, played on the same fears of miscegenation expressed in *Our Goddess of Liberty* from *Frank Leslie's Illustrated Newspaper*. Both express a virulent prejudice with a long history in performative culture. Such pernicious perpetuations of blackface burlesque also permeated intellectual culture, including academic history. Writing just three years after the release of *Birth of a Nation*, historian Ulrich B. Philips claimed in *American Negro Slavery* that antebellum slaves were docile, stupid Sambos who enjoyed the benevolent institution of slavery, playing on a different but no less derogatory blackface minstrel motif.[16]

Philips was hardly alone in perpetuating blackface burlesque in historical memory. First published in 1937, *The Growth of the American Republic*, by Samuel Eliot Morison and Henry Steel Commager, was the most widely used college-level survey of American history through the 1950s.[17] Morison and Commager described slavery and antislavery thus: "Sambo, whose wrongs moved the abolitionists to wrath and tears . . . suffered less than any other class in the South from its 'peculiar institution.' The majority of slaves were adequately fed, well cared for, and apparently happy. Although brought to America by force, the incurably optimistic negro soon became attached to the country, and devoted to his 'white folks.'" The "average" slave, they concluded, was "childlike, improvident, humorous, prevaricating and superstitious," and "there was much to be said for slavery as a transitional status between barbarism and civilization."[18] Morison and Commager, both distinguished Ivy League historians, not only unquestioningly used the derogatory "Sambo" but also depicted docile slaves enthralled to white folks, reminiscent of the supplicant blackface slaves appealing to the revolutionary-era goddess for their liberty. Although in the *Growth of the American Republic* the slaves were grateful for their slavery rather than for their liberty, the historians nonetheless made a direct link between abolitionists and the submissive slave who must be fitted for freedom by the influence of white civilization. Despite criticism, the authors did not remove the Sambo passage until 1962, in the fifth edition of the textbook.[19]

These twentieth-century examples reveal how the eighteenth- and nineteenth-century cultural and intellectual heritage has profoundly influenced modern historical memory of race, slavery, and antislavery. The persistence of the grateful slave and the bestial, lustful black freeman, which had their start in eighteenth- and nineteenth-century popular culture, raise several questions of historical and topical relevance: What happens when issues of social reform are embedded in commercial popular culture? Can commercially popular performances play

a role in altering peoples' views on social issues? Some eighteenth- and nineteenth-century commentators thought so. British theatrical commentator James
Plumptre, reacting to the 1807 abolition of the slave trade, was convinced that
the London theater had played "a very considerable part in influencing the public
mind with respect of the *Negroes*, and the infamous traffic of the *Slave-trade*."[20]
Plumptre's assertion of theater and popular culture's influence on "the public
mind" is not quantifiable. But what can be concluded is that British and American cultural interlocutors not only brought debates about slavery and race into
popular consciousness through the far reach of theater, visual, and aural culture
but also helped set the terms of the debates through the lexicon of images, characters, and conventions they jointly developed.

These eighteenth- and nineteenth-century performances of race, slavery, and
antislavery still have lasting resonance in the twenty-first century. On the one
hand, the use of blackface performance as light entertainment has endured, as
Spike Lee satirically underlined in his film *Bamboozled* (2000), a fictional depiction of a modern televised minstrel show featuring African Americans donning
blackface makeup and performing minstrel characters for mass entertainment.
Lee's premise was not far-fetched: blackface minstrel shows had a vestigial bloom
as recently as the United Kingdom's popular *The Black and White Minstrel Show*,
which aired on television from 1958 to 1978. Moreover, recent examples abound
of modern brown- and blackface film performances, like Alec Guinness's comically obsequious brownface Professor Godbole in *A Passage to India* (1984) and
Robert Downey Jr.'s performance as Kirk Lazarus in *Tropic Thunder* (2008).
While Downey's character embedded a critique of blackface—the film's storyline is of a white actor, played by Downey, who dons blackface makeup to win a
role—many were nonetheless offended by the performance. The continued use
of brown- and blackface would seem to suggest a perplexing historical amnesia
about the troubled history of blackface performances of slavery and race. On the
other hand, some contemporary thespians have chosen to remember but authori-
tatively *revise* this history by reviving eighteenth-century plays featuring slave protagonists. In 1999 the Royal Shakespeare Company staged *Oroonoko* for the first
time in 150 years. A few years later in 2006, the Chicago Opera House staged
Isaac Bickerstaffe's *The Padlock*. Cast with African American, Afro-Caribbean,
African, and African British actors in roles historically played by white actors in
blackface makeup, black thespians substantially rewrote these plays to rebut racist stereotypes and reflect contemporary understandings of the brutal history of
slavery and the slave trade.

The reader began this book by visiting productions of George Colman Jr.'s

Inkle and Yarico in 1787 London and 1792 Philadelphia. Take a trip with me now to Barbados, 1997, where *Inkle and Yarico* is taking the stage at the Holders Performing Arts Festival roughly 170 years it had previously graced the transatlantic stage. As we have not seen this play for some time, let's remind ourselves of the story. An English merchant, Inkle, shipwrecked off the coast of Barbados, is rescued from death by Yarico. Depending on the production, Yarico is variously depicted as Native American or African. After Inkle recovers he makes Yarico his mistress, only to then heartlessly sell her into slavery. But in Barbados in 1997, we find that the Holders Company has given the story a new twist: haunted by guilt and remorse over selling Yarico to a slave trader, Inkle confesses all to the abolitionist William Wilberforce. Wilberforce then publicizes the story of Inkle and Yarico, which is made into an opera that has a great effect in mobilizing public opinion behind the antislavery movement. In 1807, aided by the propagandistic use of the story of Inkle and Yarico, Wilberforce puts through a parliamentary bill abolishing the slave trade and Inkle finds redemption, or so the 1997 story goes. Individual moral change engenders a popular antislavery tale, the performance of which mobilizes public opinion behind political change. The Barbados reproduction attributes a powerful role to popular culture in transmuting individual antislavery sentiment into a massive political constituency. While popular performative culture can certainly be channeled into frivolous racial mimicry that seemingly abets willful historical erasure, it can also be a potent medium for the conscious rewriting of our cultural memories and contemporary understandings of race and slavery. Eighteenth- and nineteenth-century Britons and Americans knew this when they endlessly revised and rewrote plays, images, and characters to create a recognizably British Atlantic lexicon of race and slavery that intertwined with topical views yet also powerfully worked to reshape them.

Abbreviations

BL	British Library, London
HL	Huntington Library, San Marino, CA
HSP	Historical Society of Pennsylvania, Philadelphia
LCP	Library Company of Philadelphia
LCPlays	Lord Chamberlain's Plays collection, British Library
NA	National Archives, London (former Public Records Office)
Thcts	Theatre Cuts collection, British Library

Introduction · Political and Cultural Exchange in the British Atlantic

1. William Wilberforce to his sister, Nov. 26, 1787, in *The Correspondence of William Wilberforce*, vol. 1, edited by Robert Isaac Wilberforce and Samuel Wilberforce (1840; reprint, Miami: Mnemosyne, 1969), 50.

2. Elizabeth Inchbald, "Remarks to Inkle and Yarico" (1787), in *Remarks for the British Theatre*, ed. Cecilia Machevski (New York: Scholars' Facsimiles and Reprints, 1990).

3. Inchbald, "Remarks to Inkle and Yarico," in George Colman, *Inkle and Yarico, an Opera in Three Acts: As Performed at the Covent-Garden, Hay-market, and New-York Theaters* (New York, 1806).

4. *Daily Register*, Aug. 6, 1787; *Lloyd's Evening Post*, Dec. 1791.

5. *The London Stage, 1660–1800*, part 5: *1776–1800*, ed. C. B. Hogan (Carbondale: Southern Illinois University Press, 1968), 3:clxxiii.

6. Inchbald, "Remarks to Inkle and Yarico" (1806).

7. Frances Maria Kelly, diary, BL MS 42920 fols. 120–210b.

8. The songs were published in the *Times*, Aug. 5, 1787, and the *Morning Chronicle*, Aug. 6, 1787. Examples of Yarico's story as the basis of antislavery poetry include John Anketell, *Poems on Several Subjects; by [. . .] John Aketell. To which are added, The epistle of Yarico to Inkle* (London and Dublin, 179?), and John Wolcott, *Yarico to Incle* (London, 1793).

9. Gary B. Nash, " Reverberations of Haiti in the American North: Black Saint Dominguans in Philadelphia," *Pennsylvania History 65: Explorations in Early American Culture* (1998): 44–73, 50.

10. *Gazette of the United States* (Philadelphia), Dec. 31, 1791. For the impact of the Saint Domingue refugees and their recalcitrant slaves on the northern cities of the early American republic, see Nash, "Reverberations of Haiti," and Ashli White, *Encountering Revolution: Haiti and the Making of the Early Republic* (Baltimore: Johns Hopkins University Press, 2010).

11. William McKoy, "Long Syne Papers," originally published in *Poulson's Daily Advertiser* 2 (n.d.): 34, and reproduced in *Poulson's Scrapbook of Philadelphia History* (Philadelphia, 1828), 4:16. William McKoy published essays under the signature "Long Syne" in *Poulson's Daily Advertiser*; his essays, along with other materials, were republished in 1828 as *Poulson's Scrapbook of Philadelphia History*.

12. Charles Durang, *History of the Philadelphia Stage from the Year 1749 to the Year 1855*,

Partly Compiled from the Papers of His Father, the late John Durang (Philadelphia, 1854), 1:fol. 25.

13. Ibid., 1:fol. 75.

14. *Pennsylvania Packet*, May 17, 1790.

15. George Colman Jr., *Inkle and Yarico* (Philadelphia, 1792).

16. Playbills for *Pennsylvania Packet*, May 17, 1790; *Pennsylvania Journal*, May 1790; *Pennsylvania Journal*, June 27, 1792.

17. *Pennsylvania Packet*, May 17, 1790.

18. *Gazette of the United States*, June 1797; *Pennsylvania Daily Advertiser*, June 1797.

19. *Pennsylvania Journal*, June 27, 1792.

20. *Gazette of the United States*, June 1797; *Pennsylvania Daily Advertiser*, June 1797.

21. Durang, *History of the Philadelphia Stage*, 3:fol. 261.

22. Comte du Buffon, *Historie naturelle: dediee au Citoyen Lacépede, membre de L'Institute, Matières Générales Tome Huiteme* (Paris, 1799).

23. Roxann Wheeler, *The Complexion of Race: Categories of Difference in Eighteenth-Century British Culture* (Philadelphia: University of Pennsylvania Press, 2000), 9; Felicity Nussbaum, *The Limits of the Human: Fictions of Anomaly, Race, and Gender in the Long Eighteenth Century* (Cambridge: Cambridge University Press, 2003), 2–3 and 254–55.

24. Robert Nowatski, *Representing African Americans in Transatlantic Abolitionism and Blackface Minstrelsy* (Baton Rouge: Louisiana State University Press, 2010), 2. Sarah Meer, *Uncle Tom Mania: Slavery, Minstrelsy, and Transatlantic Culture in the 1850s* (Athens: University of Georgia Press, 2005).

25. *Morning Chronicle*, Oct. 27, 1788.

26. Olive Logan, *Before the Footlights and Behind the Scenes* (Philadelphia, 1869), 87–88. Logan was an actress who had a long career before writing her memoir. Although she was not on stage in the 1790s, she references iconic blackface characters in plays first performed in the eighteenth century, from Wowski in *Inkle and Yarico* to Mungo in Isaac Bickerstaffe's *The Padlock*, another comic blackface slave character, suggesting that a tradition was established early on for how and which characters should be "blacked up."

27. *Theatrical Censor*, Feb. 3, 1800.

28. Edmund Burke, *The Writings and Speeches of Edmund Burke*, vol. 3: *The French Revolution*, ed. L. G. Mitchell (Oxford: Clarendon Press, 1989), 119.

29. Thomas Paine, *Rights of Man*, part 2, in *The Complete Writings of Thomas Paine*, ed. Philip Foner (New York: Citadel Press, 1945), 2:426.

30. Jürgen Habermas, *The Structural Transformation of the Public Sphere: An Inquiry into a Category of Bourgeois Society*, trans. Thomas Burger and Frederick Lawrence (Cambridge, MA: MIT Press, 1991).

31. By 1776, Philadelphia had a population of 23,700, while London had been a metropolis of half a million since 1700. Wilfried Priest, *Albion Ascendant: English History 1660–1855* (Oxford: Oxford University Press, 1998), 99; Dennis Clark, *The Irish in Philadelphia: Ten Generations of Urban Experience* (Philadelphia: Temple University Press, 1973), 9.

32. Folarin Shyllon, "Blacks in Britain: A Historical and Analytical Overview," in *Global Dimensions of the African Diaspora*, ed. Joseph E. Harris (Washington, DC: Howard University Press, 1993), 232–36; Seymour Drescher, *Capitalism and Anti-Slavery: British Mobilization in Comparative Perspective* (New York: Oxford University Press, 1987), 28 and 185n10;

Gary B. Nash, *Forging Freedom: The Formation of Philadelphia's Black Community, 1720–1840* (Cambridge, MA: Harvard University Press, 1988), 137.

33. Nash, *Forging Freedom*, 137.

34. Christopher Leslie Brown, *Moral Capital: Foundations of British Abolitionism* (Chapel Hill: University of North Carolina Press, 2006), 2, 29; Linda Colley, *Britons: Forging the Nation 1708–1837* (New Haven, CT: Yale University Press, 1992), 352.

35. Kariann Akemi Yokota, *Unbecoming British: How Revolutionary America Became a Postcolonial Nation* (Oxford: Oxford University Press, 2001), 1–2; Leonard Tennenhouse, *The Importance of Feeling English: American Literature and the British Diaspora, 1750–1850* (Princeton, NJ: Princeton University Press, 2007).

36. Frances Trollope, *Domestic Manners of the Americans*, 2 vols. (London, 1832), 1:v.

37. "So Long Mammy: Opera Says Farewell to Blacking Up," *Observer*, Nov. 20, 2005.

Chapter 1 · Celebrating Columbia, Mother of the White Republic

1. *Aurora General Advertiser*, Dec. 26, 1807.

2. David Hackett Fischer, *Liberty and Freedom: A Visual History of America's Founding Ideas* (Oxford: Oxford University Press, 2005), 233–34.

3. Philip Deloria, *Playing Indian* (New Haven, CT: Yale University Press, 1998), 29–30; E. McClung Fleming, "From Indian Princess to Greek Goddess: The American Image, 1783–1815," *Winterthur Portfolio* 3 (1967): 37–66, 37.

4. Deloria, *Playing Indian*, 17–18.

5. Cornelius Vermeule, *Numismatic Art in America: Aesthetics of the United States Coinage* (Cambridge, MA: Belknap Press of Harvard University Press, 1971), 9; David Hackett Fischer, *Liberty and Freedom: A Visual History of America's Founding Ideas* (Oxford: Oxford University Press, 2005), 137–38.

6. Francis Hopkinson, *America Independent; or, The Temple of Minerva* (Philadelphia, 1781).

7. Carla Mulford, ed., *John Leacock's The First Book of the American Chronicles of the Times, 1774–1775* (Newark: University of Delaware Press; London: Associated University Press, 1987), 14; J Bennett Nolan, *Printer Strahan's Book Account: A Colonial Controversy* (Reading, PA: Bar of Berks County, 1939), 20.

8. David Waldstreicher, *Runaway America: Benjamin Franklin, Slavery, and the American Revolution* (New York: Hill & Wang, 2004), 244.

9. Leacock owned slaves as late as 1773, evidenced by tax records and his advertisements to sell them published in *Pennsylvania Gazette* on Nov. 13, 1760, and Sept. 10, 1767. By 1774, Leacock was no longer a slave owner, according to the tax records in "Proprietary, Supply, and State Tax Lists of the City and County of Philadelphia for the years 1769, 1774, and 1779," *Pennsylvania Archives*, 3rd ser., vol. 14, ed. William Henry Egle (Harrisburg, PA, 1897). The provincial taxes for the county of Philadelphia, Lower Merion Township, for 1769, list Leacock as owning two "servants," but by 1774 he longer owned them.

10. John Leacock, "The Goddess of Liberty," in *The Fall of British Tyranny; or, American Liberty Triumphant* (Philadelphia, 1776), vi. For Leacock's critique of slavery in the play, see Jenna Gibbs, "Slavery, Liberty and Revolution in John Leacock's Pro-Patriot Tragicomedy, *The Fall of British Tyranny; or, American Liberty Triumphant* (1776)," *Journal for Eighteenth-Century Studies* 31, no. 2 (2008): 241–57, and Mark Evans Bryan, "The Rhetoric of Race and

Slavery in an American Patriot Drama: John Leacock's *The Fall of British Tyranny*," *Journal of American Drama and Theatre* 12 (2000): 41–54.

11. John Parish, *Remarks on the Slavery of the Black People; Addressed to the Citizens of the United States* (Philadelphia, 1806), 9.

12. Benjamin Rush, *An Address to the Inhabitants of the British Settlements in America on Slavekeeping* (Philadelphia, 1773), 25.

13. Thomas Paine, *African Slavery in America* (1775), in *Human Rights Reader: Major Political Writings, Essays, Speeches, and Documents from the Bible to the Present*, ed. Micheline Ishay (New York: Routledge, 1997), 130–33.

14. Gary B. Nash, *The Unknown American Revolution: The Unruly Birth of Democracy and the Struggle to Create America* (New York: Penguin, 2005), 152–53.

15. Act of the Legislature of Pennsylvania for the Gradual Abolition of Slavery (1780), HSP, Cox-Parrish-Wharton Collection.

16. Gary B. Nash, *Forging Freedom: The Formation of Philadelphia's Black Community, 1720s–1840* (Cambridge, MA: Harvard University Press, 1988), 104–5, and *The Unknown American Revolution: The Unruly Birth of Democracy and the Struggle to Create America* (London: Viking Penguin, 2005), 152. For Thomas and Samuel Mifflin's membership in Sons of Saint Tammany, see Francis Von A. Cabeen, "The Society of the Sons of St. Tammany of Philadelphia," *Pennsylvania Magazine of History and Biography (1877–1906)* 25, no. 4 (1901), American Periodicals Series (APS) Online, 439, 449; for their involvement in antislavery, see John G. Whittier, "Article 7," *Friends Intelligencer* 32, no. 8 (1875): 125, APS Online; for the formal incorporation of the PAS, see Act of Incorporation, Statutes at Large (1789), 424–32, HSP, Cox-Parrish-Wharton Collection.

17. Alexander Hamilton, "No Bill of Rights is Needed," Federalist Papers #84, in *Major Problems in the Era of the American Revolution, 1760–1791*, ed. Richard D. Brown, 2nd ed. (Boston: Houghton Mifflin, 2000), 450.

18. Francis Hopkinson, "The New Roof: A Song for Federal Mechanics," first published in the *Pennsylvania Gazette* in 1788 under the title "The Raising: A New Song for Federal Mechanics." In his 1792 collection of works, Hopkinson retitled the poem.

19. Paul Finkelman, "The Problem of Slavery in the Age of Federalism," in *Federalists Reconsidered*, ed. Doron Ben-Atar and Barbara B. Oberg (Charlottesville: University Press of Virginia, 1998), 145.

20. Ibid., 146.

21. James Madison, *Notes of Debates in the Federal Convention of 1787, Reported by James Madison* (1966; reprint, New York: W. W. Norton, 1987). Capitalized in original.

22. John P. Kaminski et al., eds., *The Documentary History of the Ratification of the Constitution* (Madison: State Historical Society of Wisconsin, 1976), 13:432–33.

23. Lillian B. Miller, ed., *The Selected Papers of Charles Willson Peale and His Family* (New Haven, CT: Yale University Press, 1983), 1:509.

24. Albert Boime, *Art in the Age of Counterrevolution, 1815–1848* (Chicago: University of Chicago Press, 2004), 519.

25. Peale, "Letter to Gentlemen of the Acting Committee to Prevent the Distress of Negroes," July 2, 1787, in Miller, *Selected Papers*, 1:481.

26. Peale, diary 5, part 3, Dec. 13, 1778, in Miller, *Selected Papers*, 1:299.

27. Miller, *Selected Papers*, 1:509.

28. Francis Hopkinson, *Account of the Grand Federal Procession in Philadelphia, July 4, 1788* (Philadelphia, 1788), 1–32.

29. Hopkinson, *Grand Federal Procession*, 8.

30. Shane White, "It Was a Proud Day: African Americans, Festivals, and Parades in the North, 1741–1834," *Journal of American History* 81, no. 1 (1994): 13–50, 33.

31. Rigal, *American Manufactory*, 23.

32. Hopkinson, *Grand Federal Procession*, 1–2.

33. Rigal, *American Manufactory*, 23.

34. Hopkinson, *Grand Federal Procession*, 4–7, 11–12.

35. Gary B. Nash, *First City: Philadelphia and the Forging of Historical Memory* (Philadelphia: University of Pennsylvania Press, 2006), 114.

36. "Oration of James Wilson, esquire," in Hopkinson, *Grand Federal Procession*, 16, 17.

37. Hopkinson, *Grand Federal Procession*, 10, 13.

38. Mitch Kachun, *Festivals of Freedom: Memory and Meaning in African American Emancipation Celebrations, 1808–1915* (Amherst: University of Massachusetts Press, 2003), 25.

39. Simon P. Newman, *Parades and the Politics of the Street: Festive Culture in the Early American Republic* (Philadelphia: University of Pennsylvania Press, 1997), 137.

40. William McKoy, "Long Syne Papers," first published in *Poulson's Daily Advertiser* 2 (n.d.): 34; republished in *Poulson's Scrapbook of Philadelphia History* (Philadelphia, 1828), 4:16.

41. *Pennsylvania Gazette*, May 11, 1791.

42. Alexander Reinagle, "A Federal Song," *Albany (NY) Journal*, Aug. 4, 1788.

43. Deloria, *Playing Indian*, 44–45; Alan Taylor, *The Divided Ground: Indians, Settlers, and the Northern Borderland of the American Revolution* (New York: Vintage, 2007), 10–11.

44. McClung Fleming, "Indian Princess to Greek Goddess," 46.

45. Pamela Scott, *Temple of Liberty: Building the Capitol for a New Nation* (New York: Oxford University Press, 1995), 17.

46. Ruth H. Bloch, "The Gendered Meanings of Virtue in Revolutionary America," *Signs: Journal of Women in Culture and Society* 13, no. 1 (1987): 37–58; Jan Lewis, "The Republican Wife: Virtue and Seduction in the Early Republic," *William and Mary Quarterly* 44 (1987): 689–721; Linda Kerber, *Women of the Republic: Intellect and Ideology in Revolutionary America* (Chapel Hill: University of North Carolina Press, 1980), 189–231.

47. Kerber, *Women of the Republic*, 174, 184.

48. Rosemary Zagarri, "The Rights of Man and Woman in Post-revolutionary America" *William and Mary Quarterly* 55, no. 2 (1998): 203–30, 208.

49. Noah Webster, *A Collection of Essays and Fugitiv [sic] Writings* (Boston, 1790), 27–28.

50. Smith, "*Liberty Displaying the Arts and Sciences*," 88.

51. Minutes of the Proceedings of the Library Company of Philadelphia (1790), 3:195–97. Quoted in Smith, "Liberty Displaying the Arts and Sciences," 89.

52. Ibid., 206–7.

53. Smith, "*Liberty Displaying the Arts and Sciences*," 100.

54. Ibid., 84, 93.

55. George Richardson, *Iconology; or, A Collection of Emblematical Figures; Containing Four Hundred and Twenty-Four Remarkable Subjects, Moral and Instructive*, 2 vols. (London, 1779); cited as the key source for eighteenth-century depictions of liberty in Vivien Green

Fryd, "Hiram Powers's America: 'Triumphant as Liberty and in Unity'" *American Art Journal* 18, no. 2 (1986): 55–75, 58–59, and in Robert C. Smith, *"Liberty Displaying the Arts and Sciences*: A Philadelphia Allegory by Samuel Jennings," *Winterthur Portfolio* 2 (1965): 85–105, 97.

56. Thomas Branagan, *The Penitential Tyrant; or, Slave Trader Reformed: A Pathetic Poem, in Four Cantos*, 2nd ed. (New York, 1807), x. All citations hereafter are from this edition.

57. Branagan's other writings on slavery include *Avenia; or, A Tragical Poem, on the Oppression of the Human Species and Infringement on the Rights of Man* (Philadelphia, 1805); *A Preliminary Essay, on the Oppression of the Exiled Sons of Africa* (Philadelphia, 1804); and *Serious Remonstrances Addressed to the Citizens of the Northern States* (Philadelphia, 1805). All quotes from these texts are from the editions listed here.

58. Branagan, *Penitential Tyrant*, 53, 80.

59. Ibid., 51.

60. Nash, "Reverberations of Haiti in the American North," 56–57.

61. Ibid., 52, 60–62.

62. Nathans, *Early American Theatre from the Revolution to Thomas Jefferson: Into the Hands of the People* (Cambridge: Cambridge University Press, 2003), 78–81.

63. McKoy, "Long Syne Papers," 2:33–34.

64. Ibid., 34–35.

65. *Address of a Convention of Delegates from the Abolition Society to the Citizens of the United States* (New York, 1794), 1.

66. William Dunlap, *Diary of William Dunlap (1766–1839): The Memoirs of a Dramatist, Theatrical Manager, Painter, Critic, Novelist, and Historian* (New York: New-York Historical Society, 1930), 1:120–22.

67. Dunlap to Thomas Holcroft, July 1797, reproduced in Dunlap, *Diary*, 1:119.

68. Nash, *Forging Freedom*, 135–39.

69. On development of black denominationalism in Philadelphia, see ibid., 112, 172–211; for the expansion of black freemasonry in Philadelphia, see 218–20.

70. Margaret Jeffery, "As a Russian Saw Us in 1812," *Metropolitan Museum of Art Bulletin*, N.S., 1, no. 3 (November 1942): 134–40, 134. I am grateful to Gary B. Nash for directing my attention to Pavel Petrovich Svinin's watercolors of Philadelphian street life.

71. Branagan, *Preliminary Essay*, "Dedication," and 100–101.

72. Nash, *Forging Freedom*, 178. Nash cites James D. Essig, *The Bonds of Wickedness: American Evangelicals against Slavery, 1770–1808* (Philadelphia: Temple University Press, 1982), 199n72.

73. Branagan, *Serious Remonstrances*, 17–18, 73.

74. Ibid., 17–18, 22–25, 36–37, 51–52.

75. *New York Evening Post*, July 10 and 12, 1804, copied from the *Freeman's Journal* (Philadelphia), quoted in Nash, *Forging Freedom*, 176, and in Kachun, *Festivals of Freedom*, 25. My brief recounting of the events of July 4 and 5, 1804, comes from Nash, 175–77, and Kachun, 25–26.

76. Absalom Jones, *A Thanksgiving Sermon, Preached January 1, 1808, in St. Thomas's; or, The African Episcopal Church, Philadelphia: On Account of the Abolition of the African Slave Trade* (Philadelphia, 1808).

77. Davies, *Parades and Power*, 45–46.

78. Michael Fortune, "New Year's Anthem" (1808), in Jones, *Thanksgiving Sermon*, 1.

79. The *Aurora General Advertiser* advertised performances of the piece at the New Theatre on Dec. 12, 1808, and again on Feb. 22, 1809.

80. McKoy, "Long Syne Papers," in *Poulson's Daily Advertiser*, Mar. 21, 1828; *Poulson's Scrapbook*, 4:16.

81. Henry Wiencek, *An Imperfect God: George Washington, His Slaves, and the Creation of America* (New York: Farrar, Straus & Giroux, 2003), 219. Wiencek, with no footnote, claims that during Washington's presidency, his chef, Hercules, and two of his slaves, Ona Judge and Austin, "went by themselves to the theater." I am grateful to Gary B. Nash for directing me to this work.

82. David Grimsted, *Melodrama Unveiled: American Theater and Culture, 1800–1850* (Chicago: University of Chicago Press, 1968), 52.

83. *Aurora General Advertiser*, July 5, 1807.

84. William Dunlap, *History of the Rise and Progress of the Arts of Design in the United States* (New York, 1834), 2:246.

85. William Dunlap, *The Glory of Columbia, Her Yeomanry!: A Play in Five Acts* (New York, 1817). All citations are from this edition.

86. Phoebe Lloyd Jacobs, "John James Barralet and the Apotheosis of George Washington," *Winterthur Portfolio* 12 (1977): 115–37, 117–18.

87. See playbills in *Aurora General Advertiser* dated July 5, 1807; July 23, 1807; Jan. 30, 1808; Dec. 12, 1808; and Feb. 22, 1809.

88. Steven C. Bullock, *Revolutionary Brotherhood: Freemasonry and the Transformation of the American Social Order, 1730–1840* (Chapel Hill: University of North Carolina Press for the Omohundro Institute of Early American History and Culture, 1996), 154.

89. William A. Carpenter, *The Exemplar: A Guide to a Mason's Actions* (Philadelphia: Grand Lodge F. & A. M. of Pennsylvania, 1985); see esp. chap. 3, "Masonic Symbols," 64–79.

90. Charles Coleman Sellers, *Charles Willson Peale* (New York: Scribner, 1969), 99, and "Charles Willson Peale with Patron and Populace," *Transactions of the American Philosophical Society* 59, no. 3 (1969): 1–146, 25.

91. Bullock, *Revolutionary Brotherhood*, 154–55.

92. Nash, *Forging Freedom*, 218–19.

93. Scott, *Temple of Liberty*, xiii; Sarah Luria, *Capital Speculations: Writing and Building Washington, D.C.* (Durham, NH: University of New Hampshire Press; Lebanon, NH: University Press of New England, 2006), 32.

94. Quoted in Constance McLaughlin Green, *The Secret City: A History of Race Relations in the Nation's Capitol* (Princeton, NJ: Princeton University Press, 1967), 33; Orlando Ridout, *Building the Octagon: Octagon Museum, August 1, 1989–September 30, 1989* (Washington, DC: American Institute of Architects Press, 1989), 98; and Luria, *Capital Speculations*, 33.

95. Jesse Torrey, *A Portraiture of Domestic Slavery, in the United States* (Philadelphia, 1817), 37. Italics in original.

96. Paul Goodman, *Of One Blood: Abolitionism and the Origins of Racial Equality* (Berkeley: University of California Press, 1998), 15.

97. W. E. B. DuBois, *The Suppression of the African Slave-Trade to the United States of America 1638–1870* (New York: Longmans, Green, 1904), 109–11.

98. David Brion Davis, *The Problem of Slavery in the Age of Revolution, 1770–1823* (Ithaca, NY: Cornell University Press, 1975), 331.

99. Nash, "Reverberations of Haiti," 56–57, 60–62.

100. James Forten, *A Series of Letters by a Man of Color* (Philadelphia, 1813), in *A Documentary History of the Negro People in the United States*, ed. Herbert Aptheker (New York: Citadel Press, 1951), 64.

101. The expression "literary blackface" comes from David Waldstreicher, *In the Midst of Perpetual Fetes* (Chapel Hill: University of North Carolina Press for the Omohundro Institute of Early American History and Culture, 1997), 337.

102. For this point, I am grateful to Philip Lapsansky, emeritus curator of Afro-Americana at the Library Company of Philadelphia.

103. Isaac Bickerstaffe, *The Padlock* (1767), in Jeffrey Cox, ed., *Slavery, Abolition and Emancipation: Writings in the British Romantic Period*, vol. 5 (London: Pickering & Chatto, 1999). For the performance dates of this afterpiece, see "Day Book of the Philadelphia Theatre," in Thomas Clark Pollock, *The Philadelphia Theatre in the Eighteenth Century Together with the Day Book of the Same Period* (Philadelphia: University of Pennsylvania Press, 1933).

104. William Dunlap, *History of the American Theatre* (New York, 1832), 31; Durang, *Philadelphia Stage*, 1:fol. 14–15.

105. *Pennsylvania Gazette* advertisements for the "songs of the Padlock, Lionel and Clarissa, and many more opera songs," on Dec. 30, 1772; Sept. 6, 1775, and July 14, 1778. Music and songs from *The Padlock* were also included in *The American Songster: Being a Select Collection of the Most Celebrated American, English, Scotch, and Irish Songs* (New York, 1788).

106. Peter Tasch, *The Dramatic Cobbler: The Life and Works of Isaac Bickerstaffe* (Lewisburg, PA: Bucknell University Press, 1971), 152.

107. Between 1785 and 1793 Algiers captured and held as slaves some 120 American sailors. Robert J. Allison, *The Crescent Obscured: The United States and the Muslim World, 1776–1815* (New York: Oxford University Press, 1995), 87; Benilde Montgomery, "White Captives, African Slaves: A Drama of Abolition," *Eighteenth Century Studies* 27 (Summer 1994), 615.

108. Durang, *Philadelphia Stage*, 1:fols. 14, 29.

109. Dunlap, *History of the American Theater*, 31.

110. John Murdock, *The Triumphs of Love; or, Happy Reconciliation, a Comedy in Four Acts*, 1st ed. (Philadelphia, 1795); *The Politicians; or, a State of Things* (Philadelphia, 1798).

111. Dale Cockrell, *Demons of Disorder: Early Blackface Minstrels and Their World* (Cambridge: Cambridge University Press, 1997), 13–14; Heather Nathans, *Slavery and Sentiment on the American Stage, 1787–1861* (New York: Cambridge University Press, 2009), 44–45.

112. Nathans, *Slavery and Sentiment*, 44–45.

113. *Pennsylvania Gazette*, Dec. 1770.

114. Genêt had angered Philadelphian Federalists with his demands of increased supplies for French troops, which if complied with would have jeopardized America's official stance of neutrality in the war between Britain and France.

115. See, for example, John Sylvester Gardiner's pro-Federalist *Remarks on the Jacobiniad: Revised and Corrected by the Author; and embellished by Carricatures* [sic] (Boston, 1795). The engraving that accompanied this account of a supposed debate at a "constitutions society at Boston over whether or not to admit a black man, 'Citizen Prince,'" featured a black man dressed as Mungo peeping around the corner of the door at a Democratic-Republican debate, clearly seeking entrance to the party.

116. Cabeen, "Society of the Sons of St. Tammany," 439–40.

117. Leacock, Tammany song in *The Fall of British Tyranny*.

118. Donald A. Grinde Jr. and Bruce E. Johansen, *Exemplar of Liberty: Native America and the Evolution of Democracy* (Los Angeles: American Indian Studies Center, University of California, Los Angeles, 1991), chap. 6, "An American Synthesis: The Sons of St. Tammany or Columbine Order"; Roger D. Abrahams, "White Indians in Penn's City: The Loyal Sons of St. Tammany," in *Riot and Revelry in Early America*, ed. William Pencak, Mathew Dennis, and Simon P. Newman (University Park: Pennsylvania State University Press, 2002), 179–204, 119.

119. Abrahams, "White Indians," 193.

120. DeLoria, *Playing Indian*, 17–18.

121. From a 1795 speech quoted in Abrahams, "White Indians," 191–92.

122. "African Tammany Society Celebration," *Tickler* (Philadelphia), July 19, 1809.

123. See, for example, "To de Public," *Tickler*, Aug. 22, 1809, and "Dialogue between Sambo and Cuffy," *Poulson's*, Jan. 2, 1813.

124. Waldstreicher, *In the Midst of Perpetual Fetes*, 294–349; Joanne Pope Melish, *Disowning Slavery: Gradual Emancipation and "Race" in New England, 1780–1860* (Ithaca, NY: Cornell University Press, 1998), 163–210; Shane White, " 'It Was a Proud Day': African Americans, Festivals and Parades in the North, 1742–1834," *Journal of American History* 81 (June 1994): 13–50.

125. Goodman, *Of One Blood*, 10.

126. "Oration of James Wilson," in Hopkinson, *Account of the Grand Federal Procession*, 17.

Chapter 2 · Abolitionist Britannia and the Blackface Supplicant Slave

1. James Powell, *Furibond; or, Harlequin Negro* (London, 1807), in *Slavery, Abolition, and Emancipation*, ed. Jeffrey Cox, (London: Pickering & Chatto, 1999), vol. 5. All further citations from the play come from this edition, in which the play's authorship is, however, listed as anonymous. The attribution of the play to James Powell comes from David Worrall, *Theatric Revolution: Drama, Censorship, and Romantic Period Subcultures, 1773–1832* (Oxford: Oxford University Press, 2006), 280–82.

2. *London Evening Post*, Dec. 1775–Jan. 1776, quoted in Dror Wahrman, *Making of the Modern Self-Identity and Culture in Eighteenth-Century England* (New Haven, CT: Yale University Press, 2004), 244.

3. Kathleen Wilson, *The Sense of the People: Politics, Culture, and Imperialism in England, 1715–1785* (New York: Cambridge University Press, 1995), 274–76, 282–84.

4. Marcus Wood, *Blind Memory: Visual Representations of Slavery in England and America, 1780–1865* (New York: Routledge, 2000), 24. See also Wood, *The Horrible Gift of Freedom: Atlantic Slavery and the Representation of Emancipation* (Athens: University of Georgia Press, 2010), 35–89.

5. Linda Colley, *Britons: Forging the Nation, 1707–1837* (New Haven: Yale University Press, 1992), 354–55.

6. David Hackett Fischer, *Liberty and Freedom: A Visual History of America's Founding Ideas* (Oxford: Oxford University Press, 2005), 233–34; "Britannia on British Coins," www.24carat.co.uk/britannia2.html.

7. Edmund Burke, "Speech on the Declaratory Act, 3 February, 1766," in *The Writings*

and Speeches of Edmund Burke, vol. 2: *Party, Politics and the American Crisis, 1766–1774,* ed. Paul Langford (Oxford: Clarendon Press; New York: Oxford University Press, 1981), 47.

8. Amelia Rauser, "Death or Liberty: British Political Prints and the Struggle for Symbols in the American Revolution," *Oxford Art Journal* 21, no. 2 (1998): 153–71.

9. Samuel Johnson, "Taxation No Tyranny: An Answer to the Resolutions and Address of the American Congress," in *The Works of Samuel Johnson* (New York: Pafraets & Company, 1913), 14:116.

10. Ambrose Serle, *Americans against Liberty; or, an Essay on the Nature and Principles of True Freedom, Shewing That the Designs and Conduct of the Americans Tend Only to Tyranny and Slavery* (London, 1775).

11. Ibid., 33–34.

12. Philip Curtin, *The Atlantic Slave Trade: A Census* (Madison: University of Wisconsin Press, 1969), 3–13; Paul Lovejoy, "The Volume of the Atlantic Slave Trade: A Synthesis," *Journal of African History* 23 (1982): 496–97.

13. James A. Rawley, *London, Metropolis of the Slave Trade* (Columbia: University of Missouri Press, 2003), 18–19.

14. Roger T. Antsey, *The Atlantic Slave Trade and British Abolition, 1760–1810* (London: Cambridge University Press, 1975), 243–45.

15. BL Lyceum Theatre newspaper clippings, Thcts 44.

16. William Cowper, *The Task* (London, 1785), 2, line 47. Cowper wrote several other antislavery poems, including *Pity for the Poor Africans* (1788) and *The Negro's Complaint* (1788).

17. John O'Keefe, *Recollections of the Life of John O'Keefe* (London, 1826), 2:55.

18. John O'Keefe, *The Young Quaker,* V.2, HL MS227892. All further citations of the play are from this manuscript.

19. Ibid., V.4.

20. Felicity Nussbaum, "The Theater of Empire: Racial Counterfeit, Racial Realism," in *The New Imperial History,* ed. Kathleen Wilson (Cambridge: Cambridge University Press, 2004), 78.

21. *Lloyds Evening Post,* Oct. 5–7. Reviewer's remarks contained within the play billing.

22. Harold MacMillan, ed., *The London Stage, 1660–1800* (Carbondale; Southern Illinois Press, 1960–1968).

23. J. R. Oldfield, "The *Soft Ties of Humanity:* Slavery and Race in British Drama, 1760–1800," *Huntington Library Quarterly* 56, no. 1 (Winter 1993): 9.

24. At a masquerade ball held at the Haymarket Theatre Royal in 1768 in honor of the visiting Danish King, for example, "the character of Mungo in *The Padlock* was very excellently assumed by Mr. Mendez." "Account of the Masquerade at the Opera House in the Haymarket, for the Danish King," *Gentlemen's Magazine,* Oct. 1768.

25. Wahrman, *Making of the Modern Self,* 238.

26. Seymour Drescher, *Capitalism and Anti-Slavery: British Mobilization in Comparative Perspective* (New York: Oxford University Press, 1987), 30.

27. *London Chronicle,* Sept. 29–Oct. 2, 1764; *London Chronicle,* Oct. 18–22, 1764.

28. *London Chronicle,* Mar. 13–16, 1773.

29. William Austin's *The Duchesse of Queensberry and Soubile* (1773) also referenced Mungo to castigate interracial relations. The cartoon featured the Duchess of Queensbury's black house servant—also infamously her sometimes public companion—fencing

with the duchess and pricking her breast with his fencing saber. The caption read, "Mungo here, dere . . . what you lady tink of me now?" Austin thus lampooned Soubile's social and sexual ambitions using Mungo's enduringly popular lyrics from *The Padlock* to highlight Soubile/Mungo's slave status.

30. One of the earliest satirical prints featuring Dyson as Mungo was a 1769 print designed and engraved for the Political Register: *Mungo*, British Cartoon Prints Collection, Library of Congress, PC 1-4267.

31. Horace Walpole, *Memoirs of the Reign of King George the Third*, ed. Sir Denis D. Le Marchant, reedited by G. F. Russell Barker (London, 1894), 3:211; Arthur Murphy, *Life of David Garrick* (Dublin, 1801), 293; Peter Tasch, *The Dramatic Cobbler* (Lewisburg, PA: Bucknell University Press, 1971), 157.

32. For an insightful discussion of some of these prints, see Catherine Molineux, *Faces of Perfect Ebony: Encountering Atlantic Slavery in Imperial Britain* (Boston: Harvard Historical Studies, Jan. 2012).

33. Cassandra Pybus, *Epic Journeys of Freedom: Runaway Slaves of the American Revolution and Their Global Quest for Liberty* (Boston: Beacon Press, 2006), 81.

34. Vincent Caretta, *Equiano the African: Biography of a Self-Made Man* (Athens: University of Georgia Press, 2005), 229.

35. Henry Smeathman, *Plan of a Settlement to Be Made Near Sierra Leona* (London, 1786).

36. Pybus writes that very few of the women in the first Sierra Leone expedition were black; 70%, she estimates, were white (*Epic Journeys*, 111).

37. Kathleen Wilson, *The Island Race: Englishness, Empire, and Gender in the Eighteenth Century* (London: Routledge, 2003), 46.

38. Pybus, *Epic Journeys*, 113.

39. *Times* (London), Jan. 1787.

40. Folarin Shyllon, "Blacks in Britain," in *Global Dimensions of the African Diaspora*, ed. Joseph E. Harris (Washington, DC: Howard University Press, 1993), 230; James Walvin, *Black and White: The Negro and English Society, 1555–1945* (London: Allen Lane the Penguin Press, 1973), 148; Peter Fryer, *Staying Power: The History of Black People in Britain* (London: Pluto Press, 1984), 195.

41. Caretta, *Equiano*, 232; Drescher, *Capitalism and Anti-slavery*, 60–61.

42. Members of the Pennsylvania Abolition Society, Act of Incorporation (1789), 424–32.

43. Gretchen Gerzina, *Black London: Life before Emancipation* (New Brunswick, NJ: Rutgers University Press, 1995), 188.

44. Wahrman, *The Making of the Modern Self*, 238.

45. Felicity Nussbaum, *The Limits of the Human: Fictions of Anomaly, Race, and Gender in the Long Eighteenth Century* (Cambridge: Cambridge University Press, 2003), 158.

46. Thomas Clarkson, *History of the Rise, Progress and Accomplishment of the Abolition of the African Slave Trade by the British Parliament* (London, 1808), 67–69.

47. "Opera House Masquerade," *London Chronicle*, May 19–21, 1789, 483.

48. "The Masquerade: Containing a Variety of Merry Characters of All Sorts: Properly Dressed for the Occasion, Calculated to Amuse and Instruct All the Good Boys and Girls in the Kingdom," *Gentleman's Magazine*, Oct. 1768, 38.

49. John Dent, *The Triumph of Liberty; or, the Destruction of the Bastille: A Musical Entertainment of One Act, as Performed at the Royal Circus of Saint George's Fields*, 2nd ed. (London, 1799), 34–35.

50. Kenneth O. Morgan, ed., *The Oxford Illustrated History of Britain* (Oxford: Oxford University Press, 1997), 433.

51. On Aug. 17, Astley's Amphitheatre featured *Paris in an Uproar; or, The Destruction of the Bastille*, and by the end of the month Sadler's Wells presented *Gallic Freedom; or, Vive la Liberté*, which boasted "an affecting Representation of the SUBTERRANEOUS DUNGEONS of that once terrific prison—the situation of the Prisoners in their state of confinement, and the Actual Descent of the Citizens and Soldiers to their release"; playbill, Sept. 1, 1789, reprinted in Dennis Arundell, *The Story of Sadler's Wells* (London: Hamish Hamilton, 1965), 44.

52. BL MS Larpent Collection 845.

53. Ibid.; Dawn B. Sova, *Banned Plays: Censorship Histories of 125 Dramas* (New York: Facts on File, 2004), 126–27; L. W. Conolly, *The Censorship of English Drama, 1737–1824* (San Marino, CA: Huntington Library, 1976), 87–88.

54. BL MS Larpent Collection 848; *Times*, Nov. 5 and 7; Conolly, *Censorship of English Drama*, 89–90.

55. Edward Royle and James Walvin, *English Radicals and Reformers, 1760–1848* (Lexington: University Press of Kentucky, 1982), 43.

56. Frederick Reynolds, *The Life and Times of Frederick Reynolds, Written by Himself* (London, 1827), 2:54.

57. Melvin D. Kennedy, ed., *Lafayette and Slavery: From His Letters to Thomas Clarkson and Granville Sharp* (Easton, PA: American Friends of Lafayette, 1950).

58. William Roberts, ed., *Memoirs of the Life and Correspondence of Mrs. Hannah More*, 3rd ed. (London, 1835), 2:294, 385–86.

59. Edmund Burke, *Reflections on the Revolution in France*, ed. J. G. A. Pocock (Indianapolis: Hackett Publishing, 1987), 9.

60. Robert Dozier, *For King, Constitution, and Country: The English Loyalists and the French Revolution* (Louisville: University Press of Kentucky, 1982), 1.

61. Robert Isaac Wilberforce and Samuel Wilberforce, *The Life of William Wilberforce* (London, 1838), 2:18.

62. *Speech of the Earl of Abingdon on His Lordship's Motion for Postponing the Further Consideration of the Question for the Abolition of the Slave Trade* (London, 1793), 5, quoted in James Walvin, "The Impact of Slavery on British Radical Politics," in *Comparative Perspectives on Slavery in New World Plantation Societies*, ed. Vera Rubin and Arthur Tuden (New York: Annals of the New York Academy of Sciences, 1977), 29:399; *Slavery, Abolition, and Emancipation: Writing in the British Romantic Period*, vol. 2: *The Abolition Debate*, ed. Peter J. Kitson (London: Pickering & Chatto, 1999), xx; and David Brion Davis, *The Problem of Slavery in the Age of Revolution, 1770–1823* (1975; reprint, New York: Oxford University Press, 1999), 345.

63. Eugene Genovese, *From Rebellion to Revolution: Afro-American Slave Revolts in the Making of the Modern World* (New York: Vintage, 1979), 20–22.

64. "The Maroons," *Oracle and Public Advertiser*, Mar. 21, 1796.

65. Burke, *Reflections*, 31–33.

66. Thomas Clarkson, *The True State of the Case, Respecting the Insurrection at St. Domingo* (Ipswich, UK, 1792).

67. Reynolds, *Life and Times*, 2:132.

68. Conolly, *Censorship of English Drama*, 68–69, 107.

69. Michael Booth, *English Melodrama* (London: Herbert Jenkins, 1956), 44.

70. George Daniels, "Memoir of Mr. Quick," in John Cumberland's *British Theater*, vol. 26. (London, 18—?).

71. See, for example, William Macready's farce, *The Irishman in London; or, The Happy African* (London, 1799), which debuted in 1792 and featured Cubba (the eponymous happy African) who insisted that "Missee so good since she buy me, me no wish to go back [to Africa] though my fader great King" (II.1).

72. *True Briton*, May 1, 1797; *Monthly Mirror*, June 1797.

73. Rowlandson's conservative image extolling British liberty and decrying the supposed depravity and violence of French was one of many. See, for example, Isaac Cruikshank's *A Picture of Great Britain in the Year 1793* (Published by J. Alexander, London, 1794), BL, which featured Britannia in her temple and was "dedicated to the Associations for Preserving Liberty and Property against Republicans and Levellers."

74. Playbill, *Times*, Nov. 17, 1803.

75. James Stephen, *Buonaparte [sic] in the West Indies; or, The History of Toussaint Louverture, the African Hero* (London, 1803), 2, 16.

76. Colley, *Britons*, 354–55.

77. Drescher, *Capitalism and Anti-Slavery*, 89.

78. James Stephen, *The Crisis of the Sugar Colonies; or, An Enquiry into the Objects and Probable Effects of the French Expedition to the West Indies* (London, 1802).

79. Ibid., 76–77, 99, 201.

80. Kitson, *Slavery, Abolition, and Emancipation*, 2:xxi.

81. Paul A. Pickering and Alex Tyrrell, eds. *Contested Sites: Commemoration, Memorial, and Popular Politics in Nineteenth-Century Britain* (Aldershot, UK: Ashgate Publishing, 2004), 148.

82. N. B. Penny, "The Whig Cult of Fox in Early Nineteenth-Century Sculpture," *Past and Present* 70 (Feb. 1976): 94–105. For a description of the Temple of Liberty at Woburn Abbey, see 96–98.

83. Ibid., 96.

84. Jeremiah Holmes Wiffen, *Verses Written in the Portico of the Temple of Liberty at Woburn Alley: On Placing before It the Statues of Locke and Erskine in the Summer of 1835* (London, 1836).

85. David Worrall, *Theatric Revolution: Drama, Censorship, and Romantic Period Subcultures, 1773–1832* (Oxford: Oxford University Press, 2006), 290; James Walvin, *Fruits of Empire: Exotic Produce and British Taste, 1660–1800* (Bastingstoke, UK: Macmillan, 1997), 45.

86. For James Powell's career as a government spy, see Worrall, *Theatric Revolution*, 280–85. For Powell's spying role in the OP riots, Worrall cites Marc Baer, *Theatre and Disorder in Late Georgian London* (Oxford: Clarendon Press, 1992), 94, but notes he was unable to find corroborating evidence. For the United English and their ties with the United Irish, see Peter Linebaugh and Marcus Rediker, *The Many-Headed Hydra: Sailors, Slaves, Commoners, and the Hidden History of the Revolutionary Atlantic* (London: Verso, 2000), 248–82.

87. Royle and Walvin, *English Radicals and Reformers*, 101.

88. John O'Brien, *Harlequin Britain: Pantomime and Entertainment, 1690–1760* (Baltimore: Johns Hopkins University Press, 2004), 94–117.

89. *The History of the Blacks of Waltham in Hampshire; and Those under the Like Denomination in Berkshire* (London, 1723), 9; *The Lives of the Most Remarkable Criminals, Who Have*

Been Condemn'd and Executed; for Murder, Highway, House-Breakers, Street-Robberies, Coining, or other Offences (London, 1735), 1:353. Both sources are quoted in O'Brien, *Harlequin Britain*, 127–28.

90. O'Brien, *Harlequin Britain*, 129.

91. Worrall, *Theatric Revolution*, 290.

92. Gillian Russell, *The Theatres of War: Performance, Politics, and Society, 1793–1815* (Oxford: Clarendon Press; New York: Oxford University Press, 1995), 16. Russell cites Lucyle Thomas Werkmeister, *A Newspaper History of England, 1792–1793* (Lincoln: University of Nebraska Press, 1967), 42–43.

93. Peter Thomson, "Drury Lane, Theatre Royal," in *The Cambridge Guide to Theatre*, ed. Martin Banham (Cambridge: Cambridge University Press, 1995), 309–11.

94. Raymond Mander and Joe Mitchenson, *The Theatres of London* (London: Rupert Hart-Davis, 1961), 66.

95. *Thespian Magazine*, Mar. 1794, excerpted in Charles Beecher Hogan, *The London Stage 1660–1800* (Carbondale: Southern Illinois University Press, 1968), 5:1569.

96. Only 800 could be seated in the pit at 3 shillings sixpence; 675 in the first gallery at 2 shillings, and 308 in the upper gallery at 1 shilling; Hogan, *London Stage*, 5:1568–69.

97. Iain Mackintosh, *Architecture, Actor, and Audience* (New York: Routledge, 1993), 34.

98. Cox, *Slavery, Abolition and Emancipation*, 5:xxiii.

99. J. M. Golby and A. W. Purdue, *The Civilization of the Crowd: Popular Culture in England 1750–1900*, rev. ed. (Stroud, UK: Sutton Publishing, 1999), 71.

100. William Blake, "The Little Black Boy," in *Songs of Innocence* (London, 1789).

101. Worrall, *Theatric Revolution*, 292.

102. *London Chronicle* 16 (Sept. 29–Oct. 2, 1764): 317; *London Chronicle* 18 (Oct. 19–22, 1764): 387.

103. Clara Reeve, *Plans of Education, with Remarks on the Systems of Other Writers: In a Series of Letters between Mrs. Darnford and Her Friends* (London, 1792; reprint, New York: Garland, 1974), 90–91.

104. Jane Rendall, *The Origins of Modern Feminism: Women in Britain, France, and the United States, 1780–1860* (Basingstoke, UK: Macmillan, 1985), 74–77.

105. Kathryn Gleadle and Sarah Richardson, *Women in British Politics: 1760–1806* (London: Macmillan, 2000), 8; Nussbaum, "Theater of Empire"; Wilson, *The Sense of the People*; and Moira Ferguson, *Subject to Others: British Women Writers and Colonial Slavery, 1670–1834* (New York: Routledge, 1992).

106. George Rehin, "Harlequin Jim Crow: Continuity and Convergence in Blackface Clowning," *Journal of Popular Culture* 9, no. 3 (Winter 1975): 682–701.

107. O'Brien, *Harlequin Britain*, 118.

108. Alan Richardson, "Romantic Voodoo: Obeah and British Culture, 1797–1807," in *Sacred Possessions: Vodou, Santeria, Obeah and the Caribbean*, ed. Margarite Fernández Olmos and Lizabeth Paravisini-Gebert (New Brunswick, NJ: Rutgers University Press, 2000), 171–94; Philip D. Curtin, *Two Jamaicas: The Role of Ideas in a Tropical Colony, 1830–1865* (New York: Atheneum, 1970), 31.

109. Alfred Hunt, *Haiti's Influence on Antebellum America: Slumbering Volcano in the Caribbean* (Baton Rouge: Louisiana State University Press, 1998), 21, 28–29; Genovese, *From Rebellion to Revolution*, 20–22; Laurent Dubois, *Avengers of the New World: The Story of the Haitian Revolution* (Cambridge, MA: Harvard University Press, 2004), 22.

110. Quoted in Arnold Rattenburg, "Methodism and the Tatterdemalions," in *Popular Culture and Class Conflict 1590–1914: Explorations in the Making of Labour and Leisure*, ed. Eileen Yeo and Stephen Yeo (Brighton, UK; Harvester Press; Atlantic Highlands, NJ: Humanities Press, 1981), 51–52.

111. Golby and Purdue, *Civilization of the Crowd*, 70–71.

112. Mikhail Bakhtin, *Rabelais and His World*, trans. Hélénè Iswolsky (Bloomington: Indiana University Press, 1984).

113. *Morning Herald*, Dec. 1807.

114. *Times*, Dec. 27, 1807.

115. *Times*, Dec. 20, 1807.

116. William Hazlitt, *The Complete Works of William Hazlitt in Twenty-One Volumes*, ed. P. P. Howe (London: J. M. Dent, 1931), 2:149–51.

117. Joshua Marsden, *The Spread of the Gospel* (New York, 1812), in *Amazing Grace: An Anthology of Poems about Slavery, 1660–1810*, ed. James G. Basker (New Haven, CT: Yale University Press, 2002), 658.

118. James Montgomery, *The West Indies* I, lines 1–10.

Chapter 3 · Spreading Liberty to Africa

1. *Thoughts on the Abolition of the Slave Trade and the Civilization of Africa, with Remarks on the African Institution, and an Examination of the Report of Their Committee, Recommending a General Registry of Slaves in the West Indies* (London, 1816), 4.

2. James Montgomery, *The West Indies*, 19 lines 211–12; 40 lines 125–28; 1 lines 1–10.

3. Isaac V. Brown, *Biography of the Rev. Robert Finley, D.D., of Basking Ridge, New Jersey*, 2nd ed. (Philadelphia, 1857) 83–96, quoted in P. J. Staudenraus, *The African Colonization Movement, 1816–1865* (New York: Columbia University Press, 1961), 21.

4. *Federal Republican and Baltimore Telegraph*, July 11, 1817.

5. David Waldstreicher, *In the Midst of Perpetual Fetes: The Making of American Nationalism, 1776–1820* (Chapel Hill: University of North Carolina Press, 1997), 296.

6. Alan Taylor, *The Civil War of 1812: American Citizens, British Subjects, Irish Rebels, and Indian Allies* (New York: Alfred A. Knopf, 2010), 134–35; Nicole Eustace, *1812: War and the Passions of Patriotism* (Philadelphia: University of Pennsylvania Press, 2012), xi.

7. Taylor, *The Civil War of 1812*, 121, 135.

8. Ibid., 457; Eustace, *1812*, xi.

9. R. David Edmunds, "Red Ascendancy," chap. 7 of *Tecumseh and the Quest for Indian Leadership*, 2nd ed. (New York: Pearson Longman, 2007), 147–72.

10. Ibid., 208.

11. Editions include London: Printed by W. Bulmer and Co. for the author, 1799; London: Printed and published by George Cawtnorn, 1800; New York: Printed and sold by J. Tiebout, 1800; Philadelphia: Printed from the London quarto edition by James Humphreys, 1800; New York: Printed and sold by Everet Duyckinck, 1813; and London: Printed for John Murray, 1816.

12. See, for example, A. B. Lindsley's *Love and Friendship; or, Yankee Notions* (New York, 1809). Lindsley's *Love and Friendship* debuted in New York at the Park Theatre Company in the theatrical season of 1807–8; its antislavery commentary rests on a contrast between the vice of Southern plantation society, with its corrupting effect on both slave and slave master, and the "innocent joys" of a bucolic Africa.

13. Gary B. Nash, *Forging Freedom: The Formation of Philadelphia's Black Community, 1720–1840* (Cambridge, MA: Harvard University Press, 1988), 100.

14. Allan Yarema, *The American Colonization Society: An Avenue to Freedom?* (Lanham, MD: University Press of America, 2006), 11.

15. Henry Clay, "Speech at Organization of American Colonization Society" (Dec. 21, 1816), in *The Papers of Henry Clay*, ed. James F. Hopkins (Lexington: University of Kentucky Press, 1961), 2:263–64.

16. Tim Fulford, Debbie Lee, and Peter J. Kitson, *Literature, Science, and Exploration in the Romantic Era: Bodies of Knowledge* (Cambridge: Cambridge University Press, 2004), 94.

17. Nash, *Forging Freedom*, 260–63.

18. Ptolemy, *Geography of Claudius Ptolemy*, trans. and ed. Edward Luther Stevenson (New York: New York Public Library, 1932); Pliny, *Natural History*, trans. H. Rackham, Loeb Classical Library (Cambridge, MA: Harvard University Press, 1938); Manuel Komroff, *The Travels of Marco Polo* (New York: Modern Library, 1953).

19. P. J. Marshall, ed. *The Cambridge Illustrated History of the British Empire* (Cambridge: Cambridge University Press, 1996), 202–3; Niall Ferguson, *Empire: The Rise and Demise of the British World Order and the Lessons for Global Power* (London: Basic Books, 2002), 123.

20. Edward D. Griffin, *A Plea for Africa: A Sermon Preached October 26, 1817, in the First Presbyterian Church in the City of New York* (New York, 1817), quoted in Staudenraus, *African Colonization Movement*, 40.

21. John Campbell, *Travels in South Africa, Undertaken at the Request of the Missionary Society* (London, 1815), advertisement, 365, 379, 380.

22. C. I. Latrobe, *Journal of a Visit to South Africa in 1815 and 1816, with Some Account of the Missionary Settlements of the United Brethren, Near the Cape of Good Hope* (London, 1818), 9, 128, 279.

23. Paul Goodman, *Of One Blood: Abolitionism and the Origins of Racial Equality* (Berkeley: University of California Press, 1998), 15.

24. E. Lord, *A Compendious History of the Principal Protestant Missions to the Heathen, Selected and Compiled from the Best Authorities* (Boston, 1813), 67–68.

25. *Proceedings of the Domestic and Foreign Missionary Society of the Protestant Episcopal Church in the United States of America, from Its First Triennial Meeting in May, 1823, to Its Second Triennial Meeting in November, 1826* (Philadelphia, 1826).

26. James Cowles Prichard, "Of the Causes Which Have Produced the Diversities of the Human Species," in *Researches into the Physical History of Man* (London, 1813); William Lawrence, *Lectures on Physiology, Zoology, and the Natural History of Mankind delivered at the Royal College of Surgeons* (1819). Both are reprinted in *Slavery, Abolition and Emancipation*, vol. 8: *Theories of Race*, ed. Peter J. Kitson (London: Pickering & Chatto, 1999), 269–308, 309–34.

27. Johann Friedrich Blumenbach, *On the Natural Variety of Mankind*, in *The Anthropological Treatises of Johann Friedrich Blumenbach* (Göttingen, 1775; English translation, London, 1865).

28. Prichard, *Researches into Physical History*, 283.

29. Bruce Dain, *Hideous Monster of the Mind: American Race Theory in the Early Republic* (Cambridge, MA: Harvard University Press, 2002), 218.

30. Lawrence, *Lectures on Physiology, Zoology, etc.*, 313, 337–39.

31. *Poems on the Abolition of the Slave Trade; written by James Montgomery, James Gra-*

hame, and E. Benger; Embellished with Engravings from Pictures painted by R. Smirke, Esq., R.A. (London, 1809). All citations from the poems are from this edition.

32. Advertisement, in ibid.

33. James Grahame, *Africa Delivered; or, The Slave Trade Abolished,* in *Poems on the Abolition,* 86 lines 39–40; 87 line 46; 84 lines 1–10; 90 lines 134–52.

34. E. Benger, *A Poem, Occasioned by the Abolition of the Slave Trade,* in *Poems on the Abolition,* 105 line 7, 106 lines 29–30.

35. James Montgomery, *The West Indies,* in *Poems on the Abolition,* 19 lines 211–12; 40 lines 125–28; 1 lines 1–10.

36. Ibid., 32 lines 273, 283; 31 lines 264, 268.

37. Fulford, Lee, and Kitson, *Literature, Science, and Exploration,* 98–102.

38. Mungo Park, *Travels in the Interior Districts of Africa: Performed under the Direction and Patronage of the African Association in the Years 1795, 1796, 1797* (London, 1799), appendix, lxxxviii. All subsequent citations are from this edition unless noted otherwise.

39. Jeffrey Cox, ed., *Slavery, Abolition and Emancipation,* vol. 5 (London: Pickering & Chatto, 1999), xix.

40. Park, *Travels,* 17.

41. Ibid., appendix, lxxxviii.

42. Ibid., 23–24.

43. William Wilberforce, "Speech on the Motion for the Abolition of the Slave Trade, 12 May 1789," reprinted in *Slavery, Abolition, and Emancipation,* vol. 2: *The Abolition Debate,* ed. Peter J. Kitson (London: Pickering & Chatto, 1999), 135–47.

44. *Times,* July 30, 1808.

45. *Literary Panorama,* Sept. 1808.

46. Henry Crabb Robinson, *The London Theatre, 1811–1866: Selections from the Diary of Henry Crabb Robinson,* ed. Eluned Brown (London: Society for Theatre Research, 1966), 38.

47. Richard Brinsley Peake, *Memoirs of the Colman Family: Including Correspondence with the Most Distinguished personages of Their Time* (London, 1841), 2:324–25.

48. George Colman, prefatory remarks, *The Africans; or, War, Love, and Duty* (Philadelphia, 1811).

49. Jeremy F. Bagster-Collins, *George Colman the Younger, 1762–1836* (New York: King's Crown Press, 1946), 209.

50. See the subscribers list in Park, *Travels,* x, xii.

51. Subscribers list in Mungo Park, *Travels in the Interior Districts of Africa* (Philadelphia, 1800), x, xii.

52. Ibid., xiii.

53. Mathew Carey, *Letters on the Colonization Society, with a View of Its Probable Results* (Philadelphia, 1832), v–vii.

54. G. B. D. Odell, *Annals of the New York Stage,* vol. 1 (New York: Columbia University Press, 1927), 93–95. For the Sons of Liberty's disruption of Philadelphian theatrical performances, see, for example, *Chronicle,* Oct. 31, 1772.

55. Jared Brown, *The Theater in America during the Revolution* (Cambridge: Cambridge University Press, 1995), 171.

56. Heather Nathans, *Early American Theater from the Revolution to Thomas Jefferson: Into the Hands of the People* (Cambridge: Cambridge University Press, 2003), 1.

57. Editorial on the New Theatre, *Aurora,* June 30 1794.

58. Reese D. James, *Old Drury of Philadelphia: A History of the Philadelphia Stage, Including the Daily Account Book [. . .] William Burke Wood* (Philadelphia: University of Pennsylvania Press, 1932), 19.

59. In James's *Old Drury of Philadelphia*, the daybook for 1812 includes tried and true British classics, such as Shakespeare's *Romeo and Juliet, Hamlet,* and *Richard III*; Richard B. Sheridan's *Pizarro*; Oliver Goldsmith's *She Stoops to Conquer*; and many more, as do the daybooks for the postwar years.

60. James, *Old Drury of Philadelphia*, 7.

61. William B. Wood, *Personal Recollections of the Stage* (Philadelphia, 1855), 187.

62. Elisa Tamarkin, *Anglophilia: Deference, Devotion, and Antebellum America* (Chicago: University of Chicago Press, 2008), xxiii; Leonard Tennenhouse, *The Importance of Feeling English* (Princeton, NJ: Princeton University Press, 2007), 19.

63. William Dunlap, *History of the American Theatre: and Anecdotes of the Principle Actors* (New York: B. Franklin, 1963), 1:168–69; William Dunlap, *Diary of William Dunlap (1766–1839): The Memoirs of a Dramatist, Theatrical Manager, Painter, Critic, Novelist, and Historian* (New York: Printed for the New-York Historical Society, 1930), 1:xviii, 60, 80–81, 119; 3:323.

64. Dunlap, *History of the American Theater*, 1:42–43.

65. Dunlap, *Diary*, 1:357–58. Dunlap employed a black man in New York in 1798. Under "Expenses of the Theater," he listed payment of 1 pound to "William the Black man" on Nov. 24, 1798, and of 10 pounds to "William the Black man" on Dec. 11, 1798.

66. Ibid., 1:119–20.

67. Dunlap, Perth Amboy, NJ, to Thomas Holcroft, July 1797, reprinted in Dunlap, *Diary*, 1:119.

68. Dunlap, *History*, 2:336.

69. Although not yet published in America in 1810, Prichard's and Lawrence's texts could, of course, have been imported. Dunlap, however, does not mention either Prichard's or Lawrence's works in his *Diary*.

70. Dunlap, *Diary*, 1:189–90.

71. Ibid., 1:19–20.

72. Ibid., 2:370.

73. Gary B. Nash, *The Forgotten Fifth: African Americans in the Age of Revolution* (Cambridge, MA: Harvard University Press, 2006), 138.

74. Dain, *Hideous Monster*, 42.

75. Thomas Jefferson, *Notes on the State of Virginia* (Philadelphia, 1794), 200. All further citations are from this edition.

76. Ibid., 270.

77. Samuel Stanhope Smith, *An Essay on the Causes of the Variety of Complexion and Figure in the Human Species* (Philadelphia, 1787), 84.

78. Ibid., 23–24 and 33–38.

79. Ibid., 38–39.

80. Nash, *Forgotten Fifth*, 138; Dain, *Hideous Monster*, 72.

81. Jefferson, *Notes*, 270.

82. Charles Caldwell, "An Essay on the Causes of the Variety of Complexion and Figure in the Human Species," *American Review of History and Politics* 2 (1811): 128–66.

83. Dain, *Hideous Monster*, 72.

84. Dunlap, *History*, 2:408.

85. The only extant manuscript of Dunlap's *The Africans* is a prompt copy held by the Houghton Library at Harvard, which is almost identical to both the London and Philadelphia editions of Colman's play of the same title. If there were significant differences in Dunlap's adaptation staged in the Park Theatre, they did not make their way into the extant prompt copy.

86. *The Africans; or, War, Love, and Duty: A Play in Three Acts by George Colman Jr., as Performed at the Philadelphia Theatre* (Philadelphia, 1811). I have compared Mathew Carey's 1811 edition of the Philadelphia-produced play with the script for Colman's Haymarket production and found them to be identical. Thus, I have utilized Colman's *The Africans; or, War, Love, and Duty* (1808), in Cox, *Slavery, Abolition and Emancipation*, vol. 5, to discuss both the London and the Philadelphia iterations of the play.

87. Staudenraus, *African Colonization Movement*, 9–11.

88. "Mr. Russell to the Secretary of State, Dated London, Sept. 17, 1812," in "State Papers Laid before Congress 12th Congress—2d Session," 1–226, in Thomas Palmer, *Historical Register*, vol. 1 (Philadelphia, 1814), 86, quoted in Eustace, *1812*, 174.

89. "True Answers," *Ontario Messenger*, Dec. 15, 1812; "Honor Calls for War," *Aurora*, June 19, 1812; both cited in Taylor, *The Civil War of 1812*, 136.

90. Taylor, *The Civil War of 1812*, 327.

91. Eustace, *1812*, 78.

92. Advertisement, *National Intelligencer*, July 4, 1812.

93. James, *Old Drury of Philadelphia*, 111.

94. Ibid., 161.

95. John O'Sullivan, "Annexation," *United States Magazine and Democratic Review*, 17, no. 1 (1845); Katherine Lee Bates (lyrics) and Samuel Ward (music), "America the Beautiful" (1895).

96. William Thomas Hamilton, *A Word for the African: A Sermon, for the Benefit of the American Colonization Society, Delivered in the Second Presbyterian Church, Newark, July 24, 1825* (Newark, NJ, 1825; Cornell University Library Digital Collections), 6–7, 8–9, 14–15, 21–22, 23, 25.

97. Nash, *Forging Freedom*, 237.

98. James Forten to Paul Cuffe, Jan. 25, 1817, in *Paul Cuffe: Black America and the African Return*, ed. Sheldon Harris (New York: Simon & Schuster, 1972), quoted in Nash, *Forging Freedom*, 238.

99. James Forten and Robert Purvis, *To the Humane and Benevolent Inhabitants of the City and County of Philadelphia* (Philadelphia, 1817), reprinted in *Witness for Freedom: African American Voices on Race, Slavery, and Emancipation*, ed. C. Peter Ripley (Chapel Hill: University of North Carolina Press, 1993), 30–32.

100. Jesse Torrey, *Portraiture of Domestic Slavery in the United States . . . and, A project of a Colonial Asylum for Free Persons of Colour* (Philadelphia, 1817), "Additional Note," 93.

101. Ibid., "Meeting of Free People of Colour," 93–95.

102. Ibid., 37.

103. Ibid., 37–38.

104. Ibid., 39–40; italics in original.

105. I am grateful to Gary B. Nash for suggesting this point. Alan Taylor discusses African Americans fighting with the British in *Civil War of 1812*, 327–28.

106. Torrey, *Portraiture*, 39–40.

107. Ibid., vi.

108. Eustace, *1812*, 169.

Part II · Emancipation and Political Reform

1. Frances Trollope, *Domestic Manners of the Americans* (London, 1832), 1:v.

2. Ibid., 1:15–16. Trollope later wrote an antislavery novel drawn from her American travels, *The Life and Adventures of Jonathan Jefferson Whitlaw; or, Scenes on the Mississippi* (London, 1836), which she dedicated to "those states of the American Union in which slavery has been abolished" (1). The novel was later reissued as *Lynch Laws* (1852).

3. David Waldstreicher, *In the Midst of Perpetual Fetes* (Chapel Hill: University of North Carolina Press, 1997); Linda Colley, *Britons: Forging the Nation, 1707–1837* (Yale University Press, 1994); E. J. Hobsbawm, *Nations and Nationalism since 1780: Programme, Myth, Reality* (Cambridge: Cambridge University Press, 1990).

4. Sam W. Haynes, *Unfinished Revolution: The Early American Republic in a British World* (Charlottesville: University Press of Virginia, 2010), 1, 133–34.

5. Hazel Waters, *Racism on the Victorian Stage: Representation of Slavery and the Black Character* (Cambridge: Cambridge University Press, 2007), 89.

Chapter 4 · Black Freedom and Blackface Picaresque

1. Pierce Egan, *Life in London* (London, 1821). All subsequent citations from Pierce Egan's original *Life in London* prose sketches are from this edition, which was a compilation of the serial installments published between 1820 and 1821.

2. Robert L. Patten, *George Cruikshank's Life, Times, and Art* (New Brunswick, NJ: Rutgers University Press, 1992), 1:222.

3. Egan and Cruikshank's contemporaries debated whether Egan's prose sketches preceded Cruikshank's cartoon illustrations or vice versa, as today's scholars continue to do. I have opted to list Egan as the progenitor because the publication of his serial prose sketches preceded the publication of the book with illustrations by George Cruikshank.

4. William Shakespeare, *2 Henry IV*, II.4. For the nineteenth-century meaning of Shakespeare's Corinthian as a "fast man about town," see listing for "Corinthian" in Ebenezer Cobham Brewer, *Dictionary of Phrase and Fable* (London, 1895).

5. Egan, *Life in London*, 1.

6. Patten, *George Cruikshank's Life*, 223.

7. Edward Royle and James Walvin, *English Radicals and Reformers, 1760–1848* (Louisville: University of Kentucky Press, 1988), 137.

8. Edward Royle, *Revolutionary Britannia? Reflections on the Threat of Revolution in Britain 1789–1848* (Manchester: Manchester University Press, 2000), 70.

9. Thomas Carlyle, *Sartor Resartus* (London, 1831), vol. 3: "The Dandiacal Body," x.

10. John Camden Hotten, introduction to *Pierce Egan, Life in London* (London, 1870), 18, quoted in Patten, *George Cruikshank's Life*, 221.

11. Egan, *Life in London*, chap. 3.

12. J. A. Mangan and James Walvin, *Manliness and Morality: Middle-Class Masculinity in Britain and America, 1800–1940* (Manchester: Manchester University Press, 1987), 4–5.

13. William Makepeace Thackeray, "Essay on the Genius of George Cruikshank," *Westminster Review* 34 (June 1840): 10, quoted in Patten, *George Cruikshank's Life*, 221.

14. Robert Wedderburn, *The Axe Laid to the Root; or, A Fatal Blow to Oppressors, Being*

an *Address to the Planters and Negroes of the Island of Jamaica*, nos. 1–6 (London, 1817), reprinted in Wedderburn, *The Horrors of Slavery and Other Writings*, ed. Ian McCalman (New York: Marcus Weiner, 1991).

15. Wedderburn, *The Axe Laid to the Root*, no. 1, "To the Editor," in *The Horrors of Slavery*, n.p.

16. Douglas A. Lorimer, *Colour, Class, and the Victorians* (Leicester: Leicester University Press; New York: Holmes & Meier Publishers, 1978), 41–43.

17. Norma Myers, *Reconstructing the Black Past: Blacks in Britain, c. 1780–1830* (London: Frank Cass, 1996), 131; Lorimer, *Colour, Class, and the Victorians*, 34; David Dabydeen, *Hogarth's Blacks: Images of Blacks in Eighteenth-Century English Art* (Athens: University of Georgia Press, 1987), 35; Fōlarin Shyllon, *Black People in Britain* (London: Published for the Institute of Race Relations by Oxford University Press, 1977), 102.

18. Patten, *George Cruikshank's Life*, 313–14, 309–10, 357.

19. Egan, *Life in London*, 181–82.

20. W. T. Lhamon, *Jump Jim Crow: Lost Plays, Lyrics, and Street Prose of the First Atlantic Popular Culture* (Cambridge, MA: Harvard University Press, 2003), 64.

21. The many iterations include Charles Dibdin Jr., *Life in London; or, The Day and Night Adventures of Logic, Tom, and Jerry* at the Olympic Theatre in 1821, *The Death of Don Giovanni; or, The Shades of Logic, Tom, and Jerry* at the Olympic in 1822, and *Green in France; or, Tom and Jerry's Tour* at the Adelphi in 1823; and Thomas Longden's *Death of Life in London; or, Tom and Jerry's Funeral* at the Royal Coburg Theatre in 1823. New adaptations appeared well into the 1830s and 1840s, such as *Tom, Jerry and Logick's Hop at Brighton* in 1834 and *Life in Dublin; or, Tom, Jerry, and Logic on their Travels* at the Royal English Opera House in 1842.

22. Preface to William T. Moncrieff, *Tom and Jerry; or, Life in London* (1821), reprinted in Charles Hindley, *The True History of Tom and Jerry; or, The Day and Night Scenes, of Life in London* (London, 1890), 78–81.

23. Patten, *George Cruikshank's Life, Times, and Art*, 229.

24. Jane Moody, *Illegitimate Theater in London, 1770–1840* (London: Cambridge University Press, 2000), 39.

25. Preface to *Tom and Jerry*, in Hindley, *True History*, 78–81.

26. Ibid.

27. Announcement for the premiere, in Hindley, *True History*, 8.

28. Preface to *Tom and Jerry*, in Hindley, *True History*, 78–81.

29. William Makepeace Thackeray, "De Juventute," *Cornhill Magazine* 2 (Oct. 1860): 501–2.

30. Harriet Arbuthnot, *Journal of Mrs. Arbuthnot, 1820–1832*, ed. Francis Bamford and the Duke of Wellington (London: Macmillan, 1950), 1:144 (Feb. 20, 1822), quoted in Patten, *George Cruikshank's Life, Times, and Art*, 230.

31. *Tom, Jerry and Logick's Hop at Brighton* (Oct. 24, 1834) BL Add MS 42928 LCPlays vol. 64 fols. 290–332b; *Life in Dublin; or, Tom, Jerry, and Logic on their Travels* (Aug.–Oct. 1842, Royal Opera House), BL Add MS LCPLAYS 42964 fols. 376–412.

32. *High Life in London* (Jan.–Feb. 1826, Covent Garden), BL Add MS 42876 LCPLAYS vol. 12 fols. 465–587.

33. Francis Courtney Wemyss, *Twenty-Six Years of the Life of Actor and Manager* (New York, 1847), vol. 1, chap. 9.

34. Playbill (June 7, 1823), Harvard Theatre Collection, Cambridge, MA, reproduced in Laurence Hutton, *Curiosities of the American Stage* (New York, 1891), 97, and George A. Thompson, *A Documentary History of the African Theatre* (Evanston, IL: Northwestern University Press, 1998), 131–32.

35. Patricia Cline Cohen, Timothy J. Gilfoyle, and Helen Lefkowtich Horowitz, *The Flash Press: Sporting Male Weeklies in 1840s New York* (Chicago: University of Chicago Press, 2008), 1, 6–7.

36. Charles Durang, quoted in Reese D. James, *Old Drury of Philadelphia* (Philadelphia: University of Pennsylvania Press, 1932), 42. See also Wemyss, *Twenty-Six Years*, vol. 1, chap. 9, for Wemyss's enthusiasm for *Life in London*.

37. James, *Old Drury of Philadelphia*, 39–41.

38. Sam W. Haynes, *Unfinished Revolution: The Early American Republic in a British World* (Charlottesville: University Press of Virginia, 2010), 1, 133–35; Elisa Tamarkin, *Anglophilia: Deference, Devotion, and Antebellum America* (Chicago: University of Chicago Press, 2008), xxvi; Kariann AkemiTokota, "A Culture of Insecurity," chap. 6 in *Unbecoming British: How Revolutionary America Became a Postcolonial Nation* (Oxford: Oxford University Press, 2010), 62–114, see esp. 86–87.

39. William B. Wood, *Personal Recollections of the Stage* (Philadelphia, 1855), 290–91.

40. Ibid., 291.

41. Excerpted in Woods, *Personal Recollections of the Stage*, 290.

42. Marsh, *Black Victorians*, 26; Nancy Reynolds Davidson, "E. W. Clay: American Political Cartoonist of the Jacksonian Era" (Ph.D. diss., University of Michigan, 1980), 58–59.

43. Tavia Amolo Ochieng' Nyong'o, *The Amalgamation Waltz: Race, Performance, and the Ruses of Memory* (Minneapolis: University of Minnesota Press, 2009), 77; Davidson, "E. W. Clay," 90.

44. Davidson, "E. W. Clay," 59.

45. Ibid.; Nyong'o, *Amalgamation Waltz*, 79.

46. See also Egerton's *The Cut Celestial* and *The Cut Infernal* from 1827.

47. Davidson, "E. W. Clay," 92.

48. Edward W. Clay, *Behold thou art fair, Deborah* (1830) LCP P.9288, print from *Life in Philadelphia* (S. Hart, Philadelphia).

49. Edward W. Clay, *Well brudder what 'fect you tink Morgan's deduction gwang to hab on our sietry of free masons?*, print from *Life in Philadelphia* (W. Simpson, Philadelphia, 1828).

50. John Fanning Watson, *Annals of Philadelphia and Pennsylvania in the Olden Time, Being a Collection of Memoirs, Anecdotes, and Incidents of the City and Its Inhabitants* (Philadelphia, 1870), 2:61.

51. Frances Anne Kemble, *Journal of a Residence on a Georgian Plantation in 1838–1839* (London, 1863).

52. Kemble, journal entry, Sept. 9, 1832, in *Fanny Kemble's Journals*, ed. Catherine Clinton (Cambridge, MA: Harvard University Press, 2000), 45.

53. Monica Miller, *Slaves to Fashion: Black Dandyism and the Styling of Black Diasporic Identity* (Durham, NC: Duke University Press, 2009), 5; Ira Berlin, *Many Thousands Gone: The First Two Centuries of Slavery in North America* (Cambridge, MA: Belknap Press of Harvard University Press, 1998).

54. Shane White and Graham White, *Stylin': African American Expressive Culture, from Its Beginnings to the Zoot Suit* (Ithaca, NY: Cornell University Press, 1999).

55. Miller, *Slaves to Fashion*, 14–15, 20–21; Shane White, "It Was a Proud Day: African Americans, Festivals, and Parades in the North, 1741–1834," *Journal of American History* 81, no. 1 (1994): 17; Mitch Kachun, *Festivals of Freedom: Memory and Meaning in African American Emancipation Celebrations, 1808–1915* (Amherst: University of Massachusetts Press, 2003), 38–39.

56. Miller, *Slaves to Fashion*, 20–21.

57. Corey Capers, "Black Voices, White Print: Racial Practice, Print Publicity, and Order in the Early American Republic," in *Early African American Print Culture*, ed. Lara Langer Cohen and Jordan Alexander Stein (Philadelphia: University of Pennsylvania Press, in cooperation with the Library Company of Philadelphia, 2012), 107–26, 109; Eric Lott, *Love and Theft: Blackface Minstrelsy and the American Working Class* (New York: Oxford University Press, 1993), 46.

58. Samuel George Morton, *The Different Forms of the School, as Exhibited in the Five Races of Men* (Philadelphia, 1830); *Crania Americana; or, A Comparative View of the Skulls of Various Aboriginal Nations of North and South America* (Philadelphia 1839); "Crania Ægyptiaca," *Transactions of the American Philosophical Society* 9 (1844).

59. Pieter Camper, *The Works of the Late Professor Camper, on the Connexion between the Science of Anatomy and the Arts of Drawing, Painting, Statuary* (London, 1794), 50, reprinted in *Slavery, Abolition, and Emancipation*, vol. 8: *Theories of Race*, ed. Peter J. Kitson (London: Pickering & Chatto, 1999), 97–117.

60. Camper, *Works*, 99.

61. See Clay, *Shall I hab de honour to dance de next quadrille* (1828) LCP P.8471.1, *Fancy Ball* (1829) LCP P.9693, and *Have you any flesh coloured silk stockings . . . ?* (1829) LCP P.2004.39.1, prints from *Life in Philadelphia* (W. Simpson, Philadelphia) and *How you like de Waltz, Mr. Lorenzo* (1829) LCP P.9697, and *What you tink of my new poke bonnet . . . ?* (1830) P.9701.5, from *Life in Philadelphia* (S. Hart, Philadelphia).

62. Paul Goodman, *Of One Blood: Abolitionism and the Origins of Racial Equality* (Berkeley: University of California Press, 1998), 161.

63. Ibid., 162–63.

64. Ibid., 226–27.

65. Clay, *What de debil you hurrah General Jackson for?* (1828) LCP P.8471.3, print from *Life in Philadelphia* (W. Simpson, Philadelphia).

66. Tench Coxe, "Considerations Respecting the Helots of the United States, African and Indian, Native and Alien, and Their Descendants of the Whole and Mixed Blood," *Democratic Press*, Nov. 25, 1820. For a full discussion of Tench Coxe's virulently racist writings, see Gary B. Nash, *The Forgotten Fifth: African Americans in the Age of Revolution* (Cambridge, MA: Harvard University Press, 2005), especially 135–38.

67. Michael Craton, *Testing the Chains: Resistance to Slavery in the British West Indies* (Ithaca, NY: Cornell University Press, 1982), 291; Edith F. Hurwitz, *Politics and the Public Conscience: Slave Emancipation and the Abolitionist Movement in Britain* (London: Allen & Unwin; New York: Barnes & Noble Books, 1973), 51–52; Mary Reckord, "The Jamaica Slave Rebellion of 1831," *Past and Present* 40 (July 1968): 108–25; Craton, *Testing the Chains*, 291.

68. Reckord, "The Jamaica Slave Rebellion," 124; Hurwitz, *Politics and the Public Conscience*, 53.

69. Quoted in Hurwitz, *Politics and the Public Conscience*, 52.

70. Jonathan Sperber, *Revolutionary Europe, 1780–1850* (New York: Longman, 2000), 357–61; Royle, *Revolutionary Britannia,* 67–79; Royle and Walvin, *English Radicals and Reformers,* 145–151.

71. *Tatler* 412 (Dec. 28, 1831).

72. Royle and Walvin, *English Radicals and Reformers,* 144–45.

73. *Parliamentary Debates,* 3rd ser., 13 (May 24, 1832).

74. Davidson, "E. W. Clay," 98.

75. The three Clay prints London engravers omitted were *Promenade in Washington Square, Fancy Ball,* and the print of two black freemasons with the caption, "Well brudder what 'fect you tink Morgan's deduction gwang to hab on our sietry of free masons?"

76. Davidson, "E.W. Clay," 97.

77. *Tregear's Black Jokes, Being a Series of Laughable Caricatures on the March of Manners amongst the Blacks* (London, 1834).

78. Davidson, "E. W. Clay," 97–99.

79. Philip Lapsansky, emeritus curator of Afro-Americana at the Library Company of Philadelphia, notes the print also relates closely to *Tention! De Bobalition of Slavery* (Boston, 1820).

80. Jan Marsh, *Black Victorians: Black People in British Art, 1800–1900* (Aldershot, UK: Lund Humphries 2005), 28–30.

81. Playbill for James Hackett, *The Times; or, Life in New York,* reproduced in Francis Hodge, *Yankee Theatre: The Image of America on the Stage, 1825–1850* (Austin, TX: University of Texas Press, 1964), 107.

82. James, *Old Drury of Philadelphia,* 566.

83. Hutton, *Curiosities of the American Stage,* 104–5.

Chapter 5 · Transatlantic Travelers, Slavery, and Charles Mathews's "Black Fun"

1. Charles Mathews, "Letter to James Smith. Philadelphia, Feb 23, 1823," in *Memoirs of Charles Mathews, by Mrs. Mathews* (London, 1838), 3:390.

2. William Macready, *Macready's Reminiscences and Selections from His Diaries and Letters,* ed. Sir Frederic Pollock (New York, 1875), 587.

3. Frances Trollope, *Domestic Manners of the Americans* (London, 1832), 1:7.

4. Tracy C. Davis, "Acting Black: Charles Mathews's *Trip to America,*" *Theatre Journal* 63, no. 2 (May 2011): 163–89, 163.

5. Reese D. James, *Old Drury of Philadelphia* (Philadelphia: University of Pennsylvania Press, 1932), 373–74.

6. Davis, "Acting Black," 189.

7. Francis Hodge, *Yankee Theater: The Image of America on the Stage, 1825–1850* (Austin: University of Texas Press, 1964), 61.

8. BL, Adelphi Theatre scrapbook, Oct. 1819, Thcts.

9. Allardyce Nicoll, *The English Theater: A Short History* (London: Thomas Nelson & Sons, 1936), 165; Raymond Mander and Joe Mitchenson, *The Theatres of London* (Westport, CT: Greenwood Press, 1979), 237, 245.

10. Edward Royle and James Walvin, *English Radicals and Reformers, 1760–1848* (Louisville: University of Kentucky Press, 1988), 139.

11. Jonathan Sperber, *Revolutionary Europe, 1780–1850* (New York: Longman, 2000), 358–59.

12. Christine Bolt, *The Anti-Slavery Movement and Reconstruction: A Study in Anglo-American Co-operation, 1833–77* (London: Oxford University Press, 1969), 2–13.

13. Royle and Walvin, *English Radicals and Reformers*, 138–139.

14. Michael Craton, James Walvin, and David Wright, *Slavery, Abolition and Emancipation: Black Slaves and the British Empire* (London: Longman, 1976), 279–81.

15. Royle and Walvin, *English Radicals and Reformers*, 140.

16. Mathews published several prose versions of some of the main skits of *Trip to America*; the one I will quote from is Charles Mathews, *Sketches of Mr. Mathews's Celebrated Trip to America* (London, 1824). See also his *Mathews in America; or, The Theatrical Wanderer* (London, 1824) and *Memoirs of Charles Mathews, by Mrs. Mathews*, which also contains reproductions of his letters written home while touring America.

17. *Memoirs of Charles Mathews*, 3:375, 442–46.

18. Ibid., 3:287.

19. Hodge, *Yankee Theater*, 70–71; *Memoirs of Charles Mathews*, 3:442–46, 448.

20. Charles Mathews to James Smith, Philadelphia, Feb. 23, 1823, reproduced in *Memoirs of Charles Mathews*, 3:382.

21. Charles Mathews to Mrs. Rolls, Boston, Jan. 4, 1823, in ibid., 3:354.

22. Ibid., 3:354.

23. Charles Mathews to Mrs. Mathews, Philadelphia, Sept. 12, 1822, in ibid., 3:307.

24. Ibid., 3:448.

25. Hodge, *Yankee Theater*, 70.

26. Ibid., 69.

27. *Memoirs of Charles Mathews*, 3:447–48.

28. *Supplement to the Vocal Gleaner and Universal Melodist: A Sketch of Mr. Mathews's Entertainment, Entitled "A Trip to America," as Now Performing with Great Éclat at the English Opera House* (London, 1824), 152–53.

29. Ibid.

30. Mathews, "All's Well at Naxhitoches!" part 3 of *Sketches*.

31. William Hazlitt, "Mr. Mathews at Home," *London Magazine* 5 (May 1820): 179–83.

32. *Literary Gazette*, Mar. 27, 1824.

33. Richard Brinsley Peake, *Jonathan in England; or, Americans Abroad* (1824), BL Add MS 42868 LCPlays fols. 17–57. *Jonathan in England* was approved "after some omissions and alterations" on Sept. 1, 1824, by George Colman Jr., who had succeeded John Larpent as the official government censor. All citations of the play are from this manuscript.

34. Quoted in Hodge, *Yankee Theater*, 72.

35. Charles Durang, *History of the Philadelphia Stage, 1854–1863* (Philadelphia, 1854), 3:fols. 356.

36. James Hackett, *Jonathan in England* (Philadelphia, 1831). For a thorough account of Hackett's version of the piece and its transatlantic reception, see Hodge, "Hackett Expands the Repertoire," chap. 8 of *Yankee Theater*.

37. George Dibdin Pitt's *The Black Spartacus; or, Toussaint L'Ouverture* (1846), a staging of the Haitian Revolution features an American overseer named Jonathan, a character Pitt used to disparage American slavery (for more on this work, see chap. 7).

38. Trollope, *Domestic Manners*, 15–16.

39. Celia Morris Eckhardt, *Fanny Wright: Rebel in America* (Cambridge, MA: Harvard University Press, 1984), 27–28.

40. James, *Old Drury of Philadelphia*, 56–57.

41. Ronald Schultz, *The Republic of Labor: Philadelphia Artisans and the Politics of Class, 1720–1830* (New York: Oxford University Press, 1993), 212, 214–16.

42. Ralph Waldo Emerson, *Journals of Ralph Waldo Emerson*, ed. Edward Waldo Emerson and Waldo Emerson Forbes (Boston: Houghton-Mifflin, 1909–14), 1:185–86.

43. Robert J. Connors, "Frances Wright: First Female Civic Rhetor in America," *College English* 62, no. 1 (Sept. 1999): 30–57. For Wright's educational background, see esp. p. 34. The physical description of Wright at her lecture performances in Philadelphia also comes from this source, esp. p. 30.

44. Frances Wright D'Arusmont, *Biography, Notes, and Political Letters* (New York, 1844), 11.

45. Frances Wright, *Views of Society and Manners in America* (London, 1821), 267.

46. Frances Wright D'Arusmont, *Course of Popular Lectures*, 2:x, quoted in Connors, "Frances Wright," 43–44.

47. Helen Heineman, *Restless Angels: The Friendship of Six Victorian Women* (Athens: Ohio University Press, 1983), 25–26.

48. Trollope, *Domestic Manners*, 1:17–18.

49. Quoted in Eckhardt, *Fanny Wright*, 151.

50. Ibid., 207, 211–12.

51. Frances Wright, *A Lecture on Existing Evils and Their Remedy: As Delivered in the Arch Street Theater, to the Citizens of Philadelphia, June 2, 1829* (New York, 1829).

52. Trollope, *Domestic Manners*, 2:45.

53. Ibid., 2:45–46.

54. Frances Wright, *Address to the People of Philadelphia, Delivered in the Walnut Street Theater, on the Morning of the Fourth of July, 1829* (New York, 1829), 4, 5, 8, 13, 15.

55. Eckhardt, *Fanny Wright*, 204.

56. Trollope, *Domestic Manners*, 2:63.

57. "Female Charms," *Godey's Magazine and Lady's Book* 33, no. 52 (1846): 9.

58. Thomas Branagan, *Excellency of the Female Character Vindicated: Being an Investigation Relative to the Cause and Effects on the Encroachments of Men upon the Rights of Women* (New York, 1807), 277–88, quoted in Barbara Welter, "The Cult of True Womanhood: 1820–1860," *American Quarterly* 18, no. 2 (Summer 1966): 151–174, 154.

59. Lyman Beecher, *Lectures on Political Atheism* (Boston, 1852), 92–93, quoted in Connors, "Frances Wright," 42.

60. Sandra M. Gustafson, *Eloquence Is Power: Oratory and Performance in Early America* (Chapel Hill: Published for the Omohundro Institute of Early American History and Culture by the University of North Carolina Press, 2000), xvi.

61. Charles Mathews, *The New Comic Annual for 1831* (London, 1831), 147–60.

62. *Memoirs of Charles Mathews*, 4:79.

63. Ibid., 90.

64. Charles Buxton, ed. *Memoirs of Sir Thomas Fowell Buxton*, 3rd ed. (London, 1849), 113.

65. Edith Hurwitz, *Politics and the Public Conscience: Slave Emancipation and the Abolitionist Movement in Britain* (London: Allen & Unwin; New York: Barnes & Noble Books, 1973), 30–36.

66. *Report of the Agency Committee of the Anti-Slavery Society Established June, 1831* (London, 1832), in Hurwitz, *Politics and the Public Conscience*, 126–32.

67. Ibid., 51.

68. *Anti-Slavery Reporter* 5 (Sept. 24, 1832).

69. *Memoirs of Charles Mathews*, 4:74–79.

70. Ibid., 4:76.

71. Mathews, *New Comic Annual*, 150.

72. Ibid., 153, 159.

73. Ibid., 148–50.

74. Ibid., 157.

75. Ibid., 161.

76. *Memoirs of Charles Mathews*, 4:169.

77. Ibid.

Part III · Radical Abolitionism, Revolt, and Revolution

1. *Proceedings of the General Anti-Slavery Convention [. . .] 1840* (London, 1841); *Proceedings of the Convention [. . .] 1843* (London, 1843), 120ff, 14.

2. Thomas Paine, "LIBERTY TREE, a New Song," *Pennsylvania Magazine*, June 1775. The poem was reprinted in *Pennsylvania Ledger*, Aug. 12, 1775, and in other colonial newspapers.

3. David R. Roediger, *The Wages of Whiteness: Race and the Making of the American Working Class* (London: Verso, 1991); Dale Cockrell, *Demons of Disorder: Early Blackface Minstrels and Their World* (Cambridge: Cambridge University Press, 1997); Eric Lott, *Love and Theft: Blackface Minstrelsy and the American Working Class* (New York: Oxford University Press, 1993); William J. Mahar, *Behind the Burnt Cork Mask: Early Blackface Minstrelsy and Antebellum American Popular Culture* (Urbana: University of Illinois Press, 1999).

4. Robert Toll, *Blacking Up: The Minstrel Show in Nineteenth-Century America* (New York: Oxford University Press, 1974); Alexander Saxton, "Blackface Minstrelsy and Jacksonian Ideology," *American Quarterly* 27, no. 1 (1975): 3–28.

5. Michael Pickering, "White Skin, Black Masks," in *Music Hall Performance and Style*, ed. J. S. Bratton (Milton Keynes, UK: Open University Press, 1986), 81–85; Pickering, "Mock Blacks and Racial Mockery: The 'Nigger' Minstrel and British Imperialism," in *Acts of Supremacy: The British Empire and the Stage, 1790–1930*, ed. J. S. Bratton (Manchester: Manchester University Press, 1991); J. S. Bratton, "English Ethiopians: British Audiences and Black Face Acts, 1835–1865," *Yearbook of English Studies* (1981), 127–42; George Rehin, "Blackface Street Minstrels in Victorian London and Its Resorts," *Journal of Popular Culture* 15, no. 1 (Summer 1981): 19–38; Rehin, "Harlequin Jim Crow: Continuity and Convergence in Blackface Clowning," *Journal of Popular Culture* 9, no. 3 (Winter 1975): 682–701.

6. W. T. Lhamon, *Jump Jim Crow: Lost Plays, Lyrics, and Street Prose of the First Atlantic Popular Culture* (Cambridge, MA: Harvard University Press, 2003); Sarah Meer, *Uncle Tom Mania: Slavery, Minstrelsy, and Transatlantic Culture in the 1850s* (Athens: University of Georgia Press, 2005); Robert Nowatzki, *Representing African Americans in Transatlantic Abolitionism and Blackface Minstrelsy* (Baton Rouge: Louisiana State University Press, 2010).

7. Russel B. Nye, *The Unembarrassed Muse: The Popular Arts in America* (New York: Dial Press, 1970), 162–80; Toll, *Blacking Up*, 274.

8. Rehin, "Harlequin Jim Crow," 682–700.

9. Charles Haywood, *Negro Minstrelsy and Shakespearian Burlesque* (Hatboro, PA: Folklore Associates, 1966), 78–79.

10. Edward LeRoy Rice, *Monarchs of Minstrelsy, from "Daddy" Rice to Date* (New York:

Kenny Publishing, 1911). Rice, a minstrel performer himself, compiled a catalog of minstrel performers that supplies their places of birth and death, which is the basis of my assertion.

11. Lawrence Levine, *Highbrow Lowbrow: The Emergence of Cultural Hierarchy in America* (Cambridge, MA: Harvard University Press, 1988), 14–16.

12. Haywood, *Negro Minstrelsy,* 87–90.

Chapter 6 · Spartacus, Jim Crow, and the Black Jokes of Revolt

1. Thomas Carlyle, *Sartor Resartus and the Revolution of 1830* (London, 1830), 178–79.

2. Jonathan Sperber, *Revolutionary Europe, 1780–1850* (New York: Longman, 2000), 354–57.

3. "Appeal to Organize the First American Anti-Slavery Society," in *Letters of Theodore Dwight Weld, Angelina Grimké Weld, and Sarah Grimké, 1822–1844,* ed. Gilbert H. Barnes and Dwight L. Dumond (1934; reprint, Magnolia, MA: Peter Smith, 1965), 1:117–18.

4. Frances Anne Kemble, entry for Dec. 7, 1832, in *Journal of America* (London, 1835), reproduced in Catherine Clinton, *Fanny Kemble's Civil Wars* (New York: Simon & Schuster, 2000), 156–57.

5. *Southern Advocate* (Huntsville, AL), Oct. 15, 1831, cited in Herbert Aptheker, *American Negro Slave Revolts* (New York: International Publishers, 1974), 301.

6. Seymour Gross and Eileen Bender, "History, Politics, and Literature: The Myth of Nat Turner," *American Quarterly* 33 (1971): 487–518, 490, reprinted in *Articles on American Slavery: Rebellions, Resistance, and Runaways within the Slave South,* ed. Paul Finkelman (New York: Garland Publishing, 1989).

7. On the *Confessions of Nat Turner,* see Randolph Ferguson Scully, *Religion and the Making of Nat Turner's Virginia: Baptist Community and Conflict, 1740–1840* (Charlottesville: University Press of Virginia, 2008), 197–98, 211–14.

8. P. J. Staudenraus, *The African Colonization Movement, 1816–1865* (New York: Columbia University Press, 1961), 180–81.

9. Louis B. Filler, *The Crusade against Slavery: Friends, Foes, and Reforms, 1820–1860* (Algonac, MI: Reference Publications, 1986), 22; Stephen B. Oates, *The Fires of Jubilee: Nat Turner's Fierce Rebellion* (New York: Harper Perennial, 1990).

10. Frances Anne Kemble, entry for Dec. 7, 1832, in *Journal of America* (London, 1835), reprinted in *Fanny Kemble's Journals,* ed. Catherine Clinton (Cambridge, MA: Harvard University Press, 2000), 156–57.

11. David Walker, *Appeal . . . to the Coloured Citizens of the World,* excerpted in *Antislavery: The Crusade for Freedom in America,* ed. Dwight L. Dumond (Ann Arbor: University of Michigan Press, 1961) 114–15; Peter Hinks, *To Awaken My Afflicted Brethren: David Walker and the Problem of Antebellum Slave Resistance* (University Park: Pennsylvania State University Press, 1997).

12. Julie Winch, *Philadelphia's Black Elite: Activism, Accommodation, and the Struggle for Autonomy, 1787–1848* (Philadelphia: Temple University Press, 1988), 81–82.

13. *Liberator* (Boston), Jan. 1831.

14. Winch, *Philadelphia's Black Elite,* 41–42.

15. Marc M. Arkin, "The Federalist Trope: Power and Passion in Abolitionist Rhetoric," *Journal of American History* 88, no. 1 (June 2001): 75–98, 75.

16. Richard Harris, "A Young Dramatist's Diary: The *Secret Records* of R. M. Bird," *Library Chronicle* 25, no. 1 (Winter 1959): 10.

17. Ibid., 10–11.

18. Robert Montgomery Bird, *Sheppard Lee* (New York, 1836), 2:181–211, Bird Collection, Van Pelt Special Collections, University of Pennsylvania, Philadelphia. I am grateful to Christopher Looby of the UCLA English Department for directing my attention to *Shepard Lee*. See also Harris, "A Young Dramatist's Diary," 22 n. 9.

19. Kenneth S. Greenberg, ed., *The Confessions of Nat Turner and Related Documents* (Boston: Bedford Books of St. Martin's Press, 1996).

20. Some modern critics have already suggested as much. See, for example, Maria Wykes, *Projecting the Past: Ancient Rome, Cinema, and History* (New York: Routledge, 1997), 59–60, and John Daniel Collins, "American Drama in Antislavery Agitation, 1792–1861" (Ph.D. diss., University of Michigan, 1963), 114–15. Other scholars, however, have argued against antislavery intent on Bird's part; see, for example, Margaret Malamud, *Ancient Rome and Modern America* (London and Oxford: Wiley-Blackwell, 2009), 44; Jeffrey Richards, ed., *Early American Drama* (New York: Penguin Books, 1997), 247.

21. Robert Montgomery Bird, *The Gladiator*, MS copy dated Philadelphia, Apr. 1831, with pencil notes, Van Pelt Special Collections, University of Pennsylvania.

22. Abbé Raynal, *Philosophical and Political History of the Settlements and Trade of the Europeans in the East and West Indies*, trans. J. O. Justamond (London, 1783), 5:307–10.

23. Douglas R. Egerton, "Gabriel's Conspiracy and the Election of 1800," *Journal of Southern History* 56, no. 2 (May 1990).

24. *Baltimore Gazette*, Feb. 14, 1803, quoted in Alfred N. Hunt, *Haiti's Influence on Antebellum America: Slumbering Volcano in the Caribbean* (Baton Rouge: Louisiana State University Press, 1988), 35.

25. *Pennsylvania Gazette*, Sept. 24, Oct. 15, and Oct. 22, 1800. I am most grateful to John Davies for sharing his list of dates for articles on Gabriel's rebellion and trial.

26. Thomas Jefferson, *Notes on the State of Virginia* (London, 1787), 228–30.

27. Mary Mayer Bird, *Life of Robert Montgomery Bird, Written by His Wife, Mary Mayer Bird, Edited from the manuscript by C. Seymour Thompson* (Philadelphia: University of Pennsylvania Library, 1945); Arthur Hobson Quinn, *A History of the American Drama from the Beginning to the Civil War* (New York: Harper & Brothers, 1923), 221–23.

28. Bird, *Life of Robert Montgomery Bird*, 36–37.

29. Richard Moody, *Edwin Forrest: First Star of the American Stage* (New York: Alfred A. Knopf, 1960), 215–17.

30. Moody, *Edwin Forrest*, 98–101.

31. Reese D. James, *Old Drury of Philadelphia: A History of the Philadelphia Stage, 1800–1835* (Philadelphia: University of Pennsylvania Press, 1932), 61.

32. Charles Durang, *History of the Philadelphia Stage 1854–1863* (Philadelphia, 1854), 3:f. 302.

33. William B. Wood, *Personal Recollections of The Stage* (Philadelphia, 1855), 463, italics in original.

34. John Neal in *Blackwoods Magazine* 26 (1824): 567, quoted in Harris, "A Young Dramatist's Diary," 9.

35. Durang, *History of the Philadelphia Stage*, 3:fol. 258.

36. Playbill quoted in ibid., 3: fol. 266.

37. Bird, *The Gladiator*, II.3, in Richards, *Early American Drama*, 166–243. All quotes hereafter from the play are from this edition.

38. William Sumner Jenkins, *Pro-Slavery Thought in the Old South* (Chapel Hill: University of North Carolina Press, 1935), 139–40; Paul Finkelman, *Defending Slavery: Proslavery Thought in the Old South, a Brief History with Documents* (Boston: Bedford / St. Martin's, 2003), 29–31.

39. Edmund Ruffin, *The Political Economy of Slavery* (1853), in Finkelman, *Defending Slavery*, 61.

40. William Blair, *Inquiry into the State of Slavery amongst the Romans: From the Earliest Period till the Establishment of the Lombards in Italy* (Edinburgh, 1833); review in *American Quarterly Review* 25 (1834): 91.

41. George Bancroft, "Review of 'The Influence of Slavery on the Political Revolution in Rome.' A Lecture Delivered before a Society of Young Men in Massachusetts," *North American Review* 39 (1834): 423–24, 437.

42. *Brooklyn Eagle*, Dec. 26, 1846, quoted in Collins, "American Drama in Antislavery Agitation," 115. Collins also cites Cleveland Rodgers and John Black, eds. *The Gathering of the Forces, 1846–1847* (New York: G. P. Putnam's Sons, 1920), 2:331–32.

43. Quoted in Tice L. Miller, *Entertaining the Nation: American Drama in the Eighteenth and Nineteenth Centuries* (Carbondale: Southern Illinois University Press, 2007), 71.

44. Heather Nathans, *Slavery and Sentiment on the American Stage, 1787–1861: Lifting the Veil of Black* (Cambridge: Cambridge University Press, 2009), 176.

45. Richards, *Early American Drama*, 247.

46. Durang, *History of the Philadelphia Stage*, 3:fol. 302.

47. Ibid., 3:fol. 302, 4:fol. 301.

48. *United States Gazette*, Oct. 30, 1831.

49. In Philadelphia *The Gladiator* became a staple of the repertoire of the Northern Liberties, Arch Street, Walnut Street, and Chestnut Street theaters and was performed almost every season from its debut in 1831 until the mid-1850s. See the calendar of plays in Arthur Herman Wilson, *A History of the Philadelphia Theater 1835–1855* (Philadelphia: University of Pennsylvania Press, 1935).

50. Woods, *Personal Recollections of the Stage*, 363.

51. Jonathan H. Earle, *Jacksonian Antislavery and the Politics of Free Soil, 1824–1854* (Chapel Hill: University of North Carolina Press, 2004), 19–27.

52. Earle, *Jacksonian Antislavery*, 25–26; Collins, "American Drama in Antislavery Agitation," 123.

53. Quoted in Collins, "American Drama in Antislavery Agitation," 124.

54. William Leggett, *A Collection of the Political Writings of William Leggett*, ed. Theodore Sedgwick Jr. (New York, 1840), 2:232–36.

55. *Plaindealer*, Feb. 25, July 29, 1837, quoted in Earle, *Jacksonian Antislavery*, 25.

56. Earle, *Jacksonian Antislavery*, 25.

57. "Robert Montgomery Bird," *Philadelphia Gothic*, www.librarycompany.org/gothic/bird.htm.

58. Richards, *Early American Drama*, 168.

59. Moody quotes Bunn and cites Jones's London advertising campaign on Forrest's behalf; Moody, *Edwin Forrest*, 145–46.

60. Quoted in ibid., 149.

61. Dale Shaw, *Titans of the American Stage: Edwin Forrest, the Booths, the O'Neills* (Philadelphia: Westminster Press, 1971), 31–32.

62. *Times*, Oct. 1836 [exact date unknown], reprinted in full in Durang, *History of the Philadelphia Stage* 4:fol. 301.

63. Charles Rice, "Review, Drury-Lane Theatre, October 19, 1836," in *The London Theatre in the Eighteen-Thirties*, ed. Arthur Colby Sprague and Bertram Shuttleworth (London: Printed for the Society for Theatre Research, 1950), 6–7.

64. Jacob Jones, *Spartacus; or, The Roman Gladiator* (Bath Theatre, Mar. 1827), BL Add MS LCPlays 42955 fols. 94–128b.

65. Jacob Jones, preface to *Spartacus; or, The Roman Gladiator*, in ibid. and published in edition from James Ridgway & Sons (London, 1837).

66. Jerry Lukowski and Hubert Zawadzki, *A Concise History of Poland*, 2nd ed. (Cambridge: Cambridge University Press, 2006), 157.

67. Sperber, *Revolutionary Europe*, 356–57.

68. For some of the key installments of Mathews's *New Comic Annual for 1831* and the reproductions of Clay's prints, see *Atkinson's Saturday Evening Post*, Jan. 7, 1832; Jan. 21, 1832; Feb. 4, 1832; Feb. 18, 1832; Mar. 2, 1832; Mar. 10, 1832; Mar. 31, 1832; and Apr. 7, 1832.

69. Gary B. Nash, *Forging Freedom: The Formation of Philadelphia's Black Community, 1720–1840* (Cambridge, MA: Harvard University Press, 1988), 275.

70. *Atkinskon's Saturday Evening Post*, Jan. 21, 1832.

71. Quoted in Nash, *Forging Freedom*, 246. Nash cites Leon F. Litwack, *North of Slavery: The Negro in the Free States, 1790–1860* (Chicago: University of Chicago Press, 1961), 39.

72. Hazel Waters, *Racism on the Victorian Stage: Representation of Slavery and the Black Character* (Cambridge: Cambridge University Press, 2007), 89.

73. George Rehin, "Harlequin Jim Crow: Continuity and Convergence in Blackface Clowning," *Journal of Popular Culture* 9, no. 3 (Winter 1975): 682–700.

74. Lyrics in Isaac J. Greenwood, *The Circus: Its Origin and Growth Prior to 1835* (Washington, DC: Hobby House Press, 1962), 121–22.

75. Dale Cockrell, *Demons of Disorder: Early Blackface Minstrels and Their World* (Cambridge: Cambridge University Press, 1997), 63; Noel M. Ludlow, *Dramatic Life as I Found It* (St. Louis, 1880), 332.

76. Durang, *History of the Philadelphia Theater*, 3:f. 316.

77. E. Riley, "The Original Jim Crow" (New York, 1832), in W. T. Lhamon, *Jump Jim Crow: Lost Plays, Lyrics, and Street Prose of the First Atlantic Popular Culture* (Cambridge, MA: Harvard University Press, 2003), 95–102.

78. William J. Mahar, *Behind the Burnt Cork Mask: Early Blackface Minstrelsy and Antebellum American Popular Culture* (Urbana: University of Illinois Press, 1999), 102.

79. *Virginia Mummy* (Alabama, 1835; London, 1836), BL Add MS LCPlays 42940 vol. 76 fol.1007; *Bone Squash Diablo* in Lhamon, *Jump Jim Crow*, 178–210.

80. Lhamon, *Jump Jim Crow*, 4.

81. *Spirit of the Times*, Mar. 5, 1842.

82. William Whipper, *Eulogy on William Wilberforce, Esq., Delivered at the Request of the People of Colour of the City of Philadelphia, in the Second African Presbyterian Church, on the Sixth Day of December 1833* (Philadelphia, 1833).

83. "Circular Relative to the Formation of a National Anti-Slavery Society" (c. 1830–32), HSP, Rawle Family Papers, no. 536, box 5, fol. 87.

84. The appeal called upon American abolitionists to follow the "examples of similar organizations . . . that have speedily risen to great influence. Especially . . . the National

Anti-Slavery Society of Great Britain"; Gilbert H. Barnes and Dwight L. Dumond, eds., *Letters of Theodore Dwight Weld, Angelina Grimké Weld, and Sarah Grimké, 1822–1844* (New York: D. Appleton-Century, 1934), 1:117–18.

85. *Declaration of Sentiments* (Philadelphia, 1833), in Louis Ruchames, ed., *The Abolitionists: A Collection of Their Writing* (New York: Putnam, 1963), 78.

86. Winch, *Philadelphia's Black Elite*, 82–83.

87. "The Theater," *The Colored American*, Dec. 9, 1837.

88. Philip Lapsansky, "Afro-Americana: Inventing Black Folks," *Library Company of Philadelphia Annual Report 1997*, 35.

89. Cockrell, *Demons of Disorder*, 62–65.

90. Greenwood, *The Circus*, 123–24; Cockrell, *Demons of Disorder*, 65.

91. Durang, *History of the Philadelphia Stage*, 3:f. 316.

92. Playbill, Walnut Street Theatre, Mar. 1, 1833, LCP, McCallister Collection.

93. Ibid.

94. E. Riley, *New Music . . . the Comic Extravaganza, "Jim Crow, with a Full Length Lithography of Mr. T. Rice"* (Chatham, London, 1833), excerpted in Cockrell, *Demons of Disorder*, 72.

95. Ibid.

96. Cynthia Shelton, *The Mills of Manayunk: Industrialization and Social Conflict in the Philadelphia Region, 1787–1837* (Baltimore: Johns Hopkins University Press, 1986), 116–34.

97. "Jim Crow" (Baltimore, 1833), excerpted in Cockrell, *Demons of Disorder*, 2.

98. Bruce Laurie, *Working People of Philadelphia, 1800–1850* (Philadelphia: Temple University Press, 1980), 58–61.

99. Nash, *Forging Freedom*, 226.

100. Samuel Emlen Jr. to Samuel Emlen, Oct. 5, 1795, LCP, Dillwyn Letters; see also *To the Free Africans and Other People of Color in the United States . . . Convention of Delegates from the Abolition Societies Established in Different Parts of the United States* (Philadelphia: Printed by Zachariah Poulson, 1796).

101. Nash, *Forging Freedom*, 246–50; Dennis Clark, *The Irish in Philadelphia: Ten Generations of Urban Experience* (Philadelphia: Temple University Press, 1973), 17–18.

102. Laurie, *Working People of Philadelphia*, 62–63.

103. Nash, *First City*, 201; Harry Reynolds, *Minstrel Memories: The Story of Burnt Cork Minstrelsy in Great Britain from 1836 to 1927* (London: Alston Rivers Ltd., 1928), 72.

104. T. P. Taylor, *Jim Crow in His New Place: A Burletta in One Act* (London, 1838), BL Add MS LCPlays 42950 vol. 2 xxxvi, fols. 593–602B; *Cowardy, Cowardy Custard; or, Harlequin Jim Crow and the Magic Mustard Pot* (London, 1836), BL Add MS LCPlays 42938 vol. 74, fols. 719–29; *Otello the Moor* (London: 1838) in Lhamon, *Jump Jim Crow*, 342–85.

105. Henry Mayhew, *London Labour and the London Poor: A Cyclopaedia of the Conditions and Earnings of Those That WILL Work, Those That CANNOT Work, and Those That WILL NOT Work* (1851; reprint, London: Frank Cass, 1967), 3:51–71. Mayhew includes interviews with Punch and Judy puppeteers and a script and song lyrics from a Punch and Judy show that prominently featured Jim Crow.

106. Lhamon, *Jump Jim Crow*, 64.

107. W. L. Rede, *Life in America: The Flight, the Pursuit, the Voyage* (London, 1836), BL Add MS LCPlays 42939 vol. 75 fols. 444–79.

108. *Jim Crow's Collection of Songs to Drive Away the Blue Devils* (London, n.d.), BL Add MS LCPlays 77512.0.

109. James Montgomery, *An Essay on the Phrenology of the Hindoos and Negroes, Together with Strictures Thereon by C. Thompson, M.D.* (London, 1829).

110. Samuel George Morton, *Crania Americana; or, A Comparative View of the Skulls of Various Aboriginal Nations of North and South America* (Philadelphia; London, 1839).

111. Joseph Clark Nott, *Types of Mankind; or Ethnological Researches* (Philadelphia, 1854); Joseph-Arthur Comte de Gobineau, *Essai sur l'inégalité des races humaines* [Essay on the inequality of the human races] (Paris, 1853), translated into English by Henry Holz (commissioned by Joseph Nott) as *The Moral and Intellectual Diversity of Races* (Philadelphia, 1856); Robert Knox, *Races of Men* (London, 1850).

112. George Cruikshank, *Phrenological Illustrations; or, An Artist's View of the Craniological System of Doctors Gall and Spurzheim* (London, 1826).

113. David Claypoole Johnston, *Phrenology Exemplified and Illustrated, with Upwards of Forty Etchings: Being SCRAPS no. 7, for the Year 1837* (Boston, 1837).

114. Quoted in Philip Lapsansky, *Library Company of Philadelphia Report 1997*, 34–35.

115. Eric Lott, *Love and Theft: Blackface Minstrelsy and the American Working Class* (New York: Oxford University Press, 1993); Noel Ignatiev, *How the Irish Became White* (New York: Routledge, 1995).

116. Michael Pickering, "White Skin, Black Masks," in *Music Hall Performance and Style*, ed. J. S. Bratton (Milton Keynes, UK: Open University Press, 1986), 88; Jonathan Schneer, *London 1900: The Imperial Metropolis* (New Haven, CT: Yale University Press, 2001), 97.

117. Duncan J. MacLeod, *Slavery, Race, and the American Revolution* (New York: Cambridge University Press, 1974), 166; David Grimsted, *Melodrama Unveiled: American Theater and Culture, 1800–1850* (Chicago: University of Chicago Press, 1968), 52.

118. Ibid. The bracketed comments on the audience's reaction to Rice's speech are the theater critic's and are in the original article.

119. "The Theater."

120. *Pennsylvania Gazette*, Aug. 15, 1834.

121. *Philadelphia Gazette*, July 14, 1835.

122. Nash, *Forging Freedom*, 277.

123. C. Peter Ripley, Roy E. Finkenbine, Michael F. Hembree, and Donald Yacovone, eds., *Witness for Freedom: African American Voices on Race, Slavery, and Emancipation* (Chapel Hill: University of North Carolina Press, 1993), 12.

124. James Forten and Russell Parrott, *Resolutions and Remonstrances of the People of Color against Colonization to the Coast of Africa* (Philadelphia, 1818), 5–8, in ibid., 30–32.

125. Robert Purvis to "My Dear Friend Wright," Aug. 22, 1842, in Ripley et al., *Witness for Freedom*, 12–13.

126. Durang, *History of the Philadelphia Stage*, 3:fol. 316.

Chapter 7 · Revolutionary Brotherhood

1. Simon Gikandi, *Maps of Englishness: Writing Identity in the Culture of Colonialism* (New York: Columbia University Press, 1996), 59–62.

2. Ibid., 59–62; David R. Roediger, *The Wages of Whiteness: Race and the Making of the American Working Class* (London: Verso, 1991), 65–95.

3. Thomas Paine, "LIBERTY TREE, A New Song," *Pennsylvania Magazine*, June 1775.

4. The black population in Britain, which in the late eighteenth century was between

ten and fifteen thousand had declined by 1830s and 1840s, possibly to less than five thousand. Folarin Shyllon, "Blacks in Britain: A Historical and Analytical Overview," in *Global Dimensions of the African Diaspora*, ed. Joseph E. Harris (Washington, DC: Howard University Press, 1993), 232–36; Seymour Drescher, *Capitalism and Anti-Slavery: British Mobilization in Comparative Perspective* (New York: Oxford University Press, 1987), 28, 185 n. 10.

5. Douglas A. Lorimer, *Colour, Class, and the Victorians* (Leicester, UK: Leicester University Press; New York: Holmes & Meier, 1978), 41–43.

6. *London City Mission Magazine* 22 (Aug. 1857): 217.

7. Thomas Carlyle, *Chartism* (London, 1840), 60; italics in original.

8. Dwayne Brenna's "George Dibdin Pitt: His Life and Work" (Ph.D. diss., University of London, 2000) includes a discussion of *The Black Spartacus*. See also Hazel Waters, *Racism on the Victorian Stage: Representation of Slavery and the Black Character* (Cambridge: Cambridge University Press, 2007), 118.

9. Betty Fladeland, *Abolitionists and Working-Class Problems in the Age of Industrialization* (Baton Rouge: Louisiana State University Press, 1984), 121.

10. Alan J. Rice and Martin Crawford, eds., *Liberating Sojourn: Frederick Douglass and Transatlantic Reform* (Athens: University of Georgia Press, 1999), 2–8.

11. "The Anti-Slavery That Might Succeed," *Spectator*, July 25, 1846.

12. Quoted in Hugh Thomas, *The Slave Trade: The History of the Atlantic Slave Trade, 1440–1870* (London: Picador, 1997), 734.

13. Llewellyn Woodward, *The Age of Reform 1815–1870* (Oxford: Oxford University Press, 1962), 152–55. For press coverage of the debate in January to April 1846, see *The Gentleman's Magazine* 25 (June 1846).

14. Probably written by William Lovett, *All Men Are Brethren: An Address to the Friends of Humanity and Justice among All Nations, by the Democratic Friends of All Nations* (London, 1845), in *The Chartist Movement in Britain, 1838–1850*, ed. Gregory Claeys (London: Pickering & Chatto, 2001), 4:45–46.

15. Christine Bolt, *The Anti-Slavery Movement and Reconstruction: A Study in Anglo-American Co-operation, 1833–77* (London: Oxford University Press, 1969), 12–13; R. Harrison, *Before the Socialists: Studies in Labour and Politics, 1861–88* (London: Routledge & Kegan Paul, 1965).

16. Henry Solly, *The Midnight Cry: A Sermon Preached before the Somerset and Dorset Association, at Their Annual Meeting, Held in Dorchester, in June 1845* (London, 1846).

17. George Dibdin Pitt, *The White Slave; or, Murder and Misery* (London, 1845), BL Add MS LCPlays 42987.

18. John Russell Stephens, *The Profession of the Playwright: British Theatre, 1800–1900* (Cambridge: Cambridge University Press, 1992), xxi, 8, 50.

19. Dwayne Brenna, "George Dibdin Pitt: Actor and Playwright," *Theatre Notebook* 22, no. 1 (1998): 24–37.

20. See, for example, "Inquests," *Hackney Journal*, Mar. 1842: "An inquest was held at the Britannia on Wednesday 23rd by W. Baker, Esqu., Coroner, on the body of Sarah Parker, a charwoman, aged 67 . . . : Verdict: Found Dead."

21. Playbill for *Omadhaun; or, Poor Dog Tray* and *Englishman in France* (Nov. 24–25, 1843, "for the benefit of the Friends of Unity"), Hackney Council Archives BK/18-792.35, London. For a discussion of the Britannia's political milieu, see also Clive Barker, "The Audiences of the Britannia Theatre, Hoxton," *Theatre Quarterly* 9 (Summer 1979): 35.

22. For a full print of the National Union of the Working Classes' "Declaration of the Rights of Man," see *The Penny Papers for the People* (London, 1830–31), 302–3.

23. See BL Add MS 27821 fols. 328–29, reprinted in "Papers, 1841–2," in D. J. Rowe, ed., *London Radicalism, 1830–1843: A Selection of the Papers of Francis Place* (London: London Record Society, 1970).

24. Barker, "Audiences of the Britannia Theatre," 28.

25. Charles Dickens, "Two Views of a Cheap Theatre," in *The Uncommercial Traveller* (London: Chapman & Hall, 1907), 39.

26. Brenna, "George Dibdin Pitt," 64.

27. "Songs Written for the Annual Dinner of Hackney Debating Society," *Hackney Journal*, May 1842.

28. "Police Intelligence," *Chartist*, Feb. 2, 1839.

29. NA, Lord Chamberlain's Papers LC7/5 and LC7/6, London MSS.

30. A. L. Crauford, *Sam and Sallie* (London: Cranley & Day, 1933), 143–49, 152–55. As Clive Barker has pointed out, Crauford's information must be taken with a pinch of salt. He provides no footnotes, and his factual information is sprinkled with anecdotal hearsay.

31. See, for example, Britannia Saloon mixed playbill for *Mary Clifford, the Foundling Apprentice Girl!, or, The Victim of Mother Brownrigg!, Nigger Sleep Walker; or, The Black Ghost!,* and *Kathleen, the Maid of Munster!; or, A Soldier's Bride!* (Aug. 14, 1848); Britannia Saloon playbill for *Lady Hatton!: The Suicide's Tree!: A Legend of Bleeding Heart Yard, Luke Ashburne!; or, The gibbet of an innocent man!,* and *The Heart of a True British Sailor!* (Feb. 25, 1850); Britannia Saloon mixed playbill for *Arcadia, or, The Freaks of the Passions, La Prima Ballerina!, The Student's Grave, The Hunchback,* and *Uncle Tom's Cabin* (July 25, 1853), East London Theatre Archive, Theatre Collections production file: Britannia Saloon, www .elta-project.org/browse.html?recordId=955. See also Barker, "Audiences of the Britannia Theatre," 35, for a discussion of the Britannia as the "People's Theatre."

32. George Dibdin Pitt, *Toussaint L'Ouverture; or, The Black Spartacus* (June 14, 1846), BL Add MS LCPlays 42995 fols. 225–53b. Subsequent quotations are from this manuscript.

33. David Turley, "British Unitarians, Frederick Douglass and Race" in *Liberating Sojourn: Frederick Douglass and Transatlantic Reform,* ed. Martin Crawford and Alan Rice (Athens: University of Georgia Press, 1999), 55–72.

34. Audrey Fisch, " 'Negrophilism' and British Nationalism: The Spectacle of the Black Abolitionist Movement," *Victorian Review* 19 (Summer 1993): 20–47; Sarah Meer, "Competing Representations: Douglass, the Ethiopian Serenaders, and the Ethnic Exhibition in London," in Rice and Crawford, *Liberating Sojourn,* 141–65, 142.

35. Marcus Rainsford, *An Historical Account of the Black Empire of Hayti: Comprehending a View of the Principal Transactions in the Revolution of Saint-Domingo; with Its Ancient and Modern State* (London, 1805), 4.

36. Quoted in Jan Nederveen Pieterse, *White on Black: Images of Africa and Blacks in Western Popular Culture* (New Haven, CT: Yale University Press, 1992), 49.

37. *The Britannia Diaries of Frederick Wilton,* ed. Jim Davis (London: Society for Theatre Research, 1992), 3.

38. For Aldridge's performances at the Britannia Theatre, see A. E. Wilson, *East End Entertainment* (London: Arthur Baker, 1954), 159, 173.

39. Cited in Bernth Lindfors, " 'Nothing Extenuate, Nor Set Down Aught in Malice':

New Biographical Information on Ira Aldridge," *African American Review* 28, no. 3 (Autumn 1994): 457–72, 458.

40. Surrey Theater playbill, Apr. 22, 1833, BL Thcts. For Aldridge's reception at the London minor theaters, see Bernth Lindfors, "'Mislike Me Not for My Complexion . . .': Ira Aldridge in Whiteface," *African American Review* 33, no. 2 (Summer, 1999): 347–54, 351.

41. For Aldridge's performance of "Opossum up a Gum Tree" on the English stage, see Charles Rzepka, "Introduction: Obi, Aldridge, and Abolition," *Romantic Circles Praxis Series* 4 (Aug. 2002), www.rc.umd.edu/praxis/obi/rzepka/intro.html.

42. *A Sketch of Mr. Mathews's Entertainment, Entitled "A Trip to America,"* (London, 1824), 146. See also James Hewlett's letter published in *The Times,* July 10, 1824, in which Hewlett objects to Mathews's parody as offensive and racist.

43. Paul Lawrence Dunbar, "We Wear the Mask," in *The Collected Poetry of Paul Laurence Dunbar,* ed. Joanne M. Braxton (Charlottesville: University Press of Virginia, 1993).

44. Herbert Marshall and Mildred Stock, *Ira Aldridge, the Negro Tragedian* (Carbondale: Southern Illinois University Press, 1958); Lindfors, "New Biographical Information on Ira Aldridge," 458.

45. "Ethiopian Serenaders—St. James's Theatre," *Daily News,* Mar. 18, 1846, quoted in Meer, "Competing Representations," 150.

46. Bratton, "English Ethiopians," 128; Meer, "Competing Representations," 143.

47. R. J. Blackett, *Building an Antislavery Wall: Black Americans in the Abolitionist Movement 1830–1860* (Baton Rouge: Louisiana State University Press, 1983), 160.

48. George Dibdin Pitt, *The Revolution in Paris* (Mar. 3, 1848), BL Add MS 43009 LCPlays fols. 831–949. All quotations from the play are from this manuscript.

49. I am grateful to Geoffrey Symcox for suggesting that Pitt may have been referencing the revolt of Masaniello at Naples in 1647.

50. Pitt, *Revolution in Paris,* II.8.

51. Stephens, *Profession of the Playwright,* 69.

52. 1832 report, NA, Lord Chamberlain's Papers, fol. 393.

53. Dawn B. Sova, *Banned Plays: Censorship Histories of 125 Stage Dramas* (New York: Facts on File, 2004), 228–29.

54. Stephens, *Profession of the Playwright,* 59.

55. 1832 report, BL Add MS 219, fols. 3945–46.

56. First anonymously published as an article in *Fraser's Magazine for Town and Country* 40 (Feb. 1849) and reprinted as a pamphlet four years later with the title *Occasional Discourse on the Nigger Question,* Carlyle's revised 1853 tract was reproduced again in three installments under the title "Fifteen Years of Emancipation in the West Indies" in *The Old Guard: A Monthly Journal Devoted the Principles of 1776 and 1787:* 4 (Apr. 1853): 239–245; 5 (May 1853): 308–311; and 6 (June 1853): 372–377; available online at http://cruel.org/econ thought/texts/carlyle/odnqbk.html (accessed Oct. 5, 2013); quote at 239.

57. Carlyle, *Occasional Discourse,* 372.

58. John Stuart Mill, "The Negro Question," *Fraser's Magazine for Town and Country* 41, (Jan. 1850), reprinted in *Little's Living Age* 24 (1850): 465–69, 465.

59. Carlyle, *Occasional Disourse,* 375.

60. Mill, "The Negro Question," 465.

61. *Reynolds's Newspaper,* Apr. 10, 1853.

62. Richard Oastler, *British Labour Struggles: Contemporary Pamphlets, 1727–1850* (New York: Arno Press, 1972), 173.

63. Charles Dickens, *American Notes for General Circulation* (London, 1842), 225–26.

64. *Punch*, Mar. 4, 1865, 86.

65. Henry Mayhew, *London Labour and the London Poor* (1851; reprint, London: Frank Cass, 1967), 1:1.

66. David Reynolds, *George Lippard* (Boston: Twayne, 1982), 1.

67. See, for example, "Centralization," *United States Magazine and Democratic Review* 26, no. 142 (Apr. 1850): 289–305; "Review of Carlyle's *Latter Day Pamphlets*," *Southern Quarterly Review* 2, no. 4 (Nov. 1850): 313–56; and "British and American Slavery," *Southern Quarterly Review* 8, no. 16 (Oct. 1853): 369–411.

68. Quoted in David R. Roediger, *The Wages of Whiteness: Race and the Making of the American Working Class* (London: Verso, 1991), 71.

69. George Fitzhugh, *Cannibals All! Or, Slaves without Masters* (Richmond, VA, 1857).

70. Roediger, *Wages of Whiteness*, 70.

71. See ibid.; Eric Lott, *Love and Theft* (Oxford: Oxford University Press, 1993); Alexander Saxton, *The Rise and Fall of the White Republic* (London: Verso, 1990); and Noel Ignatiev, *How the Irish Became White* (New York: Routledge, 1995).

72. Ignatiev, *How the Irish Became White*, 2–3.

73. Ibid., 7–8, 99.

74. Quoted in Russell F. Weigley, "A Peaceful City: Public Order in Philadelphia from Consolidation through the Civil War," in *The Peoples of Philadelphia*, ed. Allen F. Davis and Mark H. Haller (Philadelphia: University of Pennsylvania Press, 1965), 155–74, 165.

75. Roediger, *Wages of Whiteness*, 72.

76. George Lippard, "Women Wage Slaves," excerpted in *George Lippard Prophet of Protest: Writings of an American Radical, 1822–1854*, ed. David S. Reynolds (New York: Peter Lang, 1986), 213–14.

77. Ibid., 213.

78. Timothy Helwig, "Denying the Wages of Whiteness: The Racial Politics of George Lippard's Working-Class Protest," *American Studies* 47, no. 3–4 (Fall–Winter 2006): 87–111, 87, 89–90.

79. His working-class figures are decidedly multiethnic in, for example, the *Nazarenes; or, Last of the Washingtons* (1844), *Quaker City* (1845), *Blanche of Brandywine, Legends of the American Revolution; or, Washington and His Generals*, and his last unfinished novel, *Eleanor; or, Slave Catching in the Quaker City* (1854), a pointed condemnation of the Fugitive Slave Act.

80. David Reynolds, "Radical Sensationalism: George Lippard in His Transatlantic Contexts," in *Transatlantic Sensations*, ed. Jennifer Phegley, John Cyril Barton, and Kristen N. Huston (Aldershot, UK: Ashgate, 2012), 93.

81. Lippard's diary, entry for Oct. 4, 1852, LCP in HSP, Brotherhood of the Union Collection MSS, vol. 1.

82. Reynolds, "Radical Sensationalism," 77–79.

83. Ibid., 1.

84. Reynolds, *George Lippard, Prophet of Protest*, 227.

85. George Lippard, *Thomas Paine: Author-Soldier of the American Revolution* (Philadelphia, 1852), 6.

86. Lippard, *Thomas Paine*, 8.

87. Advertisement for "A new series by George Lippard," *Saturday Courier*, July 4, 1846, front page.

88. John Bell Bouton, *The Life and Choice Writings of George Lippard, with a Portrait, and Facsimile of a Portion of a Letter Written in the Early Part of His Illness* (New York, 1855), 61.

89. George Lippard, *Blanche of Brandywine; or, September the Eleventh, 1777: A Romance of the Revolution* (Philadelphia, 1864), 344–45. This 1864 publication is a reproduction of the 1846 edition. All quotes hereafter are from this edition.

90. Ibid., 35.

91. Ibid., 18.

92. Ibid., 111–12, 114–15.

93. Heather Nathans, *Slavery and Sentiment on the American Stage, 1787–1861: Lifting the Veil of Black* (Cambridge: Cambridge University Press, 2009), 1–2.

94. Lippard, *Blanche of Brandywine*, 293.

95. Ibid., 223.

96. Ibid., 344–45.

97. Lott, *Love and Theft*, 80; Shelley Streeby, "Opening Up the Story Paper: George Lippard and the Construction of Class," *Boundary2* 24, no. 1 (1997): 202. Helwig disagrees in "Denying the Wages of Whiteness," 93–94.

98. Lippard, *Blanche of Brandywine*. See, for example, Lippard's descriptions of Sampson in these terms on 59, 112, and 223.

99. Ibid., 66–67.

100. Moira Ferguson, *Subject to Others: British Women Writers and Colonial Slavery, 1670–1834* (New York: Routledge, 1992); see esp. chap. 2, "*Oroonoko*: Birth of a Paradigm," 27–50.

101. William J. Mahar, "Black English in Early Blackface Minstrelsy: A New Interpretation of the Sources of Minstrel Show Dialect," *American Quarterly* 37, no. 2 (Summer 1985): 260–285, 262.

102. Lippard, *Blanche of Brandywine*, 18–19.

103. Ibid., 97–98.

104. J. G. Burnett also adapted *Blanche of Brandywine* in 1858 for Laura Keene's Theatre in New York, but this production does not seem to have traveled to Philadelphia. His version includes the Black Sampson character but reduces him to a bit part and servile comic foil.

105. David R. Brigham, *Public Culture in the Early Republic: Peale's Museum and Its Audience* (Washington, DC: Smithsonian Institution Press, 1995), 26.

106. See LCP McCallister Collection of playbills, McA5761.F.

107. Playbill, Peale's Museum, Apr. 9, 1846, LCP McAllister Collection, McA 5761.F.

108. John Leacock, *The Fall of British Tyranny; or, American Liberty Triumphant* (Philadelphia 1776); William Dunlap, *The Glory of Columbia; Her Yeomanry* (New York, 1806; Philadelphia, 1807).

109. "The Stage," *Saturday Courier*, May 29, 1847.

110. Reynolds, *George Lippard*, 15.

111. See Lippard's diary, entries for Dec. 12, Dec. 19, 1852, and Jan. 2, 1853, LCP Brotherhood of the Union Collection MSS; vol. 1.

112. "The Stage" [review of Mrs. Ward's *Blanche of Brandywine*], *Saturday Courier*, May 29, 1847.

113. Lippard to M'Makin, in *Saturday Courier*, May 8, 1847, italics in original. Lippard published this open letter to M'Makin to complain that other authors were plagiarizing his *Legends* and to defend his work.

114. George Lippard, *The Legends of the American Revolution: "1776" or, Washington and His Generals* (Philadelphia, 1876), 13–22. All quotes hereafter are from this facsimile edition republished after Lippard's death.

115. Ibid., 352.

116. Ibid., 355, 360.

117. Ibid., 363, 365.

118. Ibid., 364.

119. Ibid., 363.

120. Ibid., 361.

121. Ibid., 361–62.

122. Ibid., 362–63.

123. Timothy Mason Roberts, *Distant Revolutions: 1848 and the Challenge to American Exceptionalism* (Charlottesville: University Press of Virginia, 2009), 3–4, 48.

124. Ibid., 49–51.

125. George Lippard, *Adonai: The Pilgrim of Eternity* (1849; revised, 1851), in Reynolds, *George Lippard*, 134–35, 140–41, 148.

126. Ibid., 148–50.

127. *Quaker City Weekly*, Oct. 29, 1849, quoted in Reynolds, *George Lippard*, 19.

128. Reynolds, *George Lippard*, 19–20.

129. Ibid., 21.

130. O. L. Drake to "the circles and brothers" of the Brotherhood of the Union, Mar. 15, 1854, LCP Brotherhood of the Union Collection MSS, vol. 1, emphasis in original.

Conclusion · Uncle Tom, the Eighteenth-Century Revolutionary Legacy, and Historical Memory

1. Christine Bolt, *The Anti-Slavery Movement and Reconstruction: A Study in Anglo-American Co-operation, 1833–1877* (London: Oxford University Press, 1969), 13.

2. Nils Erik Enkvist, *Caricatures of Americans on the English State Prior to 1870* (Port Washington, NY: Kennikat Press, 1968), 111–12.

3. Jeffrey H. Richards, ed., *Early American Drama* (London: Penguin Books, 1997), 369–70.

4. Eliza Vincent, *Uncle Tom's Cabin; or, The Fugitive Slave*, BL Add MS LCPlays 52934 1852 F; E. Fitzball, *Uncle Tom's Cabin*, Add MS LCPlays 52934 1852 G; J. Courtney, BL Add MS LCPlays 52934 1852 K; W. Brough, *Uncle Tom's Cabin; or, Nigger Life in London*, BL Add MS LCPlays 52935 1852 J; H. T. Taylor and M. Lemon, *A Slave Life from Uncle Tom's Cabin*, BL Add MS LCPlays MCP52936 1852 A; anonymous, *Uncle Tom's Cabin*, BL Add MS LCPlays MCP52936 1852 Q; F. Neale, *Harlequin Uncle Tom; or, Britannia the Pride of the Ocean and Guardian Genius of the Slave*, BL Add MS LCPlays MCP52936 1852 AA. This list mentions only a few adaptations of Stowe's novel but is by no means exhaustive; there are many other Uncle Tom plays in the British Library's collection of the Lord Chamberlain's Plays.

5. "American Slavery: English Opinion of 'Uncle Tom's Cabin,' Evils of Slavery—Method of Its Removal—Dangers of Agitation—Colonization, &c.," *London Times*, Sept. 3, 1852, emphasis in original.

6. *New York Herald*, Sept. 3, 1852.

7. Douglass praised *Uncle Tom's Cabin* in "The Anti-Slavery Movement: A Lecture by Frederick Douglass before the Rochester Ladies' Anti-Slavery Society," Mar. 12, 1855, and attacked blackface minstrelsy and its audiences in his *North Star*, Oct. 27, 1848, quoted in Sarah Meer, *Uncle Tom Mania: Slavery, Minstrelsy, and Transatlantic Culture in the 1850s* (Athens: University of Georgia Press, 2005), 71.

8. John Penington, diary, Jan. 31, 1864, HSP, Edward Carey Gardiner Collection, no. 227A, box 31, p. 161.

9. *New York Herald*, Sept. 3, 1852.

10. Dale Cockrell, *Demons of Disorder: Early Blackface Minstrels and Their World* (Cambridge: Cambridge University Press, 1997), 13–14; Isaac Goldberg, *Tin Pan Alley: A Chronicle of American Popular Music* (New York: Frederick Ungard, 1961), 35–36.

11. *London Times*, Jan. 2, 1853.

12. *London Times*, Sept. 3, 1852.

13. George Dibdin Pitt, *Uncle Tom's Cabin: A Nigger Drama in Two Acts*, BL Add MS 52935 1852 I. The play was intended for representation at the Royal Pavilion Theatre on Saturday, Oct. 9, 1852; the MS was received on Oct. 7 and the license granted on Oct. 9.

14. Montrose Moses, introduction to *Uncle Tom's Cabin*, in *Representative Plays by American Dramatists* (New York: E. P. Dutton, 1918), 2:612.

15. Gary B. Nash, *First City: Philadelphia and the Forging of Historical Memory* (Philadelphia: University of Pennsylvania Press, 2002), 200.

16. Ulrich B. Phillips, *American Negro Slavery: A Survey of the Supply, Employment, and Control of Negro Labor, as Determined by the Plantation Regime* (1918; reprint, Baton Rouge: Louisiana State University Press, 1966).

17. Gary B. Nash, "Why Is the Story of Quakers and Slavery Neglected or Unknown" (paper presented at the LCP, June 16, 2012), 18; to be published under the title "The Hidden Story of Quakers and Slavery," in *Quakers, Slavery, and Abolitionism*, ed. Brycchan Carey and Geoffrey Plank (Urbana: University of Illinois Press, forthcoming).

18. Quoted in ibid., 20. Samuel Eliot Morison and Henry Steele Commager, *Growth of the American Republic*, 2nd ed. (New York: Oxford University Press, 1937), 1:423.

19. Nash, "Why Is the Story of Quakers and Slavery Neglected," 21. Nash cites Jonathan Zimmerman, *Whose America: Culture Wars in the Public Schools* (Cambridge, MA: Harvard University Press, 2002), 111.

20. James Plumptre, *Four Discourses on Subjects Relating to the Amusement of the Stage* (Cambridge, 1809), 41.

My research for this book began by locating collections of printed and manuscript plays; digital and archival cartoons, playbills, broadsides, and ephemera collections; and printed travelogues, diaries, memoirs, and theater calendars. I also examined newspapers and journals, sermons and hymns, poetry and speeches, and other printed and manuscript matter including tax records, police records, correspondence, and the minutes and published writings from British and American abolitionist organizations.

Printed, manuscript, and digital collections and catalogs of plays were crucial sources. The 1737 Licensing Act required that all narrative dramas that debuted in London be submitted to the Lord Chamberlain's Examiner for censorship and approval, and the manuscripts of these submissions are still extant: the British Library (BL) and the Huntington Library (HL) both house the Larpent Collection of play manuscripts (1737–1824). Despite changes in the licensing laws in the mid-nineteenth century, playwrights were still required to submit manuscripts for approval well into the twentieth century, and the BL also holds the Lord Chamberlain's Plays, a collection spanning from 1824 to 1968. The BL's Daybook Registers of the Lord Chamberlain's Plays (1824–1897) are also a rich manuscript resource. Of even greater value, however, is *The London Stage, 1660–1800* (Carbondale: Southern Illinois University Press, 1960–68), a five-part, eleven-volume calendar of London plays compiled by Charles Beecher Hogan et al., which includes excerpts from reviews and playbills.

As no official body of censorship existed in Philadelphia there is no comparable manuscript collection. But the Library Company of Philadelphia (LCP) has an extensive printed collection of eighteenth- and nineteenth-century plays. And the University of Pennsylvania Press has published three volumes of daybooks compiled by Philadelphia theater managers; these provide eighteenth-century play calendars of the Philadelphia theaters and nineteenth-century calendars that also include the theatrical circuits of Baltimore, Washington, and Alexandria: Thomas Clark Pollock, *The Philadelphia Theatre in the Eighteenth Century, Together with the Day Book of the Same Period* (1933), covering 1700–1800; Reese D. James, *Old Drury of Philadelphia: A History of the Philadelphia Stage, 1800–1835, Including the Dairy or Daily Account Book of William Burke wood . . . of the Chestnut Street Theatre* (1932); and Arthur Herman Wilson, *A History of the Philadelphia Theatre, 1835–1855* (1968). These volumes combine the daybooks for the main Philadelphia theaters for all the years between 1700 and 1855 except for 1800–1810, for which no play calendars are extant and I culled the play dates, therefore, from newspapers and playbills.

Playbills, cartoons, broadsides, and ephemera are invaluable sources for researching transatlantic theatrical culture and its linkages to print and popular media. The LCP holds the McAllister Collection of playbills and ephemera and a larger graphics collection in the print department, which includes the *Life in Philadelphia* prints and engraved frontispieces for printed pamphlets and plays. The Prints and Photographs Division at the Library of Congress offers phenomenal digital resources for cartoons and theatrical ephemera, as do the Lewis Walpole Library at Yale University and the Digital Library Collection of the New York Public Library; these extensive image collections are available to researchers online. LION (Literature Online) and ECCO (Gale-Cengage Eighteenth-Century Catalog Online) also have large banks of eighteenth-century plays, poetry, and pamphlets for scholars whose institutions subscribe to these databases.

Theatrical memoirs and diaries proved fruitful for investigating theater and popular culture in the revolutionary British Atlantic. Actress Francis Maria Kelly's diary (BL MS-42920); playwright/actor John O'Keefe's *Recollections of the Life of John O'Keefe* (London, 1826); playwright/actor Frederick Reynolds's *The Life of Times of Frederick Reynolds, Written by Himself* (London, 1827); reviewer Henry Crabb Robinson's *The London Theatre, 1811–1866: Selections from the Diary of Henry Crabb Robinson*, ed. Eluned Brown (London: Society for Theatre Research, 1966); and playwright/theater manager Richard Brinsley Peake's two-volume *Memoirs of the Colman Family* (London, 1841) are important diaries and memoirs pertinent to the London setting. *Memoirs of Charles Mathews, by Mrs. Mathews*, 4 vols. (London, 1838) and William Macready, *Macready's Reminiscences and Selections from His Diaries and Letters*, ed. Sir Frederic Pollock (New York, 1875), span the transatlantic stages. For Philadelphian and American theater, see especially stage manager Charles Durang's *History of the Philadelphia Stage from the Year 1749 to the Year 1855* (Philadelphia, 1854); theater manager William B. Wood's *Personal Recollections of the Stage*; playwright/theater manager William Dunlap, *Diary of William Dunlap [. . .] 1766–1839* (New York: New York Historical Society, 1930) and *History of the American Theatre* (New York, 1832); Francis Wemyss, *Twenty-Six Years of the Life of an Actor and Manager* (New York, 1847); actress Olive Logan's *Before the Footlights and Behind the Scenes* (Philadelphia, 1869); and John Fanning Watson, *Annals of Philadelphia and Pennsylvania in the olden time*, 2 vols. (Philadelphia, 1870).

An array of other printed and manuscript sources made their way into this book: travelogues, correspondence, speeches, sermons, poems, journals, newspapers, tax records, police records, and pamphlets among them. Eighteenth- and nineteenth-century newspaper and journal collections at the LCP and British Newspaper Library were especially useful, not only for playbills and reviews, but also for investigating the cross-fertilization between historical events and cultural productions. Frances Trollope, *Domestic Manners of the Americans*, 2 vols. (London, 1832); and Frances Wright, *Views of Society and Manners in America* (London, 1821); Fanny Kemble, *Journal of America* (London 1835); and Mungo Park, *Travels into the Interior Districts of Africa* (London, 1799), as well as an assortment of mission reports held by LCP and BL, were crucial to understanding British-American contestation over slavery. Compilations of letters, papers, and poems include James Barker, *Amazing Grace: An Anthology of Poems about Slavery, 1660–1810* (New Haven, CT: Yale University Press, 2002); Lillian B. Miller, ed., *The Selected Papers of Charles Willson Peale and His Family*, 5 vols. (New Haven, CT: Yale University Press, 1983); Peter Ripley, ed., *Witness for Freedom: African American Voices on Race, Slavery, and Emancipation* (Chapel Hill: University of North Carolina Press, 1993); and Peter Kitson and Debbie Lee, eds., *Slavery, Abolition, and Emancipation: Writings in the British Romantic Period*, 8 vols. (London: Pickering & Chatto, 1999). Other useful manuscript and printed resources include a cache of letters by James Forten held by the Historical Society of Pennsylvania (HSP); the HSP also holds all the records from the Pennsylvania Abolition Society. The counterparts from the London Society for Effecting the Abolition of the Slave Trade, the British and Foreign Anti-Slavery Society, and the World Anti-Slavery Conventions can be found at the BL, Rosenfeld Library at the University of California Los Angeles, and also at Dr. Williams's Library and Centre for Dissenting Studies (London). The HSP, LCP, and BL also have deep collections of eighteenth-and nineteenth-century sermons, pamphlets, and political tracts. Taxes for Philadelphia found in *Pennsylvania Archives* and police and other public records for London (found in what used to be the Public Records Office and is now the National Archives) are also valuable resources.

This book intersects with multiple fields of scholarship: slavery, abolition, and revolution; theater and politics; blackface minstrelsy; discourses of race; print, politics, and civic performance; and the question of national versus Atlantic cultural identities. An exhaustive overview of each of these historiographies is not possible in this short essay. Instead, I have highlighted selected works, beginning with scholarship on British, American, and transatlantic slavery, abolition, and revolution.

In the American context, important works related to the eighteenth-century revolutions and their impact on slavery, liberty, and polity include Gary B. Nash, *Race and Revolution* (Madison, WI: Madison House, 1990) and *The Forgotten Fifth: African Americans in the Age of Revolution* (Cambridge, MA: Harvard University Press, 2006); Paul Goodman, *Of One Blood: Abolitionism and the Origins of Racial Inequality* (Berkeley: University of California Press, 1998); Richard Newman, *The Transformation of American Abolitionism: Fighting Slavery in the Early Republic* (Chapel Hill: University of North Carolina Press, 2002); and Paul Finkelman, *Slavery and the Founders: Race and Liberty in the Age of Jefferson* (Armonk, NY: M. E. Sharpe, 1996). Douglas Egerton, *Death or Liberty: African Americans and Revolutionary America* (Oxford: Oxford University Press, 2009), reveals the revolution's impact on African Americans, while Joanne Pope Melish, *Disowning Slavery: Gradual Emancipation and "Race" in New England, 1780–1860* (Ithaca, NY: Cornell University Press, 1998), explores the cultural ramifications of abolition and emancipation.

For British slavery, abolition, and emancipation—including the debates over the linkages between antislavery sentiment, industrial capitalism, and shifts in moral and political economy that placed greater value in free labor—see essays by Thomas Haskell, John Ashworth, and David Brion Davis in Thomas Bender, ed. *The Antislavery Debate: Capitalism and Abolitionism as a Problem in Historical Interpretation* (Berkeley: University of California Press, 1992). Leo d'Anjou, *Social Movements and Cultural Change: The First Abolition Campaign Revisited* (New York: Aldine de Gruyter, 1996), offers a good analysis of abolitionism in the context of structural social changes and social reform movements. Seymour Drescher, *Capitalism and Antislavery: British Mobilization in Comparative Perspective* (New York: Oxford University Press, 1986), and Betty Fladeland, *Abolitionists and Working-Class Problems in the Age of Industrialization* (Baton Rouge: Louisiana State University Press, 1984), help situate British abolitionism into economic and class-based realities. J. R. Oldfield, *Popular Politics and British Anti-Slavery: The Mobilisation of Public Opinion against the Slave Trade, 1787–1807* (London: Frank Cass, 1998), and Elizabeth Kowaleski Wallace, *The British Slave Trade and Public Memory* (New York: Columbia University Press, 2006), are particularly pertinent to the interactions between performance, politics, and public opinion. Christopher Brown, *Moral Capital: Foundations of British Abolitionism* (Chapel Hill: University of North Carolina Press, 2006), demonstrates powerfully how the American Revolution effected a shift in public sentiment and cultural mores about slavery and antislavery.

Brown's work intermeshes with transatlantic analyses pertinent to the discourses of slavery and antislavery in the revolutionary British Atlantic. A lasting benchmark in this field is David Brion Davis's magisterial two-volume study, *The Problem of Slavery in Western Culture* (New York: Oxford University Press, 1966) and *The Problem of Slavery in the Age of*

Revolution, 1770–1823 (Ithaca, NY: Cornell University Press, 1977). His *Inhuman Bondage: The Rise and Fall of Slavery in the New World* (Oxford: Oxford University Press, 2006) and Seymour Drescher, *Abolition: A History of Slavery and Antislavery* (Cambridge: Cambridge University Press, 2009), take a pan-Atlantic purview on slavery and abolition in the revolutionary era that includes both Latin and North America. Similarly, Ashli White, *Encountering Revolution: Haiti and the Making of the Early Republic* (Baltimore: Johns Hopkins University Press, 2010), and Cassandra Pybus, *Epic Journeys to Freedom: Runaway Slaves and Their Global Quest for Liberty* (Boston: Beacon Press, 2006), both demonstrate the Atlantic-wide impact of the eighteenth-century revolutions on discourses and praxes of polity, slavery, and race. For transatlantic analysis of mid-nineteenth-century abolitionism, see Christine Bolt, *The Anti-Slavery Movement and Reconstruction: A Study in Anglo-American Co-operation, 1833–1877* (London: Oxford University Press, 1969), and R. J. Blackett, *Building an Antislavery Wall: Black Americans in the Atlantic Abolitionist Movement, 1830–1860* (Ithaca, NY: Cornell University Press, 1989).

I also found studies of the black communities in London and Philadelphia particularly useful for contextualizing discourses of race, slavery, and abolition in relation to the lived realities of African Americans and Britons: see, in particular, Gary B. Nash, *Forging Freedom: The Formation of Philadelphia's Black Community, 1720–1840* (Cambridge: Cambridge University Press, 1988), and Gary B. Nash with Jean Soderlund, *Freedom by Degrees: Emancipation in Pennsylvania and Its Aftermath* (Oxford: Oxford University Press, 1991). Key studies of the London black community include Gretchen Gerzina, *Black London: Life before Emancipation* (New Brunswick, NJ: Rutgers University Press, 1995); Douglass Lorimer, *Colour, Class, and the Victorians: English Attitudes to the Negro in the Mid-Nineteenth Century* (Leicester: Leicester University Press; New York: Holmes & Meier, 1978); and Norma Myers, *Reconstructing the Black Past: Blacks in Britain, 1780–1830* (London: Frank Cass, 1996).

The discursive backdrop for the performances of slavery and freedom in print, theater, and politics was not only revolution, but also a shift away from eighteenth-century ideas of human differences as products of environment toward ideas of biologically based physiognomic and intellectual capacities of "race." Of particular note in thinking about the development of ideas of race in relation to literary and cultural production are Winthrop Jordan's classic *White over Black: American Attitudes toward the Negro, 1550–1812* (Chapel Hill: University of North Carolina Press, 1968) and Bruce Dain, *Hideous Monster of the Mind: American Race Theory in the Early Republic* (Cambridge, MA: Harvard University Press, 2002). Roxanne Wheeler, *Complexion of Race: Categories of Difference in Eighteenth-Century British Culture* (Philadelphia: University of Pennsylvania Press, 2000), demonstrates that ideas of race were still fluid in eighteenth-century Britain but became more fixed by century's end. "Theories of Race," vol. 8 of Peter Kitson, ed., *Slavery, Abolition, and Emancipation* (London: Pickering & Chatto, 1999), offers primary sources and an excellent introductory overview. My work explicitly builds on scholarship that has examined how these new theories of race were parlayed into visual and embodied theatrical representations of slavery. For a useful examination of how race was constructed through visual representation, see Jan Nederveen Pieterse, *White on Black: Images of Africa and Blacks in Western Popular Culture* (New Haven: Yale University Press, 1992). For transatlantic analyses of visual representations of slavery, abolition, and emancipation, see Marcus Wood, *Blind Memory: Visual Representations of Slavery in England and America, 1780–1865* (New

York: Routledge, 2000), and *The Horrible Gift of Freedom: Atlantic Slavery and the Representation of Emancipation* (Athens: University of Georgia Press, 2010). Key works on theatrical performances of race and slavery include Felicity Nussbaum, *The Limits of the Human: Fictions of Anomaly, Race, and Gender in the Long Eighteenth Century* (Cambridge: Cambridge University Press, 2003); Virginia Mason Vaughan, *Performing Blackness on English Stages, 1500–1800* (Cambridge: Cambridge University Press, 2005); Hazel Waters, *Racism on the Victorian Stage: Representation of Slavery and the Black Character* (Cambridge: Cambridge University Press, 2007); and Heather Nathans, *Slavery and Sentiment on the American Stage, 1787–1861: Lifting the Veil of Black* (Cambridge: Cambridge University Press, 2009).

The rich body of scholarship on blackface minstrelsy and its relationship to class in both the British and American contexts has been particularly stimulating. Scholars have demonstrated how blackface minstrelsy was key to the formulation of American white working-class consciousness, complicating earlier scholarship that dealt with the genre as primarily about the development of racism. See Eric Lott, *Love and Theft: Blackface Minstrelsy and the American Working Class* (New York: Oxford University Press, 1993); Dale Cockrell, *Demons of Disorder: Early Blackface Minstrels and Their World* (Cambridge: Cambridge University Press, 1997); David Roediger, *The Wages of Whiteness: Race and the Making of the American Working Class* (London: Verso, 1991); and William J. Maher, *Behind the Burnt Cork Mask: Early Blackface Minstrelsy and Antebellum American Popular Culture* (Urbana: University of Illinois Press, 1999). Scholarship on blackface minstrelsy in the British context explains the popularity of minstrelsy in terms of white working-class consciousness in an imperial economy. See Michael Pickering, "White Skin, Black Masks," in *Music Hall Performance and Style*, ed. J. S. Bratton (Milton Keynes, UK: Open University Press, 1986), 81–85, and "Mock Blacks and Racial Mockery: The 'Nigger' Minstrel and British Imperialism," in *Acts of Supremacy: The British Empire and the Stage, 1790–1930*, ed. J. S. Bratton (Manchester: Manchester University Press, 1991); J. S. Bratton, "English Ethiopians: British Audiences and Black Face Acts, 1835–1865," *Yearbook of English Studies* (1981): 127–42; George Rehin, "Blackface Street Minstrels in Victorian London and Its Resorts," *Journal of Popular Culture* 15, no. 1 (Summer 1981): 19–38. These scholars have also succeeded in debunking the idea of blackface minstrelsy as a peculiarly American phenomenon, a rebuttal my scholarship confirms.

More important for my own analysis, however, is the growing body of transatlantic analysis of blackface performance and its relationship to black self-fashioning. George Rehin issued an early call for understanding blackface performance as a transatlantic genre in "Harlequin Jim Crow: Continuity and Convergence in Blackface Clowning," *Journal of Popular Culture* 9, no. 3 (Winter 1975): 682–701. Since then, W. T. Lhamon, *Jump Jim Crow Lost Plays, Lyrics and Street Prose of the First Atlantic Popular Culture* (Cambridge, MA: Harvard University Press, 2003); Sarah Meer, *Uncle Tom Mania: Slavery, Minstrelsy, and Transatlantic Culture in the 1850s* (Athens: University of Georgia Press, 2005); and Robert Nowatzki, *Representing African Americans in Transatlantic Abolitionism and Blackface Minstrelsy* (Baton Rouge: Louisiana State University Press, 2010), have all insisted on the fully transatlantic popularity of blackface performance, as do I, although I place greater emphasis on its development through transatlantic crossings from the eighteenth century onward, and on its interrelatedness to visual and print culture. In this latter regard, I am also indebted to works that analyze blackface performance in relation to African American sartorial "performances" and the ways in which these were parodied in blackface cartooning. Monica Miller, *Slaves to Fashion: Black Dandyism and the Styling of Black Diasporic Identity* (Durham, NC: Duke University Press, 2009); Shane White and Graham White, *Stylin': African American Expressive Culture From Its Beginning to the Zoot Suit* (Ithaca, NY: Cornell University Press, 1998); and Tavia Nyong'O, *The Amlagamation Waltz: Race, Performance, and the Ruses of Memory* (Minneapolis: University of Minnesota Press, 2009), were especially stimulating in rethinking whites' visual parodies of blacks.

A significant conceptual approach for my work is the idea of permeable and shifting boundaries between different cultural media, drawing on a rich body of scholarship in the fields of cultural studies, the histories of early modern Britain, early American republic, the Atlantic, and global history. Joseph Roach, *Cities of the Dead: Circum-Atlantic Performance* (New York: Columbia University Press, 1996), demonstrates the interplay between commerce and culture, ritual and performance. Steven L. Kaplan, ed., *Understanding Popular Culture: Europe from the Middle Ages to the Nineteenth Century* (New York: Mouton, 1984), and Barry Reay, *Popular Cultures in England 1550–1750* (London: Longman, 1998), have also argued for permeable and shifting boundaries between cultural media in early modern Britain. Several scholars of the early American republic have, similarly, seen a free-flowing circulation between print and politics, street and theater performances, and the commercial, intellectual and aesthetic realms: for example, Susan G. Davis, *Parades and Power: Street Theatre in 19th-Century Philadelphia* (Philadelphia: University of Pennsylvania Press, 1988); David Waldstreicher, *In the Midst of Perpetual Fetes: The Making of American Nationalism, 1776–1820* (Chapel Hill: University of North Carolina Press, 1997); Simon P. Newman, *Parades and Politics of the Street: Festive Culture in the Early American Republic* (Philadelphia: University of Pennsylvania Press, 1997); and Laura Rigal, *The American Manufactory: Art Labor, and the World of Things in the Early Republic* (Princeton, NJ: Princeton University Press, 1998).

Finally, several works have offered provocative theses about anxieties in the postcolonial relationship between Great Britain and the United States. I have benefited from thinking about the contest over the meanings of slavery, liberty, and polity in relation to the larger struggle of both nations to reformulate their post-revolutionary cultural identities. Kariann Akemi Yokota, *Unbecoming British: How Revolutionary America Became a Post-Colonial Nation* (Oxford: Oxford University Press, 2011), discusses Americans' ambivalence about losing their British identity. Sam Haynes, *Unfinished Revolution: The Early American Republic in a British World* (Charlottesville: University of Virginia Press, 2010), explores Americans' post-war "Anglophobia." Elisa Tamarkin, *Anglophilia: Deference, Devotion, and Antebellum America* (Chicago: University of Chicago Press, 2008), posits just the opposite, Americans' continued attachment to British culture. British historians have also shown how anxiety over the loss of the American war prompted Britons to redefine their political, cultural, and national identities, including John Brewer, "English Radicals in the Age of George III," in J. G. A. Pocock, ed., *Three British Revolutions: 1641, 1688, 1776* (Princeton, NJ: Princeton University Press, 1980); Kathleen Wilson, *Sense of the People: Politics, Culture, and Imperialism in England, 1715–1785* (Cambridge: Cambridge University Press, 1998); Linda Colley, *Britons: Forging the Nation, 1707–1837* (New Haven, CT: Yale University Press, 1992); Paul Langford, *Englishness Identified: Manners and Character, 1650–1850* (Oxford: Oxford University Press, 2000); and Dror Wahrman, *The Making of the Modern Self: Identity and Culture in Eighteenth-Century England* (New Haven, CT: Yale University Press, 2004).

Page numbers in italics indicate illustrations.

Drury Lane Theatre Royal, 133; about venue, 77–78, 84, 129, 270n96; stagings by, 58, 67, 72, 75, 193
Du Bois, W. E. B., 43
"dumbshew," 155
Dunbar, Paul Lawrence, 224
Dunlap, William, 35, 42, 45; as abolitionist, 104–5; *The Africans* adaptation by, 90, 104–5, 107, 275n85; *The Glory of Columbia*, 40–41, 104
Durang, Charles, 4, 44, 164, 187, 188, 191, 202
Dusty Bob, 130
Dyson, Jeremiah, 60–62

Edwin, David, 31, 32, 33, 50
Egan, Pierce, 120–31; *Life in London*, 120–21, 125, 128–30, 131, 148–49
Egerton, M., 134, 135
Elliot, John, 109
Emancipation Act (1833), 8, 143, 146, 171, 181, 207, 215, 249; slave owners and, 216; and transnational antislavery movement, 200–201
Emancipation Proclamation, 229
Emerson, Ralph Waldo, 166–67
Emmet, Robert, 225
England's Glory (play), 69–70
The English Fleet (play), 72
Equiano, Olaudah, 62
Essay on the Causes of the Variety of Complexion and Figure in the Human Species (Smith), 106
evangelism, 91–92
Evans, George Henry, 232

The Fall of British Tyranny (Leacock), 19, 20, 45, 47
Fawcett, John, 224
Federalist Papers, 22
The Female Combatants, 55, 56
Finley, Robert, 88
Finney, Charles, 92
Fitzhugh, George, 232, 244
Flaherty, Bernard, 148, 149
flash man, 131–32, 150
Flashy Nance, 130
Flight to America (Rede), 205, 206
Florian, Jean Pierre Claris de, 98–99
Forrest, Edwin, 164, 187, 188, 191–92, 212

Forten, James, 39, 42, 211; as abolitionist, 181, 184, 201; and African colonization, 107, 110
Fortune, Michael, 38–39
Foster, Hannah Webster, 28
Fourier, Charles, 242
Fox, Charles James, 67, 74, 75, 95, 96
Frank Leslie's Illustrated Newspaper, 251–52, 253
Franklin, Benjamin, 19–20, 22, 46
Fraser's Magazine for Town and Country, 227–28, 292n56
Freedom Day celebrations, 37–38, 48, 140, 146, 206
Freemasons, 41–42, 145
French Revolution (1789): abolitionists and, 52, 67–68; impact of, 26, 66–68, 220, 268n51; opposition and hostility to, 14, 35, 67, 70; Reign of Terror in, 34–35; slavery abolished by, 35; support for, 3, 34, 66–67, 233
French Revolution (1830), 144, 181, 194
Friends of Unity, 217, 219
Fugitive Slave Act, 213, 226–27, 244, 250
Fuller, Margaret, 166–67

Gabriel, 37, 186, 192
Gall, Franz Joseph, 208
Garrison, William Lloyd, 181, 184, 201, 216
Genêt, Edmond, 46, 264n114
George IV, 125, 144
Gillray, James, 71–72, 123
The Gladiator (Bird): antislavery message of, 182, 186–87, 188–89, 190–91; London stagings of, 192–94, 212; and Nat Turner rebellion, 182–83, 184–85; Philadelphia stagings of, 186, 187–88, 191, 286n49
Gliddon, George, 141
The Glory of Columbia (Dunlap), 40–41, 104
Gobineau, Joseph-Arthur Comte de, 208
Goddess of Liberty, 15, 38–39
Godey's Magazine, 170
Golby, J. M., 84
Goodman, Paul, 50
Gordon Riots (1780), 63
Gradual Emancipation Act (Pennsylvania), 8, 13, 21
Grahame, James, 95–96
Gray, Edward, 185
Gray, John, 166
Grenville, Lord, 74, 95

stagings of, 153–57; manuscript versions of, 158, 281n16; Philadelphia reception of, 164

The Triumph of Liberty (Dent), 66

The Triumph of Love (Murdock), 45

Trollope, Fanny, 9–10, 113, 153, 276n2; *Domestic Manners of the Americans,* 115; and Wright, 165–66, 168–70

Tropic Thunder (movie), 254

Turner, Nat, 181, 183–85, 186, 187, 194, 195

Types of Mankind (Nott and Gliddon), 141

Uncle Tom's Cabin (Stowe): and debate over slavery, 245–47, 248; stage adaptations of, 180, 244, 245, 250

urban dandy: Egerton sketches of, 134, *135;* flash man as, 131–32; as type, 122; white, 140, 150–51

urban dandy, black: Clay satirization of, 134, 135–39, 148; dress styles of, 140; Egan and Cruikshank depiction of, 121–22; emergence of genre, 116–17, 119–20, 249; in illustrations, *138, 149, 150;* Jim Crow as cousin of, 201, 202

urban picaresque, 10, 119–20, 134, 150; and anti-slavery discourse, 116–18; *Life in London* and, 120–31, 131–33, 156, 175; *Life in Philadelphia* and, 117, 134–43, 154, 175

utopianism: blackface minstrelsy and, 10–11, 176, 178, 179, 250; of Lippard and, 231–32, 242, 243, 250; of Paine, 13, 19, 50, 51, 214

variety acts, proto-vaudeville, 116–18, 134, 176, 199, 249; Mathews pioneering of, 116, 151, 152, 164–65, 188; and slavery question, 117, 153. *See also* Mathews, Charles

Vaux, Robert, 110

Views of Society and Manners in America (Wright), 167

Vincent, Eliza, 245

Waldstreicher, David, 117

Walker, David, *Appeal in Four Articles,* 184, 185

Walnut Street Theatre, 153, 166, 169–70, 188, 202, 286n49

Ward, Mrs. H. M., 239–40

War of 1812, 14, 88–89, 107–9, 111, 112–13

Warren, Mercy Otis, 28

Washington, George, 39–40, 42, 168–69, 263n81; theater depictions of, 235–36, 237

Washington and His Generals (Lippard), 214

Waters, Billy, 122–23, 124, 130, 149

Watson, John Fanning, 139

Webster, Daniel, 132

Webster, Noah, 28

Wedderburn, Robert, 123

Welsly, John, 218

The West Indies (Montgomery), 96–98

Whipper, William, 200, 201

The White Slave (Pitt), 217

Whitman, Walt, 190, 191, 233

Whitney, Eli, 31

Wignall, Thomas, 26

Wilberforce, William, 62, 64, 91, 103; on French Revolution, 67–68; political conservatism of, 74–75, 85; print and poetry depictions of, 71, 95, 96, 123, *124;* on slave trade, 99–100; theater depictions of, 2, 123–24, 255

Wilde, Oscar, 122

William IV, 144

Wilson, James, 23, 25, 50

Wilson, Kathleen, 63

women: black, 72, 149–50; gender restrictions on, 169–70, 233; rights of, 28

Wood, William, 104, 133, 187–88

Wordsworth, William, 98

working class: and blackface minstrelsy, 76, 200, 201–2, 204–5, 224; and black slaves, 157, 203, 204–5, 233; and Chartist movement, 178, 194, 211, 213, 214, 216–17, 218, 219; and class conflict, 213, 214–15, 217–18; Cruikshank/ Egan depiction of, 126–28; and Jacksonianism, 132, 142, 203–4; key issues facing, 156; Lippard and, 214, 233–34; London blacks' integration into, 124–25, 128, 148, 215; racist prejudice within, 158, 205, 209; and Reform Bill in Britain, 144–45, 148, 206; rise of, 121–22; and wage/chattel slavery relation, 191–92, 213–14, 216–17, 231, 232, 244

World Anti-Slavery Convention (1840), 177, 216

The World Turned Upside Down (play), 144

Wright, Fanny, 153–54, 165–70, 175, 249; biographical information, 167; opposition to slavery, 166, 167–68; on women and gender, 169–70

The Young Quaker (O'Keefe), 58–59

Zip Coon, 45, 83, 116, 148, 237, 249